Mother
Less
Child

Mother
Less
Child

Jacquelyn Mitchard

W • W • NORTON & COMPANY • NEW YORK • LONDON

The text of this book is composed in Avanta, with display type set in Typositor Deepdene. Composition and manufacturing by the Haddon Craftsmen. Book design by Marjorie J. Flock.

Library of Congress Cataloging in Publication Data
Mitchard, Jacquelyn.
    Mother less child.
    1. Mitchard, Jacquelyn. 2. Infertility, Female—Miscarriage—Adoption—Patients United States—Biography.
Patients—United States—Biography. I. Title.
RG648.M58A36   1985   618.3′92′0924[B]   84-14812

ISBN 0-393-01902-0

W. W. Norton & Company, Inc., 500 Fifth Avenue, New York, N. Y. 10110
W. W. Norton & Company Ltd., 37 Great Russell Street, London WC1B 3NU
                    2 3 4 5 6 7 8 9 0

For the two Bobbys

As I was going up the stair
I met a boy who wasn't there.
He wasn't there again today.
I wish that he would go away.

This is a true story. Only some names and identifying details of situations have been changed, to protect the privacy of those who wished it.

1

I WANT the real ambulance, the one I see gliding away from accident scenes like a jet on an airstream—swift, sure, secure, shouldering everything else on the road aside by its purpose.

This one's mined. Each bump and pit in the road detonates small new bursts of pain. My hands are locked protectively over my belly, but it seems to have rounded under the thin blanket. Each swerve sends it heaving side to side like a balloon filled with water.

"Fancy that," I say, pointing to such odd behavior from a belly. I don't want to alarm the boy seated across from me, a boy no more than twenty. In the dim light, like the lamps in the passenger cars of a train at night, he looks washed out, fearful. A sense of the spaces that stretch away around us—to the nearest city, to the nearest hospital—bears in around me. Half of me wants the real paramedic, too.

But this one looks, blinks, and grabs for the microphone hanging over his head, beside the bag of liquid running listlessly through a plastic tube into my hand. "The patient is alert . . . blood pressure seventy over forty . . . pulse rapid and weak . . . she is slightly disoriented. We are approximately thirty-five minutes away."

Disoriented, are we? "I'm oriented," I whisper, and he gives me a nervous smile. Shut up, I think; that's exactly what will make him think you're slipping.

I reach up and wipe a scrim of cold sweat from my lip; my hand looks like one of the Halloween Hazel wax molds we got as kids: pale yellow, smeared all over with Karo syrup and food coloring. So this is shock, I think, and welcome to it. It isn't half bad—it is, in fact, amazing. I feel small, drowsy, but inflated with breath. This, I think, is how the body prepares the mind to die with nonchalance.

"Can I sleep now?"

"You can sleep if you want," says the boy, who's got older—a grown man. Have we changed drivers on this stagecoach? I get ready to sleep, snuggle down a bit on the narrow shelf, when something that begins as a bright pinpoint at the back of my head comes hurtling forward, growing, illumining, until it's a headlight flooding behind my eyes and I'm sure—I'm absolutely sure—that if I go to sleep . . .

"I'm going to die," I tell the boy in as conversational a tone as I'm able, rising up suddenly like the monster's bride from the slab, arms extended straight out. "Right now."

A cramp rolls over in my abdomen like an animal flexing from a crouch. I clutch at my icy face, covering the cry. Come now. Don't make a fool of yourself. My tongue pokes out, dry and thick. Where was the damn tunnel ending in a shining door, with my grandfather and my mother, welcoming and incandescent, at the terminus? Was this any way to die, nauseous, bladder burning, terrified, and without an original thought?

Someone pushes my shoulders down; instantly my lungs are flattened. I can't get a breath. This is my bad dream, my most exquisite fear— the one that sends me flying out of saunas, bursting from crawl spaces. I'm suffocating; I shove the arms away, not with the much-hyped adrenalin rush of the mighty damaged, but with all the forward thrust of a Nerf bat. I fall back, panting.

The boy tells the driver to pull over. The driver clambers back; I haven't seen him in days. I lift my hand to wave; it doesn't lift. What, did everybody believe me? It was only a thought. I'm just a little tired now. I hear a shriek of crickets outside the wall of the truck, and think, hold on—don't die—they'll catch your soul if you do. No, that was whippoorwills. There is no question of dying now. In any case, I am not going to die thinking about the Dunwich Horror.

The boy says into the radio, "I'm putting on a monitor." A swipe of cold jelly, two little mouths below my breast.

I'm being slapped. "I'm sorry!" I cry reflexively, "I didn't mean it!" We are moving; I hear a siren. Was that why we pulled over? Did an ambulance go by? The radio crackles far off. "This is Dr. Bell," says a voice. "We are awaiting you." How polite, I think. And we shall be there anon.

". . . M.A.S.T. trousers?" the boy is asking.

"And keep the line wide open," replies the small voice crisply.

The boy is fumbling in a storage compartment under the seat opposite, steadying me with one hand, like a package. He pulls out rubberized football sweatpants—just like the ones I use to attack my thighs while I exercise. "Can you raise up? Should we put these on?"

"What will they do?"

"Oh, maybe help you stay awake?" He is joshing me; they don't take such measures to keep you brisk for the ride. I duck underwater, and the boy's face swims over me like a fish behind aquarium glass. He throws the trousers aside.

"You have to hold on," he says. He is sweating, and a drop rolls down onto my chin. "I won't let you go."

So we grip hands, soul style. I feel kindly, loving. The pain is gone; I still feel the sensation of the pain, but it has nothing to do with me. I float up and away from this boy, who keeps me anchored by one rough, warm hand. "Last turn," he coaches me. "Now the parking lot; it's a long parking lot."

We squeal, I squeal, around a last wild curve. The door flies open and an old man, his hair lovingly and precisely Brylcreamed into bluish waves, looks down as I'm whisked past. I smile up. He looks horrified.

Then a row of faces takes his place. I've seen this gang before, the night I camped out at another hospital for the never-fail old standby feature story "A Night at the Emergency Room."

It's what they call the "reception line": doctors, nurses, radiologists, technicians, lined up for the critical first look. Then, it was a boy with a gunshot wound staining his brand-new down vest. Now, I am the "bride."

And as if to cooperate with the show, my foamy levitational state deserts me. I'm wide awake, smack back inside my body; my bowels gush; I'm gagging into a plastic basin. "God! I'm so sorry! I'm so embarrassed!" A taste of old leaves pushes up in my throat.

"She has contact lenses on," a female voice says, and to me, very loudly, as if I spoke a foreign language, she says, "Honey? Can you take off your lenses? I have a jar here."

Retching, I hold up two fingers. So does she. I do it again. We give each other the peace sign. I wipe the stuff from my mouth and gasp. "Two cups. I need two cups. Left and right. Otherwise, you know . . ." Burning building, nuclear first strike, you just don't let your contact lenses get mixed up.

The doctor's presence in the room has caused everyone else's to fall back. "Good evening," he says, a real Norman Rockwell Yankee face. "When did the pains start?"

"Just now, in the ambulance."

"And before?"

"Oh, nothing much." Tubes running, swollen stomach being painted with Betadine, I realize this sounds ludicrous, "slightly disoriented," but we Mitchards like to think we scorn the physical bump, the twinge, the low-grade compound fracture. Rub a little dirt on it. Don't describe it. We reserve utter collapse for the emotional hangnail.

I have to do better. "Before, I did feel ill."

"Like bad menstrual cramps? Is that what the pains were like?"

"I've never had bad menstrual cramps."

He sighs. "Like constipation?"

I've never had constipation. But I can sense he's losing patience. "Yes," I agree. "Like that."

"Are we ready?" he suddenly asks the room at large.

But I have to tell him; I need to ask a question, and it takes enormous effort, a run to the top of a two-mile hill. I'm sweating, panting, but I cry, "Wait!" And I'm astonished. My voice rings right out. It stops people. "If it is what I think it is, does it mean I will never be able to have children?"

There is a tick of silence. Then the doctor, as if realizing nobody is going to jump into the breach, mutters, "Nonononono, it will only take longer."

And before I can ask what that means, exactly—"longer"—the nurse shoves a clipboard at me and wraps the fingers of my right hand, one by one, around a pencil. It drops. I see it land on the white sheet. Pen and sheet are snatched away. "She can't sign. Is the husband here yet?"

"The husband isn't here yet."

"Well, I am not going to wait," the doctor again. "I am going to go ahead because she is going out. She is going to go out. . . ."

Then a silvery spurt spreads up from my wrist. I flutter my fingers. All gone. Liquid sleep. And I go . . . out.

2 BLISS makes me shudder. It always has. "Bliss is unnatural." Emily Dickinson wrote that; and I believe her. I don't give the small, potbellied gods cause to notice me, to become jealous. I don't brag, and so challenge them to snatch away what I own. And now that I was pregnant, just a whisker pregnant, I was doubly so—avoiding cracks in the pavement, spilled salt, and the rind of a new moon through window glass.

But the day had been perfect. Any other word would have been unjust. It had been untimed, unruffled, full of tasty small indulgences —good jokes over breakfast, a Gauguinian sunset. We had eaten fruit and fudge on the beach, one blanket pulled around the three of us— to keep us close, to keep out the chill.

In spite of the breeze, it had been temperate underwater, in a way Lake Michigan hardly ever is. We'd spent the afternoon suspended just under the surface like porpoises, snorkeling, nicking up small hasp-shaped bits of lake floor with our fingernails, bits that later, cleaned up, might be the fossil spines of prehistoric beasties.

The direct descendant of one such now kittled over my instep as I sat cross-legged on the cold, covered toilet in our cabin, trying to figure out how I could have managed to get sunburned.

My dark skin soaked up sun with equanimity—when I let it, which I didn't. Ten years ago, I could lie on a blazing white beach for six hours with no more punishment than a pink line near the leg of my bikini that vanished by nightfall. It had been five years, for God's sake, since I'd even allowed myself the merest tan. Not vain, I told my friends, just cautious. I didn't want to greet my fortieth birthday with cheeks like a furled umbrella.

But there it was, nonetheless, on my right shoulder—achy and sullen, not a muscle pull or a bruise. No line, no redness, just two by two inches of invisible sunburn—hard to reach with a dab of Noxema and fouling my mood.

Not that that had been so terrific for the past hour or so.

I was snappy, all-overish, nursing something not quite a headache, just short of indigestion. At the restaurant where we'd stopped for a drink, I'd stood up and announced I wanted to go home.

"I just want to play one more pinball . . .," my step-daughter, age six, began to barter. I looked at my husband.

"Now," I said, and walked out. He followed me, mystified. Five minutes of pronounced silence from the back seat let me know Jocelyn was stewing. She had been away from Mommy for a good three weeks now and was about due for a little separation anxiety, and I had irked her just enough to push out her lip.

When Jocelyn was four and practically a baby, and I was twenty-six and just acting like one, we had gone through the whole elaborate Freudian wrangle over Daddy, Mommy, and the intruder in Daddy's bed and heart. In the midst of it, Jocelyn and I fell in love. Hostilities had to be suspended. But she was not an unintelligent child; close as we were, she still knew how to bust me.

Normally, I could take her periodic "Daddy, tell me how it was when you and Mommy loved each other," but today I had every ganglion out for an insult. Dan had bought me a sweater that morning, a big, oily, knobbly-knitted Norwegian thing we couldn't afford but that I convinced him would stretch out appropriately in front over the coming winter—the thought of which charmed him, and we charged it.

So now Jocelyn said, in her best Orphan Annie voice, "Daddy, did you ever buy my mommy such a nice sweater as that?"

"Jocelyn," I snapped, "just can it with that. I'm not in the mood." Which was her cue to wail. And mine. Jocelyn threw herself on her dad's shoulder, shooting me baleful looks, while he soothed her. "I know you miss your mommy, sweetheart."

"That isn't it. . . ."

"Come on, Jack." So I stared out the window, abused and forlorn, and noticed for the first time I felt truly lousy, and ruining our day was the least of it.

Now I heel-walked back to the bed, scouting for bugs. This "cabin," built by an architect and ceded in divorce to his ex-wife, a close friend of mine, boasted an original Aaron Bohrod oil over the floor-to-ceiling glass windows, a flagstone gazebo at the water's edge, a gaggle of resident bats, and a plague of sawdust beetles.

"I suppose this is a taste of what I can expect for the next eight months," said Dan, grinning in mock resignation. He'd appeared at the door, wrapping an ear of corn in foil while another rested in the crook of his arm. "One ear or two?"

"None. I feel like garbage."

"How eloquent. Lie down for a while, sweetheart, and then see. I think it was the taco sauce," he added. We had gorged on nonnutrific cuisine for lunch. "Our little baby must be allergic to jalapenos."

I lay down, and instantly felt better. The thought of my pregnancy washed me with the customary awe. My pregnancy. Mine. I could read the books now; I had a right to the lists of baby names. I could thumb racks of doll-sized dresses with something besides melancholy.

After the first month of trying, I had been worried. After the second month, distraught. After the third month, sterility was a given, divorce an option. The fourth month, my period didn't come. My temperature on my compulsively accurate basal temperature chart stayed high.

I had known about this baby, by home test and repeated home test, by urine test, by blood test—known absolutely for sure—for exactly eleven days, and already I was indulgently, elegantly among the initiated. A pregnant lady. Her serene expectancy. I bought big, sleeveless summer shifts for our trip that still hung straight down on my body like flags without wind.

But it was all show. I didn't feel pregnant; granted, I didn't know how to feel pregnant. I knew more about triple-bypass surgery than about the first trimester; at least I had written about it.

Nothing my veteran friends told me to expect had come over me. No thickening of the hair, no skin eruptions, no—to quote from *The New Baby Book*—"sense of promise and excitement coupled with hormonal changes, that might result in morning sickness for a few weeks."

I had nothing—nothing except rock-hard breasts and a kind of peculiar deadness below the waist.

And some guilt. A little guilt, because several months before, doodling with my own anxiety and with an ear out to the murmurings of a trend around me, I had begun researching a series for my newspaper on infertility—on the growing numbers of couples who couldn't conceive a pregnancy or sustain one. I wasn't sure why the idea seemed so urgent, why I pressed it on my editor like the invention of the wheel. It would be six months before *Newsweek* and the other big guns of the press would deem the phenomenon worthy of an all-out spread in color. They were still concentrating on the "older mothers" craze—on famous women who regarded pregnancy as something they had recently invested. The feature section of our medium-sized daily in Wisconsin was filling its share of columns with it, too. Every woman in the newsroom who was childless was drinking in news of the "biological time clock" with her morning coffee.

Perhaps I was, as my grandmother used to call it, "seeky." I may have felt that the act of writing about less fortunate others would propitiate the little potbellied gods. Maybe, more likely, it was simply curiosity, professional for once dovetailing with personal—the yen to get a jump on a timely, absorbing story. I'd begun by contacting Karen Sussman, one of the women who headed the local infertility support group. I'd learned long since that the best way to open up an interview subject was to offer an unvarnished chunk of your own life, so I had confided my own worries. "We keep trying and trying to get pregnant and it isn't working. And I'd like to do a series of stories . . .."

She'd been willing, even welcoming. We'd discussed future meetings. Then the second time I'd called, just before leaving on vacation, to set up interview times, I'd had to hesitate. I gulped, and admitted, "Well, for me it's good news. I just found out I'm pregnant."

There was a lull, an almost imperceptible drawing away. Then Karen's warm, slow voice said, "That's wonderful." And we made a date.

So how, I thought, do I come to be lying on the bed in what I was now thinking of ironically as a fetal position, a tightening in my abdomen strengthening, then shivering away, saying to myself, "This is ridiculous. This is absurd."

Life may imitate art, I thought, but it hardly ever bothers with journalism. You don't lie down on a bed to read a paperback about pregnancy—filing this bit away mentally for the series, this bit for the baby growing inside you—you don't read in *The New Baby Book* that "any sharp abdominal pain is a danger signal during the first three months of pregnancy," and then pull up, roll over, and feel a sharp abdominal pain.

You wanted symptoms; you're having symptoms, I told myself. You will stand up, and you will march yourself into the bathroom, and return five pounds lighter and a whole lot less silly.

The rope around my belly didn't stretch as I stood; it caught and held. So I walked, unnoticed and Quasimodo-like, across the hall and sat down on the porcelain stool, jumping at its icy smoothness. Head down, I realized abruptly I wasn't bound up, I was nauseous. I held my head over the sink; out with the bad guacamole, in with the good Northwoods water.

Jocelyn was tapping on the door with growing urgency. "I have to go! I really have to go!" I smiled, imagining her performing the dance of the seven Pepsis in her tennies.

I rushed out. She rushed in. The phone rang. I was grateful for the distraction. The phone rings in a summer cottage: Who could it be? Who knows we're here? Who died?

"Jocelyn! It's Mommy!" Dan called.

Ah. I pulled my friend Susan's old quilt up over my head. So much for who died. I had planned to take some kind of delight in this call from my divorce-in-law: this regular enough woman, prettier than a few, smarter than some, whom I had set up as a plaster Madonna.

But no more. Now I also would be "the mother of my child," deserving of homage and tithings. But when I heard Jocelyn say, "Guess what?" all I felt was foreboding; the shit was poised for the fan, and Dan was standing directly under it. Joan had no use for me, she'd made that clear enough, and didn't all the literature say the true rending of the old marriage came when the new one produced offspring?

But there was Dan beside me, smiling, unbothered, rolling his eyes. I could never anticipate him, I thought with sudden, sharp affection. The room was darker. Had I been asleep? I rocked myself back and forth tentatively, to find a place that would accommodate what was now unarguably, observably, pain.

"I think I have the flu," I told him. And we laughed. In this friend's cabin, in this maple bed, we had spent our honeymoon a year to the week before, sweaty and tingling as teenagers even after four years of cohabitation. And here in this bed, on this honeymoon, I'd spent two days alone, shivering and slugging cough medicine, while Dan skipped rocks on the beach.

"The odds against that are amazing," he said, pushing up my bangs, his voice husky and fond. "You're just having the willies, B." It was our dumb name, our pet name, short for "baby," which we used only in our closest times together.

Well, he was the gestation expert, not me. We were settling into a hug when I threw Dan aside and plunged past him, barely making the bathroom, seeing the smile drain from his face as I passed, as if I had pulled it along behind me.

"I'm better now. I'm better," I told him, as he hesitantly backed off to Jocelyn's urgent "Mommy wants you." I will treat this, I said sternly to myself, as I did the swollen glands that were Hodgkin's disease, the mole that was melanoma. Like so much stuff. I am better.

But I wasn't better. I was quaking, my ribs running with sweat. I had to get to Dan. But first, a rest. I lowered myself down on a bit of damp hall runner, touching my cheek to a place I wouldn't have touched with my toe an hour before, and thought, damn the sawdust beetles, I have to have a nap.

"Stepme?" cried Jocelyn. "Stepme?" How long had she been there, anxiously chirping the name she used for me, sometimes to score points, other times to express emotions her loyalties wouldn't permit her?

"Get Daddy," I gasped. She got Daddy. "Get a doctor," I ordered.

I could hear him fumbling with the telephone book, rude with fear. "It's Friday night in a resort town, you've got a gas pain, and I'm supposed to find a doctor. I'm trying to find a doctor to tell my pregnant wife she needs some prune juice. . . . Hello! Fucking recording! Jocelyn! Get me a pencil, get Daddy a pencil.

"Hello, is this a doctor?" His voice collected itself, civilized itself audibly. "My name is Dan Allegretti; my wife is six weeks pregnant and we're on vacation just outside Sister Bay." The good reporter—just facts, with economy.

"Honey? Can you stand up? You have to stand up. Are you okay?" Okay? Me? I'm a titan, a healthy horse. Of course I'm okay, my scared darling. When I was thirteen, during the course of a routine examination, Dr. Interlandi had told me that with my pelvic structure, I could pop out six babies like marbles. I'd gone home and cried for two hours. I am fine, I said, of course I am fine.

Looking into Jocelyn's wide, coaly eyes, I said, "I'm *fine.*"

Dan dressed me, putting one leg, then the other, into underpants, each arm into a sweater. "Jocelyn, get your shoes on!" And Jocelyn, who could make getting dressed look like a Debussy ballet choreographed on the theme of languor, appeared, already laced and hopping with anxiety.

We rattled along in our truck, narrowly missing a cow. "Did we graze a cow?" I asked, giggling. Jocelyn hid under a sleeping bag in the back and whimpered. How could I comfort her, my poor girl? She'd spent the last week studying Ms. Egg and Mr. Sperm, taken all of the books with drawings of bubble-headed fetuses out of the library, marked her "brother's" birthday on her Ranger Rick calendar, and wondered why our baby, as pictured in a book, looked rather like a pinkie-sized hippo.

A bolt of pain rocked through me. I looked up, and the darkening sky was a photo negative, white trees against whey-gray sky. But this was better. For the last five miles, I realized, I had not seen at all.

"Dan, I can see again!" I told him, and his face turned cheesy white in the dimness of the truck.

"You couldn't see?" he asked, terribly slowly.

We slammed into the parking lot of the small clinic, stopping directly in front of a young man, the doctor, rumpled in cutoffs and a madras shirt. He took my hand. "Are you bleeding?" No bleeding. I asked to use the washroom and took a little fall.

The doctor helped me onto a table, chatting cheerily, fastening a blood-pressure cuff onto my arm. As he pumped it, the chatter stopped. I tried to head it off. "I normally have low blood pressure."

"Normally seventy over forty?"

The room whirled and slowed down. I dangled my legs over the edge of the examining table like a kid at a creek. My husband leaned on a piece of tubular apparatus and talked to me animatedly. His mouth formed lazy ovals; I was too dreamy to consider why no sound came out. The doctor headed for the phone.

I woke to stabbing; two men in blue uniforms, paramedics, each had a hand, each a spoke. "This isn't going to work," I told them frantically, suddenly weeping. Didn't they see my veins were perdition as a matter of course, that nobody could get blood out of me?

Didn't they notice? Left hand, right hand, left forearm, right inner elbow. Blood squirted onto the paper sheet, onto the floor; the tiles were slick with it. Jocelyn came skipping around a corner, dangling a Little Golden Book she'd found in the waiting room, and caught sight of me, her little face stretching in terror, a pale, Munch-painting child's face.

I tried to tell them, "Wait, not in front of her . . ." But the switch had been set to fast-forward. No one heard.

The young blond paramedic's face was puffed, red with exertion. "We have to do something," he said. "We have to get a line in."

They were going to do something, they were going to cut, but then . . .

"No," said the young doctor's voice, dropping like syrup onto the roiling mess, "because it's in. I just got it in." He held my battered right hand, with its dangling quill, and helped place me gingerly on a stretcher.

He ran beside me, quickstep, as we jogged toward the door, my head flopping back against someone's warm stomach. We turned the corner, oddly at this odd vantage point, a child's eye level, and—whoops!—we passed a child. But I was past Jocelyn before I could reach out to her tears, my arm twitching uselessly in space.

I smelled, rather than saw, the parking lot—new tar, a high, hot smell. I felt the little cortege stumble; and a part of me hit the open door of the ambulance. I was embarrassed, but Dan and the doctor darted forward, adjusting tubes and throwing up trailing blanket ends, accommodating each other like longtime partners.

I thought, as they tossed me onto the narrow shelf inside the ambulance without ceremony, without care, only with haste—they are in too much of a hurry. This isn't standard.

The door snapped shut on my husband's face. I craved that face, but there wasn't room for all of us; someone had to drive to the hospital so far away—for later on, when I would come home, too late for dinner, but tomorrow . . .

We jolted to a start; I grabbed with my knees. Then a brake, the doctor poked his head in the passenger door. "The results of the hematocrit are good," he said, "so we might be wrong. It might not be what I think."

Nearly a year later, the doctor, Bill Meyer, would tell me he knocked on wood that night, in the parking lot, in his cutoffs. Doctors, like others, he would say, aren't immune to hope. "I knew it was an ectopic right away," he would say. "It was clear you were losing blood fast, and when the EMTs came, we thought of putting on pressure trousers. But that would have taken up to fifteen minutes and . . . you didn't have fifteen minutes to spare."

Even then I would still feel too young, too close to fearless immortality, for that not to seem a shock.

The trousers, he would explain, would have kept my body's fluid, stocked by the Ringer's solution running through a wide-open line into my veins, circulating around vital organs. "The solution is a saline solution, much like the contents of your circulatory system. You keep it pumping—well, you see why. First, the kidneys fail. And then the brain . . . there can be a stroke."

"Which would have killed me?"

"At your age, and in your physical condition, maybe you could have gone on an hour and survived. But the kind of survival, the quality of it . . ."

Bill Meyer would tell me it was my husband, not him, who saved my life. He would enumerate for me what husbands could do wrong.

Dan could have called for the ambulance service directly, and waited while the ambulance waved slowly over dirt roads, its light searching out a little cabin hidden in a copse of birch trees, only one of two houses on a crazy road that hacked off abruptly into the woods like a cow track.

He could have told me to go lie down. And I could have lain there, in the darkened bedroom, while what had begun slowly hurtled to a conclusion. What was happening, though I could not know it, though I had no knowledge in particular of the conduits and cavities inside me and what havoc was occurring there, was that one of the slender, curving, four-inch tubes that carry an egg from ovary to uterus had swollen, swollen and finally burst—spewing out, along with a fountain of blood, some tiny, gelid "products of conception," six weeks old and having no business there in the first place.

By the time I reached the hospital, forty-five miles away, I had lost a third or more of my blood.

But all I knew, and only by instinct, as I was sped along, was that nothing that felt so bad as this ever got better on its own.

And though I tried to push it away from me, a bit of half-learned doggerel read long ago in some forgotten women's magazine snaked around my mind, under the siren's sound: Dear babe that almost was / but could not be / dashed against rocks / swept out to sea.

THE SUN warmed my closed eyelids, but beneath my shoulders, the sand was chilly. I opened my eyes a crack. Not the sun—a lamp, a nursery night-light, yellow and glowing. I was little, and waking was a struggle up through dense fathoms of child-sleep. I surfaced, opened my eyes all the way. Bewilderment. Inventory. I am here, I am me, here are my arms, there is a lady, the lady is a nurse, this is a hospital room.

The nurse laid her fingers on my cheek. Delicate feathers, I'm not sure I haven't imagined her. "Are you awake now, hon? How do you feel, hmmmmm? Pretty punk?" Dan and Jocelyn sat at the foot of the bed, father and daughter, foreheads identically furrowed, hands identically clasped. The baby was gone. A given. What else was gone? Better not ask.

There was a bizarre diorama below the neck. I was not little; I was huge, clefts, mounds, and islands of white. Olive Oyl, courtesy of Macy's. An arm floated there, dressed out on a board, and from it up to an upended bag of blood ran a shining display of clear tubes, spliced with clips of yellow and blue. Over there an enormous, white-swathed, pregnant-seeming belly, rising up, mounding the sheets. I had the urge to laugh—"She's come out of the seventh-month coma, doctor! Just in time to deliver!"—but my belly of the past had been flat; okay, not *flat*, not Jane Fonda flat, but reasonable.

Oh come on. Dan. "Dan!" He cradled my free hand, like a small animal, stroking and cuddling.

"The baby's gone," he said, then quickly, "the *pregnancy's* gone. You knew that."

You knew that. Well, of course I knew that. I knew that from the first grab of pain. From the day the test was positive . . . because it stands to reason, doesn't it, dear, that if the truth be told, if you want a thing so badly, so nakedly, if you fasten wish and will onto it, it just stands to reason you will not actually have it. "You wanted it too much," my mother said. "You seized up." The poetry medal. Fourth grade.

"Yes," I said. "I knew that." So formal, so careful. He asked me how

I felt. I wasn't sure. We spoke as if words cost, as if words could do more injury. Dan looked awful; his cheeks pasty, eyes smudged. How did I look? How far did this go? What was this unfinished . . . this too-soon feeling? I closed my eyes and tried to start over.

But Jocelyn. I had to see Jocelyn. "What time is it?" I asked Dan.

"Midnight." Hour of closure, hour of lead—who belongs to that quote?

"Jocelyn?" She came creeping up to the bed, wan and whipped-looking, my lordly little borrowed daughter. Poor thing. She is thinking about the sweater, the Mommy-taunts. Kids think for an instant, oh, why don't you just go away and die! Poor Jocelyn. It had really happened.

"My sweetie, my pic-face," I whispered. She would know it was fine with us. It's me in here, Jocelyn-Pocelyn. See? "Are you sleepy?"

"Yes," she nodded, "and hungry, too."

"Couldn't you have got her something to eat?" The edge, the good old edge. Dan brightened up. She nags; therefore, she is.

"We could hardly run out for a Big Mac with you in surgery. . . ."

"But a doughnut, a bag of Fritos . . ." But Jocelyn didn't care about doughnuts.

"Jackie?" I knew instantly she had not heard a word her father had said, had chosen not to. She had to hear it from me. I breathed in, held it. "Is the baby all right?"

"Oh, sweetheart, the baby . . . died." How do I word this? "The baby died because I had a sickness inside, and the baby started to grow. . . ." Wait a minute. The pain is awake. A quirt, a punch, a gut wallop. "But we will have another."

"Are you sure?"

"I'm sure the baby died." I had begun to pant, Lamaze-style. "Daddy knows." Daddies know. Stepmothers have lips like galoshes and brush-fires in their bellies. I didn't even want to see what lay under the dressing. They'd made the incision with a trowel, with bare hands. I'd been torn and patched, a burst bag of skin. Dan couldn't even be sure what kind of incision it was; he thought for a while such procedures were accomplished by entering through the vagina. Daddies know most things, Jocelyn; the number of casualties at Chickamauga, what James thought of self-determination; but we're all kind of out of our depth here. Except for the car wreck, the night we slid on the icy country road, and it was only a mailbox we hit, but my cheekbone caught the dashboard . . . except for that, Daddy and I have never been sick. It doesn't seem so to you, but we're really rather young and, actuarially at least, in terrific health. The truth is, this kind of thing doesn't happen to us.

The nurse came wheeling around the corner of the door with smooth-hipped efficiency and rolled me to one side, talking all the while, as I swallowed a scream. The only hope was not moving at all. . . . "This will make you feel better," she said. "You came through just fine. You're very lucky."

Who's lucky? How close had this call been? "You were already in the operating room when we got here," said Dan. "They couldn't wait for me to sign the forms. I drove as fast as I could, of course, the ambulance just flew ahead. I only stopped," he employed his boy-face here, "for cigarettes."

I was exasperated, he could tell. He has heart-attack genes on one side, colon-cancer genes on the other side; smoking for him is like stunt flying for another man. And I hated it when he fell off the wagon. But I had to pet him and hold him—fear and relief had reconstructed him; everything was up near the surface. "Oh, baby, you're all right. Jesus, I'm so glad you're all right. Thank God you're all right."

We were more than four hours' drive from home; halfway down the thumb that made Door County into Wisconsin's small Cape Cod. It was Saturday morning, more or less, and we were due back in our newspaper office Monday morning. "They'll just have to do without us," Dan said stoutly. But he looked uneasy. It was not so big a place that the loss of two reporters didn't short-staff it, and we'd already been gone more than a week.

"Well, you can just go back tomorrow, I'll be fine," my father's side of the family suggested stoically. "But maybe I do need you; do you think you can stay here all night?" cried my mother's side.

The nurse gaped at us. "Can't you work this all out *tomorrow?*" she asked crisply. We were sheepish. "He can stay right here," soothing now.

The Demerol was coursing through me like balm. A good calm fog. I was able to figure again. And I figured I might as well know. The nurse had begun moving about the room, wadding up towels, checking the bag of clear liquid over my head, giving it an energetic shake. I asked her as she passed, "Did I have a hysterectomy?"

"Why, what made you think that?" Wrong answer.

"Well, did I?"

"No, no!" A starchy reprimand. "Nothing like that." The doctor would explain things in the morning. She didn't know.

"You do know, but you can't tell." She gave me a distinctly unprofessional grin. I felt better. What happened to nurses who told? What befell a nurse who just hazarded a guess? A year before, I had interviewed a nurse educator whose feminist health concerns had neatly knocked her out of the running for a managerial post at one of the city hospitals. Twenty years before, she said, when she had been in training, nursing students had internalized this tenet: Never discuss a patient's condition with a patient. Temperature, yes. Food, yes. Pillow too hard? Fix it right up. But, Nurse, am I gonna die? "Now why would you think that?"

Might an anecdote about my interview subject, the rebel Lillian, who was once reprimanded for not getting to her feet when a doctor entered the room, shake loose some confidential information? Watching my nurse, admiring her compact motion, I had to doubt it.

So sleep.

Dan stayed with me for the grisly insertion of a nasogastric tube—which went down like a garden spike, but was supposed to assuage my nausea—and my second blessed shot of painkiller. Even after he was sure I was sleeping, my moaning ran on like a motor, he said, constant. Periodically I would let out a drugged shriek and half rise, and Dan would half rise, and then sink back down, his strength seeping.

He went into the lounge and sat absently patting Jocelyn as she lay curled into determined sleep, clutching a wash-faded hospital blanket a nurse had tucked round her, under her chin. Her Chou-Chou dog was packed away in the truck. Good girl. She had not fussed for it. She had not insisted on her ritual hug, kiss, and pet of the hair, though she probably had needed all of them desperately this night. Funny. Jocelyn was smart, even wise, and yet so timid, timid as a fox kit. Dan thought, sometimes, the divorce had made her so.

He had not wanted another child, he thought. But he had wanted this child we had lost. There was a difference. He remembered last spring, driving along a road, searching the shoulder for some obscured trout stream, when an idea had occurred to him. Just bolt, he had said to himself, light out for the territories—drive on, away, stopping for sleep and coffee, growing younger and less encumbered by the mile.

There had been the dread of the interrupted nights, the panicky hours in emergency rooms with a wailing bundle, the mounting bills, the abstract tension, the exhausted nightly refusals. He had been there, the whole route. And he had been a younger man then.

We would no longer be able to decide to take a weekend in the woods, and just leave on Friday night after work, taking a change of jeans and telling no one. We would no longer have the luxurious dull Sundays, spent with bagels and unhurried lovemaking on the living room rug, surrounded by newspapers and shed clothing. We would be lashed together, forever, no matter how we changed, no matter how threadbare the passion wore.

But then there had come a morning when I had awakened him before dawn. I had been up for two hours, staring into the dark, getting up every fifteen minutes to glance at the bookcase where a little test tube filled with first morning urine sat. Obsessively, squinting, I had watched it—had it changed? Would it ever? Then it did. Glory.

I had crawled into the disarray of summer coverlets and put my head on his chest, rubbing my cheek against the soft mat of hair until he groaned and opened his eyes, and then whispered, "I'm pregnant."

He had taken a single deep, dissolving breath, and felt the slurry of conflicts rise up in him, and out. They had gone, replaced by a strong peace. There it was, then. Decided. Nights of smoky tavern laughter and lazy weekends, the ease of not planning, were gone. Traded for carpets strewn with trucks and plastic farm animals and the listening, from another room, for small cries. For pony-back rides and tiny baseball caps. A family man. Again, and this time for good.

He had never doubted it. He had never wanted it more than he did in these long, leaden hours, as the nurses brushed to and fro like ghosts along the tiled corridor.

Was this awful mischance some wage for his early misgivings? He dismissed it. Pragmatism was his badge. He scoffed at signs and portents, had no use for them. But as he watched the dim outline of me in the bed take shape in the rainy predawn light, like a dread photo developing before his eyes, he allowed himself regret.

WE WAITED until 7:00 A.M. and then called my grandmother. Neither of us relished the idea. She would faint outright. If she did not faint outright, it would nonetheless become family legend that she had. Her heart would beat fit to break her ribs; she'd drop ten pounds in an afternoon. Dan wetted a bit of gauze and swabbed my mouth. I could swallow nothing. "I don't want you to try to talk," he said. I nestled down, feeling cherished. "Gram?" he said, "the first thing I want to tell you is that Jackie is fine; she's right here, resting. But she had a miscarriage." I listened to the assurances, the calming monosyllables. Since my mother's death, I had taken the part of family yenta—speeding to Chicago to hold a hand, lend a buck, bring a baby present. Now I was the center. It wasn't bad.

"Just *don't* call her father," Dan was saying, "Jackie needs to rest. She can't talk on the phone too well, because she has a tube . . . that's right. Okay? Gram?" Pause. "Thank you. We love you, too."

He put the phone back in the cradle and looked up at the wall clock. We counted. Five. Four. Three. Two. One.

The phone rang in precisely six minutes. My father wasn't about to be satisfied with some son-in-law's assurances. He was a man who suspected everyone—all his relatives, all my mother's relatives, his golf partners, his accountant, the postman, the man at the sanitary landfill. So he had to hear, from my own lips, that I was not dead.

Then he said, "Jesus. Baby. This is shitty." In everyday matters, my father's emotional profile rampaged from chilly to tepid; but this was crisis. The complete emotional package came out, in primary colors—rage, love, rage.

"I'm okay, Dad," I said, "I really am." Mitchards never said otherwise.

The previous weekend, minutes before we'd left on our trip, I'd snatched up my desk phone and called him on impulse. Damn the superstition. I was marvelously healthy. Nothing would happen to this baby. I'd vowed to wait out the first trimester—the miscarriage period—before telling a soul. But.

"How would you like to be a grandpa?"

He had been silent. Then, "I hope you know what you're getting into," he said by way of congratulation. "I hope this is really what you want, dearie."

My dad's way of saying "dearie" always made it sound something like "sucker."

Three months after I left the hospital, a woman friend of his would make a throwaway remark; and I would learn that he had gone to his club that Friday and told every person he'd met, including the hat-checker and the maître d', that he would soon be a grandfather. He didn't think he was old enough, he'd said. He was delighted, he'd admitted.

But he never told me. My boss, Carol, had a legendary relationship with her father back in Michigan. They were like sweethearts; he wrote her poems for her birthday, embossed with silly caricatures, sent her flowers when she got a promotion or opened in a repertory show—she was something of a small-city star of musical comedy.

Carol's father remembered her twelve-year-old wisdoms and quoted them, endearingly. She called him when she was blue. My father and I circled each other like tigers, protecting our haunches. I envied Carol like crazy.

Okay, Pop, I thought. This is your big chance. Go bonkers. Demand a conference with the surgeon. Drop everything and catch the first plane to Sturgeon Bay.

He asked me to call him when I got home. I said I would. "There's *absolutely* no reason to come up before next weekend." Last hope. Of course, he said, he knew that. We hung up.

But my grandmother clearly was off and smoking. We would later get calls from my aunt in Louisiana, my cousin in Florida, my brother in Illinois, Dan's sister, Dan's brother, Dan's sister's mother-in-law.

But first we had to call the office. It was 7:30 A.M., daybreak for an afternoon paper. There might not be a single reporter in the place, I fussed. "Todd will be there," Dan said.

Bright, literate, and wholly compulsive, Todd Shier was Dan's investigative partner and best friend. Todd kept his little plastic boxes of paper clips and rubber bands inside one big plastic box. He would be there.

"How are you, you big asshole?" So it was Todd; Dan would not have been so affectionate with anyone else. "No, I haven't seen one in days. He did? On the record? Well, what did he say to you?" Dan's eyes flickered around the room, seeking his missing notebook and ballpoint. I sighed. Dan gathered himself visibly. "Listen, Jackie lost the baby. We're in a hospital in Sturgeon Bay. About nine last night. We didn't know what to think. They operated, and took out one of the tubes, the Fallopian tubes. The right one—why? What are you doing?"

Todd was writing it down.

He would hang up the typed note on the office corkboard after he had put down the phone, and slowly everyone would gather, first the copy desk, then the feature section—my boss shouldering her willowy five feet and ten inches through the crowd—then the editors from their cubicles.

You could, I later learned, take any twenty intelligent adults and ask them to tell what they knew about ectopic pregnancy and watch about nineteen intelligent mouths drop open. But, not many months before, a wrinkle of chance had made our office a virtual pool of knowledge on the subject.

There was a sportswriter, Paul Williams—a big, gangly ex-jock who had a wife named Marilyn. Marilyn was the kind of beauty who made other women gasp. And anyone who could get past her looks was smitten on the rebound by her brains. Marilyn was a Ph.D., a talent, an artist, who had charm without trying. She taught at a university a few hours drive from Madison, and kept a little apartment there for weeknights. On weekends she drove home to be with Paul. It wasn't an easy arrangement for a fairly young marriage, but it wasn't to be permanent, either. Because Marilyn and Paul were going to have a child.

One spring day near the end of the college term, Marilyn had, someone later conjectured, rolled out of bed early to take her morning run and collapsed between her small single bed and her nightstand. Later, too pitifully long later, the colleagues who found her said she hadn't even been able to crawl to the telephone a few feet away. It had been that swift. And I, we all, had surmised it had been painless—a brief ebbing into nothingness. But now I knew it had not been; it had been cruel and incomprehensible.

Paul had gone off his shift that day when someone from the school called the newspaper; the sportswriters clocked in at 3:00 A.M. some days and were done by ten. We had all stood around, stupid with sorrow, until our boss, Elliott, tossed on his jacket and set off to Paul's house to bring him the news.

I wrote about Marilyn, whom I had met only once, in my weekly column. "The waste was underscored by an irony," I had written, "that something so simple and hopeful as a much-planned pregnancy could take such a cruel twist. There is not one good thing to say about Marilyn Williams' death, not one saving element, and to think of her life, or the off-hand tenderness between a husband and wife, is too much to bear. . . ."

The writing was tossed salt, crossed fingers. Had the little gods had their fill? Could they strike twice in one spot? Of course not. They would take their fierce demands elsewhere. I wrote about Marilyn to stem my helplessness, to burn off my bitterness, yes, but also selfishly to protect my own soon-to-be-conceived baby.

We learned all about ectopic pregnancies that week—about how a fertilized egg, making its two-day-or-so trek down from the ovary to its home in the uterus, could get blocked by some shred of scar or some other minute obstacle and latch onto the side of one of those twisting, slender tubes, and begin to grow. And finally, there would be no more room to grow.

Marilyn Williams had been only thirty-two.

So Dan and I already knew the gist of what Dr. Bell had to tell us when he showed up later in the morning. But we weren't prepared for his opening remarks.

"We had to bail," he said. "You were full of blood." With the unwavering gray gaze of a Nantucket preacher, he pointed his clipboard at me. "Did you have any pain in your shoulders during any of this?"

The sunburn. Mystifying. He nodded, made a mark on the chart, held it out at arm's length with a satisfied snap. "Pain in the shoulders is one of the indicators of abdominal distress on the corresponding side."

Given the circumstances, Bell went on crisply, everything was jake. Big, rawboned, in his sixties, he was a figure of awe to some of the nurses. Lynne, my night nurse, whom I liked, an ex–high school teacher who'd decided to become a nurse at forty, had a teenage daughter in premed who was a kind of protégée of "TEB" (Theodore Edward Bell). I'd been lucky, Lynne told me, that he had happened to be in the neighborhood. He was retiring; I would be his last surgery.

Now he told me about it. He'd clamped the tube, excised the burst part, and sutured it. The rupture had been close to the opening of my uterus; the ovary on that side had been saved. This was good. But because of it, it might take a little longer for me to get pregnant.

I was too ashamed to ask why. I am a person who has an education, after a fashion, and I should have known the answer to my question, having reached what I considered near middle age. But the process left me floundering—does the fertile egg go up the tube? Down the tube? Do the ovaries pop out eggs both at once, or take turns? I knew the terms, from a smattering of biology: oviduct, zygote, cilia. Put them all together they spell Mother, right? This is a thing normal adults aren't called upon to document.

"Now," said Dr. Bell, "do you have any questions?" I guessed I had. To begin with, what caused this? Could it happen again? How would I know? Would I be able to get pregnant again in the usual way? How soon? What was the status of the rest of my interior? Did I need a D & C? How soon could I go home?

Dr. Bell gave me a lift of his brushy eyebrows. "I don't know what caused it," he said simply. Given the look of the other tube—it looked completely normal—he reckoned it was pure bad luck. "Maybe an exceptionally large egg," he said in all seriousness. "Maybe an obstruction in that tube, something you were born with, held it up." He was not an OB man, he reminded me, he was a general surgeon. He said it with a certain pride, as if he had just pronounced himself an American bison. I would recover nicely; I was a big, healthy girl, and in a week or so, I could go home. His own daughter-in-law had had a tubal, he told me in passing, giving me a pat on my matted head preparatory to leaving. "She had it in July; and she was pregnant by October," he chuckled. "We thought she'd burst!" So I should give myself three cycles of healing, and a long leave from work. And heal up. And be patient.

I promised, a good girl. This fellow had been a doctor, by the look of him, since God was a boy. He knew. And I had not had to listen too attentively after he gave me the payoff: the other tube was "completely normal." From the bison's mouth.

Dan needed to leave; all our clothing and gear was in an unlocked cabin forty-five miles away. And he hadn't yet called Jocelyn's mother. Joan was expecting Jocelyn home today. He would call Joan as soon as he got back to the cabin.

"Why don't you just call her from here?" A flash of irritation. I was so *modern*—hey, anything you say. You have your life, I'll have mine. Our marriage will be our intersection. All bullshit. I was a counterfeit. Love, like law, I considered to be ninety percent possession. I fought it, kept it within limits. But it was there.

So Dan preferred to talk to his ex-wife in private. Not because they shared nuggets of hidden passion. But because when I listened in, it invariably ended up a three-way conversation; they, talking in tones reasonable to reasonably stressed; me, anxious, wringing my hands, sotto voce, "Why don't you tell her. . . ."

Dan would go back to the cabin, pack everything up, call Joan, and check into a motel somewhere near the hospital. Maybe Joan wouldn't mind letting Jocelyn stay the week. "I think Jocelyn needs to be with us now, don't you?" Dan asked.

I didn't think, couldn't. There was the pain, but it had become a dullish, final matter. In all, I felt good, I thought, astonished. This had nothing to do with Demerol. I puzzled over it, until I realized this exotic feeling was something I had not experienced in my adult life. It was relaxation. I was relaxed.

Relax, said the osteopath. You have to learn to relax, said the masseuse, the physical therapist, the acupuncturist, the dance mistress, the yoga teacher. But I never could. I did try. But mostly I drummed and fretted. After 2:00 P.M. I rubbed my neck and typed one-handed.

But this thing was done. It was out of my hands. There was no one to call, nothing to write, no deadline, laundry, muddy foyer, interview, magazine draft, luncheon, waiting for my attention. Nothing. If the phone rang, I could not reach it.

My life had been a shrine to worry. I decided to take advantage. And slept.

If I had been myself, I'd have spent some concern on Dan's method of breaking down our vacation home. Dan packed for trips by waiting until the middle of the night before we left, standing in the middle of the bedroom with an open suitcase for about five minutes and then bawling out, "I can't find my bathing suit!" Or new jeans. Or fresh shirts.

And now he was in a rush. He threw wet bathing suits in with dry underclothes. He slapped ketchup and oatmeal in with cheese and cold cuts—so that the perishables and the imperishables could all perish together in a big packing box. But he was not brutish. Before he left, he spread fresh pine boughs in baskets around the rooms, so the room would be freshly scented for the next vacationer. ("What happened here?" that woman would ask my friend Susan, who owned the cabin and rented it periodically. "The last people must have left in a hurry. They left four hamburger buns in the oven.")

He stopped on the way back to buy me a music box that played "Auld

Lang Syne." From some outrageously pricey room in a lodge, the only thing he could find near the hospital, he called Joan. I'll be there in the morning, she said. No, it clearly would not be good for Jocelyn to stay up there and be exposed to something like this. She wondered aloud why we had told Jocelyn about the pregnancy so soon anyway. Didn't we realize something like this could happen? Didn't we care whether it would upset Jocelyn?

And Dan, normally so patient with his first wife it made me seethe, cried, "Oh, for shit's sake, Joan, how do you think Jocelyn would feel if she *didn't* know what was going on?"

Because of all this, it was late, after the patients who were not NPO (Latin for "nothing by mouth"), like me, had had dinner, when he rounded the door to my room, Jocelyn poking up the hall behind him.

Someone had cranked my bed to a sitting position. I was lying with my face turned to the door, the shadow of the window blinds dividing my face into bars of light and dark in the fading evening.

My eyes were centered in the space of one of the light bars. Wide and fixed and feverish, staring directly at him. He was sure I did not see him. He said later, he felt he could reach out and take hold of that stare and it would have mass in his hand; and he felt a flutter of fear.

This is real, he thought. This is really happening. And I think she is starting to realize it.

5 I HAD VISITORS the next morning. The first one was the paramedic, just going off his shift, the same shift I had got off to a bang the night before.

My heart drummed, quickening, when he showed up at the door. I was absurdly happy to see him, as if he had been a relative, a cherished friend. He sat on the bed, making me uncomfortably aware that he was a good-looking guy, about twenty-five, my younger brother's age, making me aware also that my hair stuck out in spikes of blood and upchuck, and that my breath, in spite of some lemony gel a nurse had spread on my tongue, still smelled like compost. "You look good," he told me. I rolled my eyes. "By comparison. The last time I saw you, you were on the blue side."

"I don't recall a lot of it," I told him, and wondered as I said it what sort of bizarre protocol I imagined I was fulfilling by saying this—I remembered all of it. The trick would be forgetting it.

"This is real tough to have happen to you," he said. "But at least you still have your little girl." I felt my palms prickle, as they did the moment the car came to a halt after skidding on an icy exit ramp. As if a warning light had blinked on a panel. Already, though I could not know it, I was developing what would perhaps lead me into more harm than anything else in the months ahead—the paranoiac's radar for the unsaid. Had someone told this young man more than someone had told me? Was he saying, did he know, that this was it for childbirth and me?

"She's not my little girl," I told him abruptly. "I mean, she is, of course, but she's my stepdaughter. My husband's daughter."

"Oh," said the young paramedic.

"But Dr. Bell said I should be able to have more children." I searched his face for confirmation. "He saw the other tube, and he said it was completely normal." It was the first time I would say this, but how many, many times—I couldn't count the times—I would repeat it, to myself, to doctors, finally to anyone who would listen.

I would repeat it later, to my cousin Marlene, recently born again, when she called from Florida. "You know," she would say, "this is the

Lord's subtle way of letting you know you're mortal. This is a warning."
I allowed as how the Lord was hardly subtle.

And before she could even ask, I would rush on. "I will be able to have
more children," I would say. "The other tube was normal." The-Other-
Tube-Was-Normal. You only needed one. Like kidneys.

And I would repeat it to Dan over the days, each time he walked in,
like a litany that followed the chaste kiss and pleasantries.

But this was only the first time. The paramedic brightened. "That's
great, then," he said. "I guess that isn't always the case." Isn't. Always.

Bill Meyer, the doctor from the little clinic in Sister Bay, came in just
as the paramedic was about to leave. "Hey," he said. "All right."

And then he said he had some information for me, for what it was
worth. He'd spent some time last night going through his medical books.
"My wife had a terrible miscarriage the first time out," he said. This I
liked. This I wanted to hear, because it seemed to imply a fortuitous
postscript. So? And? "And now we have two kids. One three, one just
six months."

Tears pricked at the inside of my eyelids. A new father, this. A good
person. He'd driven all the way from Sister Bay to bring me aid. I wasn't
used to such largesse. The paramedic, his day finished, probably dying
for sleep . . .

My friends and I would say, "They're just people after all," when
doctors left us waiting for two hours, or introduced themselves to us
anew as if we'd never met, after years of visits. Now when Meyer, a
doctor, did act that way, just human, it left me speechless.

Readers had called to thank me when a story plucked a chord, or got
something wrong changed; what did I say? It was nothing, nothing. But
when the matter was saving a life, and then showing uncommon concern
afterward? Simple thanks impossible.

"This is going to sound stupid," I told the paramedic as he made ready
to leave, "but I'll never forget you." Immediately feeling I'd gone too
far. Sheepish. Dumb.

But he met it with a grand clarity. "Believe me," he said, "I'll never
forget you, either."

Meyer then proceeded to give me the short course in ectopic pregnancy, as best he could determine it.

"This is fairly rare, I gather, not only that you had one—I guess it's
about one in three thousand pregnancies—but that it got so far. Usually,
they're caught before they rupture."

"How?"

"There's some pain, it seems. Cramps. Some brownish blood sometimes."

I thought back. I had had cramps. Laura had told me that it was my pelvis expanding, and she, also pregnant, should know, I had thought. My cousin Marlene had told me pregnancy was a parade of little grips and grabs and that all of them made you neurotic. And I had seen brownish blood once, on the occasion of the worst of the abdominal nips. It had been in the washroom at work, me gripping the edge of the sink and telling my reflection, you're nuts. Rub a little dirt in it. But I should have listened. . . .

Meyer was saying that many of the women who subsequently suffered ectopics had had some kind of severe infection first—gonorrhea, pelvic inflammatory disease. A severe infection could leave scars in the pelvis, even on the inner surface of the tube. An egg traveling along could get hung up on an obstruction so minute the unassisted eye could not detect it.

"I never had an infection," I told him. "Not even a yeast infection, I think."

"Well, good. Then you probably won't have another tubal." Another. People had more than one. "I guess, from what I've read, that if there were some indication that you had a condition that could lead to this, there would be up to a ten percent chance that it could happen again."

But not in my case, I cut in. It was a fluke, an accident, a one-time deal. Dr. Bell had said as much. I repeated the litany. "He was the one who saw the other tube, and he said it was *completely normal.*"

"Sure," said Meyer. "When it comes to reproduction, you know, the body has a way of going all out. There have been well-documented cases when a woman got pregnant who only had an ovary on one side and a tube on the other. The egg just crossed over."

I could tell him right now this wasn't going to happen to me; my life history didn't augur well miracle-wise.

"But you'll do fine," he said. "You'll probably have five kids." Sure I would. Five abruptly seemed a good number. He left then, telling me that my risk of having another ectopic probably was about the same as the general population's. He said he would drop by again before I left. I said I would like that; I desperately did not want him to leave. "I'll be back," he said softly.

But when he did come back, I would wish he hadn't. Because when he returned, he would tell me that he guessed he'd been mistaken: ectopics seemed to occur more commonly than he'd believed, more like one in three hundred pregnancies than one in three thousand. And my risk of having another was far greater than the general population's, just on the face of having had one.

But for this time, we shook hands, held hands almost. And he told me that when I could walk, I should look at the pictures in the hall— they were a great deal more classy than the usual hospital art. Watercolors and prints and gouaches that were gratitude offerings from the artists' colony that made this small thumb of land a midwestern Cape Cod. I would like them, he said.

The physical therapist was hanging discreetly around the door, on time for a dreaded coughing session. He would not be put off. Meyer left.

One of those Zen young men health care seemed to attract in the seventies, the therapist bustled in and busily set up the little plastic machine, like a disposable bellows, on my bed tray. It was time to attempt the absurdity. Yes, I knew the lungs had to expel the remnants of anesthetic. But clearly I would split if I coughed. He could see this, could he not? A pillow beneath my gut would not hold back the purple gush of innards. Crouch. Breath out. Now cough. Let's try a nice, hard cough, huh? Come on, let it rip, said the therapist.

Good choice of words, muttered the patient. You get in here and let it rip, the patient said, daring no more than a decorous little clearing of the throat.

And all the while, thinking. Thinking about not thinking.

I will not think, said Medea. People go mad who think too much. The *important* thing is that *you're* alive. Friends who called said it. Their cards would say it. I said it. It wasn't true. The important thing was gone, taken downstairs in a cup, summarily analyzed in the pathology lab and neatly disposed of.

My baby. This is what thinking got you. My Joey-or-Lucia. My brown-eyed child who, if I let it, would tug at my breast, and cry for fear of the thunder, and make noises like a big, fierce lion, and learn what the Stop sign said, and win the spelling bee, and fall in love, and cling to me the night before the wedding—who would assume form and presence in the space of an eye blink and tear my heart in two.

No! Stop this nonsense, good 1973-Supreme-Court-decision feminist that you are. To have dying, there had to have been living. And that was no baby.

But had there been living? Some flutter of a primogenital heart, a wiggle of a bud of an elementary pinkie, a piggie, this little piggie went to market, this little piggie . . .

Stop. Cut it off. Relaxation had flown. My shoulders pushed up toward my ears. My neck felt like an andiron. The nasogastric tube had claws; it was digging raw furrows under the skin of my face. Where was Dan, anyway? Where the fuck was Dan?

The door opened. It was Joan.

I KNEW more about Joan than I knew about any other woman save my best friend of twenty years' duration. I knew the name of her favorite book, the names of her sisters, the way she liked her eggs, her dress size, the shape of her pie pans.

I knew all this though we had exchanged perhaps two dozen sentences in five years.

First, Dan and Joan had been married. Then Dan and Joan and I had been married. This baby I had just lost was to have been, to my mind, the beginning of Dan's and my being married exclusively to each other.

"Hi!" cried Joan, whose voice when she was nervous managed to be both huge and girlish at once. I had never talked to her when she wasn't nervous, and this particular situation hardly made for easeful rapport. She glanced around. "Where's Dan?"

"Good question." I thanked God for myopia. What I could see of Joan looked slim, set up, and faintly preppy. I looked like a bag of shit. She and her fiancé, Jerry, sat down at the other end of the room and said nothing.

I wondered what she was thinking. Joan's relationship with me had been this: I had no right to hate her; she had a moral obligation to hate me. I had not murdered her marriage to Dan; but I had made sure it was not resuscitated. I would not, truly, have blamed her for taking a grim satisfaction in the present state of affairs. She was a grim woman. Also a good woman. Her grimness and her goodness seemed roughly synonymous.

Because of that, and the domestic virtues that shone from her, I had enshrined Joan as our household icon. And now here she stood, the now-uncontested grand champion Mother of His Child. All the old, odd remnants of what I had felt about her over the years—regret and sorrow and sisterliness—rushed between us like a wild stream. The time seemed appropriate for some sweeping reconciliatory gesture, but the best we could manage was to stand, each of us on her own bank, and wave.

"I'm sorry this happened to you, Jackie," she said.

"Bad luck." Plucky me, phony me. I needed to spit, and was not about to ask Joan to get my encrusted little hospital basin. She nudged the tissue box unobtrusively nearer. Oh, Joan, the tables have turned with a vengeance.

"When can you try again?" she asked, as I swabbed my lips, trying to look more like Marguerite Gautier and less like an old wino. So she knew we would try again; this implied she knew we had sex. I squirmed.

"Probably in the fall," I muttered, and began a diarrhetic account of the risks involved with trying too soon, the odds of getting pregnant in any given cycle with only one tube. . . .

Until Jocelyn arrived, rescuing the moment. She nodded and wiggled her fingers at her mother, and skipped to my side. She held my hand. She kissed my palm. I was proud of her, and horrified. This was a kid who avoided the deep end of the pool like the plague, but she was wading into more dangerous waters here. And knew it. Still, in some way, she knew that for this one moment I needed her to be my own. Finally I told her, "Go to your mommy, sweetie," and she did, released, relieved, with cub rolls and bear hugs. And everyone in the room began to breathe again.

We all made hospital small talk for an interminable fifteen minutes. Jerry, a professor of anatomy at a large teaching hospital in Chicago, dredged up what he knew about ectopic pregnancy. It wasn't much. "And I don't think a whole lot *is* known," he said, looking at his fingers.

And then they left, Jocelyn having literally to be hauled away. In the car, as they pulled out of the parking lot, the child began to cry—hard, shaking sobs the promise of McDonald's just down the road couldn't halt. "I didn't want to cry in front of them," she told her mother, "but I'm very, very sad about the baby." Joan was moved, and furious.

About midweek, I became a difficult patient—that is, I crossed over from nearer death to nearer life and began demanding what I wanted. This was bittersweet for the nurses, who were like mothers and took a guilty pleasure in charges who slept all the time. I rang, rang again. "This tube has got to come out," I told the nurse. "I'm sustaining brain damage here."

Next I started on the IV lines. My left hand, then my right hand, had gone blue and puffed. I told the nurses I would give months off my life for a few big, fat, sturdy, smoothbore veins. Finally one night, after a two-person search-and-destroy mission up and down one of my purpling forearms, Lynne, the night nurse, snapped, "This is turning even my stomach." She called Dr. Bell at home, waking him. No frail traditionalist she. The lines came out.

On the last day, I stood alone in a shower stall and let the hot water pour through my hair, a triumph. I scrubbed at my arms, my legs, and all my clefts and crevices with Castille soap squeezed from little foil packets. I must have used a dozen. But the hospital smell, redolent of soft bananas and sour socks and damp foam rubber, would linger on me for days. It would seem to seep from my pores.

I was waiting at 9:00 A.M., dressed and packed, when Dr. Bell arrived. "Any questions?" he asked.

"Just, when can my husband and I have sex? Not for procreation, just for . . ." Why hadn't I skipped the codicil? I broke off, embarrassed.

Bell raised a shaggy eyebrow. "Do you think you could stand to wait a week or two?" he asked. All that sexual traffic, he suggested, in a stage whisper to the nurse, might have contributed to the interior clog-up. He pursed his lips wryly when I gasped; only kidding.

By 9:30 A.M. I was signed out, clutching a full bottle of Percodan and wearing the wrinkled dress I had worn eight nights before. I walked out. Not wheeled. It was important. Down the stairs, not the elevator, with no wheelchair. While I waited for Dan to load my things into the truck, I asked a plump, gray-haired woman in a sky-blue smock, who was watering plants in the hospital gift shop, to cut off my plastic wristband. She nipped it in two with a little shears she wore on a chain at her belt.

"What was wrong?" she asked. Unabashed candor of hospital aficionados.

"Appendicitis," I said.

We drove home, holding hands, smooching at stoplights. We'd had it with hospitals. The next time we go to a hospital, Dan said, we'll be in labor.

The phone was ringing as we walked in the door that afternoon. "Jackie!" screamed my cousin Barbara, "I've been trying to call you for a week." She lived in Michigan; we hadn't talked in months, but I remembered, sinking, the postscript I had scribbled on my last letter, mailed weeks before.

"Barb . . . wait . . ."

"It's fantastic! I'm so happy for you. And guess *what?*"

The week before, on Friday night at around eleven, while I had been in surgery, Barbara had been, too. She had given birth to her first child. A daughter.

AUGUST in Wisconsin. People actually sought this out. They stuck their boats and luggage carriers on the tops of their cars and headed north, to sit motionless over the last deep hole in a shrunken bay, surrounded by air the density of a newly drawn bath and clouds of the nation's most punitive mosquitoes. The locals had no choice.

I was cutting rhubarb. It was noon, near the end of my second week home from the hospital, and the temperature had spiked up to a historic high of ninety-six. In the house, the oven was preheating. I planned to bake a cake.

My grandmother, standing behind me with lips pursed to the size of a raisin as I hacked away at the woody green ribs, had just finished telling me I was insane. I gave her as cheery a smile as I could manage while dashing sweat out of my eyes with a forearm. "No, no," I told her, "I have to do something with all this." In our absence, the garden had come to look like the climax forest. Zucchini the size of Louisville Sluggers.

"You could do something else just for today, though, dear. Rest a little or read a book. . . ." I had had "female surgery," she reminded me mournfully. I could "rupture myself" and end up back in the hospital. Like that. For a hysterectomy next time. It had happened to her sister's niece in just that way. . . .

I covered my eyes with one grimy hand. The heat. Her voice. It filled my head with static. I couldn't stand around here explaining my activity to her. I had to *do* something. I had washed all the clothes, even the mildewed ones, and folded them. Put them away. Rearranged all the books in my bookshelves by subject and in alphabetical order by author.

Now there was nothing manifest left to do. And if I were to sit down, just sit down here in the sun even for a moment, I would think. Something had been niggling around at the edges of my mind. Some point, elusive.

I didn't know what it was, but I knew it was better left at bay, unconsidered, that it would sizzle through my brain leaving a track like a soldering tool if I focused on it. There were several strategies for avoiding it. Eating, for one. I was eating hugely, polishing off leftovers, plowing through half-gallons of maple-nut ice cream. Eating left me slow and stuporous, dazed in the wits, though the steady upward creep of pounds on the scale each morning never failed to elicit a spasm of fear.

I couldn't tell my grandmother any of this, however. I could scarcely look at her. Everything about me made her cry—the biscuity color of my face, the stoop in my walk. "Just two weeks ago," she would say, "you were so pretty. You were so gay. Where is this going to end, honey?" She expected answers. Someone had always had answers for her—my grandfather before he died, and later, me. I was her favorite grandchild, her white chicken, and she had invested me with bolts of hope. And then, behind her back it seemed, I had turned from a cherished girl full of promise to a woman, a contemporary, and a mortal woman at that. It had her unnerved. But I couldn't help. I had all I could manage just keeping people and thought and emotion at arm's length.

Since my grandmother had met us at our door, her chin quivering, I had been fighting the old strong pull. To cling to her and wail and keen. But grief was seductive. Grief had heft. It would haul me in and whirl me around and around until the sense and strength were battered out of me.

I had a system. You dribbled grief out in manageable bits. When my grandfather lay shriveled and hacking in a hospital bed, when surgeons removed, along with a tumor, the part of my mother's brain that held her wisecracks, her gorgeous vanity, I had held then. I could now.

And why so much grief I had to skirt around it, and still it sucked like a whirlpool at my feet? What had happened that I should feel so flayed? I was alive, healthy, in possession of all my organs. People lost pregnancies. Routinely. A cousin of mine had lost a child to a heart ailment, and then subsequently had a hysterectomy, and she was outwardly unchanged. She smiled. My own woes were pattycakes next to that. Postsurgical depression, I decided. Routine. Work more.

"Here, Gram," I said brightly, drenched, holding up a muddy armload of rhubarb. "All done."

I mixed up the flour and eggs. But there was no brown sugar. I had to have brown sugar for the sauce. A sob bubbled up in my throat. Careful. Well, I would just go to the store and fetch some. Just drive myself right down to the store. "Oh, no you don't," said my grandmother, pulling on the sweater she would wear hiking the Mojave.

"Gram, don't you know that only the bag ladies wear sweaters in August?"

"That's about where you've got me right now."

I sat at the kitchen table to wait for her. Put my head down on my arms. I dreamed of running toward a burning house. Something was in there I had to recover. . . .

The kitchen was filled with smoke. My grandmother, tossing the sugar down on the counter, ran around the kitchen with me, flapping towels. "It's ruined," she said, holding out the pan for me to see. The cake looked like new asphalt.

"No, it's *fine*," I told her, busily scraping. Manically piling a little brown sugar sauce like mortar in the crevices. Now cover the whole thin mass with whipped cream. Dan's car pulled in to the drive.

Feverishly I cut a slice, slapped it on a plate, and, red faced and triumphant, handed it to him before he could close the door. But he didn't feel like having a piece of cake right then. He wanted to set his things down first. I began to cry. Scraped the whole thing into the trash.

"There you are," said my grandmother. "She's overwrought."

"I am not overwrought." Speak with caution. The edge is crumbly here. "Please don't talk about me as if I'm not here." I had a terrible urge to stamp my feet.

Instead, I went out, hauled the dog off his chain, and marched slowly across the street to where the lawns dipped down to the lake. I sat throwing tufts of grass into the water. The dog paddled in slow circles, his pale gold paws churning the algae murk.

After a while, Dan came to sit beside me. He rubbed my neck. "She was only trying to help. Now you've made her feel bad." Huh. So she feels bad. We all feel bad. "You're just upset."

"I'm not upset. I just wish everyone would stop treating me as if I've lost an arm or a leg."

"That's how you're acting, baby." He blew a wide, plump smoke ring out over the water.

"I wish you could just smoke like any normal addict and not try to make an art form of it."

"Sorry." He didn't want to have the smoking fight. Always good for a day of not speaking. I had forced him to swear off once we were home again. He'd agreed to, seemed to; then he began walking the dog so often the dog was exhausted. It was just coping, he explained urgently, when I caught him out. Once this was all over, he'd give it up. For good and all. Swear on his eyes.

I called this quibbling. How craven, I told him, to use our mishap as an excuse. But I had found his stash and was nipping a couple every day before he left for work. Felt righteous about it. He'd driven me.

"Just put it out now." The cigarette hissed in the water. Immediately I regretted it. I'd have liked a few puffs.

"Jackie, we have to talk about this. I know how terrible you feel about what happened, but you're behaving strangely. . . ."

"Strangely."

"You don't want to see anyone. Our friends call you, and they want to come to visit, or have us over, and you ask me to make up some excuse."

"Now that is strange. I have a major operation and lose a baby and I'm two weeks out of the hospital and I don't feel like a few sets of mixed doubles. Very strange."

"No one's asking you to give a dinner party. But Todd and Leah, Jack. They love you. They asked us to come out for dinner Friday night. . . ."

"I'm too tired."

"All you'd have to do is sit there. Smile occasionally."

"Sit there and listen to the kids scream and watch them throw things." I saw the small, involuntary move his hand made toward his breast pocket. He checked it. Good. He would have to make it through this without his crutch. A wave of satisfaction.

Then he said, "That's it, isn't it?"

"What's it, Watson?"

"The kids. And because Leah's pregnant. That's what Todd thought. And when he called you and asked, you told him that was ridiculous. But, honey, it isn't ridiculous. I understand why you might . . ."

"It has nothing to do with Leah." I could picture her. Bloomed. Pinked. Gestating more lyrically than any other woman I had ever known. Leah could stand on a salt flat and make crops grow. No, I definitely did not want to see Leah. The way out of this was to change the subject.

"Dan?" I began speculatively. "Do you remember once saying that you found it hard to understand, knowing how I feel about children, that I had had an abortion?"

"I never said I didn't understand it. Honey, that was years ago, you were just a kid, you were in a marriage you didn't want, that couldn't work. . . ."

"Do you remember saying it?"

"What I said was that I would have had problems with it if it had been my wife, even though I approve of the right to choose. . . ."

"But it wasn't your wife, was it? Your wife was safe and sound and pregnant. It was me. But that doesn't matter. I was just remembering, today, what you'd said about it. I was remembering the whole thing. I'd never even thought about it until now. About the nurse who wouldn't let me hold her hand when I asked to, she kept writing on this clipboard, and finally she let me hold on to her thumb. I was amazed that I could recall that, because I had put the whole thing out of my mind, gone, sealed off. You know?"

"I don't see why you're doing this to yourself now."

"Oh, I'm not having regrets. It's just that I was thinking, that might have been my only chance to have a child. And thinking about the way you feel about abortion. Not the right, I mean, but the process. You disapprove. So probably it would be easy for you to think of what has happened as some kind of vindication of that. See?"

He stared. Utterly off balance. Out came the cigarettes. No pretense. I grabbed one.

"It wouldn't be so unreasonable to think, well, she's being paid back in spades. Would it?"

"Jackie, what are you saying?"

"Just that it probably has occurred to you that there is a certain amount of ironic justice here. I mean, you had no sins on your side of the ledger, so . . ."

"Jesus Christ!"

"No, Dan, look. Think about it."

"That's the most sick, the most deeply sick notion I've ever heard." Angry now. My intent. Someone has to take blame. Someone has to be called to account here. I am no believer in bolts from the blue. In routine checkups that turn out to be six-months-to-live sentences. All my dark anticipation. My doting pessimism. I had *known*. The body gives the mind a signal. But for what? If the knowing could not prevent it from happening, it should at least have prevented this misery. This wrath. Did the perceptiveness count for nothing, then? Did the expectation of the blow not even buffer the shock?

And now that it had all happened, all I feared and foresaw and more, and I was recovering, there was this new signal. This thought I kept trying to thrust away from me. This thing that intruded around the edges if I gave it the merest chance. Was it saying that this was not the end of something? That we would not be permitted to get on with happily-ever-after? Furious. It made me furious.

I turned to Dan, lips already opened on a spite. But he looked not adversarial. Tremulous, maybe. Frightened of me. I took hold of his shirt and held him against me. Inhaled his good coppery smell.

"It's okay now," he sighed. "Let's just cool out now. The two of us. Listen, honey, Jocelyn will be here tomorrow. Right? Won't that be *fun?*" I had to smile. At him attempting to humor the simple fool. "She's really looking forward to seeing you. She can't talk about anything else."

It was expected, and I knew it, that I would say I also was looking forward to seeing her. And I said it. But I was not sure. Not only had I come to prefer the company of the people on the soap operas I'd taken to watching obsessively to the company of my friends, it was Jocelyn in particular I didn't want to see.

Even I knew why I was more comfortable with Luke and Laura than with Leah and Todd. People on soap operas were never happy more than five minutes of the hour; real people were more or less happy most of the time.

But Jocelyn. Had I ever before resented her? In any serious way? No. Honestly no. I had seen her grow from a clingy whiner hiding her face in Dan's shoulder to a cheerful ham taking full advantage of her duplicate families. She could be fearsomely stubborn. Intrusive. Pouty. But she was my girl. I'd never anticipated her arrival with anything less than eagerness.

"It scares me," I said, unknowingly aloud.

"Jocelyn coming?"

"No," I answered quickly.

"What happened to you? It would anyone."

"Not that. That I can talk to you that way. That I can want to throttle Grandma. So easily. I don't talk to you that way. I never talk to you that way. Not seriously."

"You do sometimes."

"In arguments. Months apart. Not as a matter of course. I've been an ass as a matter of course ever since I got out of the hospital. I keep stepping down, level by level, with no idea of how long I can go. I'm afraid of what I might do to us. To you."

"So long as you see that . . ."

"I see it, but I don't know how to stop it." I patted a lock of his hair. "Do you know that it's still me in here? That I love you very much?"

"Of course I do."

I apologized to my grandmother, who gave me a cool embrace. We went out to dinner, at a little jazz bar in the neighborhood that my grandmother liked. I asked the combo to play "Georgia" for my grand-mother. Dan asked them to play "Scotch and Soda" for me.

But I could not help thinking about Jocelyn, her sunny face made up, with the eeriness of a police sketch, of equal parts Joan and Dan. The weeks ahead, the last weeks of Jocelyn's school vacation, loomed like a penance. Three weeks of looking into the face of the fact that Dan once had loved another woman—a normal woman, a woman who could have babies.

Dan was right, I thought. I'm losing it.

8 SHE CAME galloping up the driveway and leaped full weight into my lap. The impact on my healing incision left me breathless. But I held her, as she whispered, "Oh, my Jackie. I missed you so much."

What was this? At her most effusive, Jocelyn could never be more than cool to me the first days of a visit. I looked at Dan over her head. His grin was all but smug. As Jocelyn ran off into the yard to visit the dog, who was howling and throwing himself against his chain link pen in rapture, he said, "You see? She really loves you, Jack."

I wasn't about to argue.

"I have to lie down," I said.

I was sure I would put my life between Jocelyn and harm. I liked to ruffle her ginger-colored hair that smelled like blankets dried in the sun. She thought I sang funny.

But there was love and love. The relation between my stepdaughter and me had always been undescribed, episodic, more a jumble of Scrabble tiles than one word.

But suddenly, there she was beside me on the pillow. She hadn't slept, this kid who tapdanced in the supermarket checkout line, discoed in the shower. "I was watching you," she said, "You slept good."

I lay looking down at her, cuddled in the curve of my arm, and thought how a little death could do wonders for relationships.

She had started out as something of a novelty to me. She dressed up my love affair, made it look like pending family. I would braid her hair, let her lick the cookie bowl, timing these domestic tableaux for Dan to happen upon, and see a wife in them. I liked her; there was no hunger to it.

Later on, when both of us had grown up a little and counted for something to each other, she had given me some treats. We made up a secret language when she was five; I was "Packie." She was "Pocelyn." She was sure no one else could understand these words. She wrote down her phone number and told me, "If you ever need me, just call and ask for Pocelyn. Then I'll know it's you."

But finally, when my own baby-need had slapped me up beside the ear, and I had been battling the impulse to engulf Jocelyn, to sponge her mind of any other mother but me, she had helped me draw back, with the occasional curve ball.

Once, she had told me earnestly that she hoped very hard that her Daddy and I would never get a divorce. A surprise, since reuniting her parents was one of her favorite fantasies, often discussed. "That's so SWEET, Jocie," I had gushed.

"If you did," she had explained then, "I would never get to see the dog."

It made sense, I thought, looking at her now, diving from the blanket chest onto the bed—sweet response hadn't lasted. She had her own parents. She could not afford to adore me. Soon I will be a parent, and adored in just such a way . . . No. That was finished. At least for now.

I got up off the bed in a rush, stalked out to the kitchen. Jocelyn followed.

"Can I see your scar?" she asked.

I showed her.

"Gross." She wrinkled her scant nose. "Will it always look like that?"

"Pretty much."

"I hope I don't get one."

"You won't." Opened the refrigerator door. Grimly began inspecting the leftovers.

"That was the worst day of my life, in Door County," Jocelyn said softly. Oh, Jocelyn, you could melt granite.

"How would you like to run through the sprinkler?"

"ALL RIGHT!" Five minutes later, she and her friend Christin from next door were suited up and shrieking. I flopped down on the couch.

Suddenly Jocelyn was standing at my head, dripping. "Chris wants to see your scar, too," she said. I drew the line. She pouted a bit, then gave it up. "Then, we want to color."

"Have Daddy set a table up for you outside."

"He went fishing." Bonding by total immersion, eh, Dan?

"Okay." I found a pad of construction paper, hauled a TV tray outside. The little girls set it up and sat underneath it, their scissors and markers ranged around them.

Through the window, I could hear them talking. "What happened to Jackie's baby?"

"It died," said Jocelyn, coloring furiously. "The seed was coming down the tube, and it got stuck. Then it got too big. Then the tube blew up." Incredible. She grasped it all. "I'm done. Let's show her."

They brought me a green and orange thing, like an aboriginal flower, with strings of yarn taped to each of the tentacles. Crayoned in the corolla of the flower was "I'm sorry your baby died. I hope you get a new baby."

And then Jocelyn asked, "What happened to the baby when it died?"

"I don't know."

"Did the hospital bury the baby?"

"Ummmmmm, I don't know, Jocie. It was so small, hardly a baby at all. . . ." This room was damnably hot. To hell with ecological responsibility; I had to get an air conditioner, or knock out a wall.

"You said it was only as big as my little fingernail. Was that big enough to have a soul?" Chris spread her towel on the floor and sat on it; Jocelyn joined her. It was clear this was the essay question. Explain fetal politics to a First Communion girl.

"Well, even grown-ups don't know for sure, Joc. Some people would say yes, it had a soul and God took it home. Other people would say no, it was too little."

"But if it did have a soul . . ." She stood, chewing on the nub of a colored pencil. I could feel her wrestling. "That means it could come back, right?"

Well, I, for one, was madly in love.

After Chris went home for supper, I stashed the home-baked quiche some well-wisher from the office had given Dan and which I had planned for our meal. Jocelyn totally hated quiche, she said. It would have been the occasion for a sermonette on the value of quiche in specific and trying-new-food-even-if-you're-not-sure-you'll-like-it in general. But in the thick of one such sermonette, on sharing, Jocelyn had said, "You're too strict to be a mommy." Well, I would show her. I made her favorite, grilled cheese with chips embedded in the melt, and left the dishes to soak while I read to her from *The Yearling*. We talked about how Flag's hair probably was almost the same color as Jeb Stuart's, our dog's.

"Jeb is just your dog."

"No, he is your dog, too."

"Well, is this bed *my* bed?"

"Part."

"How about the music box?"

"Yup."

"The stereo? Is that *mine*, too?" We went through the bookshelf, the curtains, Daddy's tackle box, the Marc Chagall poster over the bed.

"And that quiche," I reminded her, "that's part *yours*, too."

"Oh, no! That can be just yours and Daddy's. I'm supposed to *share!*" Then, "All this stuff, why is it mine, too? I didn't buy it."

"Because you are ours."

"Oh." She made her gap-toothed jack-o'-lantern face. "How about your *bra?* Is that mine, too?"

"No, that's all mine," and I dug into her small taut belly with my fingers until she howled. "It's time to go to sleep now." A tuck, a kiss.

" 'Night, Jackie."

" 'Night, weenie." I began to close the door, just partway.

"I love you." Stopped short. She had never volunteered it.

"I . . . love you, too." I walked out into the living room, drenched in protectiveness. In the other room, my little one sleeps. These are the secrets parents know.

I should have sung to her, I thought. Was she too big to sing to? I had had my cradle song all picked out. "Speed bonny boat, like a bird on the wing." Jocelyn would not mind that I was singing-impaired. Children love the sound of their mothers' voices.

Fifteen minutes later. "Jackie?" I was dozing. "Jackie? I think I have a stomachache."

"Don't you know for sure?" But she wanted no jokes. Her voice stretched into a whine. "Maybe your tummy is cold inside from the soda you drank."

"No, it just hurts."

"Do you want a drink of water?"

"No." Silence. "I want my *daddy.*" Of course. She had tried. We both had tried our very, very best. I walked down over the lawns, out to the end of the pier, to fetch Dan.

"Your daughter wants to kiss you good night. She can't sleep." I tossed a bit of gravel. "I think she went a little overboard on the togetherness today." Dan made a small grimace, squeezing the corners of his lips. Handed me the fishing pole. I reeled in the line, phosphorescent in the dark water.

The day was ending in a broad metallic band from horizon to horizon. The air tasted of nickel. A storm coming.

I walked back up to the house, seeing the clear, pale squares of the back-lit windows. I was a voyeur of windows. It wasn't sex I hoped to see. It was people around dinner tables. Little boys jostling for space in front of the television. Families in their secret places. I looked up at my own house, my own lighted windows, with a stranger's yearning. Inside that house were two people who looked at each other as parents and their small children did, routinely. As if they had just happened upon the history of Western civilization. A Reims cathedral. The double helix. A Renoir. The isolation of radium.

A family. A father and a daughter. I orbited around the two of them like a cold moon, drawn and held by their force, but on my own, my separate path.

I had to make it into that circle. Had to make family. Itinerant mothering was not enough.

I HAD READ about this.

This is the way novelists inevitably choose to portray the stagnation of marital passion. Above, the husband moans and toils on some solitary fantasy; below, the wife lies motionless, reciting her mother's recipe for red flannel hash in her head.

This is worse. We're both working hard. Trying to behave as if we're having a fantastic time.

It's barely day. We had awakened before the alarm went off; or rather, Dan had, and had turned to me and lain brushing the small stray hairs from my forehead until I opened my eyes. A slow smile. The shorthand of husbands and wives. He couldn't have signaled his intent more clearly with semaphores.

I had jumped up and rushed into the bathroom to brush my teeth. Dawdled. Combing my hair. Washing my face with complexion grains. When I returned, he lay with arms jauntily propped behind his head, sheet thrown back, brown and fine planed and audacious. What the sight of that body had once done to me, I thought.

There was no help for it. No headache, no weariness, no arcane abdominal twitch to the rescue. It was nearly September; the doctor's green light date had passed without comment the week before. I was fit as a fiddle and—Dan had to assume—ready for love.

And now we're entwined, Dan balancing carefully on his elbows so as not to press on any of my sore places, doing everything the proper way, fluid and gentle. Mustn't push. Mustn't hurt. He cups the nape of my neck in one hand, because he knows I like that, brushes my breast and throat with small murmuring kisses.

I'm absorbed in my nails. Two of the blasted things have snapped off at the quick in the past week, one of them—I turn my hand this way and that on the pillow to be sure—apparently overnight.

Why doesn't the damned alarm go off? But wait, it's begun its preparatory stutter—ah. Dan reaches over and lightly flicks it off. This is our *first time*. This is major. He will be late to the office if need be. At any other time in our history, I would have been touched, grateful. Now my arms around his neck fall slack involuntarily.

He feels it. Hesitates. Perhaps it was nothing. Glances at my profile while raising his head as if midway through some fine passage of passion. "What's wrong, B.?"

"Nothing, really, not a thing." Have I looked so resolute? It seems to me that my rhythm has been normal enough—whatever sensation is not providing, memory is.

But he's not fooled. He's on edge. That minute beading on his upper lip isn't all sexual heat.

"Does it hurt? I'm hurting you, aren't I?"

I tell him no. How could he think so. But he is hurting me. Not physically. I can't feel a thing. But because he is so flushed and eager and anxious. Because last night he made me a daiquiri, and plumped up the couch pillows and slid his hand onto my bare hip under my jersey so shyly and sweetly, like a sixteen-year-old expecting to be shut down. And when he was shut down, when I pleaded fatigue, though my eyes stayed open in the dark long after he slept, his reassurances were courtly as a plumed hat: "Oh, honey, of course tomorrow is all *right*. Any day is all right. We don't want to rush this. . . ."

You could be getting a lustier romp out of the living room sofa, my dear. You, who say you cherish our lovemaking. Who use that fine old crystal word for it.

Dan can't wait any longer. And neither can I. For this to be over, already. I find a little moan somewhere. A little rote buck and thrust. This is only the third time in these so many years I've had to fake, Dan. And I have to, I apologize silently. I wanted you, I did want you, but Dan, it's amazing. It's as if all my erotic buttons have been taped over. As if my insides were covered with skin. I can't, Dan. I just can't. . . .

But now he's beaming. Running for the shower; can't go to work all musky and slidy. What's that he's saying? "I just knew it would be like it was before."

I love you a great deal. But it's not like it was before.

Never mind. I step into the shoes I stepped out of the night before, pull down the bag I wore the day before and then slept in—no spots, just a little wrinkled. It'll do.

I'm buttering my third English muffin—cheese on this one, or peanut butter?—when disgust lets down over me. It's like what a man who had been plucked, miraculously alive, from a fall into a grain silo described as the sensation of drowning in shifting nothingness, pawing, aware, sinking. Here I am—now not only fat but frigid, feeding my face.

I grab the phone with no idea whom I will call. Whom to tell that what has been one of the most stalwart pillars of my marriage—the good skin hunger that has eased over the fights and false starts and estrangements—has just buckled neatly in the middle? Madison is a nice, liberal city; there is a hotline for everything. Connubial crisis? One-sided, please.

I call Laura in Chicago. It's her bad day at work, she says. But she can talk. She can always talk, though we can count on being interrupted by at least half a dozen panicked assistants.

Laura is my best friend. We consider it a monumental relation. It has outlasted everything: time, distance, jealous lovers. Having begun back in junior high, when a girlfriend was someone you overate with when you couldn't get a date, it has endured the period when every intelligent woman wanted to be, like Dorothy Parker, the only woman at the round table; and it's come out unscathed into the seventies, when suddenly it's the vogue to have a connection of substance with another woman. We had it all along.

I never have to explain anything to her. She intuits all. Even our lives have obligingly fallen into parallel grooves. Out of the world of men, we both picked short Italians in the newspaper business, each with one child, each with one very present past wife.

And the synchroneity seemed likely to continue. Astonishingly, last spring we had become pregnant, Laura and I—as best as we could determine, in the same week. Such exaltation then. Such a gift we spoke of it in whispers. And such a heaviness now. I've talked with her only once since I've been home from the hospital. A breezy little bread-and-butter chat.

Now she is all but ridiculously relieved. I have at least brought her something of substance. If we can't talk about *it*—if we can't share morning sickness and expanding beltlines, if she can't bear even to describe those things to me—at least we can talk.

"What you feel is completely natural," she says. "You feel defaced. Anyone would. After what you've been through, sex has got to be the last thing on your mind. Dan knows that. He's not a stone." And the weight. What do I expect? I can't even move, much less work out. It will *melt* away in a month, once I'm active. And moreover, until then, she happens to *like* my bag dresses. I look . . . medieval in them. Good Laura. Up out of the strangling slough, into the clean air.

We talk about her boss, his emotional structure that of a nine-year-old who weighs two hundred pounds and has been bequeathed two million dollars. That morning, because of a typographical error in an ad, he attempted to throw his Boston fern down into Erie Street.

We laugh, loose and corky. "Anyway," she says, "it's not for much longer. Just a few more months."

"Right." And then the long-distance lines hang empty and expensive between us. She is wishing she hadn't said that, I think. I have an absurd mental picture of Laura, weeping, waving to me from the window of a train. I've lost my ticket and stand empty-handed on the platform. You need a ticket to ride. No exceptions. She can't wait for me. But I can wish her good journey.

"You know," I begin, "I didn't realize, when this all started, how rare this kind of thing is, what happened to me. . . ."

"Not so rare. This woman at the agency had a daughter . . ."

"Well, that's because you've been talking about it. That brings the tales out of the woodwork. Really this kind of stuff only happens once in a blue moon."

"They should have known," Laura says fiercely, as if to herself, "at the clinic." I hear a slow, unmistakable pull of breath.

"You shouldn't smoke. It's rotten for the baby."

"I know . . . but Jack, it didn't need to happen that way. They should have been alert to the fact that something wasn't right about that pregnancy when you took the first test."

It had been only vexing at the time. But for Laura, convinced every clinic shingle shielded a collegium of charlatans, it's taken on monstrous proportions. I'd taken a home pregnancy test—taken two, obsessive, always—and called Laura with the marvelous news. Then, on the dot of fourteen days after my missed period, I'd brought a urine sample to my clinic.

Two hours later, I phoned for results. "That was negative," a bored voice told me.

"That can't be! I took two EPTs." Or were they Daisys? At any rate. The nurse had been baffled; it was a matter of pride. She offered to have a Betascan, a test designed to detect very low levels of human chorionic gonadotropin, the chemical in blood or urine that signals a pregnancy, run on my specimen. It had been positive.

Weeks later, I'd chanced to read that that peculiar sequence of tests was one red flag to ectopic pregnancy.

"They could hardly have known," I soothe Laura. She couldn't grasp my need to excuse these medical ones. They are my bulwark. They can't be fallible; in their hands is my fertility. "What's important now is," deep breath, "that this won't be another one of our dumb coincidences. *Nothing* will happen to your baby. And I don't want you to worry. Not about that, or me. She'll be perfect, your baby, my perfect little god-daughter."

"I hate this."

"What?"

"All this. Your reassuring me. My wanting you to reassure me. But look, this will all turn out. Don't you see, Jack? By the time I have my baby, you'll already be pregnant, you'll be huge. . . ."

We say good-bye. I sit in the heat.

It had been this hot, but at night, last spring on a trip to Florida to visit Dan's family. Our first few tries hadn't worked, but the temperature charts I'd taken everywhere, stuffed in my purse, showed the time was, in a word, ripe.

But where? We were on our way to a party with old friends in St. Petersburg. No telling when we'd next see a bed. We were driving a tiny Toyota. I fretted.

All at once, Dan had wheeled the car off onto one of the innumerable little truck roads that crisscross the scrubland along central Florida's single highway. He had shaken out a scratchy army blanket in some farmer's cul-de-sac.

"Hurry," I had squealed, "hurry." The mosquitoes were feasting on my behind.

"But we have to remember this time, Jackie. We have to cherish each other. We are making our baby." And there, sweating in the powdery dirt of some stranger's field path, where tomorrow a tractor would obliterate these small imprints, we had done just that. In a swift, unexpected gust of sensation that made me shiver involuntarily, to recall. Cherish.

I played that night back in my mind, as the airless day gave over to an airless evening, and it seemed strange, historic—like a bit of old film or a childhood incident I had been told about so often it seemed like a genuine memory, but really was only borrowed.

Only a handful of weeks, barely four months, had elapsed between that night and this morning. What was missing was not simply the sexual fervor of the woman I had been then—that would return; that must return—but her arrogance, her illusioned brashness. It had seemed to her that the world was not dangerous, and life would be endless.

I wondered if that could ever come back.

ON A THURSDAY afternoon, September 8, Dan drove me to my back-to-work checkup. Both the checkup and the chauffeuring seemed unnecessary. I'd been driving around the neighborhood for a week and everything—muscle strength, reflexes, even the ruddy squiggle of scar bisecting my abdomen—seemed to have knitted up normally. If anything, rather ahead of schedule.

Dr. Bell had advised me to give myself a month off, but I couldn't afford a month. My boss had called the previous week, an edge of hopefulness in her reasoned, managerial voice. "People have been calling," she said, "wondering where your column went. You've had so much time to think up ideas I'll have to hold you down when you get back!" Pause. "You must really be anxious to get back in the saddle. . . ."

Hardly. But her phone call had meant a resumption of life in the obligatory. The same day, I had scratched out a column in my notebook and dictated it over the phone to Dan. I wrote about what had happened to me—the athematic excuse being the difference in perspective afforded by being the one on the stretcher rather than the one standing by, scribbling in a memo pad. The real reason was simpler—I didn't want all of the people who had been calling to think I'd spent the past weeks vacationing in a padded suite at the Hotel Silly.

Dan said he got tears in his eyes when I read him the column; but by the time I had actually written down the pain, the rush, the paramedic with the rough, warm hand, all of it had happened long ago, to someone else.

We pulled into the drive of the clinic, negotiating around the obligatory flower truck. "How did you get the appointment so quickly?" Dan asked. I had set it up only the day before.

"I think a tubal pregnancy gives you a certain cachet," I told him. This doctor was booked for ages on routine matters. I hardly knew him, and had him solely because he had delivered Leah's babies, and she had said a look of honest delight came over his face when he held up a newborn. Since I had been planning to have him hold up one of mine in short order, that was sufficient. I didn't know what he did about stuff like this.

"You don't have to come in with me," I told Dan. "You can go get a cup of coffee. He'll just say I'm healed, and tell me to wait awhile before going back to work, and I'll say I can't, and that will be that. I already know we can't try again until October. . . ."

We'd already planned that I would be pregnant again by Thanksgiving at the latest. Dan might be looking for a new job by then, since he believed he'd gone as far as he could at our paper, but I'd hold off; it would hardly be fair to a newspaper to hire a new reporter who was going to require maternity leave right away. If he happened to find a job so far from Madison he couldn't commute, I'd go with him, hold up my end by free-lancing. I had some bizarre regular public relations–type customers—a hospital, a drum-and-bugle corps—and had been patiently assailing *Redbook* and *The New Yorker*.

"I still can't believe how you've bounced back . . . physically," Dan said. What did he mean, *physically?* Let it pass.

"I think it was Jane Fonda."

"You'll have to write to her. 'Dear Jane, If it hadn't been for your buttock tucks, I might never have survived my recent catastrophe. . . .'"

The receptionist called my name. I got a paper gown. Dr. Cardiff was next to me before I heard him, coming up softly on creped soles. He was one of the only doctors I knew who still wore whites in the office.

"Well," he said, his unlined boy's face sliding into a grin, "the last time I saw you, you were worried about getting pregnant. Now you know you can, huh?"

This wasn't quite what I'd had in mind—I'd expected our visit to begin with a little commiseration, and a comment or two about how much I'd been through, which I had intended to scoff at in plucky fashion—but I smiled back at him.

"Did you even know you were pregnant?" I heard a small, far-off click. What, hadn't *he* known?

"Well, sure. I'd had a test. Two, actually. Isn't that in my folder?"

He glanced down, ruffled some papers, nodding his reddish curls. He looked more like a lad than ever. "Ah. Sure, here it is. Well, at least that made the diagnosis easier when it happened . . . where were you?"

"Door County."

"Nice place." He examined me busily, tunelessly humming. "Well, everything looks in order here. Do you have any questions?"

"I wanted to know when I could start trying to get pregnant again. The doctor in Door County said October, but I'm feeling so well . . ."

"Let's see. I guess you can have the test in about two months. . . ."

"What test?"

"To see if the other tube is patent . . . open." Click.

"I didn't know there was much doubt of that. You can see right there on the operating-room notes that the surgeon who saw it said it looked normal."

"A tube can look normal on the outside and still be blocked."

"It can." Abruptly, the thing that had been niggling around the edge of my mind began to jostle for front and center. But I hadn't the time for a reverie; this man could tell me things. "What's the real deal here? What do you estimate my chances of getting pregnant are?"

"They could be excellent. They could be zero."

"I see." I didn't see. All this time, I had thought of risk, if there was going to be risk, in terms of having another ectopic. Not in terms of having nothing.

"A doctor up there told me that since there was nothing wrong with the other tube, my chances of having another ectopic were about the same as the general population's." Dr. Cardiff's blue eyes widened. He must have thought I had blocked ears, never mind tubes.

"Actually, anytime someone has one of these things, there's a pretty good chance of having another one. Maybe up to thirty percent." That rang a bell. Where had I kept these numbers all these weeks? Fears were clicking across my mind like falling dominoes.

"What's the test?" He described it. It was called a hysterosalpingogram, and I was sure I would never be able to pronounce it to schedule it. Dye would be injected into the uterus—my uterus, I thought—and its spread monitored by a fluoroscopy unit to see whether the tube was open. A number of permanent X rays—*X rays!*—would be taken to show the path the dye took.

"You'll be able to see yourself on TV!"

Well goody. That *will* be fun! Am I supposed to clap my hands? I felt very weary suddenly, and snappish. I wasn't ready to go back to work. Then I recalled that Laura had had a test, after a bout with pelvic inflammatory disease, to determine whether her tubes were scarred by infection. It seemed to me it had been called a Rubin test. Gas was pumped into her, she lay back, and by and by her shoulders ached. The doctor had pronounced the tubes open. It sounded a whole lot less strenuous than what Cardiff was proposing.

"That's hardly ever done anymore," he said. Too easy to get a false result. "I strongly suggest you have the hysterosalpingogram. But you don't have to. You could just wait and try for six months." Six months. Age thirty. Not knowing.

"No, I'll have this thing."

"Good," a big smile. "Call in a couple of months and make the appointment. Okay? See you now." He gathered up the folders and prepared to leave.

"I really wanted to have this baby," I said softly.

"Well, don't forget to call in a couple of months for that appointment." He headed for the door. A bit bemused, it seemed to me. This was a whole other kettle of fish than holding up healthy newborns. I'm irrational, I told myself. He has said *nothing* to make me feel abused.

"I need a slip for my company's insurance. Your signature and all."

"Oh." He stopped. "When are you going back to work?"

"You tell me."

"Well, when do you want to?" I couldn't. Why do people leave free will at the door of the examining room?

"I've been feeling tired lately," I lied. It was clear I couldn't face life in the obligatory right then. The stiff shoulders. The shaking leg. The stack of mail.

"How about tomorrow?"

"*Tomorrow?*" We agreed on Monday. I had expected him to try to talk me out of this. I had been very, very sick, after all. . . .

Dr. Cardiff hummed, busily scratched a pen over a pad of forms. He made conversation.

"You know, there have been some studies that indicate that the total absenteeism among employees would be cut down if people, and physicians, didn't think everything should start on Monday. 'Go back on Monday,' the doctor says. . . ." A slight shake of the crisped auburn curls.

Tell me I'm wrong if I'm wrong, but I heard him saying that I, who have just almost died here, am malingering. I said nothing. He handed me the paper. I shuffled it to shake hands. He exited.

I couldn't move. I sat on the table, looking down into the sun-washed street where three nurses were having lunch on a stone bench. One of them was laughing so hard she was bent double. Young women. Shiny young women. None of them had had an ectopic pregnancy.

I had spent the morning telling myself that I was getting too cozy with my self-pity. That it was becoming too comfortable an emotion. I determined to reform.

But now. "I never want to see this guy again," I told Dan in the lobby. Irrational. What has Dr. Cardiff done? Nothing. But to hell with it.

I walked, strode, to the parking lot, Dan trotting beside me asking, "What did he say? What was it that he said?"

"I'll drive." Switched on the ignition, narrowly avoided a concrete pole. The thing on my mind, the thing that had slid to one side for so long, was assembling itself in large white letters on the center of my brain: WHATEVER WAS WRONG WITH THE TUBE YOU LOST . . .

Jerk. You came here expecting a pat on the head and a fistful of comforting reassurances to take home. You lapped it up when your dad told you that his secretary's sister-in-law had had a tubal pregnancy, followed in rapid succession by four healthy sons. Cardiff. Why should he be anything but uncomfortable with you? He delights in normal pregnancies. Didn't Leah say as much? Leah's normal. . . .

. . . IS WRONG WITH THE TUBE YOU HAVE LEFT.

I slammed on the brakes.

"Where are we going?" Dan yelled.

"To a bookstore."

It was a nice feminist bookstore. Lots of books by women. More books about women. The blue-jeaned salesperson directed us to the health shelf.

I grabbed the first book I saw with a big-bellied lady on the cover and flipped through the index. E, e, estrogen, endometriosis, ectopic pregnancy. "For up to half of all ectopic pregnancies, no cause is ever established. . . ." Right. That was me. But not what I needed.

Another book, another index. "For many women, an ectopic pregnancy is not a random event and their future fertility is forever compromised. . . ."

New book. "If it was your first ectopic pregnancy and you have one tube left, your chance of getting pregnant again may be diminished. Only fifty percent of women conceive after having had an ectopic pregnancy." The click of things falling into place was deafening.

I grabbed the second edition of a famous women's health guide.

"Only about half of women who have had . . ." I dropped the book on the shelf. The blue-jeaned salesperson stared. Another book; I didn't even look at the title. "Of these, only about 33 percent will have a liveborn child."

The booksellers were getting nervous. I could see them out of the corners of my eyes glancing at their sensible clock. The store was closing; but good feminists don't throw a sister in extremis out at the dot of 5:00 P.M. They chat between themselves, quietly. I had to find it. The why. The worst. See it and memorize it. Why only fifty percent?

And then I did: "In addition, there is an increased chance that there may be something wrong with your remaining tube, for whatever caused the problem with your first tube (such as obstructed tubes because of pelvic inflammatory disease, tubal surgery, or other infection) may also have affected your remaining tube. . . ."

There. So simple only a carefully built, leakproof, lightproof wall of denial could have failed to let it in. Logic pounds forth. Not bad luck, kindly Yankee Dr. Bell. Not a *big* egg. Not random. Inevitable.

"See this?" I showed Dan. "This is why Cardiff wants me to have a test." He read.

"None of this necessarily means a damned thing. That firsthand look counts for something. . . ."

No, dear. Don't try to lay a logical stencil over this one. I had known this for a long, long, an indescribably long time, and yet—a wonder— I still want to wail and reel and stagger. Those other people, that secretary's sister-in-law, those were miracles. This was not the movie of the week. This was us.

I made my legs move. Neatly put the books back on the shelf. In order.

The feminist booksellers looked befuddled. All that thumbing and searching and not even one selection. This wasn't a library. I fumbled around on the counter until I found a bookmark with a verse by Emily Dickinson twining in spidery script down the front. I put down my sixty-five cents. The verse made my throat burn. Emily, born on my birthday, growing up strange and estranged in a snooty town, making black cake and verses high-school kids one day would sing to the tune of "The Yellow Rose of Texas." Wise professors told me your poetry was lightweight, Emily. I love it. Neighbor kids peeked at you through the hedge, when you still walked outside; did they run away squealing when you turned your odd eye on them? You had no children.

Dan and I stood on the sidewalk blinking in the strong sun. Young bureaucrats were getting off work, yanking their ties, hopping on their bicycles. A fine day. A mother urged her balky toddler across the street. People with their little people.

I wanted wet fog and high wind and thunderclaps. I wanted the world knocked out cold. Dan reached for my hand, his face wide open, expectant.

"Cheer up," I said to that face, "you didn't want this baby anyway."

His chin jerked, as if from an uppercut. Jaw compressed, he spun and set off for the car, leaving me standing. Then, in mid-step, he turned back.

"I'm going to let that pass." He held out a hand.

"Why should you? I don't know what I could mean to you once having said that."

"You're my wife."

"Let me tell you something. That one time, the time before we were married when you walked into the house at seven in the morning and announced you'd spent the night with an old girlfriend, you thought I was hysterical. But I wasn't. I was only angry. Now I'm hysterical. You shouldn't be fooled by the fact that I'm not screaming."

"I know that."

"I pride myself on being able to take things. Roll with the punches. But this, I can't take. I'm not excusing how I've been. I just want you to know." Dan put his arm around me. "I will never," I told him, "say anything like that to you again."

In the car heading home, me leaning hard against Dan's shoulder, he drove through soothing places and spoke hypnotic words.

"You are letting yourself be tortured over what *might* be, not what will be," he said. "Everything we know about what happened, and about your history, leads us to think there will be *nothing else wrong.*"

I was doing my grandmother's trick—torching my bridges before I reached them. Didn't I come off a long line of breeders? Did not the people in my family, with few exceptions, have many children and then die at great ages in the act of nailing up siding boards to a house?

Dan made me laugh. "I know optimism is a radical departure for you, but couldn't you just try, for me, this once, letting yourself hope for the best? It couldn't hurt. You can suffer later, if the need arises. Save up for it."

I rubbed his face with my cheek. His stubble abraded.

"Shave," I told him, "if you want hot sex in the back seat."

"I'll tell you what. I'm not going to shave. I'm going to grow a beard, and I won't shave it until you're pregnant." He kissed me, pulling into our driveway. "I'm sure, Jackie, listen, I just feel that this beard won't make it to Christmas. Okay?"

Dan. Pragmatic husband. Who didn't believe in ghosts or portents, and whose family, unlike mine, wasn't webbed with hats on the bed and umbrellas left open in the house and dour imaginings. Who nevertheless, like Thomas Boswell, was willing to believe that life, given half a chance, would imitate baseball. Hitters on a streak wore the same pair of gaiters. Grew mustaches. Didn't step on the baseline. It would work for Dan, too.

"You're a very silly man," I told him. But I allowed as how I would give hope a try. For a month or two. And then I asked him, "Please tell me everything is all right."

"I know it is. These kinds of things just don't happen to me. And I won't let them happen to you."

WORK was like a gala my first day back. The copy desk applauded when I walked in the door. My boss got up from her cubicle and hugged me. My desk was full of phone messages and stroky letters from readers who had read my most recent column. Such courage, they said. Your time will come, they said. Feeling corky, I opened the last one in the pile. It was from a woman who had had a tubal pregnancy, and it made me shudder. "It was not until six months after the actual event that I began to let myself feel the loss." Poor woman. I was glad I had done my confronting.

I spent the morning setting up appointments. I would meet with the people from the infertility support group one night next week. Through them, I got in touch with a psychologist who had been part of an infertile couple, and who was trying to gear part of his practice to helping other such couples.

My interview with the local specialist in female infertility, Dr. Sander Shapiro, was set for the following morning.

My friend Priscilla, who did public relations for University Hospitals, had warned me back in June not to expect this interview to be a day at the beach. Shapiro had not been enthusiastic when she approached him. He had the scientist's suspicion of the press. Hardly unusual. One too many banner headlines on "the cancer personality." One too many draconian analyses about what genetic engineering could lead to. Stir in a little bit of advanced-degree arrogance, a little clannishness, and you had the picture.

No problem, I'd assured Priscilla. I was used to the guardedness of specialists. But, she'd told me, he wants to review your copy before publication.

That rankled. Once before, and only once, for a story larded with technology, a source of information had reviewed my copy. At *my* request. But it was hardly standard. It was my job to be accurate. I liked to think I did it reasonably well.

But there was the condition. No review, no interview. When it came to infertility, Shapiro and his colleagues were the honchos in these parts. I needed them. With misgivings, I'd given in.

Around noon of the first day back, I went to the library to prepare for it. Searched the periodical listing for recent magazine articles on infertility and found not much. I was loath to tackle the medical school's collection of journals before I was grounded enough in basics to know what I was looking for.

The first article I found came from the June 1981 issue of one of the glossier women's publications. It skimmed the whole subject of infertility, but concentrated mainly on in-vitro fertilization—or as the headline put it, "Babies from the Lab."

"You and your husband have been waiting for this appointment for a long time," it began. The couple was described filling out a questionnaire with an intake counselor. "Color of hair?" the counselor asked. "Blond," answered the wife. Eyes? Blue. Would the couple require an artificial womb, or would the woman carry the pregnancy herself? And how about a "backup" clone for the baby, in case of injury or disease? Sounds like science fiction? the article asked. It very well might be anything but; might be, in fact, part of the routine at the infertility clinic of the future.

Great. This kind of stuff a researcher could really love. I began to see Shapiro's point. I kept searching.

Two hours of digging later, I still had more questions than answers. Which was something I seemed to have in common with everybody involved with the subject. Consumer need—later marriages, older mothers, fewer adoptable babies—was combining with galloping technology to make possible advances in restoring fertility that would have been undreamed-of a generation ago.

As had sex therapy in the early seventies, the treatment of infertility was becoming a bona fide speciality, not a sideline. Virtually every large teaching hospital now had its infertility man, or woman.

But the black box still was larger than everything else that surrounded it. Even the crack authorities still had to operate, in some areas, out of a knowledge that certain things happened without knowing precisely *why* they happened.

Age was a good example. There were all kinds of reasons why a woman of thirty-five could be less fertile than a woman of twenty-five. Simply by having lived longer, she'd had more opportunity to catch something or do something or develop something that would interfere with her ability to have babies. But in the absence of any clear indicators, there just seemed to be evidence that the older the animal, the less likely she was to reproduce successfully. Opinions varied on the degree to which age affected fertility, and on the specific age after which the drop became significant, but the mechanism was mysterious.

Older eggs, suggested one biologist, an authority on the greater incidence of birth defects in babies born to women over thirty-five. Perhaps, he said, in lay terms, for the same reason that older eggs were fractionally more likely to produce imperfect babies, they also were more likely to not produce pregnancies at all, or pregnancies that didn't go to term.

There was a growing body of material on male infertility—the age of the father, the father's habits—until recently, it had been assumed that when a couple could not have babies, the problem was with the woman. But now up to forty percent of infertility problems were being linked to the male. I copied this material, on the library's Xerox machine, but didn't read it.

I kept going back to the numbers. The conservative estimate was that one in ten couples of childbearing age in this country would encounter some degree of difficulty in having children. Many sources put the numbers at somewhere around one in six. Either way, that was millions of people, hundreds of thousands more every year.

Where were they all living? Not in Madison. Every second woman in this library alone seemed to be in some stage of pregnancy.

Impossible that there should be so many infertile people when I had not, until three months ago, ever even heard of one.

I knew childless couples, of course—Dan's brother and his wife, for one. But that had been by choice. I thought. I did not know then just how difficult, how reluctant an admission infertility could be, did not know that it was a subject some couples could not bring themselves to share. Not only because it was sexual. Because it was so freighted with guilt. A failure to measure up. Some hidden stain. Some of those "childless" couples, I would learn, had had the decision taken out of their hands.

I found what I could about the causes of infertility in women. They fell into three fairly commonsense categories: "mechanical" barriers, caused by disease or heredity, in some portion of the reproductive anatomy, hormonal disorders that interfered with the menstrual cycle, and structural defects that hindered conception or led to repeated miscarriage.

I devoured anything I could find on tubes. Infections seemed to be the primary culprit—infections occult or obvious. Gonorrhea. Syphilis. Pelvic inflammatory disease. Infections secondary to IUD problems. I'd had none of them.

I found a few paragraphs in a health publication about the role of endometriosis in infertility. A couple of years before, a free-lance writer doing a story about the disease told me, "It was like all of a sudden, in 1974, God created endometriosis." But the condition in which portions of the uterine lining grew outside it, in other areas of the pelvis, engorging and shedding and bleeding with the monthly cycle just as the lining did, was not a recent invention. It had shown up as another by-product of sociology—of the "elderly" *primi gravida* (first-time mother).

By 2:00 P.M. I had a stack of copics, and was feeling the effects of unwonted activity. My incision hurt. My eyes smarted. It was nearly time for "General Hospital."

As I left, I checked out a book I had spotted in passing—it was called *Childless: By Choice or by Chance.*

"What the hell have you got that for?" Dan asked me that night, as I lay propped up in bed, reading about the way various couples lived lives without kids.

"Just in case," I told him. The little gods chuckled.

I was at the huge complex that housed University Hospitals at 7:45 the following morning. Priscilla was waiting with two cups of coffee and condolences.

"I believe in participatory journalism," I told her.

"God," she said. And then she did a thing I would become familiar with, a thing that would be done by almost every woman of a certain age, single or married, who didn't have children. She asked me with a peculiar intensity *why* it had happened. She meant, if it could happen to her.

I skimmed what had by now become a litany, and went on to tell her for what was probably the fiftieth time that University Hospital was laid out to be an analogy of the criminal mind—corridors and cul-de-sacs that wound around into themselves, doors that opened onto nothing. And she showed me, as she always did, the trusty map of the hospital layout she carried in her purse.

I had never been inside the Infertility Clinic; but it was only a series of doors. Behind the doors were some of the top surgeons and endo-crinologists the university could snare. Priscilla opened one of them, and there was Dr. Shapiro.

He looked so *mild.* Had I expected some burly fire-breather? He was a narrow man with sparse black hair and a cauliflower ear. There were papier-mâché things here and there, and a photo under glass of a couple of little children with Sander Shapiro eyes and noses.

Patients of his would later tell me Shapiro was cold. They would tell me they waited up to three hours for scheduled appointments, and they never knew what intern or resident would show up next to probe them with some steel prod taken out of the deep freeze. They would blame Shapiro for that, with cause and with the infertility patient's need to blame. But I did not find him cold—not then or later. Only . . . narrow. A specialist in the strictest sense.

We sat down, and I started the tape.

ME: As you know, I'm planning a series on infertility, not only on the physical and biological aspects, but on the emotional ones as well . . . you also may know I have something of a personal interest in this. . . . So I'd like to begin with a few questions. . . .

SHAPIRO:

ME: Well, you deal primarily with the female half of an infertile couple. Let's talk about how a workup progresses, and at what point in a couple's realization they come to you.

SHAPIRO:

Exasperated, I was about to launch into another few seconds' worth of anticipatory filler, when he began to talk. With an extraordinary deliberateness. With long pauses between phrases I found myself stumbling into.

The clinic was the court of last resort for a five-state area. Most of the couples who came here had been trying to become pregnant for some time. Most were in their thirties.

Whether or not they had reason to expect that a serious problem existed, they were usually in a state of anxiety. "By the time they get here, they want to be pregnant yesterday, and it's not unreasonable for them to have that expectation, even if we can't realize it."

Though patients who'd been to the clinic would tell me later that they'd waited months for an evaluation, and months fell useless between each successive test, Shapiro put a premium on speed. "I think the better part of an evaluation can be completed in sixty days. In a woman of thirty-seven, months can be crucial."

An evaluation progressed from the simpler (and less costly) indices through more complicated and rigorous tests. The first step, in the absence of any other red flags, was a basal temperature chart. A woman took her temperature every morning before she got out of bed, starting with the first day of her period. She must do nothing else first—even the act of "shaking down" the thermometer could lead to a false reading. I remembered the frustration of stumbling, foggy eyed, into the bathroom and flipping on the shower, only to realize, hair wet, that the thermometer was still lying on the nightstand.

If she did it faithfully, a normal cycle would show a basal body temperature that hovered around ninety-seven and a few tenths until about the middle of her cycle, when it would drop and then spike up, abruptly, to ninety-eight degrees or more. Ovulation, the cause of the heat wave, would have taken place a day or so before. Those few days before the rise in temperature were the key days for baby making.

But there were any number of ways in which this simple monthly event could go haywire. Shapiro, I had heard, was something of an "ovary" man. He described the possibility of an inadequate luteal phase—a defect in the system that prepared the uterus for implantation of the fertilized egg.

We talked about "fertility" drugs, such as Pergonal, and Clomid—which Karen Sussman from the local infertility support group in town would later tell me was the Valium of infertility. Physicians gave it, she said, on the theory that a little Clomid couldn't hurt. We discussed wedge resection, a surgical procedure by which a thin slice of an ovary was cut out and which, for some reason, seemed to stimulate ovulation. It was hardly ever done any longer, Shapiro said.

"There are people in this field who do only one thing," said Shapiro. "They stimulate ovulation, or they do tube reconstruction." He thought these self-styled specialists fell short of maximal care. The key was to do it all. He had tried mightily to refine his own training, he went on, practicing the technique of microsurgery on lab animals with instruments as fine as hairs and threads barely visible to the naked eye. He had practiced for months, on his own time, developing an ease of touch.

"The surgeon might be even more important than the microscope," he explained mildly. When it came to infertility surgery, the cures had formerly been as bad as the diseases. Delicate tissues, scarred by disease, often formed new scars after surgery that was state-of-the-art but clumsy even so. Tubes that technically were "open" didn't function; something had been damaged. The microscope was going some way toward bettering those odds.

I sat up there. Okay, so I was hoping. I might need this stuff for my life later on.

Was he top-notch, I wanted to know? I asked this in roundabout fashion. He dodged adroitly. "A person has a right to know just how often the surgeon who will be operating on her has done this before. Does he do it once or twice a month? Or every week?"

But with this whole critical mass of experts brought to bear, with all they knew clicking, how did it go? What were the realities?

Well, they were fairly hopeful, he allowed. About sixty percent of the couples would ultimately get pregnant. The remaining forty percent were also helped, he believed. I asked how. He paused.

"There may be no more fundamental thing, in our society, perhaps for a woman more than a man, than being told, 'You cannot have a child.'" The forty percent would know, at least, that they had done their best. They would never have to look back and think, perhaps. Perhaps if I had done just that one more thing, we would have a child.

Some decided to give up on their own, before Shapiro and his team were ready to give up. Others, through sheer persistence, got pregnant. Then, he said slowly, there were those who went on, from doctor to doctor, and therapy to therapy, and test to test, forever . . . or at least until they were well beyond an age where they could reasonably expect to have a child.

I felt that in my spine. There wasn't much doubt of where I would fall along that continuum. In one of those discovery games you play with lovers after conversation runs out, I had once asked Dan, if he could use only one word to describe me, what it would be.

He didn't hesitate. "Dogged," he had said.

Why, I now asked Shapiro, if infertility affected so many lives so profoundly, why did it seem that so few specialists, relative to other human problems, were devoted to it? The old, old argument: if you can put a man on the moon . . .

The answer, in a word, was money. The people with money were not the people affected by infertility. They were older, had children, or had come to terms with their lack of them. The big corporate research gifts didn't go to the concerns of thirty-year-olds, but those of fifty-five-year-olds: imploding hearts, arcane tumors.

And the winds of politics lately had blown infertility no good. In-vitro fertilization was a good example. It had been pioneered in England, though, Shapiro now said, an American physician had established the basic procedure more than a decade before Steptoe and Edwards and Baby Louise.

In 1979 a U.S. Department of Health and Human Services advisory panel had approved the procedure on scientific merit; but the steps which would have led to the critical biomedical research grant had wandered off into a dead end. The Moralfolk were screaming about the wages of tampering with the creation of life; the proposal was never acted upon.

Until Drs. Howard and Georgeanna Jones were able to establish their program in Norfolk, Virginia, through private contributions, researchers' hands remained tied. After a bouncing Elizabeth Carr, the nation's first "test-tube" baby, was born to a Norfolk couple in December 1981, more funding sources for future clinics began to shake loose. But the government still refused to touch it.

And then Shapiro abruptly gave me what amounted to a gift. The University of Wisconsin would open an in-vitro fertilization clinic, he said, perhaps as soon as three months from now. The team already was being assembled. I was caught off guard. This was news. At the time, there was not one such facility in the Midwest. I was used to bracing my feet and pulling news out of people. As I peppered him with questions—gingerly, he could clam up at any moment—I juggled a quandary.

Should I run back to the newspaper and write this now, for today's paper, or save it to dress up my series? Was it mine alone? Was he telling this to everyone who wandered down the hall?

I was halfway out the door before I remembered the one tiny, essential question I didn't want on the tape. "I'm about to have a hysterosalpingogram." Amazing. It had rolled right off my tongue. "How does one feel?"

Pause. Then a smile. "I've heard there's some discomfort."

So it would hurt like hell. I knew enough of physicians to realize "discomfort" covered everything from a twinge to being peeled off the ceiling.

"How was it?" asked Priscilla, leading me back to the parking lot.

"Fine." Amended it. "Kind of like I imagine taking your orals would be." I didn't mention in-vitro fertilization. Without consciously deciding to, I had already tucked that bit of information away in a secure pocket.

It would dress up my series at Thanksgiving. And if the worst happened, if my hope and Dan's beard didn't turn the trick, the fewer women who knew about it, the fewer names ahead of mine on the waiting list.

"MY COLUMN'S finished, in your directory. I'll get that barbecue thing to you by tomorrow morning. God, it's going to be a dreadful story. Hope the art's good."

"The art's great." My boss tapped her small even teeth with the nub of her pencil. "Can you call creative services and check on the art before you go?"

"I can call anyone you want before I go. It's not even eleven o'clock."

"What time's the test?"

"Two. We should be there at one-thirty."

"Well, go now then. I'll call creative. Go home and rest for a while first. Have a sandwich."

"Carol, it's no big deal. I don't have to . . ."

"Go!" Carol was only a year older than me and the peculiarity of her own situation had enormous bearing on the way she was dealing with mine. Divorced, and wanting a family in the worst way, she had fallen in love with a man almost ten years younger than she was. She didn't want to rush him, she said. He could not reasonably be expected to want to marry right away. But oh, the child-time gambit absorbed her. She was living this thing of mine vicariously; she had her granny, who lived in a nearby retirement complex, clicking her beads for me every night.

And she wanted to do more. So she didn't dock me for those lost hours. When I looked pasty, she sent me home. When I rested my head on my computer terminal, even for a moment, she sent me home.

September had been a long, long month. Filled with infertile people. Hours on tape and notebooks full. It hadn't been the only work I did, but only it absorbed me. I was just conscientiously overreporting, I told myself, but the word "obsession" applied.

I'd spent hours with Susan and Karen from the local support group. Each time, we scraped another layer of experience and emotion. I was in it, it was around me. All that striving and struggle, and ultimately, it seemed, failure. I had met dozens of women and men. And only one couple, just one, had finally had a child—just one child—after three years of treatment, two surgeries, and bottles and bottles of drugs.

Susan and Karen were "normal infertile." Unendurable frustration. Each of them had gone through nearly a decade of evaluations—Susan with seventeen gynecologists in two states. "All they could turn up, before I finally stopped all the medical stuff, was a little of this, a little of that. Nothing that would have stopped anybody else from having five kids." I watched her as she talked, looking for some sense of betrayal, some hint that she feigned all this wholesomeness and cheer, some indication that she gibbered nights in her closet. There was none. Susan was whole and funny and sane. But just listening to her, and to the people who had been in her groups, left me wan, unable to sleep, labile.

I took all of it home to Dan. "Read this," I would instruct him, wide-eyed. "The environment of the uterus is so fragile, all of its functions are so intimately connected, that it's practically statistically impossible that I could be all right. I know I'm never going to have a child, Dan. We'd better stop thinking . . ."

"That's a great idea. Stop thinking. I don't know if it's a good idea for you to be doing this work at this time." So I would agree to postpone the series. But back I'd go, to another book, another interview.

I called Dr. Cardiff the third week in September. "I am healed," I said, "but the emotional stress of waiting is just devastating. Is there any good medical reason why I cannot have the test now?"

He couldn't think of one. Susan and Karen told me what they could about hysterosalpingogram. I read more. Susan had heard the cramping when the dye went in was more pronounced when the tubes were blocked. I had read that some physicians premedicated patients for pain before the test; but Dr. Cardiff said that probably would not be necessary.

I didn't care how much it hurt. You could bear anything for five minutes. And when I saw the dye flow through my remaining, undamaged tube, I would be jubilant. Dan had taken out a bottle of good champagne we had been given for our wedding and washed and polished two flutes. We would drink it when we came home from the clinic, and then we would call my brother and Laura and my grandmother and tell them the good news. And then we would make love, with release and relief and stored-up tenderness.

I lay on our bed, our ridiculously huge bed with the mattress that slanted to Dan's side because that was where the weight ended up most nights—dreamily, blindly, I would gravitate from my side to his, crowding him hungrily, like a heat-seeking missile. I thought about perceptions.

I would be back here, lying on this bed no doubt, the center where we read and talked and bundled, in a few hours. Dan would be there. The same newspapers and jeans with twisted legs and the *Bartlett's* spraddled open between the blanket chest and the mattress would still be here. But how would I see them? Would I lie here and weep, or rock in celebration? Would the sorrow and the tense nights when we had each of us clung stiffly to our own spaces be ended, or would something new, something I was unable to think past the dreadful second of learning, come back with us? It was there, already mine, inside me, this answer. The fortune cookie. Nothing real about it would change over the next few hours. Only perception. Thought. A little thing.

I worried about Dan. He had worked himself into a froth of confidence. An unswerving, banner-snapping color guard of optimism. "You know how you have 'feelings'? Well, I have a feeling. You have paid. You've had all the hurt you can be expected to absorb. Now begins the good cycle. Anything else would be too cruel." Time off for good behavior, he expected. Oh, Dan. I had heard stories in the past two weeks that knocked the possibility of karma into a cocked hat. Not a loser among these people. Not a slouch or a rotter. Good people who cared about themselves and each other and had kept clean and worked hard and put off having families until they could give children all they believed children deserved. If fate counted for anything, they'd have been overrun with offspring.

Dan had been working on a story about a prostitute who had punched her two-year-old to death in a shabby highway motel room. Who was six months pregnant with another child. It made him so angry he feared the anger spilled over into his work and spoiled his evenhandedness; he didn't care to hear how tough had been the woman's adolescence, how serious her situational maladjustment. "And then I look at you, who only want . . . ," he would say. And then subside, angry.

"It's time to go," Dan said. I had been drowsing. "That's good, honey, you're so relaxed!"

"Routine," I said. He wanted so much, so very much to hear that, so I said, also, "Don't forget to put the champagne to chill."

We were handed forms at the reception desk of the clinic and directed across the indoor bridge and down the stairs to the adjoining hospital's X-ray department. The woman who changed in the room next to me also was young. Apparently sound. She emerged in the same cocoon of paper robes (one facing front, one back) as I wore. "What are you having?" she asked me. No reticence in waiting rooms. I pronounced it.

"You?" She thought a broken bone in her ankle had healed improperly. It was interfering with her running. Ah. We both studied our *Newsweeks*.

"Jackie?" A teenage technician ushered me into the X-ray suite. A dim place, with discs and arms of gray machinery hanging down like stalactites. Always amazing, the sizes given to places of business in hospitals. The waiting rooms stretch and spread, dotted with orchards of rubber plants, but the places that count are walk-in closets. I amused myself, waiting for Dr. Cardiff, by sitting on the stationary metal table and stretching my feet out to tap the wall.

Soon all of us were squeezed in there: Cardiff, the radiologist who would run the fluoroscopy unit, the little technician, and Dan in his lead apron with its snappy flowered vinyl covering.

We went over it. Cardiff showed me the trocar-like instrument that would be inserted through my cervix and through which the tubing bearing dye would run and fill my uterus, the overflow spilling out into the tubes—in my case, the tube. Just to the right of my head, as I lay back, was the "TV screen" on which the picture of my uterus would appear. The X-ray unit crouched overhead.

I winked at Dan, and Cardiff began moving the probing instrument around between my legs, positioning it. "Don't move." I lay without drawing breath. "There." Was I comfortable? I was. The dye began to run. A small cramp.

Dan could see it on the screen, rising into the tiny, triangular, purse-shaped thing that was the outline of my uterus.

"Is it working?" I asked, and was reassured, yes, of course it was. Another small cramp, then a grabber. I flinched. Cardiff was making compressed lip noises.

"Mmmmm, I'm going to give it a little more," he said, like a mechanic goosing a balky engine. His hand moved. A massive cramp. I rolled my head back, gripped the table.

"Wait . . ." The dye had gone into the tube on the right side; Dan could see it had gone in only a short way and then stopped. That was the tube that had been destroyed. On the other side, nothing.

"It doesn't appear . . ." Cardiff said.

"Maybe it's a spasm," the radiologist broke in quickly. Dim lights flicked on. He injected something into one of the veins of my right hand, explaining all the while that sometimes tubes will "clamp down," and if that was happening, this should release it.

Waiting. Waiting for it to take effect.

"That should be long enough," Cardiff said. Then the unit switched on again, the dye pumped again. The huge whirr and click of the X ray after everyone had taken shelter.

"I prayed," Dan wrote later, "if I ever could be said to have prayed; I put every particle of mental energy I could muster into making that dye rise up into the tube. I made promises I could never reasonably keep, and I promised I was not making them lightly or inadvisedly."

And then it was over.

"The tubes . . ." Cardiff began.

"I know," Dan has told me I said then, lying on the table and looking up at the ceiling. I don't remember. I had not looked at the screen once.

He would meet us up in his office when I was dressed, Cardiff said. We would discuss it then.

Dan and I rode up in the elevator facing the door like strangers. We did not touch. We sat waiting for Cardiff, staring at his degrees in their chaste black frames. We did not speak.

"This was to have allayed all her fears," Dan wrote. "It would show her she was overreacting badly. I had been listening to her for months, even before the tubal, even before she had gotten pregnant at all, and my patience was well thinned out. I simply could not understand her.

"She was literally convinced that something was wrong, during the several months we tried to conceive, and after the one false alarm, which I think was a miscarriage, and she believes was merely a late period. Each time her period would come, when Jackie prayed it wouldn't, was a setback to me, some minor, irritating bad break. For her, it was an occasion for lengthy mourning.

"To me, it was simply normal that she should not expect to conceive the first month, nor even the second or the third. I would offer statistics and give examples. But her anxiety increased geometrically. 'It's only a matter of time,' I would say. 'No,' she would answer, 'I don't know what it is, but something's terribly wrong. I think we waited too long.'

"After the tubal, I was maybe, just possibly, willing to accept she'd known something I didn't. But I played the happy clown, as she grieved

for that BB-sized fetus as if it was one she had held and nursed.
"The worst thing I could say was, 'I know you'll have another.' That
opened the gates to wild, dreadful tears. One night, after leaving the
house of my sister, who was five months pregnant, she cried. And I lost
my temper. I accused her of making a scene, of indulging in self-pity.
And she responded with some anecdotes from her eternal books, the
books she was always marking in and underlining, that said such a period
of grief was normal, that it could take months for her to recover.

"And I said to her, 'If it takes other women six months to recover,
I want it to take my wife two. I expect you to have more substance.'

"I just didn't know."

Dan reached out, now, and took my hand, curling my fingers around
his. Cardiff came in, shook his head, and spun his leather chair to face
me.

"The repair of a tube is an iffy affair at best . . .," he began. A prepared
speech for the bereft couple.

"It is, I'm sure," I found my voice, "but I haven't had tube surgery.
I've had an ectopic pregnancy, and lost . . ."

"Yes, of course. Well, it appeared that the dye went only part of the
way into that remaining tube. . . ."

"No, Doctor. I think that the tube the dye went into is the remainder
of the tube that was removed. The *other* tube, the left tube, is the one
I have left. *Read the chart.*"

He looked down at my folder.

"I'm leaving now," I told the room at large. "One question. Can these
things ever be fixed?" Cardiff brightened.

"Why, yes. Dr. Bellow does some amazing things with tubes. . . ."

"Fine." I walked out the door, leaving Dan and Dr. Cardiff still sitting
in the office. Dan made a hurried demurral; she was very upset. She had
been on a thin edge for some time. Could Cardiff perhaps recommend
a counselor? Because we might have need of one. Well, there were
several excellent . . . Cardiff began.

And the university's in-vitro program? Did he know anything about
that? Not much? Could he find out more? Could Dan call him? A
bemused yes.

And then Dan ran to catch up with me in the lobby. "Let's get a pack
of cigarettes right away," I told him.

She will begin to cry, he thought, in such a terrible way that I will
not know how to stop her by myself. And I don't want to stop her, no

one should stop her. We got into the car, and he thought, she stares, she just stares, her face is all absent. This is terrible. Oh, this is the most terrible thing—and to his shock, it was he who began to sob, suddenly and in the middle of a street, his eyes filling and streaming so that he could not see to steer. He pulled the car off to one side of a path where brown young bike riders whizzed past in colorful shorts, and laid his head on the steering wheel.

He was surprised by the sudden pressure of my arms. Surprised that they closed strong and lifting, not with the wobbling tug he had come to know when we embraced—the tug that had said, "Help me. Hold me."

I pulled him down on my shoulder and stroked his hair as he shuddered and hiccuped and finally quieted, though he still dashed at his eyes. "I'm so sorry," he said.

"You didn't know."

"You did."

"Not really. Not as I said I did."

"Yes you did. And I . . . ."

"No my dearest, my sweetheart. Stop that. It will be all right. I haven't given up hope. I'm young. You'll see. There are plenty, plenty of things to try . . . we'll adopt, or maybe in vitro; I still have ovaries, after all. . . ."

And he thought of this bizarre exchange of roles, where is she getting this? And how? She had none of it before. She could not bear to see tomorrow.

Now it's I who can't. Tomorrow. And next month, next year. The buffeting of decisions. Surgery or no surgery? More cutting, more pain. And after the pain, waiting? No, he would not have it. Could not face it. It was to have ended here, damn it. That was the deal. Not unfurled like a dropped reel of unexposed film, twisting away and over on itself and under things, spinning out so that one couldn't see where it ended or how to roll it up neatly again.

He closed his eyes against it, and burrowed closer.

13 I WAS TEMPTED to ask Dr. Bellow if he had heard the one about the one-eyed microsurgeon. Conversation is always so awkward when one is bared to the waist in the frog position; more so when it is difficult to tell which eye is looking at you. I liked, however, the fact that the physician who was to be my infertility specialist had a glass eye, the salt-and-pepper hair-comb of a TV newsman, and a natty hand-tied bow tie. He carried an air of eccentricity, which recommended him to me.

He had come well recommended from other quarters as well; Cardiff had called him "top-notch." Shapiro had said he would give me the straight dope. In any case, there had been no question of conducting a search for a specialist; Madison may be hip, but it is small. Every gynecology practice, it seemed, was now doing its smattering of infertility, but for serious work, the women from the support group had told me, it was either Bellow, here at my clinic, or the university. The lines at the university were months deep, and here I was already, just a week after my hysterosalpingogram, so I anticipated things moving along briskly.

I didn't want to linger over this passage in my life. Whatever was to be done, whatever could be done, I wanted done now. I wanted the troops home by Christmas.

So I managed to relax while Bellow conducted his deft and brief inventory of my parts, and we talked, as it always seemed I ended up talking to anyone I met outside the office, about what I did for a living. Bellow wanted to know if my personal experience of infertility was going to be part of the series I was going to write.

"Now if you take a personal experience and write about it, and then attempt to generalize from that, doesn't it lack in objectivity?"

"So long as it's identified as a personal issue, I don't see that objectivity is a problem." And I thought, why are we talking about this, why do I not just tell people I write soda-pop jingles for a living and take them off their guard and have done with it?

But then he asked me if I were going to be writing about my treatment here as part of the series, and I told him, "I always have this experience, when I'm at a party or a play or something and I meet someone new, and they find out I'm a reporter, do you know what the first thing they always ask me is?"

He removed the speculum with a little muted pop. "They always say, 'Don't quote me.' I've had bag ladies tell me, 'Don't quote me.' And I'm always moved to say—I never have, but I'm always moved to— 'Well, for heaven's sake, why would I?' "

He grinned then. "And your husband, what does he do?"

"I guess you would say he's an investigative reporter."

"But what would you say?"

"I guess I'd say the same thing."

"So what he does is perhaps, then, just a little more . . . legitimate than what you do, would you say that?"

"No, I wouldn't say that." We were on good footing now; it comforted me that we had progressed to the trading of barbs. "Just maybe sexier. To the public mind."

"The public mind. Ah."

"You know what I mean. Crime and government corruption, stuff like that. Sexier."

"I see. Now, do you know what a laparoscopy is?"

"I do."

"Then tell me."

I told him what I knew: that a lighted probe is inserted into the abdomen, inflated by a gas, through two incisions, one just below the navel, the other near the pubic bone. That this technique, pioneered to ease the process of tube tying for sterilization, had become the bread-and-butter surgery of infertility, enabling the surgeon to get a good look at the whole interior landscape.

"I see. Well, that's pretty good. For a member of the lay public." And then he brought out the medico dialect with a flourish, and told me what I would be in for on Friday when I checked into the same-day surgery unit.

After I was dressed, we talked outcomes. He told me something that made me soar, though I reined it in and looked impassive—no fate lurking about would be able to sense that I had felt a flicker of hope. He told me that in his experience, two-thirds of women who had a hysterosalpingogram like mine had come up at laparoscopy with completely normal tubes. For some reason, "spasm" being the overused term for any number of causes, the dye simply did not flow at the test.

I reminded him, ever so nonchalantly, that the one surgeon who got a look at the tube, up in Sturgeon Bay, had said it appeared healthy.

"But that can be consistent with an obstruction, too," he said, and I was back to normal, the nugget of hope handed over as he related a harrowing account of an operation he had done on a completely normal-appearing tube, sectioning and patiently resectioning sliver by sliver for seven hours to find that there was no lumen, no cavity, that something had happened to close the tube off along its whole length. Way down, near the end of the tube where it enters the uterus, he had finally found patency. But it was no good. It was too short. There would be no pregnancy.

After we made plans for a meeting the night before the surgery, he asked me if I had any other physical problems. None, I said.

"Psychological then?"

A moment. A beat of time. "Yes. Those."

"For what reason?"

"Simply that I want to have a child, I want very much to have a child, and I have great distress over this." How nicely, how formally we delineate our woes. In this arid little sentence I encapsulated last Monday night, lying rigid and dry-eyed beside Dan on the bed, the coffee cups we had emptied and emptied and emptied sitting beside us on the bureau, the brimming ashtrays, the two of us looking up at the ceiling, at a fine tracery of cobweb that I meant, every morning of my life for three years, to brush down.

And I had said, finally, waking Dan who had fallen into a heavy sleep like an ill child, "This is really it then. I am infertile. I'm not just infertile, I'm sterile. I could screw and screw and screw from now until I'm eighty, and never, no way, conceive a child."

He had been speechless. No room to disagree. But no matter. This was a soliloquy. Up on the bed, hugging my knees. "Me, Dan. Me. No frail Degas lady, me. Rubensesque. Fruitful just to look at me. I should have had a houseful of children. Dan, I never missed a period. I got off the pill, never missed a period. When I was sixteen, and everyone else was dropping one here and there from stress over heavy petting with their boyfriends, I never once missed. Only when I was pregnant. Oh, Dan, I could have had a ten-year-old child now. . . . Why? Why didn't I? I couldn't know, I never knew. . . ."

He'd roused himself then. "We don't talk about that. There's no profit in talking about that." And he was right. I didn't want the ten-year-old child of my youth; I wanted a baby, with this man as father, the stamp and reflection of this good, hard-won marriage. Oh baby, my baby. Rocking harder.

"Dan, it can't be. I'm a horse, Dan, a horse. Infertile women are frail and sickly; they're irregular and fretful." And I'd known then I was being irrational. Hadn't I interviewed dozens of women, and men, who couldn't produce children? And didn't they look as different from each other as faces along a bar are different—joggers and professors and farmers and social workers and physicians, yes, a physician, too.

But still it had lingered, the notion that there ought to be an outward sign. Don Frederick, low sperm count—I had found myself placing my subjects in categories according to their inabilities—had told me about a couple he knew growing up. "They were so nice to us, really overly nice to us kids. They'd bring us presents, and the presents would be nice things, but just a little out of season, you know, past the fashion of what kids were asking for then. And one day, my mother told me, 'Well, she can't have babies, you know.' And afterward, when I would see her, it was as if I could see through that part of her, through her middle, as if she were one of those Visible Woman models they had then, and I would imagine that the part of her where a baby would lie was hollow.

"But now I know, my father told me once, it was him. Her husband was the one who couldn't produce a child. We were so foolish, all of us then, it was just assumed a man was fertile."

Dan was. The previous week he had visited a urologist, loathing it, going at my urging, my repeated urging. Gone and taken his little plastic cup into an empty room with a stool and a curtain and masturbated, feeling helpless and foolish and alone. "And they didn't even give you a magazine to look at? A *Penthouse* maybe?" I had asked him afterward.

"It's not funny, Jackie," he had told me briefly. But the test had come back normal, quite high normal actually. Would it have soothed me to know we were both in the same boat? Had that been at the root of my insistence? But no, and yet . . .

"You could marry again, you know. Jocelyn needs a sibling. And adopting, perhaps adopting isn't right for you. You could *have* a child, Dan, you're just saddled with a woman . . ."

He had attempted to hold me then; I'd shaken him off. Mild neurosis loves company—a spoiled love affair, a dragon boss. Misery, contrary to popular opinion, wants to go it alone.

So it went on, as the clock crept past two, past three, and at one point, when I had given leave to all reason and was ranting, "I *can't* be infertile. I'm too *fat* to be tragic," Dan had asked me, "Do you see what you're doing?"

I looked down. I had been making a cradle of my arms.

"Do you think, love, that maybe you could use some . . ."

"Help, right?"

"Yeah," he said, "help."

I CHEATED. Peter Briggs was a psychotherapist, a friend of a friend. He'd also been part of an infertile couple, and the experience had so turned him around that he was attempting to tailor part of his practice to treating the same kind of psychic aftershocks he and his wife had struggled with after they had learned she was infertile.

We had set up an appointment to talk months ago, back when all of this had been more or less theoretical for me. At the time, Peter had said infertility could invade the emotional territory of a marriage in so many disguises it was difficult for even a perfectly competent therapist to sort out the dynamics. Before, long before he had known that he and Cheryl would be unable to have a child, Peter remembered seeing certain couples. Perhaps one or the other was avoiding sex. Perhaps every petty disagreement accelerated into a bitter bout of blaming. Or everyday trifles would spark furies all out of proportion. Sometimes, he said, somewhere along the line it would emerge: this couple had been trying for five years to conceive a child.

Peter didn't consider himself an authority, but he had done the reading, and he had stood in the shoes, and he knew how a couple could go round and round with a therapist—as he and Cheryl had gone round and round—who couldn't get at the infertility as a primary issue. And there was no one predictable response to infertility, he had emphasized. There was a classic response—among couples who wanted children, had never considered not having children, and then were denied them—and it was roughly comparable to the not me/why me/yes, indeed, me stages Elisabeth Kübler-Ross had set out for an individual's acceptance of terminal illness.

But what about the marriage in which one or both of the partners had serious doubts about having kids, and into which the diagnosis could come as something of a relief, but a relief freighted with guilt? Or the couple who had a long time to make up their minds on the children issue, never really putting a lot of intensity on either choice, who woke up to find themselves at the mercy of a full-blown obsession? Was it being unable to have a child that made having one so important? Or had they simply never realized how badly they wanted one to begin with?

I ran through the October drizzle to Peter's office, feeling unorganized, but a bit smug. I had done all my personal homework, found my constellation of grief symptoms in the books and underlined them with yellow marker. But Dan thought I needed—good old euphemism—to "talk to someone." Wouldn't I now be able to tell him in all honesty that I had? There would be no six-week therapeutic contract for me—instead, this neat two-bird stone: a chat with Peter and a face-on quotable interview for the series besides.

It was better so. Journalists were fierce gossips. Weren't psychotherapists human, too? Confidentiality be damned, they'd have their own grapevine, and I could picture my personal demons speeding along it if I were to enter sessions.

How would that look? A woman who set herself up weekly as simultaneous interpreter for modern life problems, who had been known to use the word "cope" up to three times in a given column, to be so exposed? I had a reputation, a sane reputation. I wished not to risk it.

In any case, I was a world-class coper. It took only a little discipline, a little compartmentalization. No more the office gadfly, drifting from desk to desk, gabbing and plotting. I now marched to my cubicle precisely at 7:30 A.M., nodded to Carol, and lined up a row of nine, not eight, identically sharpened pencils at right angles to my coffee cup. The desk had come to lend me satisfaction. Once it had been a swamp, a thicket of mail and files and messages crowding my elbows, the occasional flood of cold coffee the only incentive to cull and toss. It was neat now. No one had a neater work space. It vexed me to tears if the night cleaning staff moved my memo pad.

A change. But not strange. No. This was my system. Work was the place where I could forget about infertility. No matter that I would spend eight hours—until the pencils were blunted and the crisp new steno book filled with my loopy handwriting—talking to people about only infertility. No matter that long after, when I toted up, it would seem that sixty interviews, five books, and two dozen magazine articles for a four-part series was overreporting in anyone's ledger. That was work.

Now, *after* work, at night, I could talk about it. I could allow myself to really think about it. And talk I did. I had a regular regiment of numbers to call—Laura, my friend Mary, my sisters-in-law in Chicago

—I could talk to anyone who didn't see me during the normal routine of a day. That was the rule. Face was preserved. Who needed therapy?

It would amaze me, months later, to come upon an introspection, like a long-forgotten shopping list stashed in the bottom of a summer purse stuffed with newspaper and put on the shelf at the change of seasons. I had avoided therapy for all of the reasons I had given myself, and one I hadn't. A therapist could help you deal with your inability to have a child. Would try to do that. If it worked, if I learned to live with my infertility, then wouldn't it move in to stay?

It was in the safe, work, context that Peter and I met. He came to meet me in the lobby, lanky and blue-jeaned, the kind of a man who, though he was in his mid-thirties, could sling a stack of books on one hip and slip effortlessly back into undergraduatecy. Such men, in their liberal uniforms, were the bricks and mortar of Madison. But Peter was an original.

It took us thirty minutes to begin crying. First me. Then him. He talked about Cheryl, his wife, Cheryl Timmons, also a therapist. Together they had been through two ectopic pregnancies, followed in rapid succession by two miscarriages. The first pregnancy had been accidental; Cheryl had been only twenty-four; they weren't even sure they wanted a family. But then after the loss of a tube, and a chance conversation with a woman they met at a campground who'd also had an ectopic and whom it had taken four years to become pregnant again, they had begun to try. Rapidly, Cheryl was pregnant again, in the other tube. Richard Bellow, who also had been their physician, had managed to remove the embryo without destroying the tube. A few months, and then another pregnancy. And as Cheryl sat in Bellow's office bleeding, several weeks after the positive test, Bellow had told her, "If you can bear it, Cheryl, this miscarriage represents progress."

But Cheryl and Peter had already begun to slip backward. At first the pain had melded them. They were very much in love, and trained to empathy beyond love. "There were times," Peter said, "when I felt so helpless to console her that I wished I were the sufferer in the hospital bed instead of the sufferer in the chair." There would have been some substance to that, he said, some obviousness—instead of the relentless invisible weight of pain once removed. In the hospital after the second ectopic, Cheryl had begun to talk adoption—seriously, then obsessively. Peter had not been ready. A relentless push-and-pull began, and in the midst of it families began to spring up around them—a family baby shower made to seem mandatory for Cheryl, a brother's baby Peter couldn't bring himself to walk into the nursery to admire.

By the time they had adopted a son, a perfect, healthy son, it had been too late for them as a couple. Looking at each other had become looking at the faces of their failure. Had infertility beaten the marriage to death? Peter shook his head slowly. No, it had been a sounder that had brought up long-submerged issues.

Peter and Cheryl had gone dutifully to therapy, to a nationally renowned practitioner, and the man had somehow, for all the good he tried expertly to do, missed the real gist. Cheryl would later tell me that the therapist had asked her at one point, which did she want more, her husband or a baby? "A baby," she had answered without a moment's hesitation.

"And he *accepted* it, and Peter accepted it," she would say incredulously. "We were in trouble. The respect was gone."

Peter stretched, unpleating his long legs up on the coffee table. We had been chain-smoking; my steno pad sat, untouched, with a brown ring in its center from the Styrofoam cup soaking through. "This is what it all comes down to," I said after a moment, "cigarettes and coffee. The health generation."

He smiled then, half turning his head toward the picture of his son, a merry two-year-old, on his desk shelf. They had adopted Garrott privately, he told me. It was more expensive, more difficult, but bypassed the long, five-year-long, waits at agencies for a healthy white infant. They had written letters to everyone they knew, and told everyone they knew to tell everyone else that they wanted to adopt a baby. And quickly, surprisingly quickly, they had gotten a call. Someone's cousin's brother-in-law was a physician. A woman had given birth who wanted to place her infant with an adopting family. When Garrott was placed in Peter's arms, he was seven hours old. By the time he was walking, Cheryl and Peter were divorced.

Two hours had passed; it was storming in earnest and my work-day was finished. Peter had an appointment coming up. He said he hoped I would mention in my articles that he was willing to counsel infertile couples. I said that I surely would. But Peter's hopes for devoting some of his professional time to infertility work never really got off the ground while I knew him. Even with the recommendations of the local infertility support group, which he and Cheryl had attended, and those of his peers, people didn't seem to come—chose instead, for some reason, to hold back.

"I'm sorry it wasn't much of an interview," I told him as we shook hands.

"It was good," he assured me. "We can do the interview another time." And we did, months later, a good question and answer session in which we covered the effects a diagnosis of infertility can have on self-image, on sexuality. We talked about anger, and its inverse, depression. We talked about a phenomenon that even then seemed uncomfortably close to the mark, but which, astonishingly, I was able to put aside as irrelevant to Dan and me.

Grief and rage were intimately linked. Grief was essential to learning to live with the loss infertility represented. But it could fail you. It could fail a couple if they did not recognize their loss as real. It could fail if they were subtly encouraged by their peers to soft-pedal the loss or not inconvenience others with a discussion of a distasteful subject. We would experience some of that - I would be told that it was not, after all, as if I had a terminal illness, and I would be forced to agree.

But there was another way grief could be blocked - and here was the clincher - Barbara Eck Menning, who'd written a landmark infertility book, said some infertile couples leaped on a merry-go-round of effort aimed at reacting to the problem and trying to reverse it. Some never really faced it. These people were trapped in perpetual outrage, and they were unable to bear it, and so they projected it onto others - the doctor, the counselor, the adoption worker. The spouse.

I would write down these things, and use them, but it would be that first talk with Peter what I would always return to as my reference. I would consider it was then that Peter had communicated the best of what he knew, even though minus the therapeutic tags. Peter's marriage always would seem to me, in spite of his denials and references to other problems, to have been not the gradual erosion divorce often is, but something more akin to a casualty of war.

"Cheryl and I were such jerks," he said once. "We thought we were somehow special people, that we had superior knowledge, or education, or whatever, that would enable us to rise above what was happening to us and understand it in intellectual terms." And listening to that, I had felt for him, at the time, only sorrow—and pity, because I was sure, absolutely sure, that Dan and I really had achieved such understanding between ourselves. And I did attribute some of that understanding to the fact that I considered us bright people, evolved people, with a firm grip on the ever-so-hip principle that what you do know can't hurt you.

"If you ever need help, you and Dan, I want you to feel free to call me," Peter had said. But I did not call him, the following spring, when Dan and I, having seen the Slippery Pavement signs smack in front of our eyes in bright warning black and yellow, went hurling around the blind curve anyway. I didn't call him, because I felt like a jerk.

Sitting in the parking lot after my interview with Peter, waiting for the curtains of rain that enveloped the car to part, I went through my notes. Note, actually. I had managed to ask him only one question, and had written down only one answer.

"The presence of the hoped-for child in the household becomes as real a presence to the infertile couple as anyone who actually lives there," I had written. "The couple begin to live with an awareness of the child's presence, the presence affects their plans, how they live, how they relate to each other. Peter calls it 'the missing member of the family.' "

Well, good, I thought. That has a ring. I have a title for my series.

The rain stopped suddenly, and a hazy sun filtered down on the late afternoon traffic. I headed toward home, toward a fresh pack of cigarettes and a long night of long-distance unburdening. I had to take care of my own child who wasn't there.

THE SAME-DAY surgery unit is a circular suite of beds surrounding a small wheeled table. A nurse stands at the table taking my history. She tells me I'll be taken to surgery at 8:00 A.M.; it's now just after six. In a few minutes, Dan and I will look at a little film about the events of the day, and then Dan will leave, go to work, work a half day, and then, with half the editors and a few of the other reporters, go to Milwaukee for the American League play-offs. A friend of ours, Deb Barber, will pick me up late this afternoon at the hospital and take me home.

We have had a big row about this the night before, and we are more or less still having it. "There isn't any real reason I have to go," Dan tells me, hushed; there are three other women in the room, chatting quietly with their husbands. "There are going to be other play-off games." I feel myself gritting my teeth.

"We had an agreement; if you didn't go to the game, I wouldn't have the surgery. Dan, there's no earthly reason for you to sit here; it's not going to change the outcome. . . ."

"But I should be with you when you come home. . . ."

"Honey, listen. You've been waiting all summer for this, you had to pull nine thousand strings to get the tickets, we paid a bundle for the tickets. . . ."

"None of that is as important as my being there when you wake up and need me." There is something to this. The trick is not to let him know.

"It's not that I won't need you. But you'll be there just a couple of hours after I get home. Anything I need to tell you I can tell you then. The important thing is you've been through a lot. I've had getting healed physically to concentrate on; you've only had to brood about me. I *want* you to have a good day, and forget about all this for a couple of hours."

"Can you imagine how that makes me feel?" His voice takes on an edge that makes the woman across the room raise her head expectantly.

"That I should go sit at the ballpark while my wife is . . . under the knife?"

"Under the knife? Ye gods, Dan. There's enough melodrama in this without trotting out the Ben Casey dialogue." I'm reasonably sure that now he'll go. My brother was wrong. Over the phone, he'd said, "This sounds like the classic martyrdom situation." After twenty-three years' association, he can see through me when all but him are buffaloed. "You'll have this nice tidy pile of ammunition for the next ten years off this."

"I've *never* held a grudge. Even when I was wronged."

"But did you hear the satisfaction in your voice when you just told me Dan had decided to go to the game, *after all?*"

"Bobby! You silly ass."

"Give the guy a break, Jack. Let him avoid walking into the stickiest trap of his life. He wants to be with you, he *ought* to be with you. Don't be the ringmaster." I'd hung up, miffed. But something nagged. Personal courage always had been my top priority virtue, but recently so many people had told me how brave I'd been that I had become a junkie for it.

If someone should fail to mention my fortitude in the course of a conversation, I casually let it drop that I've gotten all my Christmas shopping done. That seals it. Choruses of "How do you manage?" and "I could never have taken this so well." Music.

But I am not all ego animal. I *want* the picture in mind of Dan on his feet, cheering, waving a paper mug of beer as the swashbuckling Brewers we both love take on the California Angels. The Brewers and, to a lesser extent, my illness have been the chief topics of conversation around the office of late. A blue-collar phenomenon, Brewers Robin Yount and Gorman Thomas have turned the uncommon light of the East Coast sporting press on the old German hometown city of Milwaukee. This delights my editor, Elliott. The Eastern literati have caught on too late; this Cinderella story belongs to the Wisconsin newspapers.

Dan and I had been to dozens of games—I, a lifelong Cub fan whose grandfather pitched on one of the Cubs' farm clubs in the 1920s, had finally bought into Dan's prenuptial condition: the children would be raised in the American League.

If there were to be children. That's why all the urgency, why I took the first appointment available, though Dan begged me to wait just until after the World Series—begged me to give obsession a few weeks off already. But there were people conceiving even as he spoke—I could feel them, in cars, in beds, on beaches. And each of those pregnancies, even if it didn't diminish the standing pool of future babies and lessen my own likelihood of catching one (and I half-suspected this), meant I was being outstripped, left behind by fertile others.

I can't afford a day's delay. I can't understand why some women I know have approached laparoscopy with such frank terror. Perhaps it is because they are young and never have had surgery before, but they worry about things I haven't even considered: anesthesia aftereffects, minute scars, and, most of all, the verdict. The verdict that I can't wait for, no matter how awful it is. The woman who wrote about her laparoscopy for the newsletter of RESOLVE, the national infertility support organization, had dithered over having it for months, and put it off twice. Surgery might change nothing, she wrote, it might only force her to face what she wasn't sure she really wanted to know. Wondering, at least, was something she had got used to. The logic dumbfounded me. It was like someone putting her tongue in a cavity for five years but putting off having it filled. Here I was with a question mark inside my body; I was mad to have it answered. I wanted to turn myself inside out and inventory the contents.

Dan is wondering aloud what the woman in the bed to my left, who looks to be only a few years older than me, is in for. "I'll bet it's the same thing," I tell him. "Don't they fit the profile?" Husband has a nice cordovan leather briefcase propped against the foot of the bed; wife neatly folded a canvas wraparound skirt and a Shetland sweater before getting into her hospital-issued gown. It's middle class persons—like these people, like us—who go after infertility with a passion, according to Karen Sussman from the support group, who had written her master's thesis on the emotional aspects of infertility. "They tend to be people who planned things, who deferred their rewards, people who probably have some college, good jobs. Life has given them no reason to expect problems without solutions. They don't take kindly to surrendering control. They've been raised to believe that enough honest hard work will get you what's coming to you." Children, such people believe, are part of what's coming to them. Denied, they fight. Blue-collar couples, in Karen's experience, seemed to have more of a handshaking acquaintance with doom, and fate. Somehow it seems more natural, she said, for them to see infertility in terms of concepts such as God's will.

I straddle this class dichotomy. Close enough to my blue-collar origins to drag the ancestral mantle of preordained doom around with me like a hair cloak, I still want to wrestle God to the mat.

The woman in the next bed then receives a phone call. The subject is school lunches, a lost banana and a granola bar too high up in the cupboard to reach. She has children, then. She's here for a Band-Aid surgery to stop the baby-making process, not facilitate it. If only we could trade, my skin or hers. Just a few days ago, Leah told me with clumsy sisterliness, "If only I could . . . donate one of my tubes to you for transplant. It seems such a waste to just have such proven tubes tied," which she intends to do after her baby is born in January. I tell her that such a surgery has been attempted once, I believe, and not in this country, and had been a rather messy failure, but that I love her for the gesture.

I take off my contact lenses after Dan and I watch the videotape. It's time for him to leave. "B., I won't be thinking about anything but you," he tells me as we embrace on the side of my bed. "I don't know why I'm doing this, I just think it's the wrong . . ."

"Go."

"Do you . . .?"

"I have Deb Barber's number," I show him the slip of paper, "and I will call her the moment I can get up." And then, I think because I love him or perhaps for some crueler reason, I add, "Did you know, Bellow said that in two-thirds of the cases where a tube appears blocked at hysterosalpingogram, there's no blockage at all? And that when the person has a laparoscopy, the dye goes right through?"

The look on his face breaks my heart, with the kind of pitiful tenderness one would feel for a nine-year-old child stoutly asserting that he believes Santa Claus is real. I want to hold and protect him, I want him to hold me. I want, I realize with a jolt, desperately for him not to go, not to work, not to the game, not anywhere that will take him a foot from my side. "But that's wonderful. Why didn't you tell me? I feel so much better." So have a nice game, then, honey. Feel the good sunshine.

The anesthetist, a graying man who looks more like an Amway distributor than an M.D., is waiting, deliberately unaware of Dan's sudden tears and mine, to explain how he will serve me this morning.

"Now I don't want you to worry." A last squeeze. "Promise? Routine, right?"

"Routine." I'm alone. And there's business to take care of.

"Let me explain something to you," I tell the anesthetist with what I hope is a reasonable smile. "I have very peculiar veins. They seem to roll and collapse. So it may be difficult for you to get a line in. Is there any other alternative?" I know there is, I once had another surgery, a bit of reconstruction following our car wreck, and was put under to the oniony smell of gas.

We will talk about that later, this fellow tells me, and then I have my pre-op shot.

I'm lying in the hall outside the operating rooms, thinking, of all things, of the red dragon kite I had as a kid—dipping and swirling— a nurse's wide moon grin passes over me, and I hear, from far off, Bellow's voice. Is he here, talking in fact, or am I in some minor drug dream? He is quoting me verbatim, "We have a young woman here who is having a great deal of stress and anxiety over being unable to become pregnant. . . ." But who is he telling? Ah, students. That's who. So we shall be a classroom, shall we, my lumpy bisected belly a showcase for all to see. I hope fiercely all of them are men. I don't want some tight-assed, shiny-haired young female intern looking down on me and wondering how I got in such bad shape if I'm as young as they say I am.

The anesthetist and I are not talking about it, as he had promised. Instead, he's making repeated attempts to start a line in my arm, blood is squirting onto the drapes covering me. I give him three tries, and on the fourth, I lift my free left arm and say, "Now wait a damn minute. I told you this would happen. Can't you put me under with gas?"

"But gas is so unpleasant, we really only use that with children. . . ."

"Well, what do you think this is? A piece of cake?"

I get the gas, but I still can hear Bellow talking. I open my eyes and he's talking with a big, red-haired woman lying on her side in a bed across the room. There is one utterly empty second, and then I realize it is over, I am back in the surgery unit, and have, creepily, actually been awake for some time without having any thoughts at all.

I glance at the clock. It's past noon, and even if I wanted to call Dan now, and I have the feeling from the way Bellow is drawing the curtains around us—he didn't curtain off the woman across the room, so her news must have been good—that I'm going to want to call Dan, I will not be able to. Because he's gone. Already on the road. So speak, Doc. Let's have it. I'm not one of the two-thirds.

And yet when he does say it, "There was an obstruction; I think we can confirm Dr. Cardiff's diagnosis," I feel a horrible sinking. I had let myself hope after all. And I have to force myself to ask. "What now?"

"Well, I don't want to go jumping into anything. You should take some time and think it over, talk to your husband. Microsurgery is a possibility. . . ."

"Can I schedule it now?" Can I have it now? Can I just go back into that deep quiet, and come out all well? Anything, anything but sitting here with this.

"Just hold on." He seems to glance at my fists, clenched at my sides. "Are you okay?" I open them, finger by finger, deliberately.

The obstruction seems to be up close to the uterine wall, perhaps in the wall itself, Bellow tells me. Cardiff said he saw what appeared to be a shadow on the X ray, a minute length of tube extending out from the shape of the uterus; Bellow did not see it. If there were such a bit of tube that could be joined with the clear portion after the obstruction was removed, there might be a decent chance. But I have the feeling that Bellow thinks the blockage is in the wall, and that the kind of surgery possible would be what is called "reimplantation"—the tube would be sectioned off and implanted in an opening cored into another section of the uterus.

He has already told me how well this kind of surgery works. "I've never had a pregnancy from it," he said.

I sit up on the bed after he leaves. This is the worst, I tell myself, after this anything that happens will seem better if only by comparison. The thing is to get home. I have difficulty getting dressed. The little incision burns and grabs. In the washroom, I clutch the stool, feel myself go light-headed. Don't faint. No time. I lurch back to the bed, put in my contacts, and call Deb Barber's number. Rings and rings. She's not in. Of course she's not in. She's a graduate student and is in school. She doesn't expect my call until after five o'clock.

I next call my grandmother, who is irritated. "I can't drive downtown," she says firmly, "you know I can't drive my car downtown. I can't handle that Beltline. You just call a taxi, sweetheart. . . ."

I'm sweating, soaking my blouse at the breastbone. "I don't want a taxi," I hiss, beginning to cry. The patients in the other beds glance over at me. "I want you. Gram, for God's sake, I just had an operation. I want to come home, and I want to come home now. For once, just forget your fear of traffic and come and get me. You're exactly seven minutes away from here. You've *worked* at this hospital. You could drive here in your sleep."

A stiff silence. Then, "All right. But if anything happens . . ."

"Right. Fine. It'll be on my head. My head is used to it." I gather my papers and bottles, stuff them in my purse, and head out to the desk.

"I'm Ms. Mitchard," I tell the nurse, who has not fifteen minutes before asked me if I would like some lunch.

"I believe she's sleeping now." The nurse is busily making marks on a chart. "She just got out of surgery a little while ago. You can see her in a . . ."

"I'm her." The nurse looks up, flustered.

"What? Oh. Oh. I see."

"I'm ready to go home now. You did say I could leave whenever I wanted."

"Of course. I'm just used to most people sleeping the rest of the afternoon. Is there someone here to pick you up?" I run through all the wrong turns my grandmother could possibly even now be sitting at, hyperventilating. I fervently hope there's someone here to pick me up.

"Oh yes, I'm sure she's here by now." I walk deliberately toward the elevator. The nurse lifts her pen to wave, bemusedly.

"Wait! The wheelchair. You have to go down in a wheelchair!" She hails a passing volunteer in a peach blazer. "Won't you take her down?" I settle myself in the chair and we ride silently to the lobby. The volunteer seems mildly miffed at having to interrupt her business to take what appears to be a sturdy-looking woman on a pram ride. Visitors and ambulatory patients in robes and slippers gaze idly at us as we cross the lounge. What do they think? That I've been in the hospital and am going home now, all healed? The *sham*, the dull illogic of the whole thing. I didn't go in sick; I haven't come out well. Only, what . . . flawed? A second, like china? A slight irregular, quite usual in appearance? Only the new small wound making itself felt on the display case of my abdomen is additional.

My grandmother is sitting, bless her, in her fourteen-year-old rust-over-turquoise Buick at the curb. She looks a wreck, her white hair standing up in spikes, whether from concern over me or the rigors of traffic I can't tell. I slide in beside her; she knows without asking. I'm not throwing my arms around her so she knows that what I have learned is not favorable.

"Now Jacquelyn," she says, after we have pulled stealthily out into the traffic on Washington Avenue and then stopped stock still, "I know how much you wanted children. . . ."

Oh God. Trust my grandmother to put it in the past already. "I think we'd better move, Gram. There are many cars behind us, all honking." My grandmother opens her window.

"Blow it out your nose!" she yells to the car directly behind her. But we begin moving, thirty feet at a time, down the street. "I know how much you wanted children, but some things in life we cannot control. If they are meant to be, they will be. It may be that the Lord wanted to spare you what I went through. Maybe it's better that you don't have children at all than have them, and love them, and then see them go the way I did." My mother and my uncle both died in their fifties.

"Do you wish you had not had them?" I asked her, feeling that if she says one more thing, I will jump out of the car with rage, so why am I asking her?

"No, darlin', I don't regret a day of my life. But if you think what you are going through now is hard, you should imagine how I felt when I saw your uncle lying in his coffin, his hair just as curly as when he was a baby. . . ."

"Grandma! I sympathize, but THIS IS MY GRIEF! I know how badly you felt when Mama and Uncle Billy died, but this is NOW! For God's sake, I'm depressed enough as it is, not to mention that I feel like throwing up. . . ."

"Don't you raise your voice to me, young woman. And don't take the name of the Lord in vain."

"Oh, help . . ." I sink back against the headrest, my voice disintegrating to a mew.

"Your problem is that you have never had the least bit of compassion for anyone else. . . ."

"Gram, I've got an idea, let's just drive the car off a bridge, you and me. I could give a shit at this point whether I live or die, and you've been saying 'This is the last time I'll see the leaves turn scarlet' for the past fifteen Octobers, so let's go. How about it?"

And as if to oblige me, she turns the car into the off ramp of the expressway. I can see cars coming at us head-on. See the small, wide O's of shock on the drivers' faces, and I think, I'm truly flipping now, this isn't happening, and I yell, "*I DIDN'T REALLY MEAN IT!* Gram, turn! This is the wrong way!"

And she does, jerking the wheel to the right at the last possible moment and taking us bumping down over the grassy embankment, scattering cars going in the opposite direction out onto the shoulders and medians, horns bleating. "Did you do that on purpose?" She gives me a look of scorn. "Of course I didn't. It's just that when I'm around you, I can't hear myself think, and I didn't even see the Do Not Enter sign!" Then both of us begin to laugh. "I'm sorry." I am sorry. "I'm too testy." We stumble into the house, leaning on each other's arms, me breathless from surgery, she from pique and emphysema and the ridiculousness of both of us.

I sit down on the couch, feel faint again, lie down. A terrible, terrible feeling, I had none of this after the other operation. "There, there," my grandmother is leaning above me, her hand papery and cool on my forehead. I cover her hand with my own. "Do you want some tea?" The heart pounding subsides, the cold sweat dries.

"Sleep, now," my grandmother says. I will be a good girl. Obey. How long can a woman sleep, I catch myself thinking as I drop off.

"I can't imagine it will be long enough," I say aloud, and my grandmother does not have any idea what I mean, but she will remember it.

She croons, "Try to rest now, it will all come out in the wash." In the wash. Late afternoon sun fingers probe dustily around the drawn shades. The television is on. I hear a burst of tiny cheers. The Brewers are winning.

Five o'clock I expected. Seven o'clock would have been all right. But when I wake up again at nine o'clock, and Dan is just walking in the door, I am as furious as someone who can't sit up straight gets. And I open my mouth to break a rule of our marriage, our marriage of two adults who never, ever have asked one another, "Where have you been?" when he kneels by the couch, full of concern and a good explanation. "David was driving, and he wanted to stop for dinner. The whole car wanted to stop for dinner. Honey, I thought you'd only be home an hour or two by now."

"You know what happened." A statement. My grandmother has waylaid him at the door and given him the news and told him to go gently.

"I know. Oh, monster," he says.

"This is what I am going to do. Tomorrow first thing, we have to go into the office so I can use the good typewriter. I have to write a letter. To Dr. Howard Jones at the in-vitro clinic in Norfolk, Virginia."

"But didn't you say there were seven thousand women on the waiting list?"

"Yes. But I have to write. I'll convince him. And I'm going to call Peter, and find out all about how they adopted Garrott. I'm not going to sit and feel sorry for myself, Dan, I'm going to do things. All the options. All the options . . ." I can hear my voice diminishing, like a child's toy winding down. "We have to plan. I'm going to get up now, and we can talk about it. . . ."

But we don't talk about it. Dan picks me up, easily, as if I were little Jocelyn, fallen asleep in the back seat of the car, and carries me to bed.

IN HER BOOK *Starting in the Middle*, the late Judith Wax confessed that she used to embarrass her friends and befuddle her husband by baking heart-shaped cakes and dressing herself up in read velvet and doily lace on Valentine's Day. I'm embarrassing at Halloween. I dress up at the least excuse; I send cards to all my friends.

Most of it is the fault of my mother, who loved the fall and the end of October in particular, and who was genuinely odd the rest of the year. She could tell you how many letters were coming in the post, and who they were from.

I had been telling Jocelyn my mother's ghost stories. About Aunt Celia—the late Aunt Celia— rustling her taffeta skirts in the pantry. About Resurrection Mary, who left her small ghostly handprints on the cemetery gate when she tried to pry the bars apart. Joan religiously de-programmed Jocelyn after every visit, pointing out that I was certainly flaky and possibly dangerous. But I was encouraged to see that Jocelyn, who was exasperatingly timid about everything in the natural world, took to the supernatural like a fish to water. It was harmless stuff: "Eat your broccoli now, and then I'll tell you about the day the three hooded monks were seen in the choir loft at Holy Family Church, right near where Daddy and I grew up." And it was the only way we had ever found to interest Jocelyn in fantasy; she had never had any use for fairy tales or pretend. Play for Jocelyn meant an elaborate board game and three flesh-and-blood playmates. A kid can get too grounded in the real, and Jocelyn was headed that way. "What do you want to do when you are grown?" I asked her one day. "You like to dance and sing and paint, so maybe you'll want to be in the theater."

"I'd like to *own* a theater," she told me.

The Wednesday before Halloween, I called Jocelyn in Chicago. "I'm so excited I think I won't be able to sleep," she said. "I can't wait until Friday." My brother and sister-in-law and an old friend of ours, Charley, came up every year for Halloween weekend, which coincided with my brother's birthday. This year for the first time, Jocelyn was coming, too.

It had taken several years of high-level negotiations; I was not to tack silver maple leaves to an outside windowsill, as my mother had for us, and then wait to see if they turned into twenty-dollar bills at the stroke of midnight. I was not to act spooky; Jocelyn had begun telling the neighbors her stepmother was a witch.

"How can I create an atmosphere?" I asked Dan plaintively.

"Forget atmosphere," he told me, "you'll sleep better."

"She won't even get a shiver."

"That's the point."

But Madison took Halloween seriously, even if I was going to have to soft-pedal it. The annual downtown party, which was nominally for the university students, drew tens of thousands in costume rain or clear, and clogged off four city blocks on Saturday night. My brother, Bobby, his wife, Sandy, and Charley and I loved these Saturday nights—a round of house parties, the press of the young crowds downtown, the bands and bonfires. Dan hated every long minute of it. But despite strenuous bitching, he annually submitted to being dressed in hoods and robes, and allowed me to powder his beard and make latex wrinkles on the face he secretly was proud still looked like a college kid's.

Halloween had seemed distant at the end of August. By Halloween I'd be better, myself again, Dan and I would be trying to make another baby. Devout pessimism notwithstanding, I had never in my deepest heart expected all this to be drawn out. Nothing in my life had been, to date; the Mitchard crisis orientation was to screech to a halt, shatter, and then rapidly reassemble and proceed as planned.

Now that the weekend was here, I couldn't summon my manic self, the eight-armed lady who baked bread and sewed on spangles simultaneously. Halloween loomed as an irritation, an interruption in my newly inaugurated one-task-a-day program. Since the laparoscopy, I had made it a point, beyond work and other business, to take one constructive step toward getting a child each day. It could be a phone call, or the finding of a hopeful address. So long as I did not let a day pass.

Not only had I written to Dr. Jones in Virginia, I had phoned Baylor University, Vanderbilt, and every other institution in the United States that had begun or was starting a "test-tube baby" program and placed my name on their lists. I had called every adoption agency in south-central Wisconsin, and learned what I already knew—that those who still were placing healthy infants (and an infant, nowadays, was any child up to age five) had waiting lists of five years and longer. Most of the agencies had suspended infant programs "indefinitely." At any rate, the home studies required were, to us, prohibitively expensive and most agencies required prospective parents to have been married longer than our eighteen months.

So I had got back in touch with Peter, and he had laid out for me the enormous task of networking and letter writing that he and Cheryl had undertaken to find Garrott. The director of RESOLVE in Milwaukee had told me two or three members had located babies in the past by writing hundreds of letters to doctors all around the Midwest, asking that they be contacted if a physician became aware of a woman who wished to place her unborn child. I had already drafted such a letter and called my friend Michael, a printer, to arrange for two hundred copies at cost.

A woman I'd interviewed back when "older mothers" were news was going to put me in touch with an attorney friend of hers who had helped couples find babies. Stephanie had had, she told me, two blocked tubes, and had begun investigating adoption when the tubes mysteriously unblocked and she became pregnant at age thirty-eight. Her son was now a year old. She was trying to become pregnant again.

Each night over dinner, I literally sat Dan down for a briefing. He would try to open the newspaper; I would slide it away, at first gently, then not so gently. I would read him the news of the day: "I met a guy . . ." "There's a doctor in New York . . ." My green spiral notebook was filling rapidly.

This double-shifting took long hours. I needed to make my personal calls during business hours throughout the time zones, so I stayed late or came in nights to give my job its due, setting my mind aside and cranking out copy, pirating an adjective here, a simile there, from story leads that I'd admired. Originality was not the point. Getting through was the point. Carol approached my desk one morning. "I've wanted to tell you how much I appreciate the volume of work you're doing," she said, "considering the strain you're under." I looked at her blankly. What I had been doing occasionally rose to the level of banal, but this was hardly peak production. Or didn't she see the difference? Or wasn't there one?

"It helps to keep busy," I said. Bosses like to hear that; it eases guilt. What could I say? That for the first time in my life, I was doing this for the money?

"You just keep coming; you don't miss a day, you don't slack off. It amazes me," she said. "If it had been me, I'd have called in that Monday after the laparoscopy. I don't think I could've faced a desk full of work after that kind of news." This disturbed me. Had I not reacted badly enough? Taking bad news to heart was a critical element of my superstition. Those who took it lightly got more. "I was so proud of you when you just walked in here that morning and settled down to it. As if nothing had happened."

My turn to feel guilty. I had been cosseted that entire weekend. It had been like an Irish wake. My grandmother brought chicken soup. My editor, Elliott, called to tell me he loved me, he was worried about us, and that he would cash every check he had to help me get a spot in the university's in-vitro program if that was the way we decided to go. "It really wasn't so bad," I murmured now into the video display screen.

"And I wanted to tell you something else, too," Carol went on. "I cried last night. I thought it was only for you. But it was *me*, Jack. I'm so scared. Seeing this happen right in front of me. It made me think, will I ever have kids? Will something like this happen to me?"

I knew what she wanted. What I would have wanted in her position. I had asked Marie, my boss before Carol, the same question in so many words when Marilyn Williams had her ectopic. Will it happen to me? Just say it won't happen to me. But I was weary. And weary, too, of being the friendly local infertility hex sign, reassuring every thirtyish woman I knew that the great majority of women have children without incident.

"It's Carol you mourn for," I told her, without thinking first. She stared, baffled. "It's a poem," I said. "You know, 'Are you grieving, over goldenwood unleaving?' Everybody looks out for number one in a given incident." Carol had retreated to her desk. "Only in the poem, it was Margaret." I got up and walked over to her cubicle. It was after all a small thing to give. Why be niggardly with comfort? "Carol, don't worry. When it comes time for you to have kids, kids you'll have." She pursed her lips, unconvinced.

After two weeks of such days, I had been exhausted. The work was not so taxing as the social life. We had gone to the World Series, spending a night in a hotel with our friends Gail and Mike and their round, achingly adorable six-month-old son. Dan had finally, without telling me, accepted an invitation to have dinner with Leah and Todd —and so out to their farm in Sun Prairie we went and there we spent three hours with their two toddler boys and Leah's newest pregnancy. I did not hear a word that was said. The wood stove crackled and glowed;

Leah brought out some home-canned cherry preserves. I felt like an alien immersed in three hours of the American myth. Todd and Leah opened their mouths and out came work and snow tires and diaper rash and normality. I opened my mouth and out came the names of gynecologists, statistical percentages of risk and success, kinds of incisions. After that night, the last face I wanted to look on this week was Jocelyn's.

"Cancel Halloween," Dan urged me, "everyone will understand. Don't push yourself so hard to relax you hate every minute of it. They know what we're going through here." He had a point there; we had not had to go through the delicate business of serially letting down our families' hopes for us. That was what I had a grandmother for. I had talked with my brother earlier in the week, and he had rather fewer questions than I would have liked. It pained him, Bobby had said, to discuss it.

But my kind of people are seized with the need to force a situation —to stand on obstacles and prop up sags and create something that at least looks stable if one does not look too closely. "You don't do that to people," I told Dan, "you go through with things."

And so all of them came. And the familiarness of the way they behaved was, after all, comforting. Bobby and Sandy got into a spirited battle Saturday afternoon on our living room carpet when my brother, a biological engineer and a compulsive, insisted that the tibia they were cutting out of white felt to paste onto their skeleton costumes was not anatomically correct.

"Look here," he pushed the medical encyclopedia he had brought under his wife's nose. "It's a mess. That looks like a fibula, not a tibia."

"Stuff the tibia," she replied, snipping furiously.

"I solved this years ago," said Charley, who had propped his feet on the coffee table and was spending the afternoon extending one good Scotch and water. "I spend thirty dollars on a single good ghoul mask. Now I can go anywhere."

Jocelyn danced around me as I dressed. "What are you?"

"A tomato." It at least followed the general outline of my present silhouette. I had stuffed down pillows into a red beach pantaloon that I'd bought last spring from the Bloomingdale's catalog, thinking it would look fetching over my round belly when we took our winter vacation near the end of my pregnancy. I also wore a red sweatshirt with green felt leaves tacked on to the hood. As costumes go, it was more warm and cheap than inspired, but it fell together surprisingly well. It also made for good laughs when, half an hour after we left the house, my stuffed tomato began to succumb to gravity.

"Hey," said Jocelyn, "*now* you look pregnant." Did my look warn her? She jumped up off the bed and hugged me. "I'm sorry."

"Don't be sorry. You can make a joke."

"I'm still sad about the baby."

"Me, too."

"But will you get pregnant by Christmas?" Why, in the first optimism, had Dan told her that?

"I'll try, Pookie." Might as well case the territory, I thought. Applying rouge in big smears to each cheek, I asked Jocelyn, "How would you like it if we *adopted* a baby?"

"A little baby?"

"Yep."

"I'd *love* it." Convince your papa, I thought. Dan had put his foot down. He wasn't yet sure how he felt about adoption; his background was even more traditional than my own. And moreover, he insisted, it would be years before we needed to exercise that option. Exhaust the medical stuff first. I want to do both concurrently, I had demanded. It took *years* to adopt a child.

"No," he had finally come down hard, "I'm going to have to be firm on this. We're under enough of a financial strain with your missing work, and you're probably going to miss more work. We can't afford to go in all these directions. And, Jackie, I am not ready. You can't do this unless both people are completely agreed. Would you want to force me?" I left off then, but things had not been easy between us since. And now I did an awful thing.

"Well, if you would like it, let your daddy know. I believe he thinks it would upset you." Jocelyn bounded up off the bed. "Not *now!* When it comes up." She nodded, grinned. She had lost another tooth.

Having used my stepdaughter, I went out into the kitchen and had a drink. I had three drinks. Then we all had some of the potion Charley had gotten from a college kid his little brother knew, and giggling like teenagers, we piled out the door, rang Mary's doorbell, and got candy from her wide-eyed children and a quizzical "What cookie jar have you folks got into?" from her. It was a good night, ending up at three with eggs and toast at a truck stop—mated skeletons, ghoul, a hangman, and what was by now a pear tomato.

But I was up at six, even before Jocelyn. I had never been much of a sleeper, and lately I slept even more fitfully. I was sitting at the table, feeling large headed, drinking coffee, when my brother shambled out of the bedroom, zipping his jeans and rubbing his eyes.

"What's up?"

"Nothing. I just couldn't sleep. But you go sleep. We practically just got home." He sat down beside me.

"I think it's fair to say the costume of choice this year was Extra-Strength Tylenol capsules." It had been a month since seven people in Chicago had died from Tylenol laced with cyanide, and the moratorium on Tylenol jokes apparently had expired.

"But that makes me think. We'll have to check Jocelyn's candy. The police have been asking people to give their names and phone numbers on slips of paper with the candy they pass out."

"Did you do that?"

"No."

"You have to have some faith in human nature."

"Oh?"

"Well, you ought to have to." He poured himself a cup of coffee. Dan, Sandy, and Charley had not stirred, and Jocelyn, sleeping with our golden retriever in the basement rec room, couldn't hear us. "She's a good kid," my brother said suddenly. "It took so long to crack her. She doesn't warm up to people. But Friday when we were driving up, she started telling me jokes. Seven-year-old-kid jokes. 'What did the cabbage say to the carrot? *Lettuce* entertain you.' And then she'd just fall over."

He loved kids. How he had wanted me to have a baby. It had represented for him the beginning of the way life should progress, in simple greens and browns, close to each other and not too far outside the warp of tradition. He amazed me, my brother, in how little college and travel and the sprawling corporate mill he now was part of had changed him. He was a good man, an uncomplicated good man, not in any dull or narrow sense; but he had none of my edges and wires. I skittered in and out of safe orbit. His ground line never snapped.

I loved him. We were close. Brothers and sisters grow out of the in-house intimacy of childhood, become genial strangers with a past, and choose their adult intimates out of their own changed lives. We had not let that happen. We'd worked at it. When my mother died, Bobby was only fourteen. I had taken over, become meddlesome, forced him to apply to the pricey out-of-state schools he would need for his oceanography degree, and wheedled my father into sending him to one. He remembered creeping up the stairs after his first drunk. I had met him on the landing, whapped him across the face with a wet towel. Then I had held his head while he retched, and inquired tenderly whether he felt all right. When he said he did, I'd let fly the towel again. "Don't you ever drink and drive." He had resented me then. How overbearing I had been! But in a noisy bar on the weekend of his college graduation, he had thanked me, oddly, for protecting the length of his boyhood, for not allowing him to grow up too soon. And we had cried together.

"Do you remember the last time we went out to steal pumpkins together?" he asked me now.

"Old man came out of the gloom with a pitchfork, and his arms out like a zombie. . . ."

"Let's take a walk," he said.

He waited until we were standing at the lakeshore, throwing stones and watching the mist rise. "I have something to tell you. Sandy and I want to try to have a baby right away." I tossed a stone; the plop was huge in the silence. "It scared the hell out of me, what happened to you. And we are rather closely related."

"You're a man," I said, too quickly. "Infertility doesn't run in families. Well, it does, but not in that way."

But they wanted a family. Always had. Bobby and Sandy's was one of the last of the childhood sweetheart marriages to work out. "And I'm afraid that if we wait as long as you did . . ."

"I didn't wait because I didn't want kids."

"There was a time when it didn't matter to you much either way. You said so." Oh, brother. You who boast you know me so well that you see through all my games. Didn't you see through that?

"That was what Dan wanted. I was trying to want it, too." My brother hooked his hands in his jeans pockets.

"Do you resent Dan for that?" he asked.

"I do. It's foolish."

"So do I," he said slowly. "Understand, I still care about him, but I *know*, I just *know*, that if you wouldn't have put it off so long . . ."

We began walking back to the house. "Is Sandy pregnant now?" I asked, elaborately casual.

He laughed. "Not that I know of. We're thinking of beginning to try right after Christmas, pay off a few bills first. . . ." I felt surrounded. Leah's pregnancy. Laura's. And now this planned one, who would put his fat arms around my neck and shine brown eyes at me—like yours,

Bobby, like mine. Perhaps the only child I would ever be related to by blood.

I can't bear it, I thought. It's horrible to think such things, horribly selfish. But I cannot. Not now. "I can't bear . . ." I said. We were standing in front of a huge wooden mailbox. I put my head down on it.

"What, Jackie?"

Think fast. A lie, but a good lie. He'll spot a flabby one. "Passing nausea," I said. "The wages of surgery." And then I said, taking his arm, "You're a good fellow to tell me first."

"We wouldn't have felt right about just springing it on you. 'Surprise! Be happy for us!' " He was silent. "I know you're the oldest. You should have been first. But not having kids would . . . sort of kill me," he said then.

"It's *fine!*" I cried. I was flapping my arms—he thought it was the cold and gave me his jacket. "I can't wait to be . . . an aunt."

I ran up the stairs, past Sandy, who already was frying bacon for breakfast. Headed for the bathroom, a pill or something. Jocelyn flung herself on my brother's back, wearing her purple Martian hat, the anemometer my mother had sewn into the crown long ago spinning crazily.

My brother and I didn't have that talk again. I waited for their announcement. Not until nearly a year later would I find out how clearly he still saw through me, how little I fooled him, and how far he and Sandy were willing to go for a friend.

THIS WAS a game board for the mettlesome of nerve. On the one side, the ovaries. They were an asset, both present and functioning remarkably considering all the recent strip-mining in the vicinity. Over there, tubes. These were the quickest route to Conception Point in the normal course of play; but on this board, there was only one, and its appearance was deceiving. A playing hazard, definitely: it put one in mind of the cruel old joke. "Madam, I have some good news for you, your child has only one eye." "Doctor, how can that be the good news?" "The bad news is that it's blind."

There was another element on the board—there, in the middle. A uterus. Uncharted terrain, an untried course. The player had to assume it worked. Even so, no matter what the level of skill of those involved, it all came down to the pack of cards lying in the middle of the board.

"And they're all facedown," I told Mary as we ran up the bike path toward Esther Beach. It was nearly five on an early November night, and the rhythm of our ragged breathing was the only sound on the street. I wasn't much of a runner. Though I went out every year and guiltily purchased the newest revised version of running shoes, I could never stick with it long enough to receive the spiritual gifts. I hit the wall right away and stumbled along it thereafter. Still, the fuel—pasta, ice cream, even trash that had held no allure for me before, like doughnuts—was going in at an alarming rate. I was so desperate to burn it off I would resort to running.

"It would be easier to decide if you were certain about the odds," Mary gasped; this was the thigh-screaming section of our course; we always tried for animated conversation at this point.

"That's just it," I told her. "Bellow places them at zero to thirty percent chance of a pregnancy, *if* a reanastomosis can be done without having to cut into the wall of the uterus. If the blockage is in the wall itself, he seems to think the odds go way down."

But Bellow had not been my sole handicapper. I had been reading the books; the salespeople at University Bookstores broke into glad smiles when I walked in the door. Barker was of the opinion that the surgery was best able to succeed *if* the blockage was in or near the uterine wall —as best as I could determine, the very scenario Bellow seemed to consider problematical. Silber wrote that when blockage occurred in the canal that joined the tube to the uterus, rather than at the fimbriated end, the interior of the tube was less likely to be damaged. Microsurgery could open up the obstruction "quite elegantly," with pregnancy rates of up to eighty percent. Graham seemed to believe that any micro-surgery, anywhere along the length of the tube, could only be expected to result in pregnancy rates of a few percent at best. And he seemed to think that the rigors the hopeful patient endured for these odds were a fairly miserable trade-off.

And then there was the anecdotal record. Susan Reese had given me the phone number of a woman from her group who had had tubal reconstruction. She'd been in surgery for seven hours, Susan said, ex-perienced a circulatory complication that forced her to drag one leg around for months, and she had not become pregnant. I had never even made the call.

"That will be my luck," I laughed as we hit the top of the hill, panting furiously. "I'll come out of this not only sterile, but unable to walk. To run! And Mary, running is my life."

She grinned. "I think you should get another opinion."

"I have. We saw Shapiro last week." The university specialist had been uncannily warm and cordial in the doctor-patient context. "He laid out the same picture. Except that he said his partner, unlike Bellow, had had a fifty percent rate of success with reimplanting the tubes into the uterus. You know what he meant? The guy has done two of them, and one of the women got pregnant."

"Ha ha. That must have made you feel loads better. Well, look, I'm going to call my doctor tomorrow and see what he says. And my sister's doctor; he does infertility. . . ."

I loved Mary. I was not the only one; she was the angel of the street. Running was more of an excuse to be with her than anything else. How had I never known her? Jocelyn played with her two kids; we nodded from our cars on the way to work each day. But over the past two weeks, I felt I had happened upon undiscovered mineral wealth two doors down. She was warm and expansive, but more than that, nothing flapped Mary. She did things about things.

Two weeks before, I had been laboring up the hill in my Nikes, when she hailed me down. "The kids told me what happened to you last summer," she said without preamble. "I hope you don't mind my finding out that way. The thing is, I had two miscarriages a couple of years ago. I *won't* say I know what you're going through. But I know some of what you're feeling, and I wanted to ask you if. . . . I could hug you for a minute." And then, before I could reply, she did. "Even having kids doesn't change that loss. It was as if I had never known what wanting a baby meant until I lost one."

The next day, when I passed her mailbox, she had been waiting, with her tennis shoes and her husband's baggy sweatpants. We plotted a run from the dead end to the beach and back—two and a quarter miles, about all either of us could bear. The run occupied an hour and a quarter —the last forty-five minutes spent with her walking me to my driveway, and then me walking her back to hers, and then her walking me part of the way back, talking nonstop.

"Dan tells me it's my body," I said. "He says he'll go any way I want to go." We were sitting on a park bench at the beach; it had grown colder, and a breeze skated across the steely surface of the bay. An open magazine flapped in the vacant lifeguard tower. Mary reached up and closed it.

"Do you know what way you want to go?"

"I want to try in-vitro fertilization. But I doubt if I'd have it here in Wisconsin. Shapiro told me that after the surgery—if I have the reconstructive surgery—there would be another hysterosalpingogram at three months. And then, if the tube was open, we would be required to try for eighteen months before we would be evaluated for in vitro. He also said it sometimes isn't necessary to do the test, because the couple get pregnant before the three months are up. Which depressed me."

"How come?"

"Because I know we'd end up having the test."

"Ahhhh, Jackie."

"I know. I know. I asked my brother a couple of days ago if he thought that I was becoming pessimistic by nature. He said, 'Becoming?' "

"So you would go to Virginia then."

"Well, I could probably do that right now. Without having to wait very long. I got a letter from Dr. Jones there a few days ago, and he gave me reason to believe he'd take me right away." The letter had come as a shock. I'd forgotten the desperate night when, still sore from the laparoscopy, I'd hobbled into the office, typed out four pages of pleading, and sent them by the night mail to the University of Eastern Virginia.

Dr. Howard Jones had sent a most human letter in return. It made my eyes fill, though it was only a few paragraphs. He'd been moved by my account of our problems—moved, even with the heart-wrenching stories that must have filled his days for so many years. And hope, any scrap of it, was so welcome these days.

In a postcript, typed by a nurse on the bottom, I was told that Dr. Jones wished me to make my appointment specifically with him. "He has asked us to be on the lookout for your records and wishes to see you personally." When I had called to ask how long I would need to wait for that first appointment, the nurse had said, "Oh, I think he'll want to see you in just eight weeks or so." I was astounded. I knew there were several thousand couples on the Virginia list. I'd anticipated a wait of years.

Dr. Jones had also suggested the possibility of reconstructive surgery. But that entailed the long post-surgical wait for recovery, then the eighteen months of trying. "I couldn't wait *eighteen months*, Mary," I told my friend. "I have to be pregnant in eighteen months. In eighteen months, I'll be nearly thirty-two."

She put her arms around me. "That's not all that old." I knew that, on some sane and distant level. Some of the best babies I'd salivated over recently had come from thirty-five-year-old bodies. But age, which had never meant much to me as any sort of yardstick of worth before, had taken on a staggering importance. I had to have two children—the two I had coming to me—by the time I was thirty-five. I had not considered an alternative. There *was* no goddamned alternative.

This was impossible to explain to Mary sanely. I tried. I told her that celebrities under the age of thirty who were parents had no moment for me. I couldn't read enough, however, about writers and athletes and movie stars who had got pregnant after thirty. Jaclyn Smith was all right, though she was gorgeous. Meryl Streep was all right. Jill Clayburgh was marvelous; she had waited to become pregnant until she was past thirty-five and had lost one pregnancy to boot.

I told her that my personal icons of late were Baltimore Orioles pitcher Mike Flanagan and his wife, Kathy. She had suffered two ectopics. But just a few months before, she had given birth to a healthy, beautiful baby girl, the first test-tube baby in the United States to be delivered naturally instead of by cesarean. The Joneses had done the procedure. I carried the *People* magazine story about the Flanagans around in my purse, refolding it so often it eventually decomposed. So fine. So hopeful. I had taken it out to read it at stoplights.

"Anyway," I told Mary, as we started for home, "the sooner I get this behind me the sooner I can go back to being normal. Being completely selfish is a big burden. And I've become the neighborhood rag."

"Oh shit," she said. "That's not true."

"It is true. At first it feels good to be self-interested. It does. You feel like women spend so much time taking care and patching other peoples' lives, you have it coming to you. It's a relief to just worry about yourself for once." I slowed to a walk.

"But then," I went on, "you get sick to death of it. You remember why you hate to get stuck with the desk next to someone who's always gloating about his next promotion, or his latest romantic coup. You remember how your eyes start to droop when someone says, 'I've really been through a lot, but now I'm getting in touch with myself. . . .' You start to see yourself becoming the kind of person you don't want to meet."

"You have never been the kind of person I don't want to know," said Mary.

"There's a lot of the good Christian in that. I think I'm your cross."

"I'm no martyr. I wouldn't be in this if I wasn't getting something out of it."

"A sore ear."

"On the contrary. I've matched you gripe for gripe."

And she had. The shame was, I didn't recall her gripes. I had listened to them, talked with her about them, and tried to help, but then put them aside. I didn't take my friends' concerns to Dan, or to bed with me, as I once had. The only person in bed with me was me, my dilemmas, my increasingly swollen self-involvement, more ardent than the most demanding lover.

I longed for the refreshment of a genuinely disinterested emotion, as the eye longs for light after a long stretch of overcast in February.

The healthy began to irk me in a serious fashion around this time. I had no patience with them. I had no patience at all with my sister-in-law Gail, who had called me at work recently to tell me that I should try to find out more about tubal reconstruction done with laser beams.

"The woman's tube on this show was blocked just like yours, and the laser beam cleaned it all out," she told me. Not only was I on deadline that morning. I had to call the clinic as soon as I was done with my story to have my records sent to Norfolk. But Gail irritated me so much, through no action of her own, that I had to pause to school her.

"There is no such thing as 'cleaning tubes out.' "

"There is so. I saw it on TV." I yearned to tell her she was mistaken, to tell her, moreover, as I had told Dan, that it was inconceivable to me that a person could have gotten to the age of twenty-five, have one child, and be pregnant with another, without even a rudimentary knowledge of how Mr. Sperm met Ms. Egg. Gail thought ovulation was only a theory. She could not get pregnant, she assured Dan and me, unless she had intercourse precisely on the fifth day after her period began. Gail embodied for me the lilies of the field, who did not sow or reap or put forth any visible effort, only sat about being gifted with beautiful healthy children. She and her husband, Nick, were generous, funny people. But they did not work in the accepted sense of the word. If they felt like a ski trip and didn't have the bread, they sold their couch and their microwave, and Nick's mother, who was well-off, bought them new ones. I worked hard. Dan worked harder than I did. What were the twisted priorities of a fate that awarded Gail, not to mention a country mile of welfare mothers, busloads of gorgeous babies and withheld from us one very small, nothing special, brown-eyed kid?

"I already asked a surgeon, a top guy, about laser microsurgery," I told Gail, bored, typing as I talked. "And he said the results were just the same as with traditional microsurgery. So it doesn't make a bit of difference."

"I still think you should check it out. This woman they had on got pregnant the first month." That would be the one they would have on "Phil Donahue," I thought.

"I wish I would have seen it." Archly, "I don't get to see daytime TV as often as you do."

"It was on '20/20.' "

"Oh." And then I ran past Gail, just for experiment's sake, the same game plan I'd earlier run past Laura. I'd seen the Joneses on the "Today" show one day when I'd started work late. With them had been small Elizabeth Carr, the nation's first test-tube baby, now ten months old. There had been a couple of dozen pregnancies since at the Medical School of Eastern Virginia, the Joneses had told Jane Pauley—who was, by the way, all right; she had had a miscarriage and was thirty-one—and they could now estimate their pregnancy rate at about thirty percent on a given attempt.

"Which is about the same, as far I can figure, taking all the opinions into account, as the microsurgery. I have ovaries. Dan has good sperm. We've put those two things together before and made a pregnancy. Why shouldn't I make maximum use of what I know I have that works, rather than risk a seven-hour surgery?" I didn't tell her what really troubled me about microsurgery: I had read a study in which a fraction of women had failed to resume ovulating after surgery. The article called the risk "minute." Well. Minute chance? Send it right over here. I was afraid I'd come out of all of it not only sterile, but menopausal.

Gail agreed; after all, I was pretty convincing. "But I still think you should call that place that uses the lasers. I think it's in California."

I told her I would. Hello, California? Can you connect me with the guy who uses lasers on tubes? It was ridiculous. But she meant well.

I did not tell Gail that over the past several days her brother, my husband, had begun to express serious disenchantment with my odds making on tubal reconstruction versus in vitro.

I was afraid that if I did tell her, she'd agree with Dan. I was afraid most sane people would.

But I did tell Mary, though I hadn't intended to, that night on our run. We had sat on the stone bench again, at the beach, me staring at the fan of wet sand spreading near our feet for about ten minutes. Finally Mary said, "I'm freezing. Also my right leg is completely solid-ified. Can we go?"

"Sure," I said, and didn't move. I thought, how does one introduce such a subject? Begin to peel away pretty wrappings. Sure, I feel as if I've known Mary forever, but the fact is, we're barely two weeks away from being acquaintances, and after I tell her what I want to tell her, I'm still going to have to live two houses down.

"Dan and I," I began slowly, "have started to be . . . at odds over this. He's not saying it's my body and my decision anymore. In fact, he wants to end any discussion of in vitro right now. And I get the feeling he means end it for good."

There it was. It sounded polite. So stated, it did not sound like three nights running of sitting up until 3:00 A.M. and voices strained through clenched teeth. It did not sound like me demanding to know why Dan would tear from me what I saw as my only dream. Mary sat back down. Up onto my shoulder came her arm. We sat, turning into one shadow in the dusk, and I told her how it had gone.

It was the lack of any guarantee, Dan had said. No, he did not want for me to risk seven hours of reconstructive surgery under anesthetic for iffy odds. He had specific horror of that, since the wife of an old friend of his had come out of a routine D & C one day with the cognitive abilities of a four-year-old. In vitro did sound exquisitely pragmatic in theory. A minor surgery—just the same thing as the laparoscopy I'd already had—instead of a major one. But he needed a guarantee.

"No, of course there's no *guarantee*, Dan," I had insisted. "But I *feel* it. I know this is the route for me. It's meant, Dan. Or else Dr. Jones couldn't have been so willing to give us a space in the program. Things wouldn't have fallen into place so well."

"Well, if it's *meant*," Dan had said thinly, holding up a sheet describing the assessment of expenses that had accompanied our application to the VIP program in Norfolk—a sheet that pointed out that each attempt would run something like four thousand dollars, a cost not covered by most insurance policies—"if it's *meant*, then maybe fate will shower down about fifteen grand on us, which is probably what we would need for this to result in a pregnancy, when you count the travel, and hotel expenses, and the work you'd have to miss."

"I can get a loan from my dad."

"Your dad, who owns half the western Chicago suburbs and who gave us fifty dollars for a wedding present? What makes you so sure this is going to rend his heart?"

"He knows how important this is to me. And he wants a grandchild. . . ."

"Hell, Jackie, he wants a grandchild about as much as he wants a new wife. It'd be nice if it happened, but he's not going to lose any sleep over it. . . ."

"That's not true."

"That *is* true. I know how much you want him to want it, but honey, the fact is that you have this big sentimental fantasy cooked up about how much your child is going to mean to your family, and the fact is your family, except Bobby, could give a shit. They're more concerned with making you feel guilty. . . ."

"Stop that. I'll convince my dad. This is different. I know he'll help."

But the next day, I had come back to Dan eager to change the subject from my dad giving us a loan.

My father had said, "I think you should just drop it. I think someone is trying to tell you something. That if this thing isn't meant to be, it isn't meant to be, and you should be leaving well enough alone. Concentrate on your career. Make some money . . ."

"We can take out a loan from the credit union," I suggested. We were having dinner, fish Dan had caught, on the coffee table in front of the television. The dining table had long since disappeared, buried under my books and files and pamphlets on infertility.

"And pay it off how? We could get a baby all right, but then we won't be able to support it." He shifted his eyes and mildly began watching "MacNeil-Lehrer." "And anyway, I'm not willing to change my whole standard of living for the hope—the slim hope, I might add—of your having a baby. It's not as if there aren't other things I have wanted for a long time."

"Like what?" Low. Almost a snarl.

"Like a boat," he said, and was lifting his fork to his mouth when I swept half the plates and all of the condiments off the table to the carpet and jumped to my feet in a wrestler's crouch.

"All you can do is throw obstacles in the path. Why Dan? Why *really?* We are talking about my life here. Not a fucking bass boat. I don't personally care if we have to sell the cars and the goddamned house to get a child, because I am not going to be happy until we get a child. . . ."

"And you won't be happy then!" He was up and advancing toward me, tripping over the mustard. I got outside the thing in that second, and would have laughed, but it was too threatening. "Do you want to know why you won't be happy? Because you're constitutionally unable to accept happiness." The lid had been lifted, and his anger rolled about the room like billows of steam.

"Stop menacing me!"

"I'm not menacing you, though I should. Listen to my side of the equation for once. You're so damned absorbed in your own condition, your own self-pity, it's like I went to the hospital and picked up somebody's invalid aunt to live with. Happy? You promised me you would be happy if only we could buy this house. And then, you'd be happy, you were absolutely sure you would be happy, if only we could get married. And then, if you could have a baby. And now, you're sure you'll be happy if only we can sell everything we have to finance this incredibly expensive and probably worthless experiment—and then what will be the ante?"

"So. Those are things you felt you ceded to me. Marriage. The house. You didn't want them as well?"

"I didn't say . . ."

"That's precisely what you said."

"I didn't mean . . ."

"Listen Dan. Let me tell you this. I know all of this is academic to you. You *have* a child. You have a child with your, your meaty nose and your eyes and she meets all your ego needs and any need you have for real love. But Dan, if we were talking about *your* wife, here, and *your* kid . . ."

"You are my wife." We stood, arms akimbo, panting, red faced, as spent as if we had fought each other with our fists—or, more sadly, terribly sadly, as if we had made love. I noticed the bottle of Tabasco sauce on its side and leaking onto the beige rug.

"I'm going to bed." I lingered in the hall, elaborately washing my face with salt and brushing my teeth. But he did not stop me. Let the quarrel hang there, then. Let it grow moss. I would not touch it.

But I was full of sorrow. "I do love him," I told Mary. "He's the man I wanted, and I never regretted that. I don't know. But he doesn't see this as his fight. He resents the fact that I'm trying to force all these solutions on him."

"Maybe he needs to recharge," Mary said. "Maybe he feels he's given all he can give for now."

"I'm not asking him to do anything but listen. Be ears for me," I said. And shell out thousands of dollars, I thought. "He can't make my decisions. Bellow can't make my decisions."

"But something like in vitro," Mary put in softly, "that has to be a decision both of you make."

I felt the need to shake her for being so sweetly rational. Why, I wanted to yell, why should it be his decision, too? It's me who can't have a kid. But I said, with a tight, small smile, "I guess it does. It wouldn't do much good to try to go through the procedure without the sperm."

"Or raise a kid without a dad."

I stared at her. "Do you think, do I give you the impression that we're that far gone?" Were we that far gone? If we were, how had I tipped Mary off to it? I stared down at the water pooling around the tips of my running shoes. "It's just that I have a need, I *need* Dan not to be bored with my problem. I need him to see it the way I do."

"He can't do that. Dan feels like he's doing what he can to make it better in his own way."

"He's not making it better. He can't."

"Well, there's something to that. Correct me if I'm wrong, because I don't know Dan that well. But maybe if he can't fix it, he wants to turn away from it. Welcome to men."

"It's because he has Jocelyn," I said.

"Who knows?" said Mary, standing and hiking up her sweat-pants. "Anyway, you can't make these plans without him." Maybe not, I thought. But other plans, I can make other plans without him. A bit guiltily, I recalled that I had set up an appointment for the following week with Dave Porterfield, an attorney who'd handled private adoptions of children from Mexico. I had mentioned the fellow to Dan, but Dan did not know I was meeting with him. Adoption was another thing Dan wanted to wait and see about. Wait and see while nothing changed, I thought. Wait and see while years bled away.

I was not going to get a baby by waiting and seeing. So there was a breath of deception about this meeting with the attorney. Dan would try to talk me out of it. Better he should find out about Dave Porterfield after I had met with him.

"Let's motivate," said Mary. "My kids are even now crying for their Tuna Helper."

And Dan, I thought. Dan will not be home at all when I get there. He'd taken to staying out until dark every evening. Fishing, he said. Fishing and thinking. It had occurred to me to suspect otherwise. But what kind of cur would cheat on his sterile wife? "Honey, what can I say? My wife has had all these surgeries, and I feel sorry for her, you know, but she's not what you would call a sexual person anymore. . . ."

Stupidness. And yet it would not have been the first time infertility had made for strange, sad bedfellows. An infertile man I'd interviewed —who did ultimately father two children—had remembered the low points after his diagnosis: "I went out once," he told me, "when I was out of town for work, and met a woman in a museum. We went back to my hotel. She was worried about becoming pregnant, which was exactly what I wanted. I told her that I had fathered two kids, and had had a vasectomy. Afterward, I couldn't look her, or Ellen, my wife, in the eye."

Mary was disappearing into one of the dark banks of shadow that now extended down from trees to pavement. Only the sky had light. "It's downhill on the way back," she called. She sounded very far away. I jumped up and ran after her.

Bellow listened patiently, twirling his pen, while I laid out my assessment of the game board. "So, what I'd like you to do," I concluded, "is write to the insurance company, and point out to them that in vitro is one of my options given the kind of obstruction I have, so that they'll perhaps cover some of it. Also, please give me a referral to Norfolk."

"If that's what you want." He picked up the bictaphone and began to speak. Then he stopped. "Do you want to dictate what I should say?" he asked affably.

"I'm not that aggressive!"

"Oh. You've changed, then?" He dictated a brief memo. "Now," he said, "it seems to me that you are going about this backward. From what I know of the procedure, it takes most people who eventually do get pregnant three attempts. That's six laparoscopies, one each time to make sure the ovaries are accessible, and one to retrieve the egg for fertilization. How many laparoscopies can one person take?"

I sat silent. "And," he went on, "the odds of getting pregnant by in vitro at this point are about ten percent, perhaps a little more, no matter what the Joneses say. But they are improving, and a year or two from now, with the way things have been going, it's a reasonable assumption that they'll be better still. I think what you ought to do is have the surgery, and keep in vitro as a fall-back measure if the surgery doesn't work."

"What about possible damage to my ovaries? I've read that some people don't ovulate again afterward."

"In my experience, the chance of that happening is negligible. I have never had a single woman fail to ovulate after surgery—providing that woman had had no problems with ovulation before."

"Why do you do this kind of thing?" Bellow fixed his bifurcated gaze on his philodendron.

"A great deal of what I do is . . . boring," he said. "This is interesting." He smiled slowly. "And I suppose I want to prove something to the two-eyed bastards as well."

If he had said that he did it because he hoped in some small way to contribute to the welfare of humanity—if he had said it was because the plight of the infertile woman so moved him he simply had to do something about it—I would not have trusted him. I would have been able to say, there, that's it, that is whence my doubts arise. But Bellow was straight with me; he always was straight with me. My doubts arose from elsewhere—or perhaps from nowhere. Perhaps what I called doubt was no more than my refusal to believe that—however I shook them or tunred them—the odds for this surgery's succeeding would've looked lousy on a racehorse.

Dan was fretting, tossing over piles of old *Newsweeks* in the lobby when I emerged. He pressed his lips, shook his head. I'd left him there for two hours; he was nauseous from cigarettes. "I'm having the surgery November nineteenth," I told him.

"I thought . . ."

"He convinced me."

"How do you feel about it?"

"Lousy."

DAVE PORTERFIELD'S office had a stamp as unmistakable as a fraternity handshake. At a law office of a certain elevation, there seemed to occur a paradox: the greater the volume and prestige of the work powering the establishment, the less visible evidence of any work going on at all. The expanses of teak and walnut were cluttered by no over-spilling files or sloppy message boards. Two entire walls were windows given over to an unimpeded sweep, from eight stories up, of the shore of Lake Mendota.

I folded my coat and sat down. Coffee on a tray was whisked in from somewhere in the wings. We were in the master's library at his country place, I fantasized; the books were well bound, but well used. . . .

Porterfield, when he showed up, was something of a shock. I had expected a suit of three pieces at least, and a watch chain. But he was in shirt-sleeves, a man of about sixty who resembled nothing more distinctly than the ward captains in the neighborhood where I grew up, who ran to white hair and gray faces. His greeting was kindly—he asked me to call him Dave—but unlike what I was used to. He did not mention running or coping or the stress of conflicting absolutes in the workplace. He mentioned Cigarillos, of which he had run out, and produced a pack of evil-looking, olive-colored cigarettes he'd bummed from someone. This was a man, I thought, who'd spent a day or two outside Madison. The impression deepened when he opened the discussion by asking whether I realized how dark skinned Mexican children were.

"Of course," I answered. But I hadn't. In my circle, in my personal tradition, one didn't think about such things—or at least admit to thinking about them.

"That's good," he said, "because not every American family can successfully adopt one of these kids. They all look like Lee Trevino."

I had recovered myself by now and was able to point out that for us, and here I was speaking for me, and giving Dan's family and my own the benefit of the doubt, the Indian-mix background of most Mexican kids was a plus for us, not a minus. As he could see, I was on the brown side. I was American Indian, more than a trace, on my mother's side. "I'd like a brown baby," I said.

"That's good then," he said again, "because the fact is, these kids do very well. They are accepted into the mainstream circle without a hitch, and I don't give a damn what anybody says to a kid, that's important." He had to agree, he said, with the national trend toward making an effort to place black kids with black or part-black families. "It might sound harsh, but with Mexican kids in white families, that crisis of identity in the teenage years doesn't hit so hard. In fact, in my experience it doesn't hit at all. When a white family adopts a black child, with some marvelous exceptions, the kids don't do as well, or else they go through a period of intense doubt. And an adopted kid has to deal with enough contrary emotions."

He leaned back in his leather chair and lit one of the long cigarettes. He offered one to me. They were vile. He hadn't located a child for fifteen years, he said. "The last girl I helped place is coming out of high school now—the other ones are in college. And they're doing terrific, all of them. I think this girl especially, she's popular, she's bright." He smiled. "I like to see her."

A dozen years before, the process had been relatively uncomplicated. He wasn't sure what it was now. He'd got wind of some rumblings about more difficulties with immigration quotas; he'd given it only half an ear because he frankly didn't expect to do this kind of work again.

"Let me point out right now," I told him, "I'm aware just sitting here that we can't afford you."

"Well," he said. It was an inclusive "well." Finding a child for a couple to adopt was rather outside his everyday routine of business. Without ever saying so, he made it clear that he considered these to be acts of good heart—and the fees for such cases would be a secondary consideration.

"So what is the process, at least as you remember it?"

The process was simple, he said. You found a Mexican attorney—a good one who was willing to secure every tendril of red tape required by both government bureaucracies. Not, he said, one of those happy fellows who lived for the next festival.

"You're going to find this harsh of me," he said, "but mañana is the flaw in the national character down there. The tendency to smile and cut corners. And when you're dealing with two governments, and with immigration matters, you can end up looking at a godawful mess if someone slips up."

He'd often worked with a former classmate of his—a Mexican lawyer educated in the United States. But that man had died. He had also, in the past, worked directly with an orphanage outside Mexico City, a place run by a group of Catholic nuns. So far as he knew, it might still be possible to make a contact there. If not, he and his associates would make an attempt to find a social worker who had an interest in placing orphaned children with families in the United States.

The same process, he pointed out, noting my husband's last name, might also be possible in other large, predominantly Catholic countries in which the standard of living did not always match the demands of the population. Italy, for example.

I had not thought about that. The more I thought about it, the more attractive it seemed. An Allegretti child on whom the name would sit comfortably. "I have no special preference," I told Dave. "The reason we decided to investigate this route is that, while we do have some time, and we're not sure whether we'll be able to have children in the usual way, we've been discouraged by the long waits for adoption—even foreign adoption—through agencies." I paused. "And we don't know how agencies would feel about the fact that Dan is a divorced father, and that he and I have only been married a little over a year."

"Then let me tell you something about my experience with children available for adoption in Mexico," he said. "If you adopt a child in the United States, chances are pretty fair that the child is not, in fact, an orphan. The child may have parents who mistreated him, or be the child of an unmarried mother. These children who end up at orphanages in Mexico may be orphans in fact. The standard of health among poor families isn't too great; parents can be overworked and underfed. In a very Catholic country, the stigma attached to an unwed mother is still very present. So that baby may end up outside the family. Or a baby simply may be the extra mouth to feed that would drag down the whole family structure."

Unless we were able to get a newborn, and that probably would not be possible, we should not expect a rosy baby in the picture of health, he warned me.

"I am not saying that these kids won't thrive—generally all they need is some good food and vitamins and the kind of pediatric care we take for granted here. But almost any child you get will be suffering from intestinal parasites, or a certain amount of malnutrition. Let me tell you what I saw the last time I went down there to pick up a baby."

The orphanage was a paltry structure. The children, even the infants, slept on mats on bare floors, though there often was a double bed or two for the nuns, who would try to put the youngest ones in with them at night. "The sisters, in my experience, are saints who live in the world," he said. "They do their best, on very limited resources. But there just isn't enough to go around."

A nun had told him that children in her care died, early and often, from the kinds of diseases a shot of penicillin from a hospital only a few miles away could have cured.

"I didn't know any of this when I made my first trip," he said. He had gone, with an interpreter who also was a social worker, to pick up an eighteen-month-old boy. And he had brought a gym bag full of hard candy to pass out to the other children. "Well, they seized on the candy eagerly, and their faces just lit up. But within a few minutes, a lot of them were crying in pain. Their teeth were so bad that the sugar in the candy hurt them."

There had been one little girl, he said. He turned his chair so that he was looking out over the lake. She was very little, perhaps no more than three, but she was bright and friendly, even though terribly thin and obviously ill. "She kept tugging at my arm," Dave said, "and trying to tell me something.

"I asked the interpreter—I don't speak Spanish—'What does she want? What is she saying?' Well, the fellow, he was a good fellow, but he was fairly eager to get on with it, said, 'Oh, well, she thinks that you are a doctor.'

"But I persisted. 'Tell me what she's saying,' I told the guy. And finally he got this look on his face and he said, 'She is saying, "Please doctor, I don't want to die." ' "

I put my head down on his glass-topped desk. "How long do you think it would take?" I asked.

"Well, you're just at the stage of looking into this," he said. "Once you're ready to proceed . . . "

"I'm ready." I will have to explain this to Dan, I thought, because this is urgent, children are sick, and he cannot disagree, he must not disagree. . . .

"I didn't tell you these things to urge you in any way."

"I know that. But you must know that hearing them makes a difference."

"It did to me," he admitted.

The process would take some looking into, Dave said. He would first begin to open contacts with other firms in Mexico. The adoption itself would take place in a Mexican court, and the child then would enter the United States as the child of an American citizen. Later the baby would become a naturalized citizen himself.

"Some of the fees would be the attorney's down there, and ours, and immigration paperwork, and, of course, plane fare for our representative and for the child."

"Would we not be required to go and process the adoption ourselves?"

"You would probably not need to. It could be done by proxy. And you wouldn't have to. A parent . . . " he said hesitantly, "would want to take a dozen of the kids, you see. You would hate to leave them."

I did see. Dan had said only the night before that I would willingly adopt the entire third grade at Lincoln School if I could find a gym to raise them in.

"Do you want to pursue the other option? Italy? I don't know how that would work, but . . . "

I hesitated.

"Well, we can check it out, but I think we'll want to go with a Mexican adoption." He nodded, and we rose. I took a moment to treat myself to his view—a single boat near the opposite shore, nearly hidden by the gray November mists. "What happened to the little girl?" I asked him then.

"Oh, I'm not sure." His signal light was blinking insistently. "It was so long ago." He put his hand on the receiver, and then turned to me. "Actually, I'm sure. I took the trouble to check, thinking maybe I could find a family for her." I knew what he would say before he said, "But she had died. Three days after I visited."

"And then she said, 'Please doctor, I don't want to die,' " I told Dan that night. We were having dinner. He put down his fork.

"Why did you tell me this?"

Because I am shameless, I thought. Because I want a baby so desperately. But I said, and with some truth, "Because I couldn't bear knowing it alone."

Dan got up and flicked the television on. And then off. "Oh, my God," he said. I spewed emotions out like an uncapped hydrant; Dan's were deep and slow-rising. But he was a father before he was, perhaps, anything else. And he saw Jocelyn's face in the story. "Well, maybe you should look into it, then. I'm still against adopting too precipitately. . . . " I started up. "*Not* because I don't want one of these children, but because any way you cut it, it would be easier and more economical and all that just to have kids. And we don't yet know that we can't."

"I know we can't."

"Well, you're crazy. Why would you be willing to go through another surgery and all that hell, if you didn't think there was a good chance of restoring your chance to have your own child?"

"I don't know. It seems . . . charted for me. As if I have to do it. The die is already cast."

"You are so full of shit sometimes."

"But it's okay then?" I prompted him. He made a warning gesture. "At least to begin to begin pursuing it? It'd take months in any case, Dan." He didn't answer. This was what your parents used to do; silence meant assent, grudging assent.

That night, late, a young woman named Gerry Becker called me. She was, she said, an associate of Dave Porterfield's, and he had assigned her the legwork for our case. "I don't know anything yet," she told me, "except one thing. The Italian option isn't going to fly." Relief. Surprising relief. "Italy, it seems, is a first world country, whatever its economic woes. And the infertile couples in that country take care of most of the available babies."

How did she know? I asked. Well, she had a cousin who was a priest in New Mexico, but he had spent a lot of time in Italy, and she called him, and he called another guy he knew. . . . "You did all this *tonight?*"

"Well, yeah."

"Didn't all those calls cost a ton of money?" My money, I thought.

"Well, that expense isn't necessarily going to be passed along to you." This was news. Lawyers passed every word they said along to you, at a dollar a word. "Dave and I have decided that we're going to do everything we can to help you and before we start charging you for anything, we're going to find out if we really can help. I . . . price out normally at about seventy-five dollars an hour, so this really is the way to go. If we can't help you, then there'll be some nominal fee, maybe two hundred dollars. Will that be okay?"

"Of course. That's more than fair, really. I appreciate it."

She said she would be getting back to me as her investigation progressed. She had a list of phone numbers of Mexican attorneys, and had got the name of a husband and wife, both social workers, who had indicated a special interest in placing Mexican children with American families in the past. "I have a special interest, you might say, in this," she said then. I could barely hear her.

"How so?"

"I'm . . . thirty-two, and I just had a miscarriage about six weeks ago. I had read your column about that happening to you, and my doctor wonders whether there might not be some problem. You see, it was kind of a peculiar situation, the pregnancy never really developed. . . ."

We talked for an hour.

SHOCK INSULATES; it moves one from day to day. People listen, at first, actively and empathetically; they seek you out only to listen. But it doesn't last long enough. The mind refuses to remain dormant. The body rights itself. The price of natural gas kept on going up, the storm windows needed painting, it was time to update the résumé, and people were beginning to treat me as they always had—which is to say my debilitation was not the first thing on their minds, or, they assumed, on my mind when they spoke with me.

It was time to give shock up, to pack away the new psychic baggage that was going to be part of my traps and get on with it.

I could not. The essentially unchanged stuff of my life surrounded me, made as if to lift me out and up, and I resisted. I was still too psychologically disarranged, or deranged. It showed physically. Mascara was a chore, getting a haircut an ordeal. I needed a new incision, another convalescence. Something visible to pull up my shirt and show to my friends who expected me to be more or less well.

"Start thinking about work," Todd suggested one day at lunch. Work was Todd's panacea for everything. "You haven't done anything really good lately but the series. Your columns have been run-of-the-mill. I know you still feel bad, but I hope you're not going to let this thing overtake your whole life."

"I think I might," I replied, and it was as if he hadn't heard.

"Jackie, it's a disappointment. Life is full of them. But having kids, important as it is, hardly is the most important thing in the world. And even if it is important, it's not worth destroying yourself over. . . . "

"Oh, I think maybe it is."

"I don't know what to make of you anymore. All I am trying to say is that there are worse things . . . "

"Name two."

"A terminal illness."

"I'll grant that."

"And what about a complete life-style change? What about losing your way of making a living?"

"Worse than having no kids? Are you nuts? I really hate it when you start to act like the Type A American male, Todd. Work is what you *do*, that's all."

"Okay, okay. I just hope that you're not going to keep dwelling on it until . . ."

"I rather thought I would, actually, and if you don't want to hear about it, it's okay if you don't ask me how I feel." I stopped. "I didn't mean that. That was bitchy."

"It's all right."

"It's not all right. It's not all right to snipe at your friends."

"I understand. I just think you're overreacting."

"Look, it's probably very difficult for you to say how you'd react in my situation. You're speaking from the security of your two kids and another one on the way. You have your family."

"I know I wouldn't let it tear me apart."

"*How* do you know?" I walked, stalked, away from the table. Todd was safe. Nick and Andy and pregnant Leah made him safe.

There was a receptionist at an office I had to visit every week or so as part of my job. I knew the woman only slightly. We would chat. I had marveled in the past that this woman seemed to be six months pregnant more or less all the time, but it had never irritated me before when she spoke of this next one as being "a surprise" or "an accident."

"You know," she told me, about three weeks after I came back to work, "if you look at it one way, you're lucky. I wish I were like you."

"Don't be silly."

"No, really. Kids are great. But they're expensive, they're messy, they're endless; you can kiss your sex life good-bye."

Such scorn I felt I barely could conceal it. "They don't seem to have done your sex life any harm."

"Ah," she said, "I only have to look sideways at my husband and I'm off again! I wish I were like you." I noticed then that though she wasn't chewing gum, she was one of those women who always appeared to be chewing gum. I noticed that I hated her.

"When I leave, take a minute and think about what you just said."

"What? All I said comes down to that right now you think you have all the problems, but people with kids have problems, too."

"I know they have problems. I'm not stupid. But their problems are the problems I want."

"You can say that now. Come back in a couple of years if you get one, and I have no doubt that you will, and tell me if you wouldn't rather be like you are now, or better yet, single. . . . "

"Oh, Maureen," I told her, "but I never could be single again. I'd always be negative one."

"What?" I walked out the door and left her staring at my back. Then I walked back in.

"You're a very silly woman," I said.

Paul James, who'd known Dan since Dan was a boy, came to visit one night on his way up north. He set his beer mug on the table and looked around him. "You know," he began affably, "you guys have the life. Look at this. The lake, the boat, the camper, go anywhere you want, good jobs . . . "

I had been mixing paint in the sink. "Well, Paul, we can't have babies. So you see, it all balances out."

Paul reddened. Dan pursed his lips at me across the room, telegraphing displeasure. So screw him. Paul's wife, Marjorie, was pregnant with their third. And the anger had got good on me. I couldn't stop it up.

"So if you'd like to trade," I began, deceptively cordial, "we can work something out. When that one on the way comes along, you just sign the papers and you can have the boat." Paul blinked. Frightened. He thinks I am nuts, I realized. And so I am. "And if it's a boy, we'll throw in the water skis."

After he left, Dan asked me, "Do you have a picture up in the attic that's turning all twisted and ugly?"

"Huh?"

"I mean, you look all right, so it's got to be coming out somewhere. I figured you might be like Dorian Gray."

The breakthroughs came increasingly. The hop toads spilled out of my mouth and would not stay put. "I'm flipping," I told Dan one night.

"Indeed," he replied, reading.

This wasn't working. I wanted a rise, an emotional blanketing, or else a balls-out fight. "Is that book *Zelda?* I thought you just started reading that last night."

"I did."

"But you're in the middle already."

"I skipped to the good parts. I wanted to read about Hemingway."

I smiled at him slowly. My head was going to explode.

"You *skipped* to the *good parts?*" Wasn't this like him? He'd always read history from the high points out, and it never had particularly annoyed me. This was different. This was such a character flaw I couldn't bridge it. "You started in the middle of a biography? A person's life? Doesn't it impress you at all that people live lives from beginning to end and that you at least should have the grace to read about them that way?"

Dan looked at me mildly. "It doesn't matter. It's clear she was a madwoman anyway, and that it was her madness that ruined Scott Fitzgerald more than anything else." Then he asked for it. "Remind you of anyone?"

"What about him ruining her? You'd know about that little dimension if you'd bothered to read about the first twenty-one years of her life. But causes don't matter to you, Dan. Effects matter to you, Dan." I stomped into the bathroom, turned on both the taps full blast, ranting above the roar of water about "galloping misogyny." The face in the mirror was fairly horrible, purpling and huge, a vein pulsing in the forehead, eyes slitted. A face that could have come bursting out of Rochester's secret room.

"I don't think I can live with you," I told Dan.

"Because I read from the middle out? That's perfectly understandable. What isn't understandable is how you have such colossal arrogance as to assume it's any of your business what I read, or how I read. . . . "

But of course it was my business. I had to live with him, didn't I? I had to look at his face. I had to listen when he sang "Tim Finnegan's Wake" in the shower every morning of the world. I had to watch him, my jaws chattering with rage, while he rubbed his eyes on the bed sheet in the morning, watch him stab his salad greens as if they were alive and liable to escape. Give him his room-temperature watermelon. Wonder how I'd managed not to brain him with a lamp the first or the fifth or the fiftieth time he'd told me, "I lost track of time." Find the sugar for him as he stood with the cupboard door open, staring directly at the box.

I had to live with him, and watch things that had years ago filled me with yearning—back when I wanted to be the one to pick up the socks he left balled under the sofa—now fill me with murder. How had Joan borne him? If not for the infertility, would I have gone on forever under the illusion we were well mated?

There were long spaces in the day when I was sure that the infertility had nothing to do with it at all, but that marriage was the world's oldest bad joke and that everyone knew the punch line but stupidly, unbelievably, fell for it anyway.

And yet there were spaces when I loved him. Or thought I loved him. Was my love that, or simply the need to cling wetly to the one person bound by law to put up with me? To listen in the night? One by one, the fresh ears had dropped away. What, after all, did you say after you said you were sorry? What did a friend, even my nearest, have to say to someone who was past comfort but not past caring about what had happened to her?

Even to long-suffering ears, I could not divulge everything. Not outrageous things. Such as the nagging, galling sense that this . . . assault had been a forecaster—not only for parenthood but for what my life would be. That it had robbed me of my magic. I had been a grasper, a getter. I worked for what I wanted, but I made it look effortless. Making it look effortless was primary. The golden college girl, swathed in honors, ringed by scholarships and suitors. Me, the gifted high-schooler, the one about whom teachers said, not covertly, that she would take off one day like a comet. I was never better than any individual at that individual's specialty; but I'd always been a little less than the best at just about everything. Did I not have the right—didn't my history win it for me —to be a bit less than the best mother as well? Frantic but funny, adored by my brood—children about whom I could affect nonchalance, but who really were, observably, better than average children? Was it to be chipped away bit by bit now—earning power, looks, sensuality . . .

And the mean-spiritedness. I had the potential for it. Under the apparent openhandedness, it was my family's scaliest trait. Envy the Millers' fence, their car. Mutter darkly about how if *we* stooped to cheating on our income tax . . .

Laura's little sister, Meghan, was pregnant. Their other sister, Theresa, who was single and living in Los Angeles, was behaving badly. Laura couldn't understand it. "She just can't bring herself to be happy for Meghan. She can't say one kind word without this, this bitterness leaking into it. Meghan is the closest person in the world to her. If you love someone, if you really love someone, you have to glory in that person's happiness, don't you?"

Oh Laura, I thought. Glory indeed. I don't glory. Not for Meghan, whom I've known since she was a tot, not even for you, and you are my twin if I could choose a twin. I put up even with you, Laura. "I know exactly how Theresa feels," I'd told Laura. "The reason it puzzles you is because you'd never allow yourself to feel that way. You're all good, Laura. I'm not all good. If I were Meghan I'd feel the same way." Jealous, Laura. Go ahead and look at me. I'm poisoned with the stuff.

"You would? You *wouldn't*. Don't put yourself down like that. You're saying it, but you're not like that at all."

But I was. More lousy emotions in a day than Laura had in a year.

It was when Meghan, only a week later, suffered a miscarriage that I forced myself to look down the well, and I saw that whatever selflessness I had once owned, if it still gleamed down there in the murk, was invisible to me. Because I was not as unhappy as the situation warranted. I was not glad, but as Cheryl Timmons, Peter Briggs' wife, had once said to me, it did not distress to know that there was someone else in the world, better yet in one's own circle of the world, who had not gone from A to Baby with maddening ease.

As soon as I hung up the phone with Laura the night of Meghan's tragedy, I had got a call from a reader. She had wanted to talk about the column I had written when I lost the baby. But that had been months ago. Why was she calling now? She told me her name, and then she told me how she had loved the column for the part about the feelings of loss that lingered. "I hope you don't mind me calling you at home," she said, "but I've been thinking about it for a long time. I'm infertile. I found out a long time ago." Three years, I thought. Time doesn't fly. "It was so hard, when my husband just wanted to turn away from it, stop thinking about it. He just wanted to go on."

"I know. But wasn't there anything you could do? I mean, there are so many new treatment options. . . . "

"Honey," she said, "I'm sixty. I found out I was infertile in 1956." And then her voice broke, and blurred, and I knew she was crying. So that is how long it lasts, I thought. I'm doomed. She at length finished her call and I sat at the table in the dark, and it took an hour to begin squeezing out tears for Meghan, and then I was not at all sure that they weren't, some of them, for my caller, and for me.

Tears didn't soothe. There was, the next day, still no ease in me.

"I'm going to go on feeling these things, you know," I told Dan. We were lying in bed one Saturday morning, in the dark. I had a few minutes left before Dan would have to get up for work. "This is going to be one of those lives."

"So jump off a bridge," Dan said. He threw the covers back. He did not like predawn repartee. He loved his sleep, and he hadn't been getting much of it.

"Maybe not a bridge. But I could take something. Do we have anything?"

"You're such an ass. It's practically the middle of the night and you have to start this?" I realized with a shock I'd been thinking along these lines for some time. Considering options. Drugs were out—I had such a stalwart tolerance for drugs I could have run down the road to the nearest police station eight hours after ingesting eighty Seconal. Poison was hard to come by, awful, and iffy. I knew from covering a bizarre murder trial a few years back that people who ingested cyanide died slowly, strangling cell by cell. I had read about a woman who was discovered on her kitchen floor, covered with blood from about thirty stab wounds. An inquest had come back with a verdict of suicide. The judge ruled that she had been working up to the fatal wound. So stabbing was out. Hell, I didn't want to mutilate myself. I just wanted . . .

What? Peace? To not know the stuff I had to wake up every day knowing about myself? To not be required, ever, to admire another newborn? To not get any more of those you'll-never-guess-what-I-have-to-tell-you long-distance phone calls? A fine and private place where the phone would be off the hook for good?

Most people think about suicide. If you ask, they probably will tell you they have never considered it, and in all honesty, they probably never have. But they have thought about it. In some dark serves-everyone-right fantasy. In the wide-awake jitters of depression, they have thought about how lovely it would be to go to sleep and not to dream. To make the great, showstopping, renunciatory gesture.

I had done my share of thinking about it, too. When Dan's divorce was dragging out. When we fought. But it had been goofy stuff. Sort of a picture of me floating down to three-tiered Camelot, Dan looking down (with Joan, no doubt) from some nearby battlement and cursing himself.

But then there was the everything else of my life. Who would take care of my dog, who was so obnoxious no one else could bear to be around him? Who would clean under the rim? Bobby would be hurt. But he'd get over it. My space would close over.

"Dan?" He was now up, despairing of sleep, and dressing for work. "Do you realize I don't know how to use your gun?"

"To shoot yourself?"

"Of course not. But what if there was a home invasion while you were out of town?"

"You could talk at the invaders. They'd leave." I saw him glance at the closet, at the vinyl sleeve that held his shotgun, unloaded and mostly unused. Dan wasn't much of a hunter; he took the dog out every year a couple of times, and he and the dog walked around. No birds ever died because of it. "But if you want to know, it's rather simple. You take off the safety . . . oh, shit, Jackie, you're so goddamned obvious. I know what you want. You want me to talk you out of killing yourself. But you don't want to kill yourself. . . . "

"I don't want thirty or forty more years of my company." It would do no good to run away. I was inescapable. I could be infertile in Paris. I could be infertile in Nome.

"I don't want thirty more minutes of your company when you're like this. But what you really want is for me to know that you feel so bad you wish you were dead. I think it's nuts for you to feel that way. But I know you do. Okay?"

When he came home from work that day, we began carting up the winter coats and boxing up our summer clothes to put into the cellar. "Are you still suicidal?" Dan asked me.

"No. But didn't you ever think about it? Even once?"

"Not even once."

"You were never that depressed? Even when we broke up?"

"Especially not then." I got behind him and tried to shove him into the huge chest where he was kneeling, unpacking blankets. Then, "Look at this," he said, all the banter gone from his voice.

It was a pair of tiny moccasins we had bought in a leather shop in northern Wisconsin before we were married—just before. "For Baby-foot," Dan had said back then, "whenever he comes."

He smiled now and slipped the little shoes onto two of his fingers and began padding them around on the bed like a puppet. "She has your eyes," he said. One of the moccasins slipped off. "And your coordination."

"But the Allegretti schnoz. Not nice on a girl. I'd hoped she'd escape it."

"We'll have to have a plastic surgeon over to dinner."

"If I could only remember her," I said. "What she looked like, what toy she slept with, the things she wouldn't eat." Then I could cry in a useful way, I thought, and it would be done. "I love you," said Dan.

"And I need you with me. I don't want you to blow off your head."

"How about my toes? You hate my toes."

"Not even those." And we lay on the bed, among the sweaters in their plastic bags, Dan holding my toes, and my legs and my belly and my hands, and saying, "I love this. I like this, too, and this."

We made love. Good sweaty love, with much slapping of thighs. To the limits of us. For the first time in months, and, we later realized, for the last time for many more months to come.

I would enshrine those few hours as some sort of special acknowledgment Dan had given me—one time, it would seem, that we were on equal footing with the hurt. And for days afterward, I felt almost normal. I felt permitted, by Dan's shouldering some of it, to worry about the kinds of things I used to worry about. Refreshing things. Money. The rust on the car. A new apartment for my grandmother. Work. Mundane worry. A pleasure.

20

"I DON'T THINK I should write about what happened to me," I told Carol. "I don't think it's appropriate. This isn't a column."

"I don't see how you can write the series honestly *without* writing about what happened to you."

"It smacks of the confessional." She thought about it, lighting her dozenth cigarette of the morning.

"It does," she said. "But it's moving, and it's real, and it gives the work a whole different perspective."

I went back to my desk. It was laid out like a war room. I hated a series; writing a newspaper story is a fairly simple proposition, but pulling together months of interviews and research is awful. It means going over all the tapes and index cards, and outlining, and then paring and stripping the material—and then writing, and then paring and whittling the whole thing once again. Common wisdom on most newspapers has it that a reader can absorb only what he's able to read in one sitting; and afternoon newspapers are at a disadvantage. When our paper arrived, the kids were crying, the dog needed a walk, dinner was in the oven, and the television was going full blast. It was hardly the Sunday Style section of the *Washington Post*; we wrote lean.

Oddly enough, the actual writing of the series, which I dreaded, came as something of a blessing. It occupied all my daytime hours, and I needed the slack hours I spent juggling adjectives and switching paragraphs around, since the date of my surgery had been switched.

When the nurse had first called, I had been furious. Bellow had been going over my records, she said, and the November 19 date was, he determined, too close to the expected date of my period. Any complicating factor that could increase the possibility of postsurgical infection and possible scarring had to be taken into account in any surgery. In a surgery so delicate as this, such factors were critical.

"What about the following week?" I had asked.

"The doctor will be out of town then," she had answered. Of course. So would any normal person. It would be Thanksgiving week.

"But don't you remember telling me I wouldn't have to wait until December? Remember telling me I would only have to wait a couple of weeks?"

She had sighed, genuinely sympathetic. I had got on such a first-name basis with all of the OB/GYN personnel at the clinic that they recognized my voice on the phone before I gave my name. "I know, Jackie, and I'm really sorry." We set the date for December 1. I hung up, too curtly, and stomped over to Dan's desk to bum a cigarette. Damn it all! It meant restructuring everything.

Getting another six weeks' leave of absence had not—albeit unpaid —been easy. There was only one full-time feature writer in our department—me—and my absence meant a greater load fell on the arts writers and reviewers. David, our managing editor, whose job it was to handle the vagaries of personnel, couldn't understand the urgency. "Why don't you just wait until after the first of the year, when you can use vacation time and get paid for it?"

There was no logical answer for that, so I didn't try for one. "Think if you didn't have Kris and Danny," I told him. "When you are starting a family at my age, even a month makes a difference." Relented wasn't the word; David was a softy.

What I couldn't explain to him was the psychological dimension; I had trained for this surgery mentally as a marathoner trained for a race. A secure timetable helped quell the doubts. The date assumed mythic proportions. At night I had sat alone in the bedroom, lights dimmed, practicing "visualizing"—Peter Briggs' wife, Cheryl, told me how, after her ectopic, she had imaged a clear tube, the egg passing through the tube. She didn't know if it had done any good, but it had helped keep her primed and positive, and Cheryl had got pregnant.

Carol had been splendid, even though she was in the midst of her first year in management, the only female editor on the staff, and feeling herself to be the object of some scrutiny.

Now all the dates had been changed. I couldn't have blamed my editors for being exasperated. But they were not. "The important thing is that you get the best care you can," said Elliott, "and time everything right."

But I felt knocked off balance. Something grim would come of it.

There was, to boot, the matter of Dan's professional crossroads. He was nearing his middle thirties and had been at the paper five years. Valued and well respected, he nevertheless balked at following the normal tenure track into middle management that some of the editors hoped he would choose. He liked being a writer and wanted to continue at it. Still, the paper was feeling a financial pinch, and so, necessarily, were the reporters. Dan had begun, with the support of his bosses, putting out the first tentative feelers for jobs on larger newspapers. He had begun stringing for the *Washington Post*.

We didn't know where a move might take us—not too far from Jocelyn, we hoped. But I was feeling the primordial attachment infertile women can come to feel for their clinic, their town, their specialist. I had caught myself thinking about Bellow, wondering whether he was married. For reasons on some level personal, I wanted the surgery done while we still lived in Madison.

I put my broodings aside and set to work on the infertility series. The first three parts had gone swimmingly; they were technological and organized themselves—all I'd had to do was translate.

Now I was facing down writing the fourth part—about the emotional effects of infertility. And Carol was right. I need not sob all over the page, but there needed to be some personal insight. I wrote, "When I began work on this series last summer, I did not know I was an infertile woman. . . . During the time I was scouring the library and setting up interviews, I became pregnant, and lost my baby, and learned hopes for becoming pregnant again were dim. . . . Yet, this series is not significantly different in concept or scope than it would have been. Only I am different.

"My marriage is different than it was six months ago, and so are my plans. Infertility changes the look of the world. It isn't set up for childless couples."

I drew a deep breath, turned off the machine, and called my sister-in-law. "Now, what did you say was the name of that doctor who uses laser beams?"

I spent the next two hours on the phone. I called the offices of "20/20"; they didn't know what I was talking about. I called my sister-in-law back. Perhaps, she now said, the segment had been on "That's Incredible!" That scared me. I had once written stories for "That's Incredible!" back when it was supposed to be called "Super Sunday Night" and challenge "60 Minutes." "The story ideas have to be more *bizarre*," the programmer had kept telling me.

Still, I phoned ABC, and then the programmer, who was by now a different programmer, herself. "The name of that doctor is Dr. William

Heiss," she told me, "and he is in New Orleans. Here is a toll-free number you can call." I called the number.

"What you must do," the woman who answered told me, "is send your medical records to the Omega Infertility Institute, and then they will be evaluated, and the doctors will determine if your problem is one of the ones that can be helped by laser microsurgery." That would take some weeks, she told me.

"Look," I pressed her, "I know what my problem is and where it is and what needs to be done. Give me the number of the doctor." She hesitated.

"That's not usually how it's done."

"Nevertheless."

I called the New Orleans number she gave me, and went on the offensive: "I know that there is usually a process of evaluation for any case. But I have had a tubal pregnancy, a hysterosalpingogram, and a laparoscopy, and I know I have a cornual obstruction of my remaining Fallopian tube . . . "

She listened patiently. Then she said, "Okay, honey, why don't you tell the doctor? Hold on while I get him." She got him. I was in shock. Could anything be this simple?

"This is Dr. Clarke."

We talked odds. Clarke was one of three surgeons who used the laser; he was the junior member of the team. Surgeons Heiss and Mark Julius had pioneered the technique in this country. I described my concern about the blockage being located in the uterine wall, and the technique that would be used if that were the case.

"I knew the fellow who created that technique," said Clarke. "It doesn't work. Even he doesn't do it anymore." Ice walked along my neck.

"And what do you do?"

"We use the laser to bore into the uterus at the point the tube is attached. There's no need to make another opening, and the tissue damage is less." He explained, cursorily, how the laser worked; it raised the temperature of the cellular liquid to the point of vaporization, so cells were removed without cutting. The light beam could be focused with such precision that single cells could be eliminated with little or no effect on surrounding tissues. "So there naturally is a reduced danger of scars forming at the site."

"And how do you do? How well?"

"We probably could say the rate would be about fifty percent. Maybe better. Depending on what we see when we get in there." Bellow was giving me thirty percent tops; this guy, fifty or better. On the other hand, I didn't know this guy from Adam.

"How long would I be in surgery?"

"About an hour and a half. It's much more quickly done with the laser." That had been the big snag, the one my positive thinking could not flow past: the seven hours of medicated nothingness that traditional microsurgery virtually ensured. There was a moment of plain panic. Then I jumped.

"When can you take me?" He could take me before the holidays—after the first of the year, they would be booked for many weeks. At least, I thought, that's a sane reason for not waiting that I can offer to my bosses when I change dates yet another time. We set up an appointment to meet December 7. The surgery would be December 9, the day before my birthday. Clarke's nurse told me which of my records to send and said that the forms I would need would be in the next day's mail.

I put down the phone, and finished writing the fourth part of my series in an hour. My hands, my brain, felt limbered; I was satisfied with the first draft. When I finished, I called my sister-in-law and thanked her.

I called Dan on the interoffice line. "I'm going to New Orleans," I told him.

"Oh," he said. "Why?"

"It's nice this time of year."

148

21 I AM doing this as a gift to Dan, who thinks he's doing it for me. So both of us feel virtuous. The real gift has been from my grandmother, who gave us extra hours of sleeping in. She has been up since dawn. Through the comforter over our heads, and the discreetly closed door, I hear her say, "I have two turkeys this morning. And they both weigh twenty-six pounds!"

"I weigh forty-six pounds!" A muffled pounding and heavier thuds sound up the hall—the dog follows Jocelyn everywhere. "No, I weigh forty-eight pounds. Come here, Jebbie, let's see how much you weigh. Get on the scale. . . . "

But back to business. It wasn't always a chore. In the past, a morning invitation suited me fine. The day's tensions still ahead, I was warm and refreshed. And poor Dan, who slept hard and would wake looking like a prizefighter, would turn away with a groan. He doesn't anymore. Anytime. Anyplace. When he wins the connubial tug-of-war, he savors it. And I cannot find it in my heart to blame him.

Still, it's nearly ten. The families are on the way. The wreath of sentimental perfumes filling the house reminds me of fifty things I have to do. The windows above the bed spill with white light—so, it snowed after all. The walk will have to be shoveled. And a fracas is developing between my grandmother, who is saying Jeb must take his wet feet right outside and stay there, and Jocelyn, who is whining that the poor thing will catch a cold out there. They need a referee.

Dan rolls us over from my perch on top; we lock at hip and thigh with the ease of long practice. I remember really feeling all this. Remember the hot shuddering spike that would snake through my abdomen when he came to the bedroom naked after a shower, ruddy and furry, my lean muskrat, his hips and belly still hard and flat though he did nothing to preserve them. I can still see him this way, but it stops at the head. The body wants nothing to do with the impulse.

Lately my avoidance of sex has taken on a new color. I have fitted New Orleans into it. I'm saving it, I tell him, for after I'm reassembled, when there will be a chance that our couplings can count for something. Soon, B., I tell him.

"What if you were to find out you could never get pregnant?" he shouted at me a few evenings before, after I had rebuffed, through clenched teeth, the forays he had begun making beneath my robe as I rinsed the dinner dishes. "Would you simply never want to do it again?" I did not answer him. That is exactly what I would want.

But I am unfair to him; with the surgery just two weeks away and Dan able, as he says, to see the light at the end of the tunnel, he has eased off on the sexual nagging that is now a staple of our marriage. In return, I've eased off as well. Under pressure, I agreed to tell Gerry Becker to put off her efforts toward arranging a Mexican adoption for us until after I know the outcome of the surgery. No other way would Dan support me. "If the primary need is for a child, adopt now and put the surgery off for a year," he reasoned. "We can't go the distance on all the options all at once. Not financially or any other way."

He does not know the horror with which the thought of waiting a year —for anything—now fills me. A year is a year to Dan; we are not children, after all, for whom the days until the end of school loom impossibly long, but adults, who have learned to defer. I backed off only because I need Dan now. This is no time to dig in; we need to be in tune.

Putting the pieces together for the surgery has been like lobbying a minority bill through Congress. Dan and I are high on the possibilities, which is a good thing, since everything but the omens has lined up against it.

We did not know how high the price tag on newfangled technology would be until the packet from the Omega Institute arrived. We had to sit down. The surgery itself would cost at least thirty-five hundred, perhaps more, and the surgeon would require a deposit of half that amount mailed in advance. On the day of admission, we would need to put down eight hundred dollars up front to the hospital. Our assurances that our insurance was good for it cut no ice.

"Cancel," Dan had said. "There's no way." But I was already figuring. Money was never a good enough reason not to do anything; you could always get the money. Dan would not agree to dissolve the account he had set up for Jocelyn's education—furiously murdering aphorisms, he had said, "We can't throw the existing baby out with the bathwater" —and the rest of our lackadaisical savings portfolio would hardly cover half of what we needed, even if we decided to use the Christmas stash and let Jocelyn in on the straight dope about Santa. That left my dad. And I was drained by my negotiations with him, and by keeping the gist of those negotiations from Dan, who would have hated him for it, who would have accepted a loan under no circumstance.

"You're tampering with nature," my father had said. "Don't you accept that there are simply some people who aren't meant to have children?"

"I do, but I don't think I'm one of them. Not yet."

"And if this doesn't work, then what?" A person or two had made the same point to me already, in more politic terms. "More operations? More money? Do you go on having surgeries and tests until you're thirty-five? How about forty?"

"Just this. And just once. Dad, you can't refuse . . . "

"I damned well can refuse! Where's my assurance that I'll get my money back? Do you think it grows on trees? What if you die on the table? Do you really think Dan would pay me back?"

My mind raced—he didn't mean that, of course, he didn't mean that; I am his only daughter. And I wanted to hang up, to burst his ear with the crash of the descending receiver. But there was no choice, no other option.

"Dan would . . . pay . . . you back." Measured. Let no sarcasm betray you.

"Well, I'd like it in writing." This was not so different, I told myself —the college loan, the thousand for the down payment on the house; he always delivered. You just had to bleed for him a little, my brother said. And he must know I would pay him back, I always paid back, though, I had to admit, the promised interest seemed to get lost along the way.

And then he said, "It seems to me you had your chance to have a baby years ago. You didn't want it then." There it was. He had never mentioned it. "And I paid for that deal, too." How could he? Very well, he just had. I remembered the circumstances—me, half in and half out of a ten-month-long marriage I had undertaken only to please my mother, working as a waitress for fifty-six dollars a week, and pregnant because of some half-assed sentimental attempt at reconciliation on one of my husband's breaks from law school. He had been so tender then, my father. He had helped me then.

I sat transfixed, holding the phone, wordless, the side of him I truly

151

hated—Big Mitch, the hard-drinking pal, everybody's fix-it friend, who accepted Bobby's honor roll grades with a look and a nod, and then called him a pansy-ass for using school to avoid an honest day's work, looming monstrous on the other end.

"Listen," I told him now, "not a single one of your much-valued friends I hear so much about would deny his daughter the chance to have a baby if it was within his means. Don't think for a minute that I want to come around to you with my hand out and have it slapped. I have no other option."

"You make a fair amount of money every year? Where is all of it? Where does it all go?"

"To the mortgage, to the care, to the medical bills of the last six months and the lost work time . . . "

"To Joan."

"To *Jocelyn*, not Joan." It was going nowhere. We would now commence the lecture about marrying a man with a child—a lecture my father had honed to a syllable, though in fact he was fond of Jocelyn. We hung up with his grudging assent to at least consider the loan; he would discuss it further with me on Thanksgiving.

Today. I jump out of bed, out of the comfortable crook in Dan's arm in which I had almost slipped back into a dream.

"I dreamed," Dan says suddenly, in a stroke of married telepathy, "that we were together in the operating room and suddenly the lights blinked and an announcement came over the loudspeaker that doctors were to interrupt all surgeries because there was a cyclone approaching. That was the word they used, 'cyclone.' Is that a Southern word? And I walked over to the table and took you by the shoulders because you were struggling to get up, and there was a window over your head. And out that window, I could see five tornadoes in the sky approaching the hospital." He rubs his eyes on the sheet. "What do you think that means?"

"There is one cyclone approaching I'm sure of," I tell him, heading for the shower, "Tony." Dan's nephew was three. He could dismantle an entire household in fifteen minutes. I have to kid-proof the house before noon. "I think it means you're afraid of watching the surgery," I call back over my shoulder.

We had been going around on this. The Omega Institute took the enlightened approach that infertility was a couple's problem. That was good. There was a bed and a worktable for the spouse in each hospital suite, so that the nonpatient could carry on business during the hospital stay if he had need to. Husband and wife could be together throughout —the husband even permitted to carry out some of the basic tasks of his wife's care, such as helping her bathe postsurgery. The male partner's fertility was evaluated along with his wife's during the hospital stay— the goal being to turn out a couple in their best possible shape to reproduce or know the reason why. We had filled out detailed medical and personal histories and forwarded them to New Orleans. Under "Smoking," Dan, while smoking, had written "no."

"Are you going to watch?" I had asked him then.

"Not on your life."

"Don't you think it would be interesting?" The Omega Institute philosophy included allowing the husband to view the surgery on his wife through a window in the operating theater. The surgery was video-taped, and the tape returned with the patient to her home physician; most of the patients were, like me, from other states.

"I think it would be horrible beyond belief."

"You're going to watch," I warn him now.

"I'll cover my eyes," he warns in turn. "Let your grandmother watch. She gets into stuff like that." My grandmother, ever doting, was coming with Dan and me. The excuse was a visit to my aunt Patricia, the daughter of my grandmother's late sister, whom my grandmother had raised as her own daughter—mothering not having been my great-aunt Minnie's long suit. Pat lived in Lake Charles, about three hours' drive west of New Orleans.

The real reason was unclear to me. I stand, the shower on steaming, needling my face, and puzzle it over. My grandmother said she was all for the surgery; yet everything else she said indicated she was not. "What would you do," she had asked me one day, "if you woke up after the operation and they told you it hadn't worked? If you just had to give up and go home?"

"I don't know."

"And anyway," she had continued mildly, gazing around my living room in such a way that I could see the scattered leaves of newspaper, the unshelved books through her eyes, "I don't see how you could fit a child into the way you live. The way you keep this place, you and Dan. The two of you are so concerned with your own comfort, don't you think a child would be too much . . . "

"Stop that! Why do you torment me? A person can't go into surgery thinking that the outcome might be lousy, and that even if it works she isn't suited to raise a child."

"I'm not trying to torment you, sweetheart. You're the dearest thing in my whole life. I'm just very much afraid, I have this feeling, that you're heading for a big letdown. . . . "

In my green spiral notebook, I would later find that I had written, "My infertility seems somehow to gratify her. As if it is the ultimate payback for some sin of neglect I visited on her, personally, for every time I didn't call, for every sharp word. She has seemed to watch the crumbling of my touchiness with what I can only describe as satisfaction. Does she fear that with a child of my own, I would make a life that would not have time to be so tolerant of her oddities, her abuses?"

It is not so much different, I think, toweling off, as any other mother and daughter relationship. Bloody dependence brawls, love and pity. My grandmother has been my only mother for the past decade; she does double duty in my guilts. How she loves to seize on a possibility and worry it until the worst comes true. How like her I am.

Laura envisioned a half-hour sitcom called "Grandma's Place." Well-known personages would be ushered onto a set crafted to look like my grandmother's kitchen. She would be seated at the table. The action would open with my grandmother reminding the visitor to scrape off his muddy shoes and not dribble coffee on the tablecloth. "And then she would try to make them feel guilty, and they would have to try everything in their power to fight back," said Laura. "And Grandma would say, 'That's easy for you, Mr. William Buckley, you haven't been under the knife five times. You haven't spent your whole life doing for others and having them walk on your heart.' I would pit Grandma against anybody. Studs Terkel. Truman Capote. They'd all crawl away babbling idiots."

My grandmother is pounding on the bathroom door. "Am I supposed to make this whole dinner and take your phone messages, too?" Mary is calling, she says.

Mary wants, of all things, to run. Mary, who has said she thinks purgatory will be a cinder track. "Mary, I just got out of the shower. I have eight people coming to dinner in forty-five minutes, one of whom is my father. . . . "

"Just a little."

"Mary, I'm not Helen Gurley Brown. We can miss a day of exercise and I'll still live."

"Walk, then. Okay?" What is all this? Mary has a houseful of her own on the way; she has eleven brothers and sisters. I agree to meet her at the mailbox in ten minutes, fire off a round of instructions to Dan and Jocelyn, run the brush through my hair, and rush out with Jeb on his leash into the dusting of new snow.

We walk down the bike path. Jeb runs off to scatter the ducks on the fringe of the bay. I prattle on about Gail, my sister-in-law. "I don't think it will be so bad for me this time. It's like getting ready for the trip has given me a focus; I don't just sit around and fasten myself on her pregnancy."

"How is she doing now?" We have all been worried about Gail. Seven months pregnant, she has developed toxemia and can no longer work, nor barely even walk. She has gained sixty pounds and is finding it hard to breathe, and only her twenty-five-year-old constitution is hauling her through these last weeks.

"As well as can be expected. I'm going to give her my cape—the one I bought last fall when I figured I'd be expanding by now—it's never been worn, and she can't afford a winter coat. . . . " I look at Mary. Mary is crying.

"What . . . ?"

"I don't want to lose you. Your friendship means so much to me. . . . "

"Lose me? Mary, are you nuts? What . . . "

"Jack, I'm pregnant."

I have never bought the notion of conflicting emotions—you feel one thing, it's genuine, and the rest is superego, conscience, whatever, reminding you what you *ought* to be feeling.

But this is Mary. Mary had suffered. Mary deserved. In the second before I throw my arms around her, I see myself running down to the lake and into the water and walking until it is over my head, and I can look up and see the feet of the ducks, threshing like unicyclists over my head—for what? To drown? No, to hide, away from anyone who can pat my arm, and say the things I know she is saying now, since I can see her mouth moving, though I can't hear her. Away from being what I finally am—the last nonpregnant woman on earth.

I say, "That is marvelous. I'm so happy for you," in a mechanized voice, a voice a goon could see is phony.

"I know you are. You're so good. . . . "

"I'm not good."

"You are, and I know you're happy for us. Jackie, understand. I wanted to tell you before anyone else knew—I mean, Tom knows, but not even my family—so that we could talk about it together, first. And I know how hard it's going to be for you, seeing me. But I need you to see me, you're my friend. . . . "

"Of course I want to see you. Mary, I'm not crazy. . . . " I am crazy.

"I know you're not. But it seems so cruel. I didn't plan it. And I think you should know that I was sure, I was absolutely sure that I would never have another child after my last miscarriage. So if you feel that way, you can take heart from this. I *knew* I wouldn't get pregnant again, and now I am."

Take heart. I try to take heart. But what I know, deep, deep inside, is that yet another baby has been claimed from the void, and that my chances are lessened. I had never envied Mary her big children. I had a big child, or at least loan of a big child now and then. But this baby. This out-of-the-blue serendipity. Mary, you must agree, it should have been mine.

And I say, "Mary, don't apologize for heaven's sake, and you mustn't worry. It won't happen again. You won't lose it."

"I'm trying to take it a day at a time. At first, when I was late, I didn't even let myself notice. And now that I'm sure, I'm not even going to acknowledge it to myself until after three months are up. Maybe not even until the baby is born and in my arms."

"It's going to be all right, Mary. I feel it." And it's true, I do.

"And it will be for you, too. Probably before I even have this baby, you'll be pregnant. . . . "

"Of course." It's pretty to think so.

We walk back to the house, arms linked. Jeb, for once, heels decorously, his huge head brushing my knee.

Inside I extricate myself from Jocelyn, who wants to play eights, and from Dan, who wants to know where the black olives are, and go into the bedroom. I have not prayed on my knees since I was a child—no, once, on the day of my mother's brain surgery—but I arrange myself next to the unmade bed and fold my hands and wait. I close my eyes tightly and make the words in my mind. But nothing opens. I'm stifled. Dammed.

On the Friday after Thanksgiving, while Jocelyn and the teenager who cleans the house for us are rocking out to the oldies hour in the living room, I get a call from our insurance company. The man is the head of the medical review, and I can't hear what he is saying, but what I think he's saying is that there's a possibility the company cannot insure the surgery.

"Jocelyn Marie!" I shout, louder than I mean to. The radio clicks off. "Now. I was under the impression that since I had a referral from my own physician, along with the letter he sent you explaining the reasons why I chose this particular option . . . "

"We have a policy," the man begins, "to deal with what might be referred to as discretionary procedures. Cosmetic surgery might be one, for example—a surgery that strictly speaking isn't medically necessary. . . . "

"But I'm unable to have a child without this surgery."

"Well, we have made it a policy not to cover reversals of sterilization surgery. Now when you had the tubal ligation . . . "

"Tubal ligation?"

"Yes, the sterilization surgery."

"I never was voluntarily sterilized. I had an ectopic pregnancy. My remaining tube is blocked near the uterus. I hope this laser microsurgery will restore its function."

"You don't have any children?"

"No. That's the point."

"Well, we've been dealing with this as if it were the reversal of a voluntary sterilization."

"I made it perfectly clear when I first contacted you . . . "

"Yes, well, when is the surgery scheduled?"

"December ninth."

"Well, that doesn't give us much time, does it? You see, we'll have to go back to the committee. . . . " The committee would need first to approve the procedure on medical merit; then, if they did, they would stipulate what portion of the cost of the procedure insurance would cover. The man, a Mr. Bird, asks me to provide more details of the laser microsurgery. And I begin, angry because I'd already gone through this previously—and, I suspect, with the same man.

"I believe I saw something about this on television, was it on "20/20?"

"Ahhhh, yes, I think so." Let him think that; people hate to admit they watch "That's Incredible!"

"We'll have to get back to you, Mrs. Mitchard. I hope it will be in

time. I don't believe the committee is scheduled to meet until . . . "
There is a rustling of papers.

"Sir, let me point out to you that these appointments are difficult to get. This is the only hospital in the country where these things are done. I was lucky to get an appointment, because of a cancellation. If I don't get the approval, it could take months to set it up again. I'll have to rearrange my work leave. . . . " And I will have to have you killed, I think.

"I see. Of course. I'll get back to you tomorrow."

He does not get back to me. Three days later, I call him again. He is vague; the committee has not yet met. Another two days, and I call him again. He is out. I ask Dan to call him. Bird says the committee had not yet met. We are scheduled to leave in five days.

On Wednesday I call Mr. Bird. His receptionist tells me he will be out of the office until after lunch. At one o'clock I begin calling—he is away from his desk; he is in a meeting. I call four times. Finally at a quarter to five, he returns my call.

"I'm having something of a problem," he says, genuinely kindly. "You must know that we don't cover experimental surgeries—heart transplants, test-tube babies. These things are outside our coverage. And there seems to be some question in the mind of one of our physicians as to whether this . . . "

"It is not experimental. It's been performed routinely in an established medical facility on a paying basis for more than a year."

"I don't know . . . "

Dan, who is standing near the phone, coaching me, says, "He's afraid of setting a precedent."

"Look, Mr. Bird, as I explained to you, mine is a rather special problem. I don't know how many times the company will be called upon to cover such a procedure. Perhaps never again." This is a frank lie. If it works, I intend to tell every woman with a similar problem I can find. And a great many corporations, not to mention the state, use this company for their workers' group insurance.

"Mmmmmm," he says. The committee will be meeting tomorrow, he believes. He will get back to me.

I call the following evening. Mr. Bird is happy to say the committee has approved the procedure on medical merits. But it seems a copy of my referral from Dr. Bellow is missing. Panicked, I call Bellow's office. They refer me to the in-clinic insurance specialist. The referral was sent days before, she tells me in a bored voice. There is no reason it should not be there. I call Mr. Bird. He's out.

An hour later, I phone him again. "Oh, yes, it did turn up. Just now," he says mildly. He will be sure to call me tomorrow.

Dan and I do not know whether to pack or get drunk. We turn to each other—on each other. "You had to be in such a hurry," Dan says. "Now we're already out—that is, your father's going to be out—more money than we've got, and if they don't agree to cover it, we're going to have to sell the car, get a second mortgage . . . "

"Dan, be fair. I just assumed . . . "

"You *assumed.* You assume too much. Too often. Go to the phone now and cancel it. Get back as much of the deposit as you can. We'll have to eat the rest. That's all there is to it." I go to the phone. But I don't call.

The following morning, Mr. Bird is on the line first thing. Good news. The committee has agreed. They would pay—the usual and customary fee for microsurgery of this kind. Fourteen hundred dollars.

"That's not even half."

Bird pauses. "Let me check on something." He calls back, breathless. He can more or less assure us that at least three-quarters of the surgery would be covered. We were not to be overly concerned with the fourteen hundred figure, because that was intended strictly to cover the surgeon's fee itself; and often the costs quote to patients included other fees as part of the total. We could file for those later, with major medical claim forms. Surely some of it would be picked up. "Hope for the best," he says.

I put down the phone. "Pack the car," I tell Dan. "We're covered."

"Are you sure?"

"Positive." Nothing is going to stop me now. Did anyone else ever approach *surgery* this way, pain and cutting and exhaustion, as if it were a date for the ballet on a hard-to-get ticket, or two weeks all-expenses-paid in Acapulco? Rush to it this way?

"I'm worn out," Dan says. "Why did they make it so arduous? As if we were asking them to pay for some capricious, trivial . . . thing, Jack. What if you had taken no for an answer?"

I refuse to think. There remains one hurdle. To convince my father, in Chicago, waiting to drive us to the airport, to lend me the hospital deposit and cover the check we'd already mailed for the surgeon's deposit. Dan thinks it was done, taken care of, that my father had agreed in the end. He had not.

I cannot relax in the car. My heart thumps raggedly; I'm a runner who can see the tape ahead, within sight, just put one foot in front of the other. Nothing else has held my mind for weeks. The writing I have done since the series fills me with an abstract pain when I think of it —thick witted, pretentious. I have written columns I don't remember the subjects of. Blacks were rioting daily in Washington, D.C., civilians in the Shatila refugee camp in West Beirut were massacred by militiamen, and the Supreme Court was nearing its decision on governmental regulation of abortion, and the events have slipped around me like wind, invisible. I've slid. What I took pride in has slid. My marriage has slid.

All for the missing member of the family. For you, kid. And worth it. I promise. Worth it. If you'll just come. Come home to me.

My father opens the door for me when we pull up on his drive. "So," he says, "you're really going. I knew you'd find a way to pay for it." He smiles broadly. "Just had to hustle a little, right?"

"Dad," I say.

THE BANK would close in ten minutes. Yet my father was in no hurry. The bank is in the neighborhood where I grew up; my father no longer lives there, but he is not a man who makes changes readily. He cruised the side streets, pointing out to me the house in which I had been born, asking me if I still recognized it, while I fretted and squirmed.

He is waiting for one word from me, I thought. One word about it, so that he may explode. Damn him. I am set up. The bank is closing.

"Dad, it's nearly four."

"And you're worried, huh? Worried you won't get what you came for?" Here it comes, then; well, let it blow. I thought, let it scatter over my head and have done with it. So long as I get the money. "I don't know how your mind works, Jacquelyn. Tell me. Tell me so I can understand how you think. You're a grown woman, you're married, right? Isn't that what you call it?"

"That's what I call it."

"And yet here you are knocking at my door." He slammed on the brakes at the curbstone in front of the bank, throwing both of us forward. "Well, my dear, I am at my limit. You. And your brother. The well has run dry. Do you get me? Do you capish? If you want to have a kid, fine. Have ten. But don't come asking me to pay for . . ."

"No one's asking you to pay for. I'm asking for a loan. And I can't have kids without this," I said quietly. "Can you honestly say that you want to be the one thing that prevents me?" That was blackmail, but no matter. My father played dirty.

"No. I don't want to be. But don't try to make me out a wrong guy because I'm not ready to just fork it over. With no guarantee I'll ever . . ."

"You'll get it back. Jesus. You'll get it." I was steering him, as he ranted, toward the double glass doors. Inside I could see one teller cashing out. Damn him. My mother had forced him to live well. Now with her gone, he was freed, freed to measure out his life in nickels and quarters—to become a portrait of his own father, who made four kids carry their shoes to school in warm weather to save the soles. My father had become an artist of frugality. A friend of his had died not long before, leaving his wife in tough shape. My father had offered to buy all of the man's golf clothes, and then dickered with the widow over the price. My brother had told me that our father put off calling an exterminator for so long that the mice were romping about in the kitchen like poodles. "Why don't you dig a moat, Dad?" Bobby had asked him. "Then you'd never have to worry about mice, and you could look out and see if it was someone who wanted money from you before you lowered the drawbridge."

And yet hadn't he paid for a single rose on my mother's grave every summer day—summer, when she had loved to fuss with her roses? And hadn't he paid to have carved on her headstone, in a burst of something I had never known in him, "She walks in beauty, like the night"? How could she die, and leave me alone with this?

"Mom would hate this," I said to him now, shameless. "She would hate you to turn me down." He pushed open the door. I breathed the first full breath in weeks.

When we were back in the car, my father turned to me and kissed me, twice. "Good luck," he said. I tried to remember if it was Woody Allen who had written that with a schizophrenic, you at least stood a fifty-fifty chance.

We landed in New Orleans at seven o'clock that night, stepping off in our winter coats into a wet, tropical closeness. My aunt Patricia was waiting in her pickup truck, wearing a hunter's vest and blue jeans. What the Corps of Engineers had done to the Mississippi River was coming home to roost this winter, she told us. It had rained incessantly; the fields were inundated, the streets streaming. The nutria, little fur-bearing animals Louisianans regarded as sewer rats, were running amok. We rattled off toward the city, four of us crammed into the truck cab, my grandmother perched with her suitcase on Dan's lap. I loved Pat; she was of the side of my family that had a wide streak of blue-ribbon eccentricity running through it. She had had three husbands—a Chicago mobster and two career soldiers—and two kids by each. In the old days, before she moved south, she would wheel her pink Pontiac convertible into the alley and my parents would put on moony smiles and remember appointments they had to keep.

I gave her my father's regards, then bitched about him for five minutes without stopping. Pat knew my father well; they had dated before he married my mother. "Bob Mitchard," she laughed. "He would drive five miles to find a meter with time on it." She told us that she had sold her two gay bars—my grandmother sighed with relief; this had been a major family skeleton—and now had a nice middle-management job at a Lake Charles hospital. She had cut loose the last husband, but daughters and sons and grandchildren moved in and out of her house in a steady procession. They called her "Mamma," in the Cajun way; most of Pat's kids could not remember living in Chicago, or anywhere but Louisiana. "My kids are my treasures," she told me, folding me in a hard hug. "I have all the candles in St. Patrick's burning for you. I've checked out those microsurgeons with my doctors. They're top-notch. If anyone can fix you, they say, these guys can."

We went to Brennan's for dinner—a dinner that went on for three resplendent hours. Pea and oyster gumbo with crusty French bread, chicken Arno, shrimp in garlicky tomato broth, a mousse with chocolate and bourbon. My aunt told her versions of the family ghost stories. It was on the night after my great-grandmother died, she said, in the house on Walnut Street in Chicago. "Your grandmamma asked, 'Did you hear that sound?' And I did, but I didn't admit it. It was the kind of sound it would be easy to forget you heard if you wanted to forget. But I had heard it then, and again later. In the pantry. Someone unfamiliar with the house had been to dinner, washed and dried the dishes. And your great-grandmamma was in there rearranging her dishes the way they ought to be. The sound we heard was the rustle of her taffeta underskirts."

"That's great," said the waiter, who was from La Crosse, Wisconsin, and who played blues guitar down the way on the nights he didn't wait tables, guitar being the reason he was here in the first place. He kept running back to jot down names of places we should see in the French Quarter.

"Wait," I finally cried. "I only have until morning. Then I have to check into the hospital." The kid's face fell. I could hear him thinking, this poor woman has cancer, and here I am teaching her how to say "Laissez bon ton roulez."

"Don't worry," I said hastily. "I'm not sick. I'm having an operation I want to have." And then I could hear him thinking, nose? Breasts? They look okay. "To have a baby."

The waiter paused and then made the briefest suggestion of a courtly bow. "I do hope it works," he said with his best broad Wisconsin vowels, "because your baby will be beautiful beyond words."

I peeled off a bill from my own wallet, as Dan counted out the tip. "It was a good omen, what he said," I told him.

"It was good business sense," Dan answered.

We had never been in New Orleans, much less in the Old Town. How had I pictured it? Not as this miniature city, its warren of tiny streets and close-leaning buildings tucked among a forest of blue-white skyscrapers and aerial towers. We wandered, brushing a hooker in blue sequins and a raggedy staggerer in a captain's hat and muskrat coat, from Rampart to Bourbon, up Bourbon to Toulouse Street, marveling at this brassy old dowager of a city-within-a-city, her fancy laces out at the elbows. We put our fingers into the tasseled iron lace on old balconies, stood outside doorways blue with smoke and listened to the howl of jazz horn, drank pink hurricanes at Pat O'Brien's, stingers somewhere else. At one in the morning we were watching kids who couldn't have been more than ten doing soft-shoe in the mud for quarters.

"I've found my city," Dan announced, "and I'm only going to get this one small taste of it."

We took a taxi back to Metairie and the motel, and Pat pushed a pair of hurricane glasses into my hands—"birthday present," she said, and I remembered, vaguely, that my birthday was three days away—and Dan and I fell asleep to the sound of Pat and my grandmother laughing through the wall. I had never seen my grandmother so bright.

I had to check into the hospital at seven—not a lot of sleep, but I could sleep for the next week. I was looking forward to being in the hospital, any hospital, again. At a hospital it was permissible to be solemn, people there were supposed to feel sorry for you, not look at you as if you'd lost your mind. I was looking forward to being too ill to answer the phone, to having nothing to do but watch the same framed bit of landscape lighten and darken for seven days. I had brought some reading for an upcoming project, and some work correspondence, but I knew the folders would never come out of my suitcase.

The hospital was in Gretna, a suburb that had to be approached over a Mississippi River drawbridge. Dr. Clarke would later tell me the unit was being moved to Metairie because the practice actually had suffered from the local phobia: there were people who were born in New Orleans, grew up and died there, without ever crossing that bridge.

From the Omega brochures, we had been led to expect a spa—the place sounded too good to be true. In a patient newsletter we had received, a woman who had become pregnant after her surgery described the experience as "more like a vacation than a hospital stay." Omega patients would dine on "gourmet" food, have wine with meals, be able to use a kitchen set up for late-night beverages and snacks. The staff ratio would be four nurses to every patient, since there were fewer than a dozen surgical suites on the RBU (Reproductive Biology Unit).

So when we first caught sight of F. Edward Hebert Hospital, we were unsettled. It did not look like a spa. It looked like Stateville Penitentiary in Illinois. What we had not been told—there were a great many things, it later would turn out, that we had not been told—was that the whole place was set down on a surplus installation the navy did not quite know what to do with. For the next seven mornings, Dan and I would wake to the strains of prerecorded reveille from the adjacent naval base.

What we noticed first when we walked in the door were the men— all the other patients were men who did not look so much sick as seedy, sitting around in wheelchairs smoking. They were all veteran sailors in alcohol or drug abuse treatment, Clarke later told us—the five of us on the RBU that week were the only female patients in the hospital.

I glimpsed a couple of them as a nurse with the good New Orleans name of Marie Duvalle showed us to our room. We had got the lower-priced suite, which was a hospital room with a sleeper sofa along one wall. The brochure had not, however, exaggerated the deluxe accommodations. They were across the hall.

As soon as the nurse was gone, I tiptoed across to have a look and was watching a tourist paddleboat wend its way up the river (the scenery obviously was part of the deluxe ticket) when I felt a brush on my shoulder.

She was smiling, and she put out her hand to me. "I'm Jamie Lancaster," she said. "I guess you're on the other side of the hall. I guess we're *all* on the other side of the hall." Jamie and her husband, Philip, were from Little Rock, Arkansas. He was a tool and die maker; she taught elementary school. Jamie wasn't fretting about the surgery; she *knew* that would work. She was fretting about her waistline, ravaged by her two days in New Orleans. And about her classroom. "I *hate* missing school," she said. "And if they have to make a vertical incision, I'm not going to be able to wear a two-piece anymore." I tried to reassure her; the standard incision was called a bikini-line. A two-piece would hide it.

Such worries, I thought. Such confidence. I didn't care if my incision began at my neck so long as I got a pregnancy out of it. But it hit me that Jamie's was the healthier attitude. She was worried about her own person, not only her status as a future incubator.

"I have agglutinated fimbriae," Jamie said, and didn't question whether I knew what she meant. She assumed that having come this distance I was a veteran, could roll the Latin off my tongue, and would know she meant that the small tentacles on the outer ends of her tubes were fused, making the egg-retrieval function dubious. Dr. Heiss had told her that the laser could be used to separate the fimbriae and that the surgery would take no more than thirty minutes.

As we walked down to the lab to have preliminary blood drawn, Jamie told me that she and her husband—he was forty, she thirty-three—had been trying to have a baby for three years. "Philip wants one so bad," she said. "I guess I do, too, but I tell you the truth, I'm worried about all this."

There was another woman waiting outside the lab when we got there —a tall, slender, beautiful woman whose long brown hair fell curling to her waist. It was hair without a strand of gray; I figured her for thirty —panic avoids the twenties—but she told me she was thirty-eight. Her name was Kathy Freeman.

"This is the worst part for me," I confided, as Jamie went into the lab to have her blood drawn. "I have these veins . . . "

"It won't be so bad," said Kathy, whom I had never seen before in my life but who then put her arm around me and told me she would be with me. And then began to talk. At the end of the story she told me, I felt diminished, me with my tears and my hysterics.

Kathy and Paul had been married for five years. They were supremely happy in each other—except that for three of those five years, they had been trying without success to have a child. Kathy had had children, two of them, from her first, disastrous teenage marriage. They were nearly grown, since Kathy had been married at sixteen and a half, been divorced at twenty. Paul had never been married or had children. Fond as he was of Kathy's, he terribly wanted a baby of his own.

A year after their wedding, Kathy's eldest son had gone surfing with friends on a weekend trip to the shore near where Paul, who was in the air force, was stationed. He was sixteen, Kathy said, a happy, smart boy who would not have gone off surfing alone and left his friends and his mother to go mad with worry when he didn't show up after a day and a night. After three days. After five. Police found Mark's body washed up on the beach a week after he disappeared.

The grief had nearly leveled Kathy. But with health had returned her desire for another child—doubly strong. When she and Paul went to Germany on a tour, an air force surgeon began an infertility investigation with them. A hysterosalpingogram ultimately showed blocked tubes. A laparoscopy, the surgeon said, showed that all looked good and surgery was in order. It was done in July. Minute plastic tubing was inserted in each of the tubes "to keep them open," according to the doctor. He removed the tubes a month later with another surgery. Do not, he warned Kathy and Paul, attempt to get pregnant for at least three months.

At her next visit, the surgeon informed Kathy he was being discharged and returning to private practice in California. "Write and tell me if it works," he told her. "I'm curious. I've never done this before." Kathy was speechless.

"How dare you treat me as an experiment without informing me?" she raged. The rage mounted when she requested her records for transfer back to the United States and learned that at the time of the surgery, her reproductive organs had been covered with endometriosis. The physician had never mentioned it. Kathy phoned him in California. "Oh that," he said. "The only cure for endometriosis is pregnancy."

By the time a physician at Duke University got a look at Kathy, the tubes not only were blocked once again, the endometriosis was rampant. One tube, she was told, "was twisted like a pretzel." One ovary was not even visible.

The Duke surgeon called the use of the plastic rods by the other doctor foolishness, brutality. If the interior of the tubes had not been damaged, he said, it would be a miracle. And he was at a loss to explain why the military doctor had counseled them to hold off trying for three months—it was common knowledge, he said, that the chances for success were highest right after a surgery. He gave Kathy five percent odds for success with conventional microsurgery.

A year later, she heard about Drs. Heiss and Julius in New Orleans. Julius put the odds for pregnancy at forty percent with laser microsurgery. Kathy took a three-month course of hormone therapy and now was set for what she, astonishingly, did not consider her last shot. "I could still try in vitro," she said. "Some places take women over thirty-five. We've even talked about a surrogate mother. I want a baby," she said simply. "It will sleep in our room. And I'll teach it to sing."

Until she came to New Orleans, Kathy said, she knew not one other infertile woman. She supposed she was the only one subject to terrible bouts of reasonless crying, who was obsessed with other children, with her nieces and nephews, but resentful of their parents—who felt, she said, like an Olympic runner informed of a disability that would make it impossible for him ever to run again, but who no one, looking at him, would believe was disabled. People would tell him, Kathy said, that it was all in his mind. "Do you know what I mean?" she asked me. Then, "Of course you know."

We sat in the lounge together, curled up in robes, with bottles of soda from the unit galley, for most of the late afternoon. We confided in each other with the utter confidence of strangers. It was like some bizarre grown-up pajama party, except that the subjects were not school or boys, but child abuse and how it grieved us, adoption and how we despaired of it, X rays and sperm counts and hostile cervical mucus.

A woman whose surgery was not scheduled until the following week, but who was in for tests, wandered in looking small and ill at ease. "You can tell the new patients," Kathy said to her. "They're the ones in robes they just cut the tags off." The woman relaxed; she showed us a newspaper clipping a relative had given her just before she left home in Indiana —perhaps, she said, it was an effort to cheer her up.

It was an Ann Landers column, reprinted at the request of a reader who considered the essay, from a long-ago reader, one of Ann's more hilarious sallies. "There's nothing sadder than the childless couple," it began. "It breaks your heart to see them stretched out, relaxing around swimming pools in Florida or California, sun-tanned and miserable on the decks of boats, trotting off to enjoy Europe like lonesome fools— with money to spend, time to enjoy themselves and nothing to worry about."

The writer went on to put forth a laundry list of the rigors parents endure: potato chips in the rug, olives plucked out of martinis, braces ruined by peanut brittle. Satirically, she asked, "What childless couple ever shares in such a wonderful growing experience" as the night the beautiful daughter elopes with the village idiot?

"The childless couple lives in a vacuum. They try to fill their lonely lives with dinner dates, theater, golf, tennis, swimming, civic affairs and trips all over the world. . . . The emptiness of life without children is indescribable."

"I guess it's supposed to be funny," Kathy said. "I guess it's supposed to make us see how great we really have it."

"I used to think it was me," said the other woman, whose name was Annie. "I wondered, why didn't I have a sense of humor? Why couldn't I see the joke that people all over America were laughing at?"

I was holding the column in my hand. It concluded, "See what the years have done. He looks boyish, unlined and rested. She is slim and youthful. If they had kids, they'd look like the rest of us—tired, gray, wrinkled and haggard. In other words, normal."

I thought of Dan's and my own festive life. We jetted about the country—for surgeries. We spent money lavishly—on treatment. We used our work vacations for hospitalization and recovery. Was I youthful, slim, and girlish? Had the six months Dan had spent without sleep left him "rested"?

Was I only hypersensitive—all of us here and our husbands in our "vacuum"—so out of touch with everything "normal" we couldn't take a joke?

"I think it's the cruelest thing I've ever read," Kathy said. Annie folded the article and placed it back in her wallet. We all headed for our rooms.

Months later, Kathy would write and tell me the laser surgery, at first apparently successful, had failed; the tubes were again blocked.

"Paul is completely disheartened," she would write. "And even I am finding it hard to keep pushing on. He won't even discuss in vitro at this point. But I'm determined. I have a couple of good years left. I can't have gone through all this for nothing."

It would turn out, incredibly, that she had not. A year later, at Christmas, I got a card from Kathy, whose letters had grown sparse over the months. They had been building a new house, she wrote, they had been so busy with it she'd neglected her correspondence, and—she saved it, she deserved to save it, for last—"I'm PREGNANT! I'm due in March. So if you haven't yet conceived, don't give up hope! The test showed the tubes were closed, but it happened anyway."

I wrote back to her, wholeheartedly meaning it, "You're blessed. I'm completely happy for you. You had, more than I had, utter confidence, and it paid off. . . . "

By five o'clock I had been weighed and X-rayed and bled and pre sented with a copy of my electrocardiogram, and an aide had brought Dan and me dinner in our room. Chicken-fried steak. Canned peas. "I won't eat meat," I told the dietary woman. "That was on the information sheet I sent in." She went out into the hall and brought back another helping of canned peas.

"This is the gourmet food, huh?" Dan asked, flipping over the stiff, sawdust-colored slab on his tray. We did get wine, though—an airline bottle of Gallo and two paper cups. We were chuckling about it when Dr. Clarke came into the room.

We chatted about inessentials. He loved New Orleans, he said, it was some fantastic city. But it had been something of a culture shock for him, coming out of Ohio State and before that, the navy, to drop feet first into the South, where his being black still was more primary a fact to some than his being a physician.

He looked at our cooling dinner. "You don't want to eat that stuff," he said. "Why don't you take a pass and go into town for the evening and get a fine meal?"

"We paid for this," Dan said darkly, and I hurried to cover up.

"So how do you feel, now that you've looked at my records, about our chances?" I asked.

"I think they're fine. We'll fix you up, don't worry."

"You're awfully confident."

"No reason not to be." He explained again the boring procedure that would be used to reinsert the cleared tube into the uterus. "And if you do get pregnant, you probably won't have to have a cesarean, which you would if you had the traditional reimplantation that causes a lot of weakening of the uterine wall. You can probably do it naturally."

Dan wanted to know if he would have to watch the surgery, or if he could opt out of that little bonus. I gave him a shot with my elbow. "We, ah . . . aren't doing that anymore," said Clarke. "A little problem with insurance." Dan beamed at me.

We shook hands around, and Clarke left. I had found myself looking hard, lingering over his cool, coffee-colored fingers. They were firm and spatulate and steady—the whole man was steady, stocky, compact. Down to his discreet gold-rimmed spectacles, he carried with him the clean, settled sense of middle-class achievement. "I liked him," Dan said.

We left our chicken-fried steaks untouched and phoned for a cab, hanging around the darkened lobby with the smokers in their thin robes until it came.

The ride cost fifteen bucks, and we could afford none of it—not the trip, nor the oyster dinner on the terrace at Seafood Sam's overlooking Bourbon Street, not even the dollar each we paid to get in to Preservation Hall to sit on a dusty wooden floor and watch the legendary Sweet Emma Barrett, eighty-six years old and hunched in her wheelchair, lift her long thin hands to the keys of her upright piano and, cigarette jigging in one corner of her mouth, thump out the bass line to "St. James Infirmary Blues."

In spite of the surgery, or perhaps because of it, there was a fullness and a shimmer to the night—the four hours of it we had before we must report back to the hospital at midnight. It was perhaps our best time ever together.

At the end of it, while we were seeking a taxi—one driver already had told us, with a brief shake of his ponytail, "I don't drive over that bridge" —we heard a sough of low notes drift out of the darkness beyond the borders of the quarter.

We saw him, barely, in the grated doorway of a big, closed department store, a man with a saxophone, bent at the waist and blowing, alone. We walked in his direction. He was tall and thin and odd, wearing a peaked hat and overcoat though the night was too warm even for a jacket. He looked, half-turned away from us, like the silhouette of a huge praying mantis. He took a few melancholy puffs at his mouthpiece, and then slowly, yearningly slowly, he began "Stardust."

Seven years before, when Dan and I were newly in love and I wanted all the trappings, I had told him, "We don't have a song, an 'our song.' We should have one."

"What was your parents' song?" he had asked me.

" 'Stardust.' "

"That was my parents' song, too. I think it was everybody's parents' song."

"Let's have it be ours, then."

The crowd that stopped in their tracks to listen to the magical notes that seemed to come from nowhere was quiet. No one moved; there was a smoke in the air it would have been sinful to disturb. When he had finished, the sax player opened his case and put his horn away. He had come, and set up, for only that one song.

That night, from my cranked-up hospital bed, I saw a shooting star slip like a tear across the sky. "Omens," said Dan, who saw it, too. "Good omens."

"NOW you'll just hold the bag up over your head and run the line down," the nurse instructed. I was sitting curled up, on the closed lid of the toilet, getting enema instructions.

"Who's going to hold the bag up?"

"Why, your husband can do that for you." So this was part of the Omega philosophy. Well.

"Excuse me, I don't think that's going to be . . . "

Dan interrupted. After the nurse left, he said, "Well, you're just going to have to let me do it. B., you and I are married. It's not as if I'm going to get a glimpse of any part of you I haven't seen before in a different posture." He put up a palm. "I know. I know. It's difficult and embarrassing but that's the whole point. I'm not a stranger. Think of me as you would your . . . your mother. Let me care for you."

I squeezed my eyes shut. It had been a long day, full of only possibly necessary indignities. And a few others to boot. I had spent an hour arguing with the hospital's doctor of anesthesiology, a young east Indian woman. She had come to my room after seeing on my chart that I had requested a gas induction for surgery or else the kinds of measures used to start a line in children. "It's my veins," I explained. "It's always been difficult even to draw a blood sample, but lately they've been getting a lot of use and it seems to be worse. . . . "

"That is nonsense," said the young doctor. "The veins do not get overuse."

"Perhaps I didn't put that correctly. . . . " She snatched my left hand, turned it over.

"Your veins are just fine," she said after a glance. "You are only frighten."

"I'm not frightened." I felt like Jimmy Stewart in *No Highway in the Sky*. "But I do *know* my own veins, and I have had surgeries before in which the problem has developed. They are *my* veins, and I know . . . "

"It won't happen here. We are very good."

"I did not mean to insinuate anything about the training of the staff." She was looking at her watch. Her nurse, who I noticed with a kind of weird click looked just like her, was grinning at me. She was leaving. I was losing. "I don't want to have the surgery if I can't have some kind of special assurances about this. It's too stressful." There. Now she had pushed me to it. I had acted spoiled and petulant and neurotic, and I am none of these; but from the look on her face, I could tell she was thinking, ah ha. I know how to deal with this. We have a patient fastened on her frailty, who wants special treatment, a fretful Frau in her chenille bathrobe. . . .

"Is everything all right now?" the doctor asked me briskly, looking as if she were about to clap her hands.

"No. I need your assurance that special care will be taken with putting in the lines."

"I don't see the necessity."

"But really, what's it to you? Will it cost more? Will it throw the day off schedule? Is it really such an outrageous request?"

"It's not how we do it. It's difficult, I believe, for you, as a patient, to understand, but there are ways that we . . . "

This is supposed, I believed, to bring me up short. Screech to a stop and bow from the waist to the arcane authority of medical expertise the ways of which are not vouchsafed to the patient—not for any reason mundane or pietistic—but to *spare* the patient the difficulty of trying to understand what is impossible for her to understand: matters ineffable, exalted. I rose to the occasion. Acted the complete ass. Got up from the sleeper sofa, went to my hospital bed, sat down on it, and drew the curtain.

We were all the same, I thought, looking out at what passed for a parade ground on this base and yearning for a cigarette. We were individual only in that they took us one at a time—even at this place, which was a better place than most. I had asked for a photocopy of my charts for my files. "Patient began menstruation at thirteen, 28–30 day cycles, experiences dysmenorrhea, mild premenstrual tension." I had never said that. I had never had that. But women are women. *All* women had menstrual cramps. All women had tension. No matter what they said.

A resident found me and took me off for an exam, and in the course of it asked me every single question Dan and I had answered minutely on the questionnaire mailed in weeks before. "This is called replication," Dan said when I told him. "This is called everybody gets a piece of the insurance money."

The resident probed my abdomen. "Abdomen soft," he scratched on his chart, "slightly obese." Obese. God. I was five feet and four inches and 148 pounds. Hefty, certainly. Fatter than I'd ever dreamed possible, yes. But *obese?*

"God," I told Dan. "This is humbling."

"No shit." He had been fretting about having to give another sperm sample. "I don't know why they have to test me," he said. "I had the same thing a couple of months ago. I'm not the one with the problem."

"How sensitive of you."

"I didn't mean it that way." But we had no time to talk. I was whisked away for another exam.

We were savoring another gourmet delight—beef fritters and tepid scalloped potatoes—when Dr. Clarke stopped by for his presurgery call. He wanted to calm my fears. I wanted to tell him about sweet Emma Barrett.

"You're so . . . settled," he said wonderingly. "I've never had a patient who wasn't at least a little afraid the night before."

"I'm a little afraid. That it won't work. But the surgery itself—I can't wait. I wish we could do it now."

"Soon enough." He looked at our plates and shook his head. "Order a pizza," he advised. "But nothing after midnight."

I had night thirsts. At home we had developed a routine. Dan brought in the dog, turned out the lights, and brought me a glass of water before we went to sleep. I drank quarts of water that night. A nurse came to shave me. I had a Phisohex shower. Then the enema. Then another shower.

The night nurse came to say good night and put out the overhead light. Dan and I lay in silence. He read the *Times-Picayune* by the light of a small bed lamp. "You're a better columnist than this guy," he said.

But I was listening. Listening to the muffled shrillness of voices on the hall. Who was it? Behind which door were tensions fulminating? I would bet on Tina Graham. She was the fifth woman on the unit, and she was not in New Orleans to gamble on restored fertility. She didn't have a husband and seemed not to want a child. But it was difficult to tell. Tina was perennially, seriously depressed; she never dressed, but hunched along the corridor in her blue satin turtleneck robe—a twin of her mother's, who was accompanying her. Tina was on the RBU for relief. She had virulent endometriosis—painful, invasive. She had hoped the laser could burn it away, but one attempt already had failed. Tomorrow there would be a second.

She was a strange case. Sorry as you felt for her, she acted like the spoiled Hollywood brat she probably had been. Mother worked at Warner Brothers; Tina didn't work at all. Bouts of her condition, or one of ten operations—in the past five years—had kept her from maintaining work or school for so many years that she had a perpetual teenagerish quality about her, though she was nearly thirty. She swore at her mother, snapped at her, sulked. Her mother treated her with alternate contempt and smothering concern.

I tried to talk to Tina, but as often as I did, I had to flee her. Her depression sucked at me; she coaxed out and cultivated the worst of me —my fears, our fights, our shames.

"You don't know what I've been through!" a voice cried. "You don't know!" If infertility had an anthem, I thought, and slept.

I had a paper shower hat on my head and a good shot of the groggies spreading through me, and Dan was holding my hand. We were in the anteroom to the operating suite. I had to muster my wits for one last engagement; it was time to put in the lines, and "this one time," I said to Dan, "I don't want to wake up from it. I don't want to go into this sober." I recited the litany of my veins to a kind young man.

"Let me take a look." I made a fist, let it open. "The doctor was wrong," he said wryly. "My dead grandmother has better veins than you do." He turned my hand over. "But look. Relax. Out of the hat of fate you have drawn the honest-to-God artist of line-starting. Me." He used the assembly designed for pediatrics, and it was done with a small pinch.

Dan kissed my shower hat. Dr. Clarke swam into my vision above me. He introduced a man with a salt-and-pepper beard. Dr. Heiss. "Good morning," I said.

"Good morning," said Dr. Clarke. "How do you feel?"

"Fine." I felt fine. Just a nagging dryness of the tongue. "When . . . ?"

"It's all done." Clarke grinned broadly. "It went well."

"You're saying it worked?"

"Of course it worked. What did you expect?" What did I expect. I was wheeled back into our room feet first. Dan was finishing breakfast. "It worked," I told him faintly, holding out my hand. "How about that?"

"I know," he kissed my fingers, hard. "Happy birthday."

177

 IT WORKED. We thought that was all there was to it. But we were learning that infertility has one constant: there is no such thing as all there is to it. Given what could interfere, it began to seem miraculous to us that anyone ever had kids.

Late on the afternoon after surgery, Clarke came by the room to take us to the movies. He brought a couple of prospective patients, husband and wife, along to show me off. "The day after surgery," he beamed. "Look at that range of movement!" Obligingly, I got up off the bed for a clumsy pirouette. I felt splendid. Steroids, Bellow would tell me later, accounted for the physical euphoria.

"I highly recommend this fellow," I told the woman. Late thirties. Dripping with designer labels. She gave me a wan smile—one of those smiles so innocent it looked as if she had just learned how to do it. I smiled back. I could afford pity. I had been; she had yet to go. Dan and I, arm in arm, crossed the hall to the tape library.

The videotape of my surgery put me in mind of stag films I had seen —the pink and white blobs were at such close range it was impossible to tell what they were or what they were doing. But Clarke pointed out the laser, and after a moment, we could see its sizzling action nick away at the obstruction. "There it goes!" said a voice on the tape, and violet dye shot through the tube. The obstruction had been rather large, about six millimeters, but it had not been in the wall of the uterus after all. Cardiff had been right about the shadow on the X ray; there remained enough tube to make a reattachment. My original purpose in bucking for New Orleans was negated. No reimplantation. No cesarean. Absurd gratitude.

"About the length of the tube now," I started to ask Clarke, who held up one palm.

"Don't worry. There's plenty."

"What caused it?"

"Probably endometriosis. We found a few spots of it."

A few spots. Don't tell me where. Clarke sounded unconcerned. But

I knew better. Endometriosis—evil-sounding question mark of a word —was a thing no doctor liked to see. Nobody really was sure how the cells of uterine lining that grew in other areas of the pelvis got there, or why. Clarke was of the "retrograde menstruation" school, which held that sloughed-off cells of endometrial tissue moved up and out of the tubes instead of down and out of the cervix, as they were supposed to. How did it affect fertility? Nobody really was sure. But it did. More than once, I had heard of couples told by physicians who had found endometriosis, "Perhaps it's time you considered adoption." Women who had just a few tiny black specks of it could have as difficult a time conceiving as those riddled with the stuff. Did the powerful prostaglandins the deposits produced interfere with ovulation? I had read that. No one was sure, again. But endometriosis could, for sure, block tubes and corrode organs. A touch of it could double a woman over in pain at the time of her period, or a slew of it could go undetected for years.

At least, I had told myself over the months, I don't have *that*.

Clarke was telling me how he proposed to treat it. Since pregnancy seems to quell the condition—I knew that much—it was treated with a decoction of male hormones that suppressed ovulation and menstruation, creating a false atmosphere of pregnancy. I would take Danazol twice a day for six months.

"Six *months?*"

"Four to six months is the usual . . ."

"The woman down the hall had more endometriosis than you could shake a stick at and she only has to take it for six weeks." It was common practice for everyone who had the surgery to have to take a short course of the stuff, the feeling being that all the messing about and running of dyes was likely to spread some endometrial cells about. "How come I have to take it for six months for a few spots?" Was he screwing around with me? Not giving it to me straight, perhaps saving the bad news for later? I wanted to unzip my staples and see for myself.

"We want to be sure," Clarke said.

"Four months, then," I bargained. This was not me. Jackie, who went along with the program, always, like a good sheep. I felt I was fighting for days. The first months after this kind of surgery were supposed to be the prime ones. Now I was not to have them. I had been counting the days until we might try—my first fertility period, post surgery, would have been around Christmas. Now it would be spring. Months. The panic began to percolate. "This is an extremely urgent baby," I told Clarke.

"Well," he smiled. "Four months should be sufficient." Now I didn't trust that. Why did he give in so easily? Was I jeopardizing my chances? Should I recant? "You can expect some side effects," he said then. They were fairly harrowing. Weight gain. Now that was something to look forward to. Clarke said it resulted from increased appetite. I would read in months to come, swooping down on every mention of the disease in books and women's magazines, that other specialists said the drug increased muscle mass or contributed to water retention. Whatever the reason, the result would be ten or more roly-poly pounds I scarcely needed.

But now Clarke went on. Facial hair. Mainly on the upper lip, but not confined to it. Some could show up on the breasts, too. And the breasts would be tender. There'd be headaches. Cramps. This was great stuff.

And we must be careful to use birth control. Some barrier method. That meant condoms, because I would not risk even the slightest yeast infection from using a diaphragm. Clarke said the drug probably could harm an embryo. So I must not conceive, even though the drug itself probably would prevent that.

"Is that all, then?" It wasn't all. There was some indication, from the appearance of the follicle, that I had not ovulated the previous month. "Nothing to be concerned about," he went on. "The stress of upcoming surgery, anything could have interfered. . . ." I debated whether to believe him. My dependables were falling like playing cards. I knew I ovulated. My basal temperature charts were so relentlessly biphasic Bellow said it looked as if I completed one and then copied it on a Xerox machine. I would ovulate in an air raid in Lebanon.

"And we found that there was a bit of fimbrial agglutination. We separated them with the laser."

"Is that serious?"

"If I gave up on every case where it showed up, I'd give up on three-quarters of them. Don't worry." His wide smile was meant to be reassuring. "I think the prognosis for a pregnancy is excellent." Well, of course. How could he say otherwise.

I was glad, I told Dan after Clarke left, that Laura had already made her call. That she already had been able to cry happy for me. That I had talked with Bobby. That the birthday party the other patients had engineered for me—convincing the food service to come up with a cake —already was over. Because I couldn't account for what might happen now.

My grandmother had been there for the party, and my aunt, and my cousin Winona. All shining. All happy for me. And I had been gay as well. Had done some appropriate mugging. "I'm old," I had cried to the assemblage. And they had made the looked-for response.

"Nonsense," Kathy Freeman had said. "You have plenty of good years left." And I remembered having thought then, good years. About what good years means to an infertility patient. Not years in which there is personal success and health and perhaps money to travel, not years in which the world seems kind. Childbearing years. We should all have T-shirts, I had thought. Jamie—seven good years. Kathy—three good years. If I took the Ursula Andress approach, and considered forty the top limit. Which I did not.

Dan tells me that I was quiet the rest of the day, absorbed in TV. That I cooed appropriately over the nice book and pretty robe he had packed back in Madison to give me that day, but seemed not to see them at all. He had fussed about me, awkward, feeling his hands and feet were too large, helped me shower.

I had gone to sleep early. To escape the nightmares. I saw them in the room. Failure. Withering. Having come so far with the shreds of my hope gathered together in one fist. I had strung together the things Clarke had told me, and taken them apart, and strung them together again in a new order. And they still did not add up to "That's Incredible!" They added up to an outside chance.

The following afternoon, I believe I lost my mind. Dr. Julius, who was taking Clarke's rounds for the day, started it; but my father set it up.

He had called me an hour before to wish me happy birthday but also to tell Dan he needed to move our car and couldn't find the keys. "I don't know why Dan is down there in the first place," he grumbled. "Just so the two of you can spend money you don't have. So he can cut out of work . . ."

"Dad, I explained why Dan had to be here."

"What good is he doing there? Your grandmother could have done anything he did."

"She's in Lake Charles."

"Well, then all of you are nuts. You're a real trio."

"Dad, don't start. It's my birthday. I'm in the hospital. Why don't you just say you love me." Silence. "Say you love me, Dad. Come on." I began to cry. "Go ahead. Say it."

"I don't know what you're . . ."

"Say it."

A long pause. Then he said, "Okay, I love you." And a childhood memory flew up like paper against a windshield. It was a memory I did not often take out because I could not explain it, even to myself.

My mother had been busy one rainy summer evening with my baby brother; I probably was about seven. I was whining around the house with nothing to do, under my mother's feet. "Bob," she finally said to my father, exasperated, "play with her."

My father had taken me into the living room. We sat down on the matching love seats. We looked at each other. "What do you want to play?" he asked.

"House."

"Okay. How do you play that?"

I ran for my bag of old clothes and material scraps. "You be the baby and I'll be the mommy. I'm going to dress you up." He had sat, patiently enough, while I wound a strip of cotton around his head to make a bonnet, then ran into the kitchen and got a saucer of applesauce and fed it to him with a spoon. After a few minutes, I put the spoon down. "Dad," I complained, "you're not *playing.* You have to pretend to be the baby." His look frightened me. I did not think he would hurt me, but I could feel his terrible unease. I tried to teach him how to play. "Say a baby thing, Daddy," I urged. "Say 'goo goo.' That's what a baby says."

"Jackie," he said flatly.

"Come on, Daddy. Don't you want to play with me? Please? Say 'goo goo.' Then I'll pretend to be the mommy. . . ."

"No."

"Daddy. You *have* to. Come on." I began to cry, and my mother heard.

"Bob!" she shouted. "For heaven's sake!"

My father looked back at me. "Okay," he said slowly. "Goo goo. There. Are you happy?"

But I had not been happy. I cried harder, and the crying had worked its way into a fit of tears until my mother had to carry me off to bed. I had forced my father into something he didn't want, that made him miserable, and I had made both of us awkward and embarrassed and angry. I didn't know what it was I had done. The memory lasted, playing itself out with merciless clarity whenever—as a teenager, as a young woman—I had worked up the courage to send my father a funny card or kiss his cheek, every time I saw how these things unsettled him, how he did not seem to understand why I did them.

It was playing itself out yet again, when Dr. Julius came into the room, terse and tense, took a look at my chart, and said, "Ah. Endometriosis. Well. What the condition is really is a kind of cancer. Growth of abnormal cells. It usually leads ultimately to a hysterectomy. The hope is to hold it off long enough to establish a pregnancy."

He left then. It was nearly sunset, raining. I picked up a glass of cold water from my tray. The sound of the ice against the glass roared like a subway train leaving a tunnel.

"I want a pizza," I told Dan.

"Honey," he said, "we can't afford it. There isn't a pizza joint within ten miles of here. And you really shouldn't overeat."

"I want a pizza. You live on canned vegetables for a week and then tell me how satisfied you feel."

"You had some cake yesterday."

"It was terrible. Did you like it? You would like it. Sugary, cloying mess. Hard frosting. I hated it. I hate the cake." And I jumped up off the bed and tossed the remains of tonight's cake, and the rest of the meal, into the trash. "There. Now you don't have to rag me about cake."

"I didn't rag you."

"You sonofabitch." Dan gaped. I remember seeing his face swim, thinking, Christ, oh no, my love, I've lost you, and me saying, "You cur. You with your perfect first wife and your perfect daughter."

We argued. I ranted, said every mean thing I could conceive. He finally ordered the pizza after asking around about a place that would deliver, went downstairs and waited an hour and a half, and finally brought it upstairs. It was cold and clammy. I wouldn't touch it. He had paid fifteen dollars for it. It only made me angrier, but by then I was completely irrational.

Dan picked up my green spiral notebook and began to write. Furiously. He needed a witness. I snatched it out of his hands, certain he was looking for something to use against me. "I know what you're saving our money for," I cried, "to give it to Joan. To keep blessed Joan in designer jeans. . . ." I flopped on the bed. Dan started up.

"Watch out," he said. "Your incision."

"My goddamned incision." I struck myself in the stomach. It hurt terribly. "This is for my incision. Why didn't I die? Why didn't I just die?" I don't recall all the words. But Dan wrote them down. "You're still in love with her. And I can't blame you. She had your child. Do you remember the John Updike story you read me from *Playboy?* About the true wife? The first wife. You cried when you read it, Dan. You cried. You never cried for me. You never did."

"That was five years ago," he said to me. "I was in the middle of the divorce. You understood. At least you said you did."

And I had. Of course I had. "I didn't," I said. "I never understood why you would make me feel so . . . so corollary." He approached the bed then. Let down the rail. And I tried to sock him. Then I looked at my fist and what it had done in horror. "Leave. Go on, Dan. Hurry, get a plane. Get away from me. You still can. You can be happy." I grabbed the telephone directory and began feverishly to search for the Delta Airlines listing. "I'll get you a reservation. . . ."

Dan ran for the nurse. I knew she would come. Had to compose myself. Had to fool her. I practiced smiling. I ran my hands up and down my cheeks. They felt hard, calloused. Like files. I had to banish the monsters. But they would not go; they perched on my knees, grinning at me. I would need a hysterectomy at thirty-one. Dan would not love our children, even if we had them.

By the time the nurse came in, on the run, with permission from the doctor to give me a sedative, I was lying back on the pillows, my hair arranged. "Oh, sweetie, you worry so much," I said to Dan in a treacly voice.

Pam the nurse was not fooled. "Now here, honey, you take this and try to rest." Aside, she said to Dan, "The whole unit's on edge. Dr. Julius went through here like a whirlwind. It's like a night of the full moon out there. Nobody can sleep, people are having fights. . . ."

"Oh, he made too much of it," I put in.

"I did not." Dan's face had hardened, like someone preparing to take a blow. "You were scaring the shit out of me."

I was ferociously embarrassed. "Oh, now Dan . . ."

"You were!" He held up the notebook. "You brought up the shotgun again." Had I done that? Was he embellishing it for the sake of the nurse? She stood to one side; oddly, she looked as if we were discussing the seating capacity of the Superdome.

"Will you try to sleep now?" she asked.

And then I asked her, "Do you have kids?"

"No. I just got married about six months ago."

"How old are you?"

"Twenty-six." Twenty-six. What I wouldn't give for those few years. "But you know, it's odd. Working here. I think about it. Every twinge is a pelvic infection. I think, you could be me. Jamie could be me." She straightened out an edge of my sheet. "But you know what is great? Getting the pictures of the babies eighteen months later." I made a rapid calculation.

"When do most of the women who get pregnant get pregnant?"

"Some right after. Some not for a couple of years. I think it's about nine to eighteen months after surgery on the average." She gave me a pat—this twenty-six-year-old kid playing mama to a woman old enough to be her . . . her upperclassman. Pam the nurse had a round, peachy Southern face, auburn hair that fell down her back in a shining braided rope, and all the Central Casting requirements for a nurse. Efficient. Tender. Healing. Prepared. The gods would never land her in such a pickle as this. "Sleep now?" she said. "Yes." Meek.

As she left the room, Dan put his hand out to me. "Just rest now, honey, and let the sedative take effect."

And I hissed at him, "You betrayed me. You bastard. I can't believe you would do this to me. Maybe we should try to get pregnant. There's a good chance of another ectopic. You'd like that."

"A twenty percent chance," Dan whispered, clinging to real things.

"Which in my case is virtually a sure thing, you must agree." I began to sob. "Leave me. With what's left of my pride. We'll take care of your pride later, and your reputation." He had no idea what I meant. I had no idea what I meant. The room began to close like a lens. I slept.

The phone was ringing when I awoke, unable for a moment to remember where I was. The sky outside was dark, the moon set. It had been hours. I saw Dan sitting in a chair near the bed, still writing in the notebook. He didn't reach for the phone. I caught it, awkwardly.

"Listen," said my father. He turned on what I imagined to be a tape. There was a bleat, and then Shirley Jones singing " 'Til There Was You." "Do you get it?" asked my father, when the song was over.

"I get it," I told him. We hung up. I turned to Dan. "Could you forgive me?" I asked him.

He gave me a look. There was nothing in it. Nothing at all. He might have been looking at an interesting bit of geology in a museum case. "Please," I said. "Dan. I was unspeakable. I didn't mean a bit of it."

"I'm afraid of you," Dan said. "I'm afraid this thing has changed you in some irrevocable way. You were the worst person for something like this to happen to, Jackie. Your fears and your insecurities go deep. Your obsessions with Joan. I loved you, Jackie. I truly did. You just wouldn't know it. Not since you lost the baby. Because after that, no one could possibly love you enough." The past tense was not lost on me. I felt an electric spurt of fear.

Be the baby, then. The irresistible small thing. I was desperate. I held out my arms. He did not come into them. "Dan, it was the stress. The operation. All these last months coming to a head. And now these things we're finding out. That there was more wrong than we believed, more problems. That there will be more waiting. Having to bear that and thinking that I can't. I promise, it was that. Don't you believe me?"

"I considered that." He turned the pen over in his fingers. "But you haven't been right for months. You haven't been *present* for months. I believe it was the truth that came out tonight. You hate me."

"I don't hate you. I love you." He hesitated.

"I don't know if I can believe that."

"Please, Dan. A reprieve. When we're home, and back to normal . . ."

"We'll see then."

"No! I want you now! Please love me." And in answer, he made room in his bed. I crept in there and curled against him, and he lay lightly so as not to jostle my hurts, and in a few minutes, I could tell he was sleeping.

And then I inched out my hand and got hold of his notebook. In the light from the hall, I read, "She blames me. She believes if I hadn't waited so long, first to get married and then to have kids, the tubes would not have been blocked. Is she right? Does she think I blame her? That I consider her inferior, to Joan of course, first and primarily, but then to all 'normal' women? This is not true. This is a reflection of her feelings of lack, of inadequacy.

"I want a child. But I would have been happy with Jackie, without more children, if she were not so filled with hate and self-loathing over her fate. I fear she would have left me long ago if she had any hope that by doing so, by finding someone else, she could have children.

"I'm doomed to bear the brunt of this rage. How do I sort it out? She rants, she is hysterical, she apologizes. I think it's over, then it surfaces again. She is a walking contradiction."

And then, "A divorce will be difficult. She wants it, but she will fight. She will see it as a way to get back at me. I do know that it seems impossible that we can remain married. The irony is that the incidents she refers to, the things about Joan that seem to drive her the most, go back to the very time when I turned away from my own guilts and committed myself only to her."

I awakened him. "Is is morning?" he asked groggily.

"No. But Dan, Dan, I don't want a divorce. I don't want to leave you."

"Go back to sleep now," he said. "We've had enough for one night."

But I did not sleep. I lay and listened to the quiet shush of the nurses' crepe-soled shoes along the hall, squeezed my eyes shut when Pam poked her head in to check on us, and tried to put together a logical chain of what had led us to this place, a chain that if I followed it carefully could lead us back out. I wanted to believe it could lead us back out.

25

ON THE DAY we got back from New Orleans, early in the morning after Dan had left for work, I found a packet of pictures he had taken and had developed and never shown to me.

I could not place them at first. Jocelyn and I, standing by a wall in front of a sherbet sunset, overlooking what appeared to be the sea. Florida? It had been warm, because I wore a strapless dress, a dress cinched in at the waist, I noticed—I had had a waist then, whenever it was. But the Jocelyn in the photo was too big for it to have been Florida; her hair was too short, as it was now. And why would Dan tuck away photos of Florida in his underwear drawer?

It was Door County. Last summer. Only five months before. Dan had not shown me the pictures because they had been taken on the night before the night it happened. What Jocelyn had taken to calling "the terrible thing."

Memory deletes and embroiders according to its fancy, and my memory had been particularly feckless these last days. But even that could not account for how strange this woman looked to me, how bold and brown and fearless on her rock. I looked at the next one and the next —Jocelyn in an old rowboat, throwing daisy tops into the water. Me swinging Jocelyn over my head. I could not pick her up anymore. She approached me cautiously. I seemed to her always to be recovering from one thing or another. Dan said she did not leap on me any longer because she was afraid she would hurt me inside.

There were other pictures in the stack. I paged through them. Leaves turning over the lake by our house. Halloween—me in my red tomato getup, glazed merriment on my face. But I came back to the first. There was something in my face, something yielding and yet supremely arrogant—was it there, or did my mind paint it in? I looked into the camera directly, daring Dan not to love me—how could he help but love me? I was healthy and glossy and sure and I was carrying his child inside me.

I knew from poems that time is relative. For those who have a sorrow, it plods. Yet this had sped away from me, even as I had tried determinedly to stop it, telling myself and others that I had just lost a baby, long after the "just" in the sentence was a lie.

Even as I had tried to hoard them, those weeks had compressed, had become a scant handful of time, as furry around the small details as if I had lived them only in passing. Significant and vivid—and as long ago —as the week I graduated college. The week I got my first job. My eleventh birthday, when I'd knocked out two teeth riding my new bike. Not really more significant. They had fallen into place.

But still I took the pictures from the envelope, put the arm load of underwear I held on the bed, and went into the living room to find our photo album. I slid the picture in a cellophane sleeve on the last page.

There would not be a first birthday snapshot, with hats and cake. There would be no candids of a fat face smeared with strained carrots. But this was evidence. This was a record of my baby and me together. I had not managed to manipulate time; it had hurtled ahead, terribly quickly. But I would keep the picture.

On the night of December 16, the second night we were home, our dog, Jeb Stuart, was struck by a car as he ran across Highway 19 near Todd's house. It was his first sight of Dan after a week, and Dan was Jeb's whole life. "That was all he knew," Dan said when he came home that night, weeping. "That he was with me again. He was absolutely mad with happiness." Dan had opened the door to the garage where Todd had kept Jeb, and the dog dashed out, jumped on him, then took off directly into the highway. A car whizzed by, Dan heard a thump, and by the time he reached him, Jeb was gone.

The car that hit him had been driven by an elderly lady, and Dan said she put her face in her hands and cried when she saw Jeb lying unmarked and still. "I never even hit a squirrel," she pleaded.

I wrote a column about how people make progeny of their pets, comforting myself in the house that was so still and clean, so free of clumps of soft yellow hair. "He had never had an unhappy moment," I wrote. "Never a clout that stung more than a second, never a hungry night. . . . Perhaps it is because we do not know if we may ever have a child that the loss is so keen, and so absurd. He was such a lordly fool, a big, strapping, muscular locomotive, and yet he held our hands in his mouth with eggshell tenderness."

Dan and I reunited, also absurdly, over Jeb. We called Jocelyn, even though we would see her in a few days. "Darling," said Dan, "Jeb had an accident. . . ."

"I know," she said. "He's dead. He was always too wild. Oh, Daddy."

We decided not to replace him. Jeb was famous at our office and in the neighborhood. A big Secretariat of a dog, small on brains and large on looks. We had mated him with a bitch owned by Rick Krause, who ran the food service at work, and she had had two litters of ten pups. When Dan told Rick that Jeb had been killed, Rick said, "You're going to be glad to see the end of this year. Damn. That was one fine dog."

Two days before Christmas Eve, Dan came home from work and asked me if I'd like to take a drive. We were packed for Chicago, the presents wrapped, and I had a fierce cabin fever, so I agreed eagerly. We drove out through what people in that part of Wisconsin call the Ocooch Mountains—which aren't mountains at all, merely glacial hills, but which seem to tower over that flat land. There was new snow, and ice making prisms of the trees, and I cuddled against Dan as best I could with my belly stiffness. "I feel sanguine," I told him.

"Sanguine?"

"You know. After all, nobody said there was no chance we'd have a baby."

"Nobody said that at all, Jackie. In fact, they said just the opposite. You're just so conditioned to everything going wrong that possibly can, it's impossible for you to see that a ten percent chance of something going wrong means there are ninety other chances that it won't."

"You can see why."

"I can see why. But let's try hope for a while. Give it a whirl, huh?" We turned into an unfamiliar drive that led over a little creek bridge to a farmhouse.

"What's this place?"

"Rick's," Dan told me. "He thought we might like to see Kelly and the pups he kept from Jeb's last litter."

"Oh, Dan. We'll just feel bad."

"No," he said. "Look." The dogs were slipping and gamboling down the snowy hill from the barn where Rick housed them—little copper-colored Kelly in the lead, her muzzle silver from age, and, I supposed, childbearing. Kelly was the smartest dog we knew except when it came to passion. A new litter of round, black-and-white puffballs were circling her heels—the fruit of some chance overnight encounter. And after those came her purebred golden retriever pups, a male and a female, eight months old.

"Dan," I shouted, "it's Jeb. The big male looks just like Jeb." And he did, just a bit smaller, a bit darker of coat.

"And a whole lot smarter," said Dan, as he heeled the dog, and bade him fetch. I was down on my knees in the snow, fondling the head as big as a roast, getting my hands and my coat filthy with saliva. "Rick says he's a smart dog. Kelly has taught them to be smart about cars." He lit a cigarette. "So do you want him?"

"I'd love him. But Dan, we can't afford a dog like this."

"We can have him. Rick wants us to have him. Or we can take the little female. She's pretty. That is, if we even want another dog. . . ."

"When?"

"Well, anytime. I told Rick we'd come out here so you could see the dog, and he said to take him now if we wanted. But we'll want to wait until after Christmas, and think it over."

"Sure." We handed pets all around, and got into the car. As we pulled off down the drive, I looked back and saw the big male standing alone at the bridge. Kelly was herding the rest back toward the barn. "Dan," I said.

He backed up the car. And opened the hatchback. The pup jumped in. He stank to high heaven. These were outside dogs; they rolled in the cow pasture, ran down deer in the woods. "We'll have to give him a bath as soon as we get home, and get a flea collar. Do we have time to go to the vet? How many of his shots . . ."

"Jackie, are you sure?"

Dogs were a big mess. I was in no shape to take care of one that probably was not even housebroken. "Of course," I said. "What's his name?"

"They call him Josie. But he hasn't been registered."

"That's a girl dog's name."

"How about Jesse?" So we called him Jesse James (the thirty-seventh, it turned out), son of Jeb Stuart the seventh and Princess Kelly. And he was so fine a dog we felt disloyal—he knew everything without being told, with a grave and soulful attention. We bought Rick a bottle of Scotch, and packed up Jesse and the presents in the truck the day before Christmas Eve and headed for Chicago.

There was a party that night at the home of Dan's sister's mother-in-law. Ann threw great spreads—smoked oysters and huge silver bowls full of the kind of green shrimp Dan and I bought at the deli in the quarter-pound package. And wines. Cabernets and champagnes older than I was that Ann handed out like soda pop. We were fond of her not because of her largesse, but because she seemed to like life so thoroughly; she didn't hold her money close the way so many who have it do. She had fun with it. She liked to see others have fun with it. Sometimes it all got faintly decadent, as with the third birthday party for Gail's son John, when Ann bought him a real electric train big enough to ride, with a track that went around the backyard. But it was impossible to think anything ill of Ann.

We went to her house straight off the expressway. My father was there, flushed with cheer. "So it worked!" he said, hugging me. "How about that? Great news." For once he did not warn me about tampering with nature. My brother and his wife arrived and built a fire in the flagstone fireplace, and even my grandmother allowed herself a discreet brandy and soda.

For once the sight of Gail did not upset me, though she was at the stage of her pregnancy when she literally had become her unborn child. I was happy to see her, happy to see her healthy. What her obstetrician had believed was toxemia not long before had turned out to be merely an unwonted accumulation of fluid; she still had to sit often, and lying down she could barely breathe, but it seemed she would carry the baby to term without event.

Gail and I kissed. She whispered conspiratorially, "Wasn't I right about New Orleans? Wasn't I?"

Dan and I met in the foyer, in a small island of quiet as the party swirled around the edges. I rummaged in my purse and found the Christmas poem I had written for him, and called, in what I imagined to be my best *New Yorker* style, "Advent."

> We will be home tomorrow
> Before night, if the weather
> holds
> and the thin gray band that binds the road
> to sky in front of us
> does not bring snow.
> You wrote that you had found the old tinsel
> and the pepper wreathe from our honeymoon in
> Spain

and we are bringing back those fat blue candles
that drizzle wax
like rain
and smell of fruit you cannot name,
and a box of new tissue, the kind printed with stars,
a clove orange and a music box.
The rest we'll have to buy.
We will be home tomorrow.
Wait up for us, reel us in
if it should begin to snow.

"We didn't have a honeymoon in Spain," Dan said.

"Don't be so literal."

He kissed me. "All right, then. We'll have a second honeymoon in Spain. We'll take the kids. All the kids."

"Tons of kids."

"Piles of them. We'll have to rent a bus." And then a relative of Ann's came in the door, shaking off snow, with her two-month-old son in a red velvet Santa suit and a hat with a white pompon on top.

He was unexpected. He was perfect. I had trained myself for one weekend of bright-eyed tots tearing open shining packages, one Jocelyn, two pregnancies—Gail's and the harder one, Laura's, six months along, healthy and glorious, that I knew I would measure against my own lost one, which would have been at exactly the same stage. I had trained myself for that. But not for a baby, a new, fresh, just-this-minute infant, curling a hand too tiny and perfect to be real around his mommy's collar.

The baby pass began; and in time it came to my turn, and I smiled appropriately and held up two occupied hands, full of wineglass and canapes. I saw Gail watching me. Her eyes were narrow, a carbon copy of Dan's when he was angry. "I can't," I told her. She shook her head.

I had prepared myself well enough for what else Christmas would mean—the gathering of families in the most real sense, the unfolding of couples into parents, each taking their places on the ladder of generations. I didn't fit. I was neither-nor. I felt I had been busted back to the kids' table, out of my rightful position. Perpetual girl. Perpetual date. Dan's wife by virtue of vows and papers only. That Jackie. She's everywhere. You couldn't ever really imagine her settling down, with a family. I had misstepped, lost my footing on the ladder, and now someone else

—Bobby and Sandy, no doubt—would assume my place.

"That will be you in a few months," said a small, reedy voice. An elderly relative of Ann's, a woman I hardly knew, looking down at my baggy black dress approvingly. She thought I was pregnant. I could see it from her smile.

"Why yes," I said, smiling back at her, patting my belly and thinking, this is madness. Tell her. Right now. "It certainly will be."

We left the party then, not abruptly, not noticeably quickly, with hugs all around. The week before, we had left Todd's in the middle of a Risk game. I had pleaded fatigue. But it had been this. The men had gathered in the dining room, around the game board, and the women in the kitchen to talk about babies. And I had sat in between with little Andy, watching some spy movie, and heard Leah's voice—a voice that always had a laugh just beneath it—say, "I *love* being pregnant. I love everything about it. I don't want this one to end."

Dan had been winning. He had snapped at me. "You're going to have to stop regarding every woman's happiness as a personal assault."

He was mystified then, and he was mystified now, because he could not figure out why I continued to react so strongly to pregnant women and babies, to flee from them, especially since the report from New Orleans was basically favorable.

Perhaps it was the drugs I was taking; depression was among its bouquet of side effects. But more truly, it was a feeling—not unlike one of my grandmother's famous feelings—that I would not become pregnant in spite of the surgery. I would try, but I could not *see* myself pregnant in my mind's eye. I felt as if the training period was over, and now I was out on it alone; it was time for the Olympic trials. There would be no more comfortable cocoon of doctors and hospitals; it was down to us, my body and Dan's. The bodies had to perform in that oh-so-simple old way.

But they would not. I knew it would not happen. The tube would close over, and if it did not, it would be dysfunctional. I could not confide it. The last thing anybody wanted to talk about, myself included, was my condition. Everyone was happy for us. Everyone thought I had been fixed. It was crazy to think otherwise. I wanted more than anything else not to think otherwise. And yet there it was. I did.

But Dan did not snap at me as we drove away from the party. It was Christmas, after all, and we were on our way to Jocelyn. We were to pick her up for the rehearsal of her Sunday school pageant. We'd divided up the pageant; Daddy and Jackie would get the dress rehearsal, Mommy and Jerry the Christmas play itself.

Jocelyn wanted to climb into the back of the camper and roll around with Jesse. She had never seen him. "Daddy," she cried, "come on. Seriously."

"Seriously," I told her, "you'll ruin your costume." We tried to distract her. "Do you know your lines?"

"Actually," said Jocelyn, who had taken to saying "actually" a lot lately, "I don't. But the other angels do, so I'll just move my mouth and say it with them." I was struck by a vision of Jocelyn, aged fifteen, smiling bewitchingly at the boy next to her as she asked to copy his math paper.

"You only have two lines!" I cried. "How come you didn't learn them?"

Jocelyn's face was dreamy under her tinsel halo. "I had a lot on my mind."

Actually, she had. This was Jocelyn's best Christmas ever. She was old enough to understand everything but young enough to ignore the loopholes. She was worried that all the people on her mother's block were "Scrooges." Scrooges stop with trees, she explained. "Nice people" had life-sized choirboys with speakers playing carols inside their heads mounted on the lawn. They had sleighs on the roof that moved up and down. She was worried because the telephone company Santa had said over the phone that turkeys might someday cost more than one hundred dollars. "That's what my mother's house cost," she said sagely.

Sister, a veteran of more than thirty Christmas pageants, greeted us at the door of the gym. Her assistant, a star of one of Sister's early productions who now was a mommy, helped a group of bigger children mount spotlights on a position over the stage, which was set up midway between the backboard and the free throw line.

Other angels trickled in—one in an elaborate handmade gown with paper wings, but most, like Jocelyn, in bathrobes spruced up with tinsel. "That's the head angel," Jocelyn whispered to me. "She's only seven, but she can say lines like a grown-up." The head angel's lips moved slightly as she handed her coat to her reverent father.

"Somebody remembered to learn her lines," I whispered to Jocelyn, who sighed.

"Angels over here," Sister directed. Jocelyn spotted her best friend,

Jill, also in the celestial choir. Jill and Jocelyn had not seen each other in a full day. They clasped hands and jumped up and down.

"Yours is *braided*," Jocelyn said of Jill's halo. "That is so *neat!*"

"Oh, it will just help keep ours apart," Jill said, and added, in generous spirit, "I like yours better."

"I have to tell you some stuff," Jocelyn said to Dan and me, pulling us to one side of the stage. "That up there is the nativity. And there are the shepherds and there are the kings." A king in a floured black beard that reached to his knees lifted his staff and yelled, "DE-cent!" to an approaching shepherd. "And that one," Jocelyn said, "is Count Dracula."

"Count Dracula?" Had I missed something over the past couple of decades? "What is he doing in the Christmas play?"

"I don't know," said Jocelyn. "But you don't have to be scared. It's not like a monster. The kings come to see the baby, and one brings gold and one . . . oh, that's right. It's not Dracula. It's Frankenstein."

Dan swallowed a grin. "It's not Frankenstein, honey. It's frankincense. The king was from a part of Arabia, and people there used to use that for perfume and to make the room smell beautiful."

Jocelyn was disappointed. Sister was giving out the last call for angels. We had to make one quick run to the local mall, to try in vain to find some Strawberry Shortcake paraphernalia Jocelyn was sure she would die without having. The shelves in Madison had been picked clean. "Learn your lines," we hissed over our shoulders. "We'll be back by the time the show starts."

When we returned, with no Strawberry Shortcake tea set, the gym was dark and still. But then a hand-held floodlight flicked on. The face it revealed was seraphic, ringed by crisp black curls. An hour before, when we had left, this boy—a big boy—had been tugging off his vestments. "Ma, this is cutting off my air," he had said. Now his features were as of German china, rosy and still.

He said, "And it came to pass in those days that there went out a decree from Caesar Augustus that all the world should be taxed. And they went to be taxed, each to his own city." Here came Mary—who an hour before had been shy Sarah, whose dad had gone to school with Dan—poised now with the great weight of myth and motherhood. She lifted the baby doll from under the cradle onstage and tenderly wrapped him –in "waddling clothes," as Jocelyn had explained earlier, "like blankets."

And then came the head angel to center stage, to comfort the shepherds who had stopped giggling and were "sore afraid," just as they were when I was a girl, and when my mother was a girl, and her mother.

"Fear not," the head angel declared, "for I bring you tidings of great joy. Unto you is born this day in the city of David a savior, who is Christ the Lord." And suddenly there was a multitude of the heavenly host, entering through the boys' locker room. Seeing us, Jocelyn shook her head and pursed her lips, then forgave us our lateness and waved.

The angels trilled, "Glory to God in the highest" (she really didn't know her lines), "peace on earth, good will toward all people." In the dark, Jocelyn's father and I found each other's hands. Something old and slumberous in us was stirring.

The words of St. Luke triggered tricky emotions. The surge of feeling had been all but prepackaged for us by the fine old language of many Christmases, by countless cards, by Snoopy reruns. But then there was Jocelyn, with no front teeth, lip-synching them and making them new.

The kings were approaching the stage—Caspar carrying a gravy boat and Balthazar absolutely resplendent, his winged and turbaned raiments of stiff blue, green and yellow plaid. The kings leading, the children sang "Happy Birthday."

"And now," said Sister, gently lifting her hand. Then she and the young priest who had just poked his head in, his overcoat half on, and all the angels, and the big boys who had been wrestling each other on top of the scaffolding instead of moving the lights around began to sing "Silent Night."

Jocelyn had told us that last time around, everyone stopped in the middle. This time no one stopped, and no one faltered. The children's voices were as thin and sweet as meadow pipes. "This is good," said Dan. I said nothing. I couldn't talk.

Then she was running to us, her halo around her neck, showing us that yes, the bottom ruffle on her gown was almost entirely ripped off where a shepherd had stepped on it. The lights were on and we were blinking, husky voiced and brusque, trying to tell her she'd better learn those lines or else. But it was easier to hold her close and hide our faces, smelling pine and soap in her fine hair.

Dan gave me a gargoyle for Christmas, a tiny stone copy of one from the cornice at Notre Dame Cathedral that he had bought in New Orleans—slipping away one afternoon to an antique shop on Toulouse

Street while I'd slept. I had told him not to buy a thing; there was not enough money. "And anyway, the only thing I want in the world is a gargoyle," I had said.

Late one night, not long after we had returned to Madison after the holidays, Gail's husband Nick called Dan at work from the hospital, laughing and crying, barely able to tell us.

It was a new nephew.

26

THE BABY NEWS came thick and fast then.

Some of it was wonderful. In mid-January, Leah and Todd's third child and first daughter was born—an easy birth, a beautiful, black-haired baby they named Emma Rose, after great-grandmothers she'd never see. They were fatuous with joy; Todd had yearned for a daughter with the fervor men once reserved for sons. "There's no agenda with this one," he said. "I can spoil her to my heart's content."

Leah had planned to have a tubal ligation while still in the hospital after Emma's birth. At the last minute, she had put it off. Not only did it seem so final, there was the added discomfort and scarring of the laparoscopy.

"They'll be having another one soon, wait and see if they don't," I told Dan darkly.

"So what if they do?"

"They have *three*. It would be selfish to have more."

"Selfish in terms of what? If they can manage, if they think they can afford it, they can have ten kids. What's the skin off your nose?"

"None. None, I suppose." I could never catch up with Leah in any case. She was several years older, but she had the jump on me. I called her in her room the day after Emma was born. "So! Was I right or was I right?"

While Todd kept saying they were no longer making girls, I alone had held out. It would be an Emma, not a Theodore. "Oh, Jackie, you should just see her," Leah bubbled. "She's so beautiful I can't stop looking at her. She's the prettiest baby I ever had. You'll love her. She looks just like Andy."

"I'm sure I will. I just wish . . ."

"What?"

"Honestly, that I was in your place." Damn. I had taken to doing this, forcing my infertility on people if they didn't bring it up first. The protocol demanded Leah to say now, in response to my congratulations, "You'll be the next one." She didn't. She said only, "Mmmmmm. Well."

That didn't do. People were to tell me that my fears were ridiculous, that of course I would become pregnant, that I must simply be patient, rest, have faith, take my medicine, don't overexert, relax, take a vacation —dozens of soothing prescriptions I hated and needed terribly. Now, when I went casting for them, they did not come so readily. The reassurances had worn thin, tedious. After all, I seemed never to put any faith in them; in fact, I resisted them.

Didn't they realize? It was not my business to hope. I had to keep the fates at bay. Others, luckier ones, must do it for me. They had the strength. They had the inside track. They must make my denials for me.

I was too tired. For the first time in my life, I was physically depleted. I slept nine-hour nights, napped during the day, and was never rested. This last operation, so much less taxing physically than the first one, had, as my grandmother put it, knocked the stuffing out of me. The only side effect of the Danazol to put in an appearance as yet was headache, but it was relentless.

Curtains of silvery streaks shimmered before my eyes; my brow ridges felt bruised to the touch.

Even that was not so troubling as the memory. I tried to recall when I had last called Laura. Was it only a week? Yesterday? I could not remember. Could not remember very well at all. It terrified me. My memory had been my stout staff, my never-fail bag of tricks I took out to dazzle my friends. What a memory, they said admiringly. I was hell on trivia. Now something . . . something had happened. A mistake? Some stray blip or bubble in the anesthesia process, a kink in some unnoticed line? I dared not think so. It was temporary. It must be temporary. Still, if I had lost my cousin's phone number—it had fallen out of my brain so utterly that when the information operator read it to me I knew I had never heard that number before in my life —what else had I lost? I had admired a ship model on top of my brother's wardrobe. "How lovely," I told him. "Where did you find it?"

He had looked at me wonderingly. "I got it from you two Christmases ago." It was gone. I had never set eyes on the ship before.

"The hell of it is knowing I've forgotten things I need to know," I had told Mary. "They just aren't in my head any longer. No one can help me. No one else knows what they are. I feel alone with this thing."

I decided not to call Laura. I had to conserve on trusty ears. And I remembered. Now I remembered. She was lazy about calling me. Mock-serious the last time we'd talked, I'd told her, "This may be the last time

you ever hear my voice. Because next time it's going to cost you a dime."
    I didn't call. I waited days. And then one night, it was her, her voice
faint and far-off.
    "We have a bad connection," I said, laughing.
    "No we don't. I'm tired is all. I'm sorry I haven't called."
    "Don't mention it, my dear. I knew you'd crack. How are . . ."
    "I'm in the hospital. Now don't worry."
    "Don't *worry!* Are you . . . is the baby all right?" No, this is not
happening. Echoes of Dan last summer. Had I wished it? Willed it? Had
my poisonous envy sent out shoots? I made a prayer: Let mine be
enough. Don't take Laura's baby. Let the tube close over, let the endometriosis grow like moss. I love her; this is not what I meant at all,
not what I intended.
    It was called placenta previa, she said. The placenta had placed itself
in front of the fetus. Laura's and Richard's cautious lovemaking had
opened a fountain of blood. A rush to the hospital. The bleeding had
been stanched, then began again, and again was stopped.
    "So it's fine, then? It's going to be okay?" Please.
    That was the problem, Laura said, her brave laugh a feeble chirp. Her
gynecologist had told her that the British called this condition "inevitable hemorrhage." It almost always began again, and when it did, the
baby would have to be taken by cesarean. By cesarean in any case, since
labor would kill them both. I made a rapid calculation. It was too soon.
It was barely seven months.
    Casually, then, carefully. "But the doctor said the baby is far enough
along, he thinks she is developed enough? She would do well even if she
came now?"
    "It's too early."
    Wait and hope. There was nothing else for it. Laura would have to
remain in the hospital. Work was out for the duration. She could not
get out of bed; she could not move about. The longer the situation
remained stable, the more days the baby had to grow, the better the
chances. The chances did not look terrific.
    "I will come right away."
    "Don't. I'm a mess. I can't do a thing. I don't even want to see
Richard. It wouldn't be worth it, babe. All I'm doing is having tests and
monitoring. So wait, just wait." Her voice wobbled ever so slightly.
"What ever happened to the healthy, uneventful pregnancy, Jack? Meghan, and you, and me . . ."

"The odds are impossible. All of us, in one family. I mean, two in your family . . ."

"In one family. You were right the first time." How I loved her. How I wanted to fly into the phone, and pour will and grace and health over her. I could do nothing. I hung up abashed, tasting bitter shame.

And as if to atone, by nightfall I felt ill. I used my basal thermometer to take my temperature. More than 103. I was ill in fact. But this could not happen. I had been back at work less than a week. By morning I was shivering, coughing, my neck swelling out to my ears. "I have to go to work," I said to Dan, falling off the bed.

"Don't be crazy." He helped me back up.

"Tell Carol then, tell her I have got the Rangoon flu or something." The fever spiked up to 104.1. My grandmother moved into the spare bedroom and brought me clear soups I couldn't swallow. She brushed back my sweaty hair and tied it.

"Stay away," I warned her.

"Nonsense," she said, and two days later, she was hacking. The following morning, she was having difficulty breathing, and Dan and I were frantic. Dan drove her to her doctor's office just before work. He called me. "Now I don't want you to worry, but they decided to check her in to the hospital. She's older, and there's the problem of her having smoked for so long." She had given it up just two years earlier, with a magnificent effort of will, after forty years of three packs a day. "The doctor will call you later today, when she's settled."

The doctor, a man called Stein, didn't call. Finally, at three o'clock, I called him. "Ah, didn't the nurse get in touch with you?" Hair rose on my neck. "We had, ah, an incident."

"Is she dead?"

"Of course not. But she's in intensive care."

"*What?*"

"They should have called you." My grandmother had had an episode of difficult breathing; she panicked, and it worsened. There was an alert; a physician had inserted a breathing tube and placed her on a respirator.

Dan and I rushed to the hospital. "You've still got a high fever," he protested.

"Bullshit. I could easier die from the guilt." My grandmother lay in bed, impossibly small and white, the respirator wheezing and sighing like a huge toad next to her. She was in rare good spirits.

"It took SEVEN DOCTORS to save me," she wrote on a pad.

She was in intensive care for three days. Once while we were visiting, a middle-aged man in a clerical collar asked to see us in the waiting room. "It's hard to deal with these kinds of things," he began kindly.

"What kinds of things?" I asked. He made a gesture in the direction of my grandmother's cubicle. "If you mean that she is in danger of dying, yes it is terribly hard. But she is not going to die. She is going to live to see my kid."

"My wife hasn't been well," Dan put in.

"This is the limit," I said. The chaplain smiled brightly, and left.

Since I had been going to the hospital every day, I figured I might as well go back to work. I brought my cough pills—the syrups hadn't worked—and my other pills and my thermometer. If I began to feel peculiar, I would go into the washroom and take my temperature. So long as it stayed below 102, I stayed at my desk. If it rose, I went home and took a couple of aspirin and slept.

My grandmother mended slowly. There had been evidence of pneumonia in one lung, but her doctor believed he had caught it in time with intravenous antibiotics. At the end of the second week, Stein called me. "I'm beginning to consider discharging Mrs. Dvorak, but she is concerned that she will not be able to care for herself for the first few days."

"But we've already arranged that. She knows she is to come to us as soon as she gets out."

"Ah. Well, she didn't say that." Ah, indeed. Things had to fall on me like walls. My grandmother, who strung out her hospital stays across three states like rosary beads, had been pushed to the wings in the family medical drama the past few months. She had center stage now, and I suspected she would not surrender it without a struggle.

I knew for sure when she came home, portable oxygen tanks in tow. "I am not to walk," she said in greeting.

"The doctor says you're to walk a little more each day. Lying flat in bed will only contribute to fluid in your lungs."

I would come home from work and find her lying determinedly flat on her back. "I just lay down this minute."

On the morning of the third day, I got a frantic call at work from Mary.

"The fire and rescue ambulance just came for your grandma," she said. "She called me and said she couldn't breathe. But Jackie, when the paramedics got there, they didn't seem too concerned." I went to the hospital after work and found my grandmother lying in bed, nasal prongs of the oxygen apparatus in place. "It was nip and tuck," she told me gravely. "Honey, the doctor knows I was discharged too soon. I told him that was what you wanted. . . ."

"What *I* wanted?" I called Dr. Stein. He wasn't sure what the problem was; but in cases where emphysema was present in any degree, it didn't hurt to be too careful. And at any rate, he sighed, he hesitated to send her home. "It would be impossible to ask anyone who wasn't being paid for it to keep up with her demands."

The passing days seemed to make her worse instead of better.

"Are you getting out of bed?" I asked her on every visit.

"Now, Jackie, I get out of bed every day and sit right in that chair. I'm very weak." The next day when I walked into her room, I saw a portable commode next to the bed. My grandmother smiled wanly. "They don't want me to try to get to the bathroom by myself at night," she explained. "I told them I could."

I called Dr. Stein. He recognized my voice.

"Well, I have to tell you that the staff is going crazy with her. She can be ah . . . very childish and demanding. She'll buzz the nurse and then ask her to do some inane thing like move the buzzer."

The doctor would leave orders for my grandmother to get up in the afternoon. An aide would come to walk her down the hall. My grandmother would recoil. "The doctor said I wasn't to walk!" By the end of the office day, when the orders finally were checked with Stein, the night shift had come on and the floor was too shorthanded for someone to walk my grandmother.

This went on for days. Finally, I sat down on the bed and looked hard at her. She avoided my eyes.

"You think you're prolonging being taken care of," I told her. "But the fact is, you're killing yourself. Nobody can stay in bed for the better part of three weeks and not feel weak. You're going to have to get down to it, or you are going to die." A physical therapist came in to give my grandmother a breathing treatment—Stein had begun to think that her second admission had been the result of a panic attack rather than a relapse.

"Breathe in sloooowly," said the pert young girl, and my grandmother, holding the girl's hand like a child, smiled and obeyed.

"She isn't senile," I told Stein. "She works, she drives . . . she just likes being in hospitals."

"She didn't tell me she had a job."

"You see what I mean. Don't you think she can come home now?"

"So long as she keeps taking the Theo-Dur. I've given her some Percoset for pain. I think she might have suffered a bruised rib when she was being placed on the respirator."

We set her up in the spare bedroom—the oxygen tanks next to the bed. The first night she said, "I'm just bone-weary, dear. I can't get up for dinner." I brought her dinner on a tray. "I can't eat all this."

"You have to." She'd lost fifteen pounds.

"They don't do it this way in the hospital. I can't take all this food." She suggested I bring her small amounts of food in small dishes throughout the evening. "I can take it better that way." And I did, until Dan caught on when he saw me rushing in hourly with cottage cheese, then with creamed soup.

"She's going to get up and eat with the family," he insisted, out of her hearing. "You're haggard, Jack. This has got to stop." We had been up—one or both of us—two or three times a night for a week. She wasn't sure her oxygen was on; she couldn't hear the hiss. She wanted a cold cloth for her lips. A glass of water. Another glass of water. The light dimmed. So many imperatives. I began to wake reflexively, like a nursing mother, at two-hour intervals. It was when she roused me to come and move her quilt from behind her back to her shoulder that Dan exploded.

"It's not just that it's killing you. It's killing her. She's going to be an invalid for life if you let her go on this way. She won't last the winter." The next day, a Saturday, I made a brave stand.

"Gram, it's time to take a bath. You haven't had a full bath since the hospital."

"I'm not supposed to have a bath," she wailed. "I could catch a draft."

"The doctor said it's all right. I checked. I'll turn up the heat nice and warm."

"You have to put a chair in the tub, or I won't be able to get out." I looked at her. Her hair hung in greasy gray tufts. The front of her robe was soiled with food. Just a month before, she would have died sooner than appear at the supermarket before her weekly hair appointment. She had been going to a seniors' exercise class with a few other "girls" Tuesdays and Fridays. She'd been talking about getting a jogging suit.

"You can take a shower."

"After dinner," she pleaded. I roasted a capon. Made her favorite vegetables. A pudding. She took one look at the plate and put down her fork. "I can't eat this stuff."

"It's perfectly good. You like chicken."

"I'm sick, don't you see? I can't get my breath. I need to go back to bed and lie down for a while."

"No, Gram," Dan said then. "You have to eat."

"I'm going to faint " She made a sound that bordered on a howl. "Dan, you're going to have to take me back to the hospital."

"No. You're fine. You're just starting to panic. Try to be calm." I imitated the therapist. "Breathe in, slooooowly."

"God damn it!" she cried. "I need to be in the hospital! Get me the phone so I can call an ambulance! Right now!" Dan took my plate and his and went into the kitchen.

"Come in here and eat," he commanded me.

"I can't . . ."

"Come." We sat straining our ears, unable to eat, listening to my grandmother in the living room. She called on God. She ranted.

"If I die, if I go into heart failure, it's going to be your fault," she called. "Oh my God. How can you do this to a person? This is brutality." After half an hour, when she had not died, when her shouts had subsided to dire mutterings, I went back to take her plate. She had eaten the pudding.

"Shower now," I said brightly. "You promised."

"Tomorrow," she breathed, and then, leaning over conspiratorially, she whispered, "Honey. I know you're not like him." She stabbed with her fork toward the kitchen. "Just take me back to the hospital. . . ."

"For how long this time, Gram?"

"Not long. Maybe just overnight. So they can tell me how to breathe." I wanted to grab her neck and throttle her, to see her eyes pop. And yet, the pity. The terrible pity I couldn't let her see, or we would both be lost.

"Shower," I said. I half-dragged her to the bathroom. My God, if a psychologist could see me. I believe this is abuse of the elderly. Hell. I would save her or kill her. I sat my grandmother on the closed toilet and turned on the taps. "Now call me if you need anything. The shampoo is right there."

She called—she shrieked—in less than a minute. I found her swaying, her head swiveling in panic, clinging to both walls of the shower. "Get me out of here."

"Gram, try to calm down. You can stand. There's nothing wrong with your legs."

"I'll fall! I can't lift the washcloth! You're killing me!" And so I washed her. The preposterousness, the faint obscenity of this. Washed the breasts that hung like flaps, the jutting collarbones. This was the lap that had rocked me, the hands that had diapered me and dealt me firm whacks, the firm white legs she still liked to dress up in nylons and heels. I washed her, sprinkled powder on her bottom, averting my eyes, hating her for bringing both of us to this, dried her, and got her a fresh robe and buttoned it.

My baby, I thought. Leah is bathing her baby tonight, and I am bathing mine. She was mine, my grandmother, and helpless, and I dreaded it. My baby was withered. She cussed me. She was seventy-seven years old and in better health than she had a right to expect given her history; but she had decided she was to be the baby, and I had no choice but to mother her.

And when I finally got her back to bed and got her oxygen bubbling, I sat down on the floor and cried, "Gram, this isn't right. You know it isn't right. I know I may be selfish, but *you* are *my* grandmother. If you were terribly ill, even truly ill, I'd bathe you and feed you and put you on a bedpan until the skin came off my hands and you know I would. But you are putting us through this . . . humiliation for no reason. Because you won't give up. You think that somehow, by refusing to try, you're keeping me beside you. Don't you know I'd never leave you? Anyway?"

"I need more pain pills," she said, holding up the empty bottle. We had filled it at the pharmacy three days before.

"*That's* why you're so groggy! You're eating those things!"

"I am not." I slammed the door, threw myself down on my own bed face first, trying to muffle the voice I heard sobbing, "Jackie! Jackie!" At length I went back into the room.

She was sitting up on the side of the bed, reading her newspaper. "You're right," she sighed. "This is ridiculous."

The next day, she walked out to the mailbox to get the newspaper. A week later, the oxygen tanks went back, still half-filled, to the medical products firm.

Dan was less than forgiving. He did not own the bond with my grandmother that I shared. He felt his life had been seized and derailed; he had done nothing but caretaking for months and he was exhausted, sick of it. But there came a day when he overheard my grandmother on the telephone, giving an aunt of mine a sprightly description of her illness—"It was nip and tuck. They never realized how ill I was, poor dears"—and could laugh. "She's amazing," he said.

Them reconciled, I could get back to a-thing-a-day. Gerry Becker's research south of the border did not augur well for an adoption. Things had changed from the days in which Dave Porterfield paid a few visits to the good sisters. Our best bet, she told me, was sticking to the agencies; she'd copied a nationwide directory for me and put it in the mail.

I told Dan the news about Mexico. "It's just as well," he said. "I'm not ready to adopt."

"But Dan, you said . . ."

"I said that you could proceed with this lawyer connection pending the outcome of the surgery. It appears that the surgery is giving you a good chance of conceiving. Let's hold off on adoption now."

"Let me explain something to you. Say we try to get pregnant for two years." Two years. I could not believe I was hearing myself say this. I would give up after six months. "After two years, if I have not been able to get pregnant, we still probably would not be high enough up on the lists to be in line for a baby. Even most of the foreign agencies put the wait at two to three years. So what can it hurt? We don't have to adopt a child if we're offered one, if I'm already pregnant."

"I could see you refusing a child."

"I would. I just want to begin filling out some of the forms, get our name in the computers . . ."

"And start an eight-hundred-dollar home study which I don't need to remind you we can ill afford." I suppressed a smile. Eight hundred dollars would have been bargain basement. We were talking twelve, fifteen hundred dollars here, I was glad to see he did not realize.

"I don't see that we have to start a home study now. But if we should hear of a kid, we couldn't go ahead with an adoption unless we had a home study. How about if we wait until June. . . ."

"Jackie. There is something that I keep trying to say in a way that won't hurt you. I'm not ready to adopt a child. I don't know if I ever will be."

"We can wait until June at least. . . ."

"Read my lips. I'm not ready."

"I . . . well, what is it? Do you think it would be impossible for you to love a child who was adopted? Since you'd had one of your own?"

"That isn't it at all. It's not that I think it's necessary to be blood-related to a child in order to love that child. It would take some getting used to. It's just not an idea that I thought I would have to confront in my life." He began folding the newspaper into neat quadrants, as he did when he was stressed. "You know that we decided we could support only two more children besides Jocelyn. . . ."

"You decided."

"Fine. I decided. If we were to adopt a kid, you could have only one child. Period. I would not care if it was the easiest, most meaningful birth experience in history. One would be it. Less than two months ago, you went through a grueling surgery in order to have a child. And we haven't even begun to try to get pregnant, and you're already upset because the adoption waiting lists are too long. I can't go through all these changes at once, Jack."

And then he said, "Especially when I'm not sure about our future."

"*Our* future? What, have you got a terminal illness I don't know about?"

"I mean our marriage."

I took hold of the couch. We were not having a fight. We were not angry with each other. Dan did not say these kinds of things unless he was in extremis, at the outer, ragged edge of a guts-out fight. "Do . . . you mean that you don't think we will stay married?"

"I hope we will. But I'm not sure. This has been an . . . unsettling time for us. And you know that part of the reason I balked at having kids to begin with was that I had to be sure, absolutely sure, that what we had was going to last. I wasn't going to have history repeat itself. And I haven't changed my mind about that. I have to be sure."

"I thought you were sure. I'm sure."

"You're sure you don't want to be alone. I'm not sure you want to be with me." Bull's-eye, that. Karen. Whose husband left her. He'd married his lab assistant, and had two children in rapid succession. Karen wouldn't say the infertility was the backbreaking straw. But there were those two kids he was so proud of, kids Karen had to run into every now and then on the street. What could be worse than not having a child? Not having a husband. Becoming the square root of solitary. No. I would not look Jocelyn's little brothers and sisters in the face.

"Would you remarry?"

"Who said anything about remarry? We haven't even got to divorce yet." Dan grinned. "Is that all you care about? That I'd remarry someone who could have kids?"

"*No*. But I would hate it. I would hate it more than you could possibly believe."

"If that's what your major worry is, we're in more trouble than I thought."

"I didn't mean anything by it. Let's talk about what's bothering you. Is it adoption? It's just that I find it very comforting to pursue adoption simultaneously, Dan. That's natural. Isn't it? To try to assure myself I'll be able to have a child one way or another?"

"It isn't any one thing. It's just that it doesn't take a psychiatrist to tell me you're unhappy. And I don't know if having a child—adopted or not—would make much difference, even as much as you believe it would. There'd still be me."

It was the adoption, I thought. That had to be it. He had qualms. And I had been too oblivious to acknowledge them. He'd told his sister Gail, who'd told me, that when he'd tried to picture himself the father of an adopted child, he could not help but picture a healthy white infant, a baby not all that different from the baby we might ourselves have produced. And such children were as rare as midwinter thunderstorms. He'd duly looked over the photos I'd shown him, from brochures I'd sent for from the list given me by the attorney Gerry Becker. He'd kept an open mind. The east Indian children were charming. The Nicaraguan children were adorable. But to see himself as the father of one of these children?

"Jackie could mother all," he'd told Gail. "That's fine. That's marvelous. But I don't know about me." A child—particularly an adopted child, he believed—needed a family beyond parents to clasp him close. And he knew my father. His brother. Could they embrace a child so different from them? And if they could not, would it anger Dan? Would it break his heart, estrange him from his own family?

Worse yet were his fears of adopting an older child, a child with a history, quite likely a terrible history, and with memories and gestures and habits all in place. Could he be father? He didn't want to play at being father; it had to run true. He would not lie to himself, he'd told Gail.

He had told me none of this himself; we could not discuss it. Would he be more accepting, I thought, if things were as they once were between us? I liked to think so. I had to admit I did not know. It was a pocket of Dan I'd never had occasion to rifle.

But then there was that dry, pressed-out phrase: "There'd still be me." That had nothing to do with adoption. Dan, I thought, I can't figure it. This is a brand new curve. You are a man so secure it borders on obnoxious. You never feared losing me; it always went the other way. Before we were married, we'd have words and I would spend the night bawling and dialing your number, and you would set up a racquetball date with Todd and buy yourself a steak. "Are you saying that you think I don't really love you? That all I want from you is a child? Do you think I'd leave you?" I asked him now. "Do you want me to comfort you?"

"Honey, it wouldn't occur to you, would it?" he said, not bitter, only weary. "You're the only one who has fears, aren't you?"

But fretful as I was about the state of our marriage, I kept filling out forms as agencies sent them. I did not discuss them with Dan. Only a few of the dozens on Gerry Becker's list accepted single parents, and none of them for infants. I was married now, and I might as well make hay, I thought. Perhaps there was not enough left of us to patch. Perhaps I would end up without a husband. But if I waited, if I were wise and cautious, I might end up with no child as well.

One private agency near Portage, Wisconsin, required that husband and wife each submit an autobiography as part of the package. "I'm a pragmatist," I wrote under Dan's name, "and a romantic. My interest in history springs in part from my caution about the future of the planet. . . ." I signed up for the newsletter of the Holt Agency in Oregon, which specialized in placing Korean children.

"How would you like a little Korean brother or sister?" I asked Jocelyn over the phone.

"What's Korean?"

"Like Chinese."

"Oh, Jackie! She would be so *cute!* Get a little girl!" Jocelyn said. I sent for forms from the South American Missionary Evangelism organization, and from a Colorado agency that served the entire Midwest and had contacts in Indonesia and the Mariana Islands. I wrote to an agency in Montreal that found children in India.

Each of the packets arrived with a fantasy: me, walking up the ramp from a plane with a bright bundle in my arms, presenting it to Dan: "Meet your son." A social worker ringing our doorbell, a brown child with the huge eyes of an ocelot clinging to her shoulder and sucking her thumb. In the fantasy, the Oriental children were all girls, the South American children were all boys.

The fantasies crumbled in the face of the fees, and the fees were not so discouraging as the waiting times. I took an average of the twenty agencies I had contacted, and the minimum wait for an infant came to two and a half years. I would be thirty-three before I'd see those ocelot eyes. Thirty-four. Jocelyn would be ten.

So I called the local Catholic Social Services agency, though I had a good idea that the divorce in our history would render us less than ideal parents from their point of view. I told the intake worker I spoke with that I was interested in adopting an infant.

She told me, gently, that an infant nowadays was considered to be any child up to the age of five; and that if they were accepting names for that list—which they were not—we could expect to wait at least two years to begin a home study, and then after that, if we were approved, up to three more years for a baby.

But she asked if I was interested in special needs. I knew something about this program, which was called the Angels program, having written about it. "Most of these are mixed-raced babies, isn't that right?" I asked. Well, said the worker, it seemed that most of the mixed-race kids who once formed the core of the program were finding homes through the traditional placement route.

Most of the kids in special needs now were kids with handicaps. She had to amend that. Permanent and rather serious handicaps. "A very young child with a defect that might even require surgery is placed now as a non-special needs child."

Still, I asked her to forward the forms. And when I put down the phone, I thought, for the first time in any personal sense, about the ironies of the adoption roulette, with its fierce rivalry for small bundles. Dan and I would not be prime parents. And so we would be candidates to adopt what—terribly cruelly—amounted to the leavings. Children prime couples would not choose. To the prime couples would go the "best" babies.

Single parents could adopt special-needs kids. Divorced parents could adopt special-needs kids. The implication that these were somehow lesser parents, unfit to adopt the "best" babies, was never spoken by the agency representatives I talked with—they were good people, trying to use the only objective standard available to them to sort out multitudes of eager requests. And neither was the glaring irony: that special children, even more than "normal" children, would need the most special of parents, the most devoted, the most flexible, the most committed to each other.

When I got the special-needs application from Catholic Social Services, I took out a pen and began to fill it out with a will. The handicaps
were listed on a sheet, with boxes to check next to each one. Epilepsy
I checked. My mother had had epilepsy. It never held her down. Poor
eyesight. I checked it. I couldn't see my own hand in front of my face
without my glasses. Deformed arm. I checked it. So he wouldn't be a
pitcher, so what? Hearing impairment. I checked it. I knew some fantastic kids who couldn't hear. Mental retardation. I lifted my pen.

I couldn't. I'd had dreadful imaginings of giving birth to a child who
would never learn to read or write. Parents of retarded kids I knew
rhapsodized about the unforeseen bonuses, the sharing. I knew I could
not go that distance by choice. I did not check the box. Still, it was a
decent enough list.

And then, when I put down my pen, I had to look myself in the face.
There were plenty of things I could live with, and accept, but what I
wanted was a healthy, normal kid. Preferably gorgeous. Preferably bril-
liant. Dan and I were not the DeBolts, capable of adopting a houseful
of heartbreaks and turning them into joys. We were not the kind of
people about whom the parents of healthy children murmur, "They
must be such wonderful people," and then turn away, thanking their
stars, having salved their own consciences with the compliment.

The impulse was to berate myself for my small heart. I decided to skip
it. I had psychic baggage enough. There was still private adoption—
Peter Briggs had done it. It was a long shot at best, though, and
potentially a dangerous one. I had done a story about the pitfalls.
The birth parents and the adopting parents often were known to each
other, and there had been a few cases in which a birth mother had had
a change of heart and convinced a court that she had ceded her
child under duress. And the parents had been forced to give the
baby back.

And there were other dangers—the potential for abuses by the doctors and lawyers who sometimes served as intermediaries in such adoptions was always there. "The problem with intermediaries," the director
of one agency told me, "is that the line is very thin and indistinct. How
far can you go? There can be no question of actually paying for a child,
but I've heard of plenty of arrangements in which the adopting parents
gave the birth mother a 'gift,' money to finish her education, or even
a car. One birth mother wanted a truckload of antiques. And she held
out until she found a couple who would give it to her."

Still, I began to make inquiries. I wrote to an attorney in New York called Lester Cranshaw—a literary agent I knew there had given me his name. Cranshaw was well known, and had made private adoption the bulk of his practice. But his methods troubled some adoption experts; he had no qualms about encouraging couples to place advertisements in newspapers, all but soliciting pregnant girls.

Bill Kirby, a friend of ours from Madison who'd given up his medical practice and bought a sheep ranch in Costa Rica with his wife, Abigail, wrote to me and told me that it was possible to adopt the mixed-Indian children native to that country. The best avenue for doing that, a private agency headed by a Dutch woman, had closed up. Another friend of Bill's also had helped to place children; she had given it up as well, but when Bill told her our story, she reluctantly agreed to make inquiries for us, though not until spring when her own children would return to school.

Bill also told me that lawyers in Costa Rica occasionally arranged intercountry adoptions as well, drawing from the pool of street children, the children of the local prostitutes. He did not recommend that option. But there it was if we wanted to consider it, he wrote.

The investigating I was doing took time. It took time from my marriage, and time from my work. So much time that I forgot, until the day of the event, that I was to speak to a group of teachers in early February about infertility—about my own experience and about the possibility of including as part of the home economics curriculum some cursory introduction to infertility, a problem that one in ten of their students probably would encounter. I showed up for the talk with no notes, no speech. No matter. On infertility, I could wing it.

After the talk, one of the women told me, "You're so articulate on the subject. You talk about it so easily. I know that I could never have coped with it so well if it had happened to me."

The comment floored me. I was not coping well. I was not *coping* at all. I had never told a single soul, "I can't have children." I had said I might not, never that I could not. But I had set up a weird balance: I reminded myself endlessly that I could not, not ever, have children, but admitting it to anyone else would make it true.

As I drove home, I found myself thinking about the gypsy. For a Halloween story, I'd once gone to a gypsy fortune teller. She knew I was a reporter, but in order to try and throw her off, I'd worn a wedding band —I was not married at the time—and told her that I had one child, a girl.

"That is strange," said the gypsy. "I don't see a child in your hand.

But I could be wrong. Anyway, I think your little girl will be the only child you will have."

I asked Dan if he remembered what the gypsy had told me. He did. He had been hoping for months that I wouldn't come up with that particular memory. "Do you think there is something to it, Dan?" I asked him. "Don't you even wonder?"

"I wonder," said Dan, "whether there is still a French Foreign Legion. I wonder about that a lot."

THE SEX WARS began in February.

I could tell that Dan was less than satisfied. Subtle codes only a wife could decipher. Dan unzipping his fly four inches from my nose as I sat on the couch watching television. Dan grinding my rear end as I changed the trash bag. Dan initiating a full body press as I reached for my boots on the closet shelf.

I responded with an elaborate set of harry-and-retreat maneuvers. A little feely on the couch after dinner. Nothing that would embarrass a shy sixteen-year-old. Then an attack of the wearies. The recollection—oh, so suddenly—of the stack of articles I needed to read, gathering dust on the bedside table. One last kiss, a bit of tongue; I would stretch out on the couch and give his crotch a promissory nuzzle. "Tomorrow, sweetie," I would tell him. "A special. Something to write home about." I was full of good intentions. Moreover, I did not want to send him grazing among the tempting row of pear-shaped Calvin Kleins on display every morning out in the composing room.

"All you ever want to do is kiss," Dan complained. "Don't we ever just fuck anymore?" It was good natured. At first. He had read the passages I'd underlined in the books. I had just had surgery. I was not feeling particularly alluring. So he was not a beast. He could wait. He waited a month. Six weeks. Eight.

He thought about what he knew of psychology. Sexual dysfunction surfaces out of anger sometimes, he knew. Maybe she is angry with me. But why? Have I not been as compassionate as I should have been? I have been as compassionate as I could be. I have tried to keep her optimistic, and that is what she needs most.

It was not what I needed at all. But it was impossible for me to get what I needed from Dan, because the man could not be of two minds. Even given what we knew about my physical problems, he had never once, since the first hysterosalpingogram, faltered in his insistence that we would have a child. He thought there was a very good chance that it would happen on the first cycle after I finished the Danazol. Hadn't

Dr. Clarke mentioned a seventy-five percent "rebound" fertility effect? If it didn't happen then, it would happen soon after. The worst was behind us; there was no reason to worry. His capacity for denial staggered me. Mine for pessimism mystified him.

On the other hand—there was always another hand—if he had joined me on the down side, if he had begun to preface his remarks about children, as I had in the past few weeks, with "If we would have had children . . . ," I would have been desolate. Despite what I said—and I said that I believed it would be a flat-out miracle if I ever conceived —I had only just begun to admit to myself that the problems I had might not only hinder pregnancy, but preclude it. I wanted Dan to know that, to acknowledge it, and still wanted him to protest vigorously to the contrary.

Dina Fiore, a woman I had met while researching my infertility series, had told me her husband's strong-hearted denials comforted her at first. But when, after a year of discouraging tests and attempts, he still refused to admit that there was a single thing wrong with either of them, the comfort began to crumble, and resentment to build. Is he blind? she thought. Can he truly not see what is going on? Their spirits seemed in inverse proportion; the lower she sank, the higher he got. He is doing it deliberately, she thought. Finally they could no longer talk about it: what point in discussing a problem if there was no problem? By small degrees, Dina began to turn away from her husband. He would not see —he refused to see—what was presently the most salient part of her personality.

There was a friend at work. He and Dina met for drinks, for lunch. He listened. It became clear, in time, that the two of them were drifting into something more than a friendship. "It scared the hell out of my husband and me," Dina said. They went for counseling. "It was like hitting a door, pounding and pounding at a door that would not open." And then during one session, Dina's husband, Don, began to talk about his brother, who had undergone heart surgery at the age of eleven, about how it had rocked the whole family—particularly Don, who shared a room with the sick boy. "It seemed as though they had made a tacit decision to cope with the whole thing by ignoring it," Dina told me. "That had become Don's way." Later in the session, he had begun to cry.

"This is an awful situation," he had admitted. "I've been awful. I'm so sorry. I know I may never be a father."

I did not know—perhaps Dan did not know—what it was in him that did not love a heart-searching discussion. But he had had his fill of ours. He no longer tolerated the nightly briefing; he said no good could come of plowing and replowing the same small plot.

So I persevered alone in it, sharing the small scraps of adoption information, of medical information that I uncovered, with Mary and with my boss. I took my files and my pamphlets to bed with me; Dan was an intrusion, his needs an interruption of my own.

And though both of us were very careful to step around the edges of the pit we had glimpsed in the hospital room in New Orleans, we peppered each other daily with small atrocities.

Dan came stomping, sputtering into the bedroom where I was banging away at some free-lance writing on his old Underwood. I had been churning them out almost nightly, for anyone who would pay; our financial straits, because of all my lost pay and medical expenses, were growing more narrow. The bills had begun to arrive, and we still were in negotiation with the insurance company over its portion. We had worked out an assembly line: I typed the rough drafts on the bad typewriter, while Dan in the kitchen redid them on the good typewriter.

"Look at this shit," he shouted. "Trying to read this stuff is like reading Chaucer. What is this word?" I looked at it. It read "whyter."

"It's 'white.' Snow is white. Couldn't you get it out of context?"

"Jackie, this is pure and simple laziness. There's no excuse for it."

"I'm a writer, not a typer."

"You're a lazy . . . you're an irresponsible . . ."

"All this over a typo? My, my. Are we nervous?"

"You're damned right we're nervous. We live like a goddamned monk. . . ."

"Dan, I don't have to do all this extra stuff. I'm doing it for us, to take some of the strain off us financially."

"You don't give a shit about us."

"Ah."

"Us means two people, Jack. There's only one in your life."

"I see."

"Look," he began, pleadingly. "Just proofread the damn things once before you hand them to me. Make a few corrections. I can't even follow this stuff."

"Okay. I will. I'm just in such a hurry with all of them." Dan sat down beside me on the bed; I saw the look on his face, the slack, hooded look that signaled passion. I began to type furiously. He put both hands on my breasts. I kept typing. He began to knead them slowly. I felt my jaw stiffen. "Just what is it, darling, about my dirty hair and my baggy robe that brings this out in you? Can't you see that I'm doing something here? Why is it that when I want it, you're not interested, but when I'm absorbed in doing something wholly unrelated, you decide you want to get it on?"

"When do you want it? You never want it."

"Jesus, Dan. We did it yesterday."

"Sunday." Well, this was only Wednesday. Was he keeping a diary?

"Sunday, then. And if you'd just let me finish this . . ."

"You'll go to sleep. Or you'll start underlining one of your infertility books. I'm not getting any . . ."

"*Getting* any? Is that what it's come to? You get, and I give? I put out?"

"Yeah, Jack, it is. That's the best I can expect. You don't have sex with me willingly. You make me come begging."

"Great guilt, Dan. Really tops. Look, I'm beat. It wouldn't be fun anyway."

"You know what they say about sex. It's like pizza, when it's good, it's very good, and when it isn't good, it's still pretty good."

"Indeed."

His lips tightened. Anger. Available tight jeans at work. Avoid this. "Honey. Honey. It isn't that I don't want to make love. It's just that I don't want . . ."

"You don't want it with me."

I did not want it with him. But not for the reasons he thought. Sex was on my mind constantly. I fantasized in the tub, fingers busy, and in the dreams I was seventeen—the thin, brown girl I had been, whose hipbones poked seductively through the pockets of her wheat-colored HIS jeans. The boys were there—boys with no hips and fuzz on their chests. I ached over the eroticism of teenage boys fresh from the shower, full heads of wet hair curled in wisps, boys in crew-necked sweaters, smelling of Ivory and Brut, clean and hot and unaged. They were tight where you grabbed them—you did not risk getting a handful of flab, or disarranging the wisps that hid the receding hairline.

I pictured me on the seat of some father's brand-new Buick Electra, the windows nicely fogged, Levi Stubbs on the radio, his tenor soaring into the bridge of "Reach Out." Lying back against the armrest, sucking in a stomach that went concave whenever I bade it to, waiting for the hand that slipped into the waistband, ostensibly unawares. Such sex I longed for. For riding up in the elevator to class after a session in the backseat with my first husband, before he was my husband, wondering if the people riding with me could tell what I had been doing, if I smelled of it, if anyone else in the world had discovered this wonder, this fever, that sublimated gritty mattresses and three-week sheets. And if they had, how could they do anything else, how could they work, or eat or study? Sex that had nothing to do with babies, or the lack of them, nothing to do with intercourse in the prescribed position, or with intercourse at all. With touching. With waiting all day Saturday for a touch, then feeling the burn of its outline for a week.

And love. I had forgotten the incandescence of young love. Enshrining of rocks and shells and candles stuck in wine bottles, the extravagance of moony August nights.

How had I become this clenched and guarded woman? How had the change been accomplished? Abruptly or gradually? After I married Dan? Before the pregnancy? Did it happen to other people? It did, of course. Success replaced that incandescence. Or children. Or trouble.

How could I explain all this to my husband, how I suddenly needed love with the dust still on its wings, not harmed and weighted down with history and finances and ignobling familiarity?

I could not. And so I got up and slipped off my robe and said, "Here. If you want me, I want you. I do. So go ahead." We lay down on the bed with the fluidity of robots. And then I heard a whistle, a screech. "Dan," I tried to tell him; his mouth was smothering mine. "It's the furnace. The . . . filter." I could not find the word. My blasted memory gap had left me with a touch of aphasia, and when I was in a hurry, it worsened. "The filter, *Dan!*" It was the teapot.

When he came back, after taking it off the stove, I was sitting up in bed crying. Dan put his arm around me. "Don't worry," he said, "I turned the filter off."

"I feel so out of joint. As if parts of me have been removed randomly." Dan held me. He did not put the moves on me. He helped me put my robe back on. Perversely, I wanted him terribly right then. But it was no good.

I wrote in my journal for February 9, "We have moved out of the strong stone house of our marriage. We keep moving into these small straw lean-tos. None of them ever lasts. We run away, throw another one together. This scares me. Nothing's holding. Christ, what a mess."

If this moving in and out of symbolic houses did not make for sufficient domestic tranquility, we added to it, in early February, by moving out of our house in fact. We moved to Illinois, as Dan described it over the phone to his brother in Florida, lock, stock, but not quite barrel.

A decision as profound as relocating does not creep up on people? It did on us.

I had decided to take a few days of my new year's vacation time. I'd finally had to admit that the most recent surgery had left me sapped, and my flu, topped by my grandmother's, had administered the knockout blow. I simply couldn't find the physical wherewithal to get back on the daily track.

Dan was looking at several out-of-town assignments; so I knew that if I took time off, I would be spending it alone. I decided, in reconciliatory fervor, to go and stay at my father's, to make a conscious retreat into preresponsibility days, sleeping in my old room under my shelf of collection dolls.

My grandmother was between jobs—the several elderly women she had been providing home care for before she took ill had either got well enough to take care of themselves or gone, to her regret, into nursing homes.

So she decided to come along. I didn't know how this would work out; but my grandmother was all for it. She and my father had an unexplainably terrific relationship. Whenever we stayed there, my grandmother— who highly disapproved of intemperance—would spend hours with my dad at the glass-topped kitchen table, tossing back gin and tonics and dishing dirt about the relatives. The years would fall away, as the evening progressed and the squeezed limes mounted, and the two of them would be back in the days when my father and mother were young and shared a house with my grandparents.

They would talk old times. They would talk, in large part, about my mother. This to the politely concealed chagrin of whatever woman friend my father was courting at the time. This to the not-so-politely concealed delight of my grandmother. There would be tears, and laughter, and stories I still was not old enough not to consider embarrassing.

But though I envisioned plenty of this, I was glad that I would be able
to spend more than hospital-visit time with my brother and his wife, who
lived just up the block, and with Laura, who lived in the same town. In a
few days, no more than two weeks, I expected that I would be able to
reassume my full-time load. Dan would miss me, he said; but there was
more than a little relief under the statement. Dan needed a breather.
"Take the time," he said enthusiastically. "You've got four weeks of
columns in storage. Your body is saying, 'Enough already,' Jackie."

But it turned out to be more than a respite. And that it did was due
to an odd confluence of circumstances.

I was having lunch with a friend of mine—after a few days at my
father's, I began to be quite a luncher, dining out at the drop of an
invitation with anyone who would drive. This woman had written several books, and as I described the circumstances of the past few months
to her, she got a studied look about the eyes.

"You should write about it," she said.

"I did."

"I mean really write about it. A book."

"I can't write a book."

"Why?"

"I've never written a book. And anyway, who'd want to read about
my infertility?"

"Lots of people."

"I don't think so. It's not as if I beat cancer or learned to paint with
my toes or . . ."

"I don't mean an inspirational tract. Just a book."

"But I don't have time. I work."

"Couldn't you take a sabbatical?" I thought about Dave, and Carol,
and their eminent forbearance with my medical trials.

"I think I've already used up the good humor of my bosses."

"You could try." We left it at that; but the thought danced on my
mind. All the journals I had been writing could be made to take a public
shape. There would be a use for it. She was not the first to have suggested
it.

I pitched the idea to Dan when he came for the weekend. "It's a
thought," he said. "You could do it. . . ."

"I don't think I could do it."

"You could do it, but I think it might just get you fixated all over
again."

"Fixated on infertility? I'm already fixated."

"Do you think it might make you talk about it less?" I rolled him off the bed onto the floor.

But the idea of taking a leave to write a book I was not sure could ever be published was not compelling enough to someone who had lived by her weekly paycheck since the age of eighteen.

Then, one evening, I had dinner with my father and several of his friends at his club. One of them was an obstetrician. In line with what I had been writing and telling friends and relatives for the past months, I mentioned to him that we might be interested in adopting an infant. I asked him if he would spread that word among his colleagues.

"I'd be happy to," he said, patting my hand. "But it wouldn't do any good."

"I know. I've been studying. Ninety percent of unmarried mothers keep their infants, and when they don't . . ."

"I didn't mean that."

"What then?"

"If I found a baby for you to adopt, and I'm not saying I could, though I have once or twice helped couples out in my time—not for a fee, you understand . . ."

"Oh, I know, I know." Gray-market anxiety was everywhere.

"But if I did, or my partner did, you'd be living in Wisconsin. And you can't adopt a child that's born in Illinois when you live in Wisconsin. You'd have to live here."

"Who says?"

"The law says. You have to be a resident of this state for, I don't know, I think it's a year before you can legally adopt a child."

"I'd be willing to do that," I said, startling myself with my readiness. "If it came to that. And if you think there's even an honest chance."

"Well, I'll keep my ear to the ground. It's not impossible that it could happen. I've seen it happen."

It sounded impossible to me. But the next day, in the spirit of what I was by now calling "research," I called Nick the Lawyer, another friend of the family. He hit his books. Wisconsin, he said, did have a statute governing private adoption, but it mainly was intended for allowing the families of children who lost their parents to adopt them. And even if we did fulfill the requirements, the law strictly prohibited bringing a child in from Illinois to adopt in Wisconsin courts. In Illinois, private adoption was more customary. We would have a better chance. But one had to have been a resident, not for a year as the obstetrician had suggested, but indeed for six months to commence an adoption.

I turned it over that night, staring out into the street from my foldout bed in my father's living room—my grandmother had decamped me from my old room, pleading fragile constitution. What if my father's friend did find a baby for us? I could take a leave. We could live here. I could still write my column. . . . I didn't have to live in Wisconsin to write my column. That would be a little income, anyway. If nothing came of it in a couple of months, we would be no worse off. I could work on a book.

Dan could commute. But two and a half hours was a hell of a commute. Still, people in New York did it. Well, he could stay in Wisconsin a couple of days each week. We'd still have our house there. Or Dan could find a job in Chicago. I could just hear Dan. "Of course, babe, I'll just give up my job and stroll over to the *Chicago Tribune*. I'm sure I'll be welcomed with open arms. They've been begging me to come on staff. . . ."

But it was Dan, in odd fact, who turned up the last card. Or, rather, it was Ann Lombardy, who came across with what we would at first seriously, and later ironically, refer to as The Job Offer Of A Lifetime.

She needed a public relations person for her widespread development interests. She, quite unbidden, offered Dan the job. The salary she mentioned, offhand, made Dan unsteady on his chair.

And she made it plausible, by suggesting Dan give her two days a week. One day. Days of his choosing. Until he was sure it was what he wanted. He wouldn't have to give up his newspaper job at first.

"Do you think I should consider it?" Dan asked me. "Listen, you know it's not my idea of what I want to do for a living."

"Tell her so, then. Nicely."

"She's trying to be nice. She knows how much I want to live near Jocelyn. To her, any writing job is like any other writing job. Before I went into newspapers, I'd probably have jumped at it. Even now, I can't stop thinking about what we could do with the money. If I could stand it, even for a couple of years."

"But you'd be running back and forth, working weekends . . . at first, anyway."

"And I'd have to be away from you, and you're not in terrific shape."

I closed my eyes and jumped. "But here's the thing, Dan. I've been thinking that maybe it wouldn't be such a bad idea to live here. We've been talking for years about being closer to Jocelyn, especially if we had another baby. You could go on flextime at the paper. Work four long days. Or three. Other people have. And I'd . . . I'd stay here. Let me explain." I laid out my newborn book idea. My sabbatical idea. And, oh so softly, I mentioned the adoption angle.

Dan's lips tightened. "Why, God, am I so dumb? I should have figured there'd be a baby side to this. Jackie, here you are with a scar barely healed on your stomach, a tube that for all you know is now good as new, and you're already planning an adoption."

"Not for sure. But if we were living in Wisconsin, it couldn't happen. Ever. It's not the reason for doing this, just an added thought. It's like it's . . ."

"It's meant, right? It's meant we should do this."

"Are you mad?"

"No, I'm not mad. But I think Ann should have approached you with this instead of me. You're the one with the head for machinations."

But the following day, it was I who balked. I'd be away from Bellow, from Mary, from the infertility support group if I needed it. This time, it was Dan who picked up the slack. "You could still be in Madison sometimes. You wouldn't be working at a nine-to-five job. You'd have lots of flexibility."

Over the next few days, in Madison, I broached the subject with Carol, my boss. We sat a pack of cigarettes between us in a glassed-in office, and watched them disappear. "Would this be a leave? Or are you talking about quitting?"

"I don't want to quit. Not for good. I just want the opportunity to work for the paper outside the office, probably for no more than a couple of months. Do more regional things. I'd be in Chicago, but I'd come up here as often as I could. Then should the book really get serious, I'd like to take what would amount to a couple of months' sabbatical to write it."

But I would do my column in either case, I assured her. That would never miss the paper in either case. We talked about special projects I could do. Finally Carol shook her head. She smiled at me through her blue smoke haze. "There's a piece of this missing, isn't there?"

And so I told her. That the large reason for going to live in Illinois was the hope that we might soon find a baby to adopt. I told her about my father's friend, the obstetrician. "It's not much," I admitted. "But it's happened before."

And that sealed it. Carol made do. She arranged. She found ways. She embraced the untraditional on trust. If she believed Dan and I had gone around the bend for keeps, her Irish loyalty prevented her from ever saying that. She gave me a hard hug, and I packed up some of my files and left.

Within a few weeks, Dan and I had moved most of our clothes, our dog, and some of our furnishings to my father's house. My dad was not sure how he felt about the invasion; but he was stifled by the rule. It was the single rule he had never reneged upon; he swore to it often. His house, the house of my growing up, was my house. But we were testing the limits of the rule. We were talking two filing cabinets and a golden retriever, for starters.

Fortunately, it was the season when he spent weeks at a time at his condominium in Florida; and we were able to assure him that if the job Dan was trying out became a full-time endeavor, we would immediately find a place of our own.

Within a few weeks, Dan was commuting, working six days a week and more; I was readying a book proposal for an agent I didn't even have as yet; and we had, trepidatiously, begun thinking about trying to sell our house.

"Don't worry," Dan told me. "It won't sell. Nobody buys houses near lakes in the dead of winter. If we decide this isn't working out, we can go right back home. And anyway, if we have a kid, we'll need a bigger house. Wherever."

Jocelyn was crazy about the idea; she had both worlds. We could take her to see her friends in Madison, and she could be with us, or at least me, for the occasional evening during the week instead of just the occasional weekend.

She went to Madison with us on the weekend we moved our things. "Are you moving forever?" one of her friends asked her mournfully.

"No, this is going to be our summer house," Jocelyn said, with the easy archness of one to the manor born.

We assumed my grandmother would want to stay in Madison. We were wrong. "But where will you live?" I asked her. "An apartment here is going to cost more than . . ."

"Well, I just thought you might want company when Dan was out of town."

"You mean you're going to live with us."

"Don't you want me to?"

"I didn't say that. Of course I want you to."

"Well then."

Well then. It was time to put all the loose change I had spent on extolling the virtues of the extended family where my mouth was. This was to be an adventure on all fronts. But temporary, I told myself. In all probability, it would be temporary, I told myself, when my grandmother rearranged all the cabinets and appropriated all the bed pillows. My father moved the departure date for his first winter vacation up one week. "Dad," I soothed him, "there are four bedrooms. You had this many people living here when we were kids."

"Yeah, but I could tell two of them to go to bed anytime I wanted." He left, cautioning me under no circumstances to let the dog out of the basement. He called me from the airport forty minutes later. "I have the feeling that dog is in my house," he said. "Tell me I'm crazy."

"Oh, Dad," I said, "you're crazy. Don't worry." Jesse was lying on the rug at my feet, asleep. "Dad, it's only temporary." Probably temporary, I thought, as I tried to fall asleep with neon daylight outside my window, instead of pure Wisconsin dark. After all the years I'd lived away from it, I was sure I would never get used to the noise, the unaccustomed rumble of all-night traffic that had been the lullaby of my childhood but was intolerable now.

I would lie awake, homesick for my home, and think of the possibilities. Dan would not like the job and we would go home. I might become pregnant, and I would return to the paper, somehow, until it was time for my maternity leave. And things would be the same as they always had been.

But enough time would pass that I no longer lay awake. I came to the point that I didn't even hear the traffic. My ear would grow so tolerant of noise that when I visited Wisconsin, the silence would make me restless. And things were never to be the same.

Dan had every Monday off. For the first two weeks, he used it to work for Ann. But then, one Sunday, I came into the bedroom we shared at my father's and Dan was folding up his shirts. "Why so neat?" I asked.

"I'm, ah, going to go back tonight."

"How come?"

"I want to have dinner out at the Shiers'. Talk to Todd about some work stuff. I've been going back and forth so much I haven't had time to do much planning."

"You see him every day at lunch."

"You can't talk about stuff like that at lunch."

"What about Ann? Doesn't she expect you tomorrow?"

"I got a ton of stuff done today. At least it seems like that to Ann; she's used to having to struggle with the writing part. Jocelyn's in sophomore year by now," he said with a laugh—we'd been putting the extra money he earned into a savings account for Jocelyn, replacing money we'd robbed from her for New Orleans.

I subsided. Didn't ask more. But when, a week later, he did it again, I began to twitch. I said nothing. But my grandmother was not so reticent. She came into the bedroom where I was working one Sunday night and leaned against the door frame, tapping her foot. "Where's Dan?" she asked.

"He left."

"Well, I knew he left."

"Then why ask?"

Ah, shut up, Jackie, I thought. Why does my grandmother always make me want to act like a snotty ten-year-old.

"I don't know," she said. "Nothing else to do." I got the message. But I did not ask her if her having nothing to do was my fault.

"Do you want to go out or something, Grandma? We could have dinner."

"No. You save your money. Buy yourself something nice to wear for a change. What are you doing?"

"A column."

"Oh, you're doing your typing, then?"

"I like to call it writing, Gram."

"Typing, writing." My grandmother has never forgiven me for giving up teaching high school English. "So," she said then, "I want to ask you a question and I want you to give me an honest answer."

I hated this part. I said, "Fire away."

"I know there is something wrong with you and Dan. And it's something you're not telling me about. I called your house in Madison last Sunday night. And there was no answer."

"Well, Dan was with Todd, I'm sure. And he went fishing on Monday."

"Fishing? In winter?"

"Ice fishing."

"Do you really believe that?"

"What?"

"That he was fishing. Men don't spend all that time . . . fishing. For fish, anyway."

"Gram. What do you think he was doing?" My forehead was pounding.

"I don't know. But I do know this. You'd better decide what's going to happen with you two. You've turned your life upside down—you're there, you're here."

"This isn't an easy move. . . ."

"That's not the point. You better decide if you're going to get a divorce, get a divorce, because before you know it, you're going to be an old, tired woman, and nobody's going to take a second look at you."

"Dear woman, no one has taken a second look at me for six months."

"That's what I'm saying. You've let yourself go, and men will look other places. Jacquelyn, that's just a fact of life."

"Not of my life."

"So Dan's different, huh?"

"I trust Dan. Dan doesn't do anything he can't tell me about."

Or did he? I remembered how lavishly single Dan had been a few years before we married, just after his divorce from Joan. Madison, a great Friday night town, where every second person was single and a liberal, was like paradise to him. Every year or so, I would find his black satin-backed vest squirreled away in his closet. I'd take it out and ask him if he was expecting disco to come back.

But I would later find out what he had been doing on those Sunday nights. They were as much like bachelorhood for him as they were like childhood for me. Almost like. He'd watch a ball game at the corner bar with some of the editors, if they were around, later read in the tub and leave the newspapers on the floor, make waffles and let the dishes soak. He would feel calm on those following Monday mornings. He visited the library, took out books about archaeology and history. He'd even find himself planning what he'd do the next Sunday night, after he'd kissed me good-bye, and planning how he'd get enough work done for Ann to enable him to take off from Chicago early.

And then one Sunday night, he had gone alone to a bar that he'd once frequented and found out once he was inside that it had changed hands.

It was a jungle of glass and ferns and girls in leotard tops. Well, hell, he'd thought, and decided to have one drink and head home, when he heard someone calling his name.

It was the wife of a man he'd known at the office. He hadn't seen either of them since the previous summer, when they'd moved to Portage. But Lynn was back in town, she told him. She and Ken were separated, and she was sharing an apartment with the young woman who was holding out her hand to Dan now.

"Where's Jackie?" Lynn asked. "In Chicago," he said. "We're moving. Or at least we may be moving. Everything's up in the air. . . ." As Dan began to tell Lynn just the briefest outline of what had happened to us since the previous summer, he caught himself looking at her roommate. She was lovely. Long auburn hair that fell straight down her back in defiance of the corkscrew look that was in vogue. She was a graduate student, she said, twenty-six, and her name was Daryl. And as Dan, without meaning to, ordered a second drink and a third and kept on telling Lynn how hard it had been for him and for me, and how hard it was on the marriage, the young woman named Daryl had placed her hand, ever so lightly, on his arm.

"So, are you separating from your wife?" she had asked Dan, and he remembered that he had jumped as if she had lit a match to his sleeve. Was that how he had made it sound? Was that how it was? He'd mumbled something. "Listen," Daryl had said then. "Lynn's got to pick Elena up at the baby-sitter, but I'm starving to death. Do you want to grab something to eat in the dining room?" She said the place wasn't the greatest. But the shrimp wasn't bad. . . .

"Better not," Lynn had teased, lifting her coat off the back of the bar stool. "I'll tell Jackie."

"Jackie wouldn't mind," Dan said quickly, and then he put the cost of the drinks on the bar and got up. "But I'm bushed. I'd better head on home." He walked Lynn to the parking lot, suddenly chilled, suddenly terribly saddened by the idea of her and Ken parting. He thought of their beautiful dark-haired daughters, four and two years old. "Don't you think you might work it out?" he asked. "Isn't there any chance?"

Lynn shook her head. "I have to doubt it. It wasn't that we were so terribly miserable together—we didn't fight all the time or anything—but we just had to wonder whether we really were in love anymore, or whether it was just convenience." And then she asked, "How about you and Jackie? It sounds as if you're having some real problems. . . ."

And Dan had told her, "It's just the opposite for Jackie and me. We do fight all the time. But I think we still really love each other." And, he remembered thinking then, we sure aren't staying together for the sake of convenience.

He didn't mention meeting Lynn, or her young friend, when he came back to Chicago, nor for months afterward. But when I climbed into bed the following Saturday night, he said to me, "I won't be going to Madison anymore on weekends." I didn't say a word. "It doesn't make sense. You can't live in two places at once. I'm already working in two places at once." He put his arm over my back. "I don't want to sleep alone any more than I have to."

I heard the assurance he was telegraphing. "Me, either," I said.

We made the obligatory visit, to make soft noises over Dan's new nephew, who would be, to his mother's surprise, the fourth Jason on the block. Before we went to see the baby, we visited Laura, whom I had not seen in weeks, not since she was newly home from the hospital, though we talked on the phone several times each day. Her condition had astonished even the doctors. She had not hemorrhaged again; the pregnancy was proceeding normally, so she had been allowed to go home, provided that she remain in bed except to shower or use the bathroom. I had brought fancy mints and a cake with an umbrella on top, and gifts for the baby. "This is your shower," I announced as I walked into the bedroom. My face must have dropped.

"Don't say it," Laura told me. "I know I look awful." She looked not so much awful as changed into someone else. Laura is gorgeous. I had spent years walking down streets with her, watching men step off curbs and walk into poles as they passed her. I had planned to take a perverse delight in seeing her wisp of a hundred-pound self get fat in her pregnancy. But there was no delight in this. She was white, swollen from water retention, her arms and legs huge. I held her and felt her belly warm and pulsing between us.

"But this is perfect," I soothed her. "And very soon, the rest of you will be perfect as well. And I will hate you for having got so perfect again so quickly."

She unwrapped the bunting and the little soccer outfit—"Girls can play soccer, too," I told her—and I struggled with the urge to grill her. How did it feel? How did it precisely feel when the baby moved—like indigestion, like butterflies, like a muscle motion? Annie at the hospital in New Orleans had told me that her curiosity about her sister's pregnancy had verged on the creepy.

"I wanted to go into the delivery room with her and climb up on the table," Annie had said with a shiver. Perhaps because I knew Laura so minutely, body and mind—our voices even sounded alike through long association, we used the same expressions and inflections—my inquisitiveness did not seem overly bold. I had shunned pregnancies for so long I could not get enough of this one. This one I had the need to shelter. And Laura was Laura. She showed me the bulges and veins, we giggled on her bed, we ate all the mints between us, and when Dan said we had to leave, that Gail was waiting, I felt that the one supremely normal hour of the past six months was being cut short cruelly.

It put me in a mood.

Gail had lost her bloat, but she still was weak. Her husband, Nick, had arranged with Ann, his mother, to work nights painting the various apartments that she owned and rented so that Nick could be home to help Gail care for the kids during the day. New Jason was a red face over a yellow blanket. Dan and his sister prattled on about Mom's eyes and Dad's nose and your chin and my cheeks; but I looked at the baby through determinedly ordinary eyes.

Gail noticed. She bristled. If I had been a quiet woman by nature, if I had not been renowned for my mouth, the things I was not saying would not have seemed so rude to her. And yet I still wince remembering it. Gail and I were close, though our views of the world were poles apart. She had been very fond of Dan's first wife—had known Joan since she was herself no more than a child—but she had made room for me gracefully, in her life and her emotions. And I was being a shit to her.

She tried hard that day. "Are you upset?" she asked me. "Don't you feel well?"

But I was in a bloody mood. I thought that I had done nicely with Laura; I felt I had spent my tolerance for the day, and so I sat on the couch like a lump, holding Jocelyn—ever the emotional Geiger counter, who sensed I needed a baby to hold and obliged by being one—curled in my lap. I managed to ignore Jason almost entirely.

"God," said Gail, as we got ready to leave. "It's the baby, isn't it? I can't believe you're still taking all this so hard."

"Dan isn't," I said. Bitchy.

"Oh, he is," Gail told me. "It's real hard on him." Gail's husband shot her a warning look. "It's got to be hard for him just being around you."

I gave her my best brittle smile. "Jackie, you may not believe this, but this isn't all as bad as it seems. Someday you'll look back on the way you acted and laugh."

Dan gasped. "That is . . . sure an interesting way to look at it," he said quickly. We stood around, the four of us adults, all hands. Everyone kissed the various kids.

I waited until we were on the expressway, headed back for my dad's house, and then I asked Dan, "Do you think your sister would be considered of normal intelligence by any objective standard?"

"Do you really want to know? Or is that intended to be provocative?"

"Take it any way you like. It astounds me that she could consider that an appropriate comment to our situation."

"I knew you wouldn't let it pass. Let it go, Jack. She just couldn't come up with anything else on the spot, and she wanted to offer you comfort."

"Comfort! To suggest that someday I would be able to see how insignificant, no, how laughable my pain had really been?"

"Jackie. At some point you're going to have to admit that you have overreacted badly to this whole thing."

"I see. Even if I admit that it is a bit neurotic to feel that I have worked hard and kept my nose clean and not stepped on the cracks all my adult life, that I *deserve* the kids I wanted to have, and that Gail, who is dear, but also irresponsible, who has made it her business to step on all the cracks she could find, did not *deserve* two perfect, healthy boys, but instead a good kick in the ass, even admitting that that is neurotic, I still get the feeling that she and everybody else believes that what happened to me is not so bad in any objective sense, but only in the way I react to it."

"You're ranting."

"I'll tell the world I'm ranting! I'm ranting because I think it's damned unfair to tell me how I've overreacted, when it seems to me I have been decently brave, considering what I've . . ."

"What you've suffered. Ah, Jack. No one is trying to deprive you of your precious suffering. The point is, you don't seem to recover. And that is why I say that at some point you're going to have to admit that you have overreacted."

There it was. The word. He had used it before and I had let it pass. Now, I thought, all right, let's have it. Come ahead, you silly ass. Tell me how I have let losing my baby, and hope, and three surgeries in six months bother my little head too much. How I have made a mountain out of all these life molehills.

"Okay. Describe for me overreacting."

It poured from him. I had given it utter control of my life and my relationships. I had thought of nothing else. My thing-a-day program was classic obsessive-compulsiveness. I steered every single conversation I had with anyone around to the subject of children—or more precisely, my lack of children. I took every opportunity to moan publicly. And it embarrassed him. I waited until he wound down, anecdotes still popping out of him like stray notes from a played-down music box, and then I said, "What you fail to realize is that every conversation of any length you have with anyone docs come around to children, no matter how diligently you try to steer it in another direction. When you're sensitized to it, you notice. That's what's so goddamned awful, Dan. It's everywhere I go."

"Well, people have a limit, Jack. People can only give so much sympathy without asking when that sympathy is going to have an effect. You haven't even made the first attempt to get back on your feet. You're wallowing in it." He shook his head, abruptly, as if to get rid of the sediment. "I think you behaved badly. But don't worry. She's not a grudge holder. You can make it up to her by being the appropriately fussy auntie at the christening."

"I'm not going to the christening."

"You have to. There's no excuse. We live here now."

"I don't have to. I've had my fill of baby-centered occasions for the present." What did he expect? If I could not swim, would he push me into the deep end of the pool? My head took up the old cry: no one knows. No one grasps it. I opened my mouth. A hop toad popped out. "Anyway, Gail has sufficient people to look at her baby and tell her how much he looks like her, and how perfect he is. She doesn't need me."

"You're hateful."

If I hadn't been before, I was then. Hating him for not taking my side. Hating him for asking more of me than he could reasonably expect me to give.

Hating him for being right.

There was one thing sure. You are hanging by threads when even your own family is sick of you. Gail was not the only one. Even my brother asked to be forewarned when I called if this was going to be a conversation or an infertility conversation. They were sick of seeing me sitting around bleeding from the eyes. Or worse. They thought it was stage blood; and that any grief that lasted so long had to be a grandstand play.

I swallowed a lump. "I will be better," I said.

Dan said, "Good girl."

I SCREAMED, "Richard!" into the phone, and my father, asleep in his swivel chair, jumped into a combat crouch. "How is she? Is she fine?"

"She's fine," Richard told me. Such a voice he had today. Bone-tired and full of laughter. "Dopey, but fine."

"Is it Eamon or Michael Eamon?" I hoped it was Michael Eamon. Laura and Richard had finally agreed that Eamon Toscano sounded too much like Juan Epstein.

"It's a Michael!" Richard said. I looked up at the clock. It was nine-fifteen. Richard said the baby had been born at eight-thirty. I grabbed the morning paper lying on the floor and ripped off the front page. Scrawled across it in red marker, "MICHAEL'S birthday." And began addressing a manila envelope to Laura and Richard as we talked.

We had known the baby was a boy. On Laura's last ultrasound, the evidence had been clear to see, sticking right up. Laura was momentarily disappointed. Only momentarily. Was this not, after all, a miracle child —who had come within a few weeks of term in spite of all prognostications to the contrary? Laura was only thirty-one. There could be a girl in the future.

"Well, tell Laura that I love her, and tell the baby that I love him . . . wait! Is he fine? Is Michael okay?" I asked Richard.

"He's great. He has red hair like his mama, and he's really tiny . . . I can't remember the weight exactly, but not much more than seven pounds."

"That's not tiny. That's normal. He'd have been a monster if he'd gone to term."

It was a Wednesday. Laura had been back in the hospital for ten days and would have to stay at least another week. "Tell Laura that Dan and I will be there on Saturday, as soon as Dan gets home."

I could not talk to Laura, who was full of drugs, more exhausted than in any real pain. But I had to tell someone. I called Dan.

"I'm an aunt!" I told him.

"Of course you're an aunt," he said.

"No, I mean I'm an aunt again! Laura's had the baby."

There was a drop of silence.

"Are you okay?" It fell on my head then. Of course, he would have to wonder. Hadn't I grieved every pregnancy? Bewailed every birth? Rushed out of the supermarket to sit in the car if I caught sight of even a stranger near my age in a smock? And this birth Dan had feared particularly—feared unquenchable tears, a whole new catalog of recriminations.

He had steeled himself. This one would at least be justifiable. For women who have miscarried, the approach of the birthday-not-to-be is particularly bad. He had read in one of my books that I might commemorate this anniversary for years.

And though he had not told me so, he was not handling this time terribly well himself. He had caught himself thinking, we would be in Lamaze class now. Now he would be painting the spare bedroom. It puzzled him; it had been eight months. He thought he'd outdistanced sorrow.

And now here I was, grinning though he couldn't see me, like a fond fool. She will crumple tonight, Dan thought. Perhaps in the morning. Or when she sees the baby. It is not real to her as yet. "Honey, it will be okay," he said out of reflex.

"It's okay *now*. I'm happy." And a swift mental inventory proved it so, though I would have said as much had it not been—given the parameters of the situation, any other reaction would have been impermissible. But it was sheer relief not to have to fake it, to have the relief spotless, untarnished. Because I love her? Because she'd nearly lost him? Don't question it, I warned myself. Be triumphant.

We picked Jocelyn up on the way to the hospital. "Joan wants to talk to me," Dan marveled, sliding back into the car. "Joan never wants to talk to me. What do you think is up?" I tried to reckon. We were up-to-date on child support. Orthodontia was a few years off yet. Jocelyn was due for a long visit at Easter, but that had been negotiated for months.

"She wants to talk to you about the summer," Jocelyn said in a small voice. And then segued so rapidly, firing off questions about baby Michael, that I heard a gear click into place and thought, we are going to have trouble. Dan did not catch it. Dan was always surprised when someone strung a wire across his ankles.

The three of us took the elevator up eight floors; it was a huge university hospital just north of the Loop, and the high-risk floor Laura was on had fifty rooms. The first thing we saw when the elevator door opened was a monumentally pregnant woman, a woman so huge she looked as though she had an entire other torso grafted onto her middle. "Stepme!" Jocelyn breathed, lifting her hand to point. "Look at . . ." I clapped my hand over her mouth.

And then I heard a small voice at my shoulder say, "It's triplets. It only looks like a hockey team." And Laura came waddling comically into my arms looking only drawn, the terrible grayness gone from her face. She was wearing mascara, smelling of Castille soap and Chloe, not at all the svelte and self-confident executive of the recent past, but somehow more the girl of the far past, guard down, silly. "Can Jocelyn see him . . . ?"

"Of course she can. The baby isn't allowed outside the nursery during visiting hours anyway. Even David can't hold him in my room."

We walked around the corner to the Plexiglas viewing window. Laura caught the attention of the nurse, who wheeled a tiny, clear plastic gurney across the room. I thought that I had become quite an old hand at saying "What a beautiful baby" in recent weeks, but I was not prepared for Michael. He was stunning. Laura made deprecatory noises; cesarean babies are never so battered as those born by natural childbirth, and his fine rose coloring was a hospital tan, from the bilirubin lights he lay under for his jaundice. "He'll be as pasty as the rest of the family soon enough," she said.

I said, "Nonsense." I placed my hand against the glass, describing the oval of Michael's tiny head. "He is the grandest baby you ever saw and you know it." Even Dan, who shared with most men the apparent inability to distinguish one baby from another, made much of the finer points of this one.

"He is precious," said Dan.

"Ah," said Laura. "I guess so." Michael was not asymmetrical, as most newborns are, but sculpted—his forehead high and broad, his mouth a cunning coral pout. He waved his fist obligingly and made a bulldog face.

He went through his repertoire—a yawn, a blink—he did basically nothing. He needed to do nothing more to cause love than a filament needed to do to cause light. Be present. Be made of the proper elements. Nothing else.

I spoke to Michael, stroking his face through the glass. "Sweet small boy." This was the point. I had all but forgotten. Like a terminal patient casting about so desperately for cures he neglects to live, I had grown so rapt in pursuit of the means I had overlooked the end. I crooned to the baby, "Little love," and he stirred, as if to reach for the voice he certainly could not hear. There was a small whisper of memory—not grief. Sharp grief had eroded unawares into mourning and mourning into memory. Just this: my Joey-or-Lucia, you would have been this fine.

"Ooooooh, Jackie, look at his little tongue. Isn't it adorable?" Jocelyn was smitten on the spot, and that would not change. Seeing baby Michael grow would become the hit of our visits. "Laura, what does he do when he's hungry?" Jocelyn looked around for her. "Laura?"

She was running back toward her room, rushing as much as a woman who'd just had her staples removed can rush, her face in her hands. I ran after her, tears already spilling, put my arms around her, and kissed her hair.

"Such love," she cried. "Such love as you would not believe you could feel. It just came on me so suddenly. Love that is completely unqualified. I'm not a believer in total joy. Even what I feel for Richard has other things in it. But with him, with the baby, there's just this complete absorption. I want to spend every minute of every hour with him. I can't bear it! It breaks my heart. To have all this, and know that you can't have it, too. It isn't right. It isn't the hormones."

I did not know what to say. I made small mushing noises.

"I can't stand it," Laura said.

"I can't either, often. I think of it in pieces. I have had this surgery and that test and this surgery and this test is coming up, but if I ever just got up and looked down at myself and said, 'My due date would be in three weeks. My only baby is gone. I can't be pregnant anymore,' I'm afraid I would scream and scream and scream. And that would be melodramatic."

Laura did not ask me if I'd gotten some professional help. She did not tell me that someday I'd look back on this moment and laugh. She said, "You *will* be a mother. One way or another. Both of us. You and me."

This had been missing, with the other mothers, the other babies. Everything—Dan, the world, good form—bade me share in their joy, but they were not expected to share in my sorrow. As if my pain somehow could sully the moment, diminish it. Mary, on Thanksgiving Day—and I had not thanked her for it—and now Laura had done the unacceptable; they had made room in their happiness for me.

"I just want to . . . praise you," I told Laura, fumbling for large language. "For caring about me when it ought to be the last thing on your mind."

"Oh, Jackie, you ass," Laura said, wiping her face roughly with the backs of her hands. "As if you could ever be the last thing on my mind."

Jocelyn did not have to be home until seven, so we went out for ice cream, and then back to my father's to watch, for the seventieth time at least, the videotape he had made of Jocelyn's dancing class performing "Frosty the Snowman" on the "Bozo the Clown" television show.

Dan took the phone with the long cord and a fistful of cigarettes into my father's study. He called Joan. Joan didn't mince words. "Jocelyn has been talking about summer. She thinks she's going to be spending most of the summer in Madison this year, or with you here, if you're still here," she began. "How did she get that idea?"

"Well, I thought that we agreed that as soon as she was really old enough to spend extended periods of time away from her mother, we'd work out something like that. After all, Joan, you have her ten months of the year. And now that we're here, you could see her almost every weekend."

"You had her for a week at Christmas. And you're going to have her for a week at Easter."

"Right. Except for those times, and one weekend a month, sometimes two."

"So, what I wanted to tell you is that isn't going to work out."

"What isn't?"

"Jocelyn can spend four weeks with you. I'll expect to have her for at least one weekend during those four weeks. That's plenty of time." Dan had to sit down.

"Four weeks? But I had her for seven weeks last year, and we talked about it—we agreed that she thought that wasn't enough time."

"I never agreed." Her voice hardened into a monotone. "Listen, Dan. I've been very generous with you. Whenever you wanted Jocelyn for a weekend, even if you didn't call until the last minute, I let you have her. But there's no way she's going to spend eight weeks with you. It's not right, it's not good for Jocelyn. . . ."

"Not good for her?"

"I know what it was like last summer, Dan. Don't think she doesn't tell me." And then she went into a litany of perceived abuses, and Dan began to write them down as he talked, taking notes as furiously as he had ever taken them for a story, because he wanted to share them with me, and because he could not believe he was hearing them.

We let Jocelyn go barefoot. The sitter we had left her with during the day was a teenager—college student didn't matter, eighteen still is a teenager. The sitter did not structure planned activities for Jocelyn. She allowed her to watch "General Hospital." She had allowed Jocelyn and Christin to call a local rock radio station and request songs. And— "This was the killer, Jack," he would tell me later. "Wait 'til you hear this"—we fed the kid too much. Jocelyn, who wore jeans the seat of which was the width of a hand span, had come back from Madison "fat."

Dan walked out of the study looking as if he'd been smacked behind the ear with a ball bat. Joan had told him that Jocelyn's peer relationships suffered when she was with her father. "Joan, she has plenty of good friends up there, and she loves being with Jackie's family," he had pleaded. "She's with them every day."

"But this is her *home!* You don't have to deal with it when she gets back. The neighborhood kids are a very close-knit group. They won't play with her."

"Jocie," Dan asked, flicking off the television. "I didn't know that you had problems playing with your friends last summer when you got back from spending time in Madison."

"Problems?" asked Jocelyn. "What problems?"

"Well, that they didn't come to play with you, and that made you feel left out."

"Daddy, I only have problems when they all want to play with me at the same time when I get back from Madison." She preened. "They're all so glad to see me."

"Poop-face!" I laughed, and pushed her off the couch. "Go play with Grandpa Bob's poker machine for a little while. Daddy and I want to talk."

"Talk!" Jocelyn mourned. "All you ever do is talk. And all Mama and Jerry ever do is kiss. They kiss everyplace. I have to stick my hand in between them to tell them something."

Jerry and Joan had been married in January; Dan thought this had something to do with the timing. And Joan had said, "I want this thing worked out once and for all. I didn't have the resources before."

"Resources?" Dan thought she meant money.

"Financial, and emotional," Joan said.

"What are you going to do?" I asked him.

"I told her I didn't want a court battle. I asked her if there wasn't some way we could work this out. That would be awful for Jocelyn, Jack. Her parents fighting over her. You don't know what that does to kids."

"I, ah, guess I don't, no. But even a nonparent can have an imagination." The mouth. Glitch. I wanted to recall it. He didn't mean it that way.

"Don't get your back up. I didn't mean it that way. But Joan's adamant. When I suggested, hinted, that I might have to take her to court, she yelled, 'Go ahead!' She's prepared. She already has a copy of the customary family court guidelines. She's already retained an attorney. She told me the retainer was a thousand dollars."

"Jerry's got it."

"But we haven't."

"True."

"Joan says a month is what the guidelines suggest. But she generously allowed that when Jocelyn is fourteen, she can make her own decision about spending more time in the summer with us."

"Hey, great. That's only seven years."

"Exactly. I made a mistake then, Jack."

"What?"

"I lost my temper. I told her to take her list of the ways in which we supposedly hinder Jocelyn's development before a judge. I told her he would fall off the bench laughing and then award me eight weeks. I threatened to ask for a reduction in support. She told me to try it. And now I don't know what she'll do."

I hated it. Hated to see this standup guy reduced to pussy-in-the-corner out of fear of losing his kid. The child support was his ace in the hole; he could try to use it. But I knew he wouldn't. Every component would require a separate court action, and here Joan held all the aces; Jerry was on the staff—high up on the staff—of one of the largest medical centers in the Midwest. The two of them could go on endlessly. Dan and I were a step ahead of F. Edward Hebert Hospital's collection agency, in spite of the extra money he'd been earning. But he had the right. Damn. He did. Good feminist principles aside, Dan was gouged. He paid the amount of child support other men paid for three kids, for four. When the mortgage loan banker got a look at our monthly indebtedness, he reduced the amount of house the agency could finance by thirty thousand dollars. At the divorce, Joan and her attorney had asked for the outrageous—the figure they probably figured they would then have to dicker down from—and Dan, wracked by guilt, had given it. Signed everything. Retained no counsel of his own.

"I hate to say I told you so, Dan."

"But you will anyway." His laugh was a dry bark. "You told me I should try for joint custody years ago, when it was happening. But I honestly thought it would never come to this. Whatever we felt about each other, we were still parents. We could agree over Jocelyn. I thought, if anything, that when Joan remarried and had a new life of her own, it would take the edge off her bitterness. That hating me would stop being the driving force in her life."

"You underestimate bitterness."

"That's my flaw."

"How can I help? Should I talk to her? Write to her?" And as soon as this was out of my mouth, I saw it for a fabulous bit of fatuousness. Given Jocelyn's mother's oft-expressed fondness for me, my input would probably fix it so we'd never set eyes on the child again.

"No. Maybe she's just on the defensive. I put her on the defensive. Maybe she'll see reason."

"Well, let's see. You don't want to go to court, so . . ."

"But I have to. How would it seem to Jocelyn ten years down the line if I didn't? That her daddy would not fight for her? I don't want to do it, Jack, but I'm her father."

"You're damned right you are. You're a wonderful father. And you don't just want to be a big playmate to her—some kindly uncle who takes her to the lake and to the circus and buys her presents and then goes off. You have to be a parent. Participate in her discipline, her learning, shape the ways she grows . . ."

Dan held up a hand. "Whoa. I know all that."

"Sorry. I got mad, too."

He repeated the substance of this, shivering at the door to Joan's house, when he dropped Jocelyn off. "Please try to see past what you feel about me," he begged. "Think of what's best for Jocelyn."

"I am thinking only of what's best for Jocelyn. You're not thinking of what's best for Jocelyn."

He forced down the anger that made him clench his fists in his pockets. "Joan. I just want to be a father to her. A child needs a mother and a father. I don't want to be her friend. I want to be her parent."

"Don't worry about that," Joan said. "That's *my* job." And closed the door.

29 WE NEEDED an attorney. We had lived in Wisconsin so long we didn't know anyone. We had to have someone savvy in the hairy realms of the Cook County court system. My father called Nick, the Lawyer. "We'll take care of it," said the fellow. "Don't worry. I know I can get him six weeks anyway, and maybe eight. Six is half. They like to give each parent half."

"I don't doubt that you can take care of it," I told him. I was doing the dealings, since I was my father's daughter, and since the whole business made Dan sick. "What I doubt is whether we can take care of you."

"Ah, it won't cost too much. How about four hundred? We can do it for four hundred." I knew he was doing me a favor—that this was what he charged to cross the street. But lately that was an enormous amount. I began to calculate rapidly. I can do a fast bit for the credit union magazine for $200, a quickie for the hospital magazine for another $110. We can sell something. Maybe a print, or a box of books. We still had boxes of books sitting around.

"That sounds just fine. We thank you," I said.

"Nothing, kid." This definitely was one of my father's friends.

He called me the following morning; Dan was out of town on assignment. "I talked to her lawyer," Nick told me. "Are you sure Dan is on the level?"

"How do you mean?"

"The guy says he's fifteen hundred dollars in arrears on support."

"That's impossible. That's incredible. Dan has never missed a payment in his life. He's probably the only person in the world who can say that. He's been absolutely scrupulous."

"Ah, well, he said Dan never paid her when he had the kid."

Click. "He didn't. But he wasn't supposed to. That was their agreement. During the time he had Jocelyn and was paying for her day care himself, and everything else, too, he didn't pay Joan."

"Is it in the decree?"

"I don't know. I don't think so."

"Then she can make an issue out of it. If she wants to fight for it." Fifteen hundred. Plus four hundred. There was nothing to sell. Even the dog would only bring in about two hundred, tops.

Dan called Joan that night. "Are you really going to do this?"

"I've got it coming to me."

We got a letter from Joan's attorney—a copy of a letter he had written to our attorney—later that week. It gave answer to Dan's pleas for a personal meeting between his ex-wife and himself, without spouses, without Jocelyn, just the two of them over a cup of coffee on neutral ground.

"Perhaps there is a misunderstanding," the lawyer had written. "My client does not intend to communicate with Mr. Allegretti on this matter in any way. As for the question of support payments, my client cannot consider a reduction. She, in fact, intends to petition the court for an increase in support immediately."

Dan called Joan again. She did not want to talk to him. I could tell from the shift in his tone that she had handed the phone to Jocelyn. They talked for a few minutes. The dog was eating enough, he assured her. Yes, it was only a couple more weeks until Easter—oh, boy! He came into the living room after he hung up, looking as if he were about to cry.

"Do you know what Joan said, Jack? She said I wasn't starting all this because I care about Jocelyn. She said it was only because I thought we weren't going to have any kids of our own. *That* was the root of all this sudden fatherly concern, she said."

There was a party after work one Friday night for the engagement of one of our editors. It was a man I'd known well, and I took the bus to Madison for it. Dan and Todd drifted away with some of the night shift girls, who have perfected the art of appearing confused unless there is a man about. As they wandered off toward the bar, I heard Dan ask one of the women, who had just been introduced to me as Sharon, "Can I get you a drink, sweetie?" I felt myself begin to outgrow my best dress bag, my face felt like a melon; I was a Macy's balloon with a tuft of hair on top. I looked around for an avenue of escape. I needed great breaths of fresh air. Snow.

But as I did, one of the bosses' wives came up and asked me how life in the big city was treating me. She began to tell me about her new career as a student. She was in women's studies. They'd learned "all about infertility."

"Let me ask you," she said, "does it distress you to know there is a very good chance that you won't be able to conceive again? That the chance is considerably reduced?"

I clenched. Did she sincerely want to know? Was she sympathetic? Or was this women's studies field work? It crossed my mind that such a narrow designation—making studies out of women—might be dicey in the wrong hands. I answered, honestly, that it absorbed all my life for a while, less of it now, but still it depressed me. She said she expected so.

"I really didn't even know I wanted kids until I held mine in my arms. You know we had filed for adoption and then I came up pregnant. That's how it happens, you know." Did I know. Four dozen people had greeted me with this same nugget of information.

"Actually, that doesn't really happen," I said. "Studies show that the people who get pregnant after adoption only amount to a very small percentage."

"Really?" She seemed to consider this. I looked at this woman, who probably was trying to be nice, and realized I was sending out distress signals, that I was desperate for the first time not to talk about it anymore, that I had lost control of this conversation. Then Rosemary, who was forty, unmarried, childless, and raised beautiful, prizewinning silver tabby cats, wandered over.

"Jackie, maybe you should forget about having kids," she said. "Come over and I'll give you a couple of cats. I spend so much time and devotion on those cats that I know they take up all my maternal instincts. I don't think I could ever have kids now."

I declined, pleading allergy, in delicate horror at the vision of myself surrounded by fifteen cats, cooing "Mama's baby" to all of them.

But then I thought what the gesture must have cost her, exposing a potentially silly-sounding attachment to someone she really didn't know all that well. And later I remembered that Rosemary had said she would give me cats, not sell them to me. Those cats were her children, and she had offered to let me adopt two, to assuage my emptiness. And that was very human, very kind.

Karen Sussman called one night while I was typing a column. I had not talked to her, nor anyone else from the infertility support group, for weeks, and I had the panicked urge to pretend I was a recording and beep for her message.

"How are you?" she asked in her gentle way. "We haven't heard from you since you booked out of the last group. And then I heard you moved. What's up? Are you okay?"

"Fine. Really well, actually. Waiting for the next test that will show whether the tube really is open. Busy catching up on everything I've let slide."

I stammered, guiltily. I had signed up for the last session of the group and gone once, just before we left Madison. Fifteen of us, counting Susan and Karen, had sat around a long Sunday school table in a church basement. We had introduced ourselves. Every one of the women had been infertile longer than I had. They had begun losing hope after three years, five years. I was way ahead of them on that, I told myself. All I needed was to spend time pooling lost hope.

It had been easy to assure myself that I wasn't the group type, the group wasn't for me.

I had a better reason not to return as well. Every other woman in the group had been there with her husband.

And as if Karen intuited what I was thinking, she asked, "And how is Dan?"

"Oh, he's fine. He's really been great. Worn out, though."

"You're lucky," said Karen. Her own husband had been not so great. She had dragged him to counseling, but it had been too late. No physician had ever been able to discover what was keeping them from having children, but Karen's husband, she said, had been convinced nothing was wrong with *him*. She sensed he believed that what was wrong was Karen's attitude.

Was I aware, she asked, that there was an accepted body of opinion twenty years ago that held that infertility was primarily psychogenic? And that the woman who could not conceive was either "masculine," rejecting of the feminine mother role, or obsessively infantile and neurotic? And was I aware that the primary voice in this school of thought was a woman—a psychologist by the name of Helene Deutsch?

"It wasn't bad enough not to have a baby," Karen said. "The woman also had to feel it was her own crazy desire not to have a baby that was causing it."

I hadn't known that, I told her, glad we had moved off the subject of Dan, when she said, "About Dan. Why didn't he come to the group with you?"

"Dan hates support groups. He thinks Madison is a hotbed of support groups—he says he keeps expecting to see a notice in the paper for a support group for people who have bridgework, or people who are married to Iranians. He thinks people should cope with their problems on their own."

I was being polite. Dan actually had said also that he did not want to sit around with a group of mopey women trying to match each other neurosis for neurosis.

"He can cope on his own, huh?" Karen asked me.

"Yep." And then I said, "That bit about thinking it's all in your head. That still happens. Dan always manages to find the brief section of any book where it says there is a *possibility* that stress can function in infertility—that it makes the tubes clamp down or interferes with ovulation or whatever. 'See?' he says, to me."

"And so you do feel he blames you."

"I feel like I'm taking it from both ends," I said, thinking, clam up. You don't want to say any of this. You've just told her you're feeling terrific. "Sure, this thing has made me feel stressed. I'm a vegetable from it. And then Dan tells me, his sister tells me, that I'm never going to get pregnant so long as I'm so depressed. That nature doesn't work that way. Dan just doesn't believe that any woman who was halfway well adjusted would obsess around this thing so much. He keeps pointing to his brother and sister-in-law. They can't have kids, and nobody in the family even knew about it for years, they were that private about it."

"And Dan considers that the way to be, right?"

"He's a stoic. He believes you conquer negative emotions, you don't indulge them."

"Has he ever talked about this with his brother?"

"Just recently. And you know how the conversation went? Dan was telling Rick about the surgery, and all of a sudden Rick asked him if infertility was the name of what I had. And Dan said, yes, there was a lot more to it, but basically, yes. Rick said then, 'Well, I guess that's what we had.'

"And I'm sitting there, wanting to grab the phone and yell to him, Go to a doctor if you still want kids! Find out more about this! Maybe they still could have children," I told Karen. "They're only in their early thirties. Maybe it's some simple thing."

"Not everyone deals with that adjustment in the same way. Plenty of people deal with it by avoiding it. My husband sure did," Karen said. "Dan thinks nobody deals with it less well than me."

"When are you going to be in Madison next?"

"At Easter."

"Then why don't you get him to come to the next group with you?"

"We couldn't come to all of them, and anyway, even if he did, he would just be doing it for me."

"Is that so bad?"

Karen had been having some lousy experiences herself lately, which she said only proved to her that infertility is like malaria; it can recur in low-grade form years after the primary bout. There had been a couple of things—she'd hoped to adopt a child through the state, but the social worker there had finally told her that the kind of child she'd hoped for, a four- or five-year-old girl, probably would be offered to a couple rather than a divorced woman. Someone had come to her door, selling something for kids, and just assumed she was too old to have any little ones, and she was only thirty-eight. Things like that.

Her voice waxed and waned, as if the telephone wire that connected us was being buffeted by gusts of high wind. She didn't know. Perhaps, she said, it's just time to give up entirely. Let the waiting end.

I told her I'd send her all my brochures on foreign adoption. "How do they feel about divorced moms?" she asked.

"Lots of them say singles are okay. For kids that age." I wondered if I should tell her about the waiting times.

We said good-bye fairly cheerfully. "And don't forget about the group," Karen reminded me.

I went into the bedroom, where Dan was reading, and said, "Honey, that was Karen who runs the support group. How about if you go with me when it meets next? We'll be in Madison, anyway. I'd like to go. Just for the purpose of research. In case I ever really write this book."

"Sure," Dan said, without looking up. I was dumbfounded.

We collected Jocelyn the week before Easter and went to Madison. The house was immaculate; I went into shock. "Who's been staying here besides you?" I asked. "This house is suspiciously orderly."

"Nobody," Dan said, eminently smug. "It's your not being here that's kept it so clean."

Our schedule was crammed tight. We wanted to see all of our friends, and my hysterosalpingogram, to show the state of the tube after surgery, was scheduled for the same time period. I would not risk having it done by anyone but Bellow. There were omens to consider.

And then there was the group. Dan had given no evidence of having changed his mind about going. I called Joanna, who cleaned house for us, and asked her if she would stay with Jocelyn while we attended the meeting. She agreed.

On the night the group was to meet, while I was putting on my coat, Dan yawned and said, "You go ahead and go. I'm fagged out."

"Come on." He didn't mean this. I had told Karen he was coming. I had spent the last few days happily thinking that while the group might force me to confront something I didn't want to confront, I would at least have my husband beside me. "You promised."

"Jack, it's just not my style. I don't want to sit around with a bunch of depressed people and talk about depressing things. It only breeds self-pity. You go. You like self-pity."

"That's a shitty thing to say."

"Well, I didn't mean it shitty. I just, I dread this. I know I'm going to be uncomfortable and embarrassed, and I know everyone there is going to be able to tell."

I held out his coat. "But you *promised.*"

He shrugged it on with bad grace, and grumbled all the way to the church. "Let me warn you," he said, taking my arm as we walked in the door. "I'm not going to say one word. And don't try to make me say one word."

There were five couples. We went around the table and introduced ourselves, a roll call of our disabilities. We sat across from a pair of dysfunctional ovaries, and were flanked by an ectopic, and at the foot of the table were some fimbrial adhesions. The problems in this group all were with the female partners, which made it easy, one woman said to me in an aside, but not wholly representative. I didn't mind. I preferred it. I thought that a discussion of poor sperm motility would get in the way. I wanted to hear misfortunes like mine and measure them —these two are worse off; this couple have got a better chance on paper, but they've been trying longer. . . . In some absurd way, I hoped to add them all up and divide by five and come out with a statistical likelihood that it would be Dan and I, alone of these assembled couples, who would catch the brass ring. I didn't plan on caring for them as individuals. It surprised me when I did.

We began with an assessment: Karen asked what each of us hoped to get out of this. "I know what I want to get out of this," Dan said, sotto voce, so that only I could hear. "What I want to get out of this is to get out of this."

Carrie Piper, a ski instructor whose husband was a teacher at the university, wanted information. She wanted to know how others had managed to get through all this—learn their strategies. Ruth and Bill Waite, who were farmers, wanted primarily to find out about adoption. They couldn't bring themselves to consider special-needs kids. Ruth, who at twenty-nine was fourteen years younger than her husband, didn't believe it would be possible for her to mother an older child, either; she had a teenage stepdaughter who lived with them, and she couldn't bear her. "All she wants to do is lie around upstairs on her bed and listen to her stereo through the headphones. She doesn't do a lick of work. It's as if the rest of us don't exist to her," she complained. "How would you like to live with that?"

"She sounds . . . I don't mean to demean what you're saying, but she sounds pretty much like any other teenage girl," Karen put in.

"Huh," said Ruth. "I wasn't like that."

Mary and Jason Ebberly were very young; she was twenty-five, he, twenty-six. They had got an early start when Mary had stopped menstruating a year after their marriage. Mary rhapsodized about her physician—Dr. Joel at the university. "I would walk on fire for that man," she said, so fervently no one was moved to laugh. "He got me pregnant." But the pregnancy had lasted only a month, she added in a small voice. And then later there had been a problem; someone hadn't monitored her dosage of Clomid very well—not Dr. Joel, no, he wouldn't have done that—but some intern or someone, and her ovaries had begun to swell, and by the time she had been able to get anyone to see her, she had been in awful shape and spent two weeks in the hospital in pain.

She wanted to find out more about her chances to conceive—about any reading she could do. It made her feel very lonely to be infertile, and a bit ill-used as well, because—again, it was not her doctor's fault —she often had to wait months for an appointment, and then when she went, always right on time, she waited three hours, four hours, and she never knew whom she'd see.

Jeannie and Jim didn't know what they wanted. They weren't sure why they were there. Jeannie was a tiny thing, who looked like a Madame Alexander doll, and of all the group, I felt most strongly for her.

Perhaps because she, too, had got pregnant, only to have the bottom ripped out as I had, with a ruptured ectopic. Perhaps because, though it happened nearly two years ago, her chin began to quiver and her blue eyes filled when she told us about it. And when she told us that she had only one functional ovary and it was on the opposite side from her healthy tube, but she and Jim still "have more hope than ever before, because we've heard that sometimes an egg can cross over—it really can," I wanted to pick her up and cradle her. And I could tell that her husband, who sat beside her making small rueful motions with his hands, felt the same way. I caught myself thinking, how lucky that at least he still felt bad about it, too.

When it was my turn, I said, for lack of anything better, that I wanted to learn how the others in the group coped with family births and pregnancies, of which we recently had experienced a spate, and it was a big hit. Everybody agreed we would start with that.

"That's a tough one," Karen said. "You have the impulse to not want to be around anyone who's pregnant. I think it's possible that we idealize pregnancy and . . ."

"Everything in a family is set up for the ones who have kids," Ruth chimed in. "Holidays. Birthdays."

"I know," Karen replied. "When my sister had a baby, I actually felt that all of the emotion of the family was focused on that baby, and that if I couldn't produce one, I wasn't going to get any attention anymore." She smiled wryly, and I could feel Dan, next to me, suppress a groan. This was just the kind of I-need-you-need stuff he loathed.

Then Carrie spoke up. "At first, I felt like telling Art, why are we even together? If we don't have kids, why have a marriage?" There, Dan, I thought, that should impress you.

But she said then, "I used to go through tremendous mood swings, timed about like my menstrual cycles. Emotional spurts. A withdrawal, then an upswing. Right now, I feel pretty good. It's like, I fight my impulse to avoid other people's pregnancies, and after I do, I feel better. I've made myself want to be around babies."

"But how can you?" I asked. Did I really want to know? Or was I trying to defend my own position in some oblique fashion to Dan, who was beaming his approval across the table at Carrie? "I have a christening coming up, and I don't want to go to it, but I am getting a lot of pressure from Dan to tough it out. . . ."

"I don't see why you can't tough it out," Dan said. I had thought he wasn't going to say anything. I wished he wouldn't. "You refuse to make any demands on yourself. You seem to think that it would be disloyal to your depression. I understand why the christening would bother you, but not to the point where you have to avoid it entirely, and hurt other people by doing it. It's just a day, Jack. A day of sitting around . . ."

"Sitting around with a whole roomful of parents. You with your daughter on your knee. Gail with her kids . . ." I was surprised and horrified by the tears. After my last visit to the group, Karen had told me, I gave the details of our situation with a big smile on my face that never wavered.

"It was as if you could handle it so long as you kept it on a nice, cool intellectual level," she had said. "As if you could stay in control only so long as you didn't let it touch you." I looked at her now, thinking, is this better? Is this emotional enough for you?

"But aren't we really here because of kids?" Carrie asked earnestly. "Because we love kids? When I finally decided that I was more important than all the suffering I'd have to endure in order to have any chance at pregnancy, decided to give up on the medical stuff, I decided I'd have to find another outlet for my maternal instincts. I'll always want to be connected with kids in some way—teach them, or have a special relationship with my nieces and nephews."

And I wanted to pop this woman. Who was saying all the correct, sane, healthy, impossible things in such a reasonable way. I wanted to ask her if she ever really wanted kids. And if she had, how she could accept so profound a loss with such equanimity. I wanted to ruffle her, tear her peace to pieces.

"I think we're afraid to try sometimes," Carrie went on. "But you know, this doesn't have to be the end of the world. I still have me. I have Art. And now that I won't be devoting a great deal of my life to being a parent, there are a lot of other possibilities. I might be depressed again at some point, but right now, I'm actually feeling rather excited about the ways I can be creative with my . . ."

Karen's sigh was like an exploding cap. "That's great. That's all really hopeful. But . . . what did you think you'd need the group for? You seem to have done terrifically on your own." She was hostile, and she was not doing a great job of hiding it. It was on the tip of my mind to think, go get 'er, Karen, when Ruth started up, and said Carrie actually was making her feel kind of inadequate, because she couldn't be so well adjusted. And Jeannie nodded.

Carrie gazed around the table, eyes wide, and said, "But isn't this the purpose? For all of us to give each other strength?"

And I was ashamed. We'd jumped on her like a pack of dogs just because she had dared to try to be cheerful. We'd given her—given all of us—the message that ye who enter here damned well better have abandoned all hope.

We broke, because everybody was feeling unsettled, and the second half of the session largely was absorbed with listening to Bill Waite read from a paperback on holistic nutrition—he droned on about toxins and incomplete proteins, and interjected his own comments about how he believed there might be something to this, if we all ate organically perhaps we could avoid some of these problems. Everyone else doodled on pads or stared out of the window at the dark sky, unsure whether to be embarrassed or merely bored, and at length the meeting petered out.

"I know what you're going to say," I began as soon as Dan started the car. "And I agree with you. It was terrible the way they jumped on Carrie, and you're right, Karen was depressing tonight, but she has been feeling rather depressed."

"I wasn't going to say that at all. What I was going to say is, though I really can't stand that kind of format, I did see that there are plenty of other people who are just as messed up over this as you are."

"Oh, honey . . ."

"I still don't think it's normal, though."

"Oh."

The day of the hysterosalpingogram was approaching. We had not even talked about it. This time I had not peppered Dan with the incessant will-it-or-won't-it, as I had the first time around. I had done all I could, and the rest was a horse race. The single hedge I had made was getting a good haircut beforehand, knowing that if the news was bad I would not have the heart to do it later, and that looking like a mop would only depress me further. Actually I felt fairly sanguine. If endometriosis had caused the blockage, and the Danazol was doing its job, the blockage should not have recurred.

At my back-to-work checkup, Bellow had whistled when he saw Clarke's prescribed course for the medication. "Six months is pretty substantial," he said.

"I talked him down to four."

"Even that. There couldn't have been much endometriosis, Jackie. I didn't see any at the laparoscopy."

I hate when this happens. I want there to be one clear-cut diagnosis and one surefire method of treatment, and have everyone agree. The disagreement among authorities unsettles me. Until I became infertile, I had no idea what a roulette game treatment could be—solutions and styles were as various as specialists.

What would happen after I stopped taking the Danazol was a good puzzler. The information packet sent home with me from New Orleans said I could expect normal menstruation to commence in sixty to ninety days. The head nurse from the RBU, when she called to check on my condition, said generally women had their periods within three weeks after stopping the medication. One of my books said it would take four to six weeks. A nurse in Bellow's office said about a month. Was there somebody who really *knew*? I decided that after I finished the prescription in April, I would become concerned after four weeks, and panic after six.

Bellow had been going over the operating-room notes from New Orleans. "Ah ha!" he said at one point. "They didn't even use the laser."

"What do you mean?"

"It says right here—cautery. I thought that was what the laser was supposed to be best for, creating a bloodless atmosphere. They used cauterization to stop bleeding."

"They may have used it for that. But they used the laser to remove the obstruction. I saw it on the tape." I had brought him the tape. He said he'd give it a look when he could borrow a Betamax from somebody. I never got it back, never wanted it. I couldn't see it being as popular for family viewing as Jocelyn's dance number.

"But it turned out that the laser wasn't really necessary, after all, didn't it?" I felt like a little girl, gently prodded by an elder to own up to a fib.

"I guess not."

"I'm not convinced that this isn't just an incredibly costly piece of equipment that doesn't really improve the odds."

"It seems to. Theoretically."

"Well, based on whose theory? The guy who's using it, right? I'd have to see a lot more objective evidence than that."

I couldn't argue. The thing was done. But I was unable to understand why it irked him so. Professional rivalry? It didn't seem his style. However, we'd talked no more about it, and set March 18 as the date for my second dye test.

And now here I was, decked out in my paper gown, sitting in the waiting room of the X-ray facility with Dan, and fuming. We had been waiting for two hours, and I was cold. The paper robe I'd been given did not even cover my recently massive butt.

The little technician, whose name was Glenda, kept buzzing in and out. "I don't know what's keeping Dr. Bellow," she fluttered. I waved her away, shrugging.

At length she came back, looking at her shoes. "There's an emergency over in OR," she explained. "I'm so sorry. I'm supposed to reschedule you."

I blew. "So when did it become an emergency? Fifteen minutes ago? We've been here two and a half hours. I really don't mean to be rude, but this is unreal. It's as if our time were of no consequence, not to mention that my husband and I have been very, very anxiously awaiting this test for three months, and the last thing we want to do is go home and wait three more goddamned weeks, and have to come back from out of town. Why didn't they tell you, at the very least, that we were going to be canceled two hours ago?"

"I don't know." She looked contrite. Oh, hell. She was just a nice kid.

"I'm sorry," I offered. "It's just that you get ready for something in your mind, and this is something that's not pleasant, it's not fun. . . ."

"I really know." I looked at her; she couldn't really know. She looked to be about twelve. But I appreciated the gesture.

"So when can we reschedule? *Not* three weeks from now. How about Monday?" It was a Friday. I got dressed and went out to the desk where the technician was waiting with a wide smile on her face.

"How about tomorrow?"

"A Saturday?" Even I was not prepared for such largesse from modern medicine. She said Bellow had agreed to come in, that the test would be at ten.

"Okay?"

"The good witch, huh?" I smiled at her.

"Yep."

Dan and I went out for a drink, and I had four. I was drunk when he asked me, "Are you prepared? For it to be unfavorable?"

"I am. Are you?"

"I don't know. I don't feel particularly confident about it. The preparedness. Not the test." He was scared, the good fellow, to say even one word that would make me start to see the cancellation in terms of omens, afraid to topple my fragile hope cart with even a single doubt.

"Whatever the news is, I'll handle it. So you don't have to worry."

"Jesus, Jackie, I hope so. Because if it's like it was before, I don't think we can handle it."

"It's not as if even that would be the end of the road. There'd still be in vitro. We could adopt. Maybe my dad's friend will come up with something. Maybe another whack at the tube."

"You wouldn't seriously consider that again?" I looked at his face, saw the incredulity in it. Of course I would consider that. But I said, "No. Not really. That would be a little excessive."

"Even for you, who are excessive in all things."

"Even for me."

"Except sex. You're very restrained about sex."

"One must exercise some restraint." He kissed me.

We were twenty minutes early the following morning. I had picked Dan up at work, handing out promises to any editor on the short-staffed Saturday desk who would listen that this would be the last time Dan would be waltzed away to one of my medical assignations.

I lay down on the table, comforted to see the same technician was back on duty. The X-ray machine was moved over my chest. Everyone else put on their lead vests and aprons. Dan haunted the door; I had warned him to stay out this time. Not only had the last time been very hard on him, I had got claustrophobic with so many people in the room.

Bellow came in, apologized for yesterday. "Emergency cesarean," he said. "Prolapsed cord."

"Is the baby all right?" He gave me a quizzical look. "Yes. They're both all right."

"Good." Omens.

Bellow introduced me to the radiologist as a reporter—he was very conscious of it, and I found this peculiar. Did it mean I would be treated differently? He began to try to insert the speculum. "You're going to have to put your knees apart," he said.

"I'm trying to. My feet kept slipping."

"Maybe it's the socks," the technician suggested.

I laughed. "No, it's the knees. I was raised to keep my knees together." I lay back. Bellow cleaned the cervix, coated it with Betadine, talking all the while. "Other than being a reporter," he told the radiologist, "she had an ectopic pregnancy in July and tuboplasty in December. At some place in New Orleans." He began to run the dye.

"Stop!" I screamed. The cramp was excruciating.

"Breathe in and out of your mouth," Bellow said. "Deep breaths."

I breathed. It kept building; I understood the expression "climbing the wall." My fingernails raked the steel table. "The pain! Shit!"

"No shit! Breathe!"

"Stop!"

"I'm not doing anything." Bellow sounded less than patient; but he had, after all, been up most of the night. "That's just a cramp."

"Just a *cramp?*"

The dye kept flowing. "There's your cornual obstruction," said the radiologist, and I thought, oh shit, oh no . . . and then Bellow said, "That's not an obstruction. She doesn't have a tube on that side."

"I can't stand it. The pain," I hissed. I began to want to reach for the radiologist's free hand, and if he had been a woman, I would have.

"Breathe deep. Breathe deep," the radiologist said. But I couldn't breathe deep. I couldn't breathe at all.

Then Bellow's voice cut through my sweaty concentration. "There's the tube. Looks good." And I couldn't believe it. I couldn't believe that I couldn't believe it.

"You mean it worked?"

"It worked."

I reached out and touched the screen. There it was, all right, like the Colorado River on a small-scale map. "And the distribution at the end of the tube?"

"It looks fine."

I made as if to sit up. "Don't!" Bellow yelled. "All that stuff is still in you. You'll undo everything the surgery did. Lie still." He withdrew the cannula. This felt orgasmic.

"Can I sit up now?"

"If you feel okay."

"I feel terrific!"

"Do you want to see your X rays?"

"No, I don't care. I believe you."

"Do you want your husband to see them?"

"He'll believe you, too." I was up, half-mad with joy, waddling around in the breezing gown. Someone said he would go out and look for Dan. *"No!* I want to get him." But Dan was there already. At the door. I gave him the okay sign with thumb and forefinger. He hugged me. The technician hugged me.

"This made my day," she said.

There were congratulations all around. As if we'd already had the baby.

Bellow asked, ironically, "Doesn't anyone want to see the X ray?"

In the parking lot, though the cramps were getting to me still, I did arabesques around the concrete posts.

"How do you feel?" I asked Dan.

"Ten years younger. How about you?"

"Marvelous. Zippety-do-dah."

We ran into the house, where Joanna, the housecleaner, was mopping the kitchen floor. I grabbed her and swung her around in the suds. "Joanna! I'm going to be able to have a baby!"

"THAT'S nothing," says Jocelyn, tearing the tissue off the Easter gift I have given her, a lace sweater collar. "You should see what my mommy gave me." She holds up a mesh bag of chocolate shillings. Even Dan, who thinks that all children are endogenously rude and that those who amount to anything get over it as much by natural selection as by instruction, is appalled.

"Jocelyn! That's a terrible thing to say! When someone gives you a present, you give them a nice thank you—you don't make them feel as if what they gave you isn't good enough."

Jocelyn's lip juts out and begins to quiver. "Thank you, Jackie," she hisses, and takes the collar and heads for her room.

"Don't feel bad," Dan soothes me. "Naturally, you have to expect that anything a kid gets from her mother takes on some kind of special significance."

"I'm sure."

"And she has that conflict of loyalties, honey, you know."

"Are you going to explain away every rude thing she does for the rest of her life that way?"

His face goes slack. "No," he says shortly. I whirl away. I'd brought it on myself, after all. Googled at her all the way from Chicago, "Wait until you see what I've got in my suitcase for you!" Picked it out so carefully—a collar with flowers in her favorite color embroidered round it. After all, when you are seven, *anything* to wear is not so glamorous as something to eat. She felt let down. I don't blame her. So did I.

But Jocelyn has it in for me. She's mad. So I should expect what happens when Dan takes my brother and his wife—who are visiting for Easter weekend—out for a boat ride on the bay, newly opened from its ice crust, and Jocelyn and I stay behind to color eggs because the boat is too small for five.

We are having a tense little discussion. "Are we going to Mass?" Jocelyn asks.

"Yes, tomorrow." Jocelyn knows this is something of a departure. Both Dan and I are more or less lapsed Catholics, divorces notwithstanding. I had gone to confession with Mary one Saturday morning before my surgery—large events being a goad to cleansing the soul, I suppose —and was able to see through the door of the wooden confessional that the young priest was doing a needlepoint. "Bless me, father, for I have sinned," I whispered.

"When was your last confession?"

"Nine years ago." He had put down his needlepoint.

Now Jocelyn says, "It's a good thing we're going, because my mommy would go savage if she knew I didn't go to church. My mommy always goes to church. And she always," with a leveling look at me, "takes Communion."

Quibble, quibble, I think. Do not make an issue out of this. But my mouth opens anyway and I say, before I can bite it off, "She can't take Communion."

Jocelyn is up off her chair in a swivet. "She does! My mommy always takes Communion."

"She's divorced and remarried. Divorced and remarried Catholics can't take Communion."

"Can too!"

I should drop it here. I know that. It is none of my business, and dumb doctrine to boot, but it seems to me I have had Joan held up to me for measuring one too many times, and while she may make a better beef Stroganoff and sew a better patch and construct cunning bunny suits for Halloween out of scraps she had lying around, I am not willing, not at this moment, for her to be holier than me as well. And so I say, "If she does, according to Catholics, that's a sin."

And then the phone rings, and I can tell by Jocelyn's end of the conversation that it's Mary's five-year-old Susie, who has been distracted for days in her excitement about our coming up with Jocelyn for a whole week. I make it a point never to listen when Jocelyn talks to her friends—the minor verbal atrocities kids visit on each other in the course of a usual conversation are too jarring for adult ears, the urge to meddle too tempting—but now, perhaps because of something in her voice, which is lowered, or the way she is stretching the phone cord into the hall and turning away from me, I strain to over-hear.

"I'll *call* you," she is saying. "When we get done coloring eggs, if Carrie can't play, then I'll play with you." Jocelyn hangs up, comes back into the kitchen. Gives my impassive face a quick once-over. "Where's the decals?" she asks quickly.

"Never mind the decals. I heard what you said to Susie. And I thought it was awful."

"She didn't care."

"Why? Because she's the littlest one? Wouldn't you care if Susie told you she would play with you only if she couldn't get someone better to play with her?"

Jocelyn slams an egg—thankfully hard-boiled——down on the table. "But I *want* to play with Carrie!"

"Sometimes you can't do everything you want, right when you want to do it. Don't you know that? You're a big, almost eight-year-old person. Don't you understand that what you do affects other people's feelings?" Jocelyn doesn't answer. She stares determinedly out the window. "Don't answer, then. Because I think you do know that, but you chose to ignore it. You hurt Susie's feelings, and I don't want my girl to be the kind of girl who hurts other people's feelings."

"I'm *not!*"

"Well, that's good, then. Maybe you and Susie and Carrie can all play together later. . . ."

"No."

"Well, then you can't play at all." Jocelyn's eyes widen in horror.

"What?"

"You can't play at all, then. For the rest of today."

"Are you crazy?" This is novel. "This is my vacation!"

"This is your school vacation, but what this really is is some time at your other home, with Daddy, and rules go here the same as they do anyplace else."

Jocelyn bursts into tears; she throws down her egg dipper and runs into her room, slamming the door. I follow. "Do you understand why I'm doing this? I don't want you to think it's just because I'm angry with you." I don't want you to think that, Jocelyn, because it's just about entirely true. "I want you to think about what you did to Susie."

"No you don't! You just want to be mean to me. My mommy never grounds me—she just yells at me. She never makes me eat food I hate. You can't even be nice to me for one day. You're mean to me every single day!"

"Jocelyn! I can hear you. Don't scream!"

"I will if I want to! You already grounded me." This makes good sense; she might as well hang for a sheep as a lamb. "Leave me alone."

I hear her sobbing through the door. Piteously. Jocelyn is a good sobber. Occasionally she lifts her head from the muffling pillow and gives a mournful wail. I let this go on for half an hour by the clock, and one bitten thumbnail. And then, casually, I knock at the door. "Jocie? You know you don't have to stay in bed just because you can't play. You can read. Or finish the eggs."

"I don't want to do anything." Just suffer. Ah, honey. I know how that feels.

"Okay."

"Okay? You mean you just want me to stay in here?"

"Joc. Come on, now." I walk over to the bed and cradle her stiff little shoulders. "Hush a bit."

"I hate everything."

"Me, you mean?"

"No. Everything." She sits up on the bed and mops her nose with a tissue I handed her. "One thing I hate is being fought over." Ah. Ms. Sensitive. If this were a stranger's child, a study for my column, I'd have sniffed it out an hour ago.

"You mean the court thing?"

"Yes. Mommy says I might have to talk to the judge. And I don't want to."

"Why not? It won't be scary. It will be just in a little room, with Mommy and Daddy right there."

"Yeah, right there."

"Oh. I see." I brush back her sweaty hair. "You know, I think that Daddy wouldn't really mind if you only got to spend four weeks with us in the summer. I don't think it would hurt him very much at all if he knew that was what you really wanted."

"It's not what I really want."

"What do you really want?"

"I can't tell."

"Why?"

"Because you would tell Mommy."

"I wouldn't tell Mommy. I promise. But honey, maybe you should tell Mommy and Daddy yourself. Because they're doing all this, they're spending all this money, and maybe the judge is going to rule something that won't make you happy at all. And the whole point is, they both want what you want."

"No. Mommy wants me with her. She's selfish of me."

"She loves you very much."

"I know. And she thinks you and my dad don't take too good of care of me."

"Hmmmmmmm."

"I think you take okay care of me."

"That's good. So, Joc, what do you want to happen?"

"Well, I think it's fair for me to spend more time with my daddy. But I can't tell Mommy."

"Why?"

"Because her feelings are too soft. When I want to go to your house in Chicago, she cries and has to lie down on the couch." I am hit with a vision of Joan, supine with a case of the vapors, one hand gesturing weakly for a cold cloth. The vision is rimmed in red.

"But honey, you know your dad has feelings, too. He doesn't cry, because he doesn't want to make you cry. But he misses you very, very much. And that's why he's going to go to court. Because he thinks— he's not mad at your mom, exactly, but he thinks it isn't fair that you should have to spend less time with him just because it makes your mommy sad. Grown-ups have to accept some things sometimes that make them sad."

"So do kids. Like I'm sad they're divorced. I'm sad I'm grounded."

"You just have to . . . accept them."

"When I was little, I used to wish they'd get married again. But they really don't love each other anymore."

"And if they did, you'd never get to see me again." She gives me a blank look, and it stings to recognize that this isn't as big a part of her personal equation as I fancy it, when I'm blue. Still, she covers nicely.

"I could still see you. I could call you up. You could come over with Jesse. You live right by, now."

"Right. But Joc, that won't happen."

"I know."

"Daddy and I are going to stay married to each other now."

"I know. I want you to."

"Good ol' Pocelyn."

"Good ol' Packie."

She doesn't sound convinced, though. And twenty-four hours later, I am not convinced either.

Dan had not thought Jocelyn's was a grounding offense, considering what had been troubling her. He didn't countermand my decision, and he didn't bring it up while my brother and sister-in-law were around. But on Sunday evening, after church, after brunch, after Bobby and Sandy had headed home, their car loaded with stuff we were still in the process of moving, he said, "I think you were too hard on her."

"I think she deserved it. I don't punish her for breaking or spilling or even for smart-mouthing. But when a child tramples on someone's feelings, she's saying something pretty disturbing about the way she values people. And I think she deserved a lesson."

"I wish you'd check with me next time."

"You were out in the boat."

"I said next time." And we could have left it there. I would think, months later, that if we had left it there, if I had swallowed the small irritation, the lump of insecurity that welled up, we could have done with it, turned it to something else, and the stain of that night would never have spread, and Jocelyn would never have the memory, that she would recount wide-eyed, of "the time you almost got divorced, right in this very house."

But I didn't let it alone. Weariness. Or pique. Or the image of the sainted Joan. Whatever. I said, "I thought it was your aim to have me treat Jocelyn as I would my own child. That is what I did. If you object to that, I will withdraw from it."

"You mean you'll withdraw from her."

"I mean I'll leave her discipline entirely to you."

"I didn't mean that."

"Well, what did you mean? It sounds to me as though you meant she was your kid, and hands off."

"She is my kid, and you and I have . . . different styles. You're a strict woman. You're strict with your grandmother and you're strict with Jocelyn and you're strict with me." Dan smiled with his mouth. "You're not quite so strict, however, with yourself."

"So you would prefer that since Jocelyn is your kid, we use *your* style. If she was my kid . . ."

"I'd still prefer we use my style, yes. In either case."

"And what is so goddamned effective about your style? Answer me that, because I'm puzzled. Because it seems to me that between the two of you, you and Joan have managed to turn out quite a little ego-monster. . . ."

"There is my point. If she was *your* kid, you wouldn't say that. It's because she's Joan's and mine that you are so, so critical of her. She senses it. She's not stupid."

"Indeed she's not. She's smart enough to see that she can parlay this

266

trauma-of-divorce bit into a pretty cherry situation for herself."

"Jackie, listen. Really listen to what you're saying."

Jocelyn called me then. She was in the bathtub with her inflatable pumpkin, and she wanted a glass of Kool-Aid. She said that all the water in the tub was making her thirsty. I fetched the glass. "See?" I said childishly. "She only wants me when she wants something done. When she wants cuddles, she comes to you."

"That's hardly unusual. I'm her father."

"Usual or unusual. I'm weary of it. I wash that kid's clothes and make her meals and take her berrying and ice-skating and to the movies—I dote on her—and she . . . she tolerates me. It doesn't make any of this any easier. It doesn't make me feel that I have a real relationship with a child. Only that I have a part-time resident minor I work for. And it's no different in Chicago. She's more interested in the video machine than she is in me."

"Were you interested in adults when you were eight?"

"No. Yes. I was at least civilized around them." Oh, Jackie, I thought. For shame.

Dan carefully opened and folded the newspaper. "I think that your perceptions in this whole matter are, to use a technical term, warped." He grinned. "Why don't you take this newest up at the support group? With the other Sad Sarahs? Perhaps they can assure you that any bizarre emotion you have is perfectly normal and simply a function of your infertility, as though that somehow makes it all right."

It had become a sore point, and he was rubbing it hard. The next meeting of the group was Tuesday—the day before we were to close up the house again and head home for Chicago. The subject was to be adoption. It might be the last time I would see Karen and Susan. Dan already had made it clear that he would not be in attendance. He would prefer to spend the time with Jocelyn. And at any rate, he had done his bit. He had gone once.

"Dan, now that you brought it up, I'd really like to talk with you for a minute about . . ." It came down over his face like a veil, the opaque look—the look that meant he was about to go on automatic pilot for as long as the discussion of infertility lasted.

He hesitated for a beat. And then he asked, "Must you?"

"Must? No must about it. Let's skip the whole routine." I left the room and lay down on the bed. I heard Jocelyn in the bathroom.

"What's the matter with her?" she asked.

"Jackie is giving you a lesson on how not to deal with problems." He came into the bedroom.

"That wasn't fair," I said quietly.

"What?"

"Talking about me in the third person. It just makes me feel like more of a third wheel."

"You make yourself feel that way."

"Dan, Jocelyn would be happier if things were the way they used to be."

"So would I."

"I mean, if you were married to Joan again. Or if you were single."

"I don't think that's true." He sat down on the bed, his eyes fixed on a distant point. "On the other hand, maybe it would be better for all of us."

"If we separated?"

"Yes. If we separated."

How quietly we can have this talk, I thought. We are aware that Jocelyn is ten feet away, ears extended. How quietly, days after the test that showed we might be able to have a child, we can begin to take the bricks out of the foundation, and because we are not arguing, or in any other way absent reasonableness, know that we mean it.

"Do you want that?"

He didn't answer. I got up off the bed and took my suitcase off the closet shelf. I must take my contact lens solution, I thought. Then he will stop me. He didn't stop me. "I'll take the car," I said. "You two can come back on the bus when you're ready. I'll pick you up. And I'll take Jesse with me." I had heard of divorces commenced with such civility. I had never believed the tellers.

Dan said not a word.

I began packing, randomly, blinded, throwing in underwear, pillowcases, anything. Then Jocelyn was standing in the door, her towel falling off, her pumpkin clutched in front of her like a shield. "Where are you going?"

I felt guilty, as if she had caught Dan and me making love instead of sorrow. "Jocie, Daddy and I think that maybe I need a little vacation from the family. I've been so nutsy, and I'm sorry. I think maybe I was too hard on you yesterday. . . ."

"No," said Jocelyn, her eyes widening. "I was rude. I deserved it. Maybe not for the whole day . . ."

"But you know, anyway, Daddy and I think that might be best."

"Do you mean a divorce?"

"No, of course not. Not now."

"But sometime. You mean you might get divorced sometime."

"Maybe sometime. If we can't get happy again." I sent Dan a beseeching look over her head, and he refused to catch it. "We don't want to."

"Do you want to, Daddy?" She was angry, at Dan. "Are you going to let Jackie leave us?"

"Jackie has to do what she thinks is best, sweetie." I could have brained him in that moment. This was his idea. I closed the suitcase.

"Jackie?" She looked ghostly. I will never forget that drawn, small oval. "Do you really want to leave?" I dropped onto the bed and held out my arms and she ran into them, naked and small, her little fingerbones like marbles in a pocket.

"Of course, I don't. Honey, forgive me. Stepme would never, ever leave you or your daddy." We wept into each other's hair. Christ, how she cried. The shame of it. That we had let it intrude on her, in a time when she already was unsettled. All the raving I had done, once perhaps understandable—never justifiable. A tantrum a day kept resignation away. Nine months of it. Small wonder Dan was ready to throw in the towel. As if infertility had purchased for me the right to rampage over the rights of others, to make demands on Jocelyn and Dan they had no idea how to fill.

Was this what I had wanted? Proof that she cared for me? Dan stood in the doorway, his mouth working in pity and embarrassment. I held out my free arm to him. He shook his head. I used the arm to point to Jocelyn, her head still buried in my shoulder. He came then, and in a moment I could tell, by his strokes and nuzzles, that he really was there, it was not feigned.

We lay on the bed, the three of us. "It's hard for you to understand that even grown-ups feel like they can't handle things sometimes. I have been so angry. At myself, Jocie. Not at Daddy."

"Sometimes at Daddy."

"Sometimes at Daddy, true, but not always in a fair way. And never, ever at you."

"All because you can't get a baby?"

"I guess so."

"But now you can."

"Maybe, pie. But maybe not. We can't be sure until . . . until we're sure."

"I'll play I'm your baby. Until you get a baby."

"Well, isn't that nice of you."

"I'll be half your baby."

"Half a baby is better than no baby."

"If you got a divorce, you wouldn't even have me." True, I thought, Jocelyn, true.

I leaned over her to try to kiss Dan. He made a small move of avoidance. "Daddy," Jocelyn warned, "Jackie is trying to make marriage with you."

And so he kissed me, and I thought, poor Dan. You married into a whirlwind. You who love simplicity so well. We made popcorn.

Over the popping, I said to Dan, "I find I am saying 'I'm a shit' all the time. But look, I'm aware of it, how I've been. Not just this weekend, for months. I'll earnestly try to be better. I don't want to harm you." But then I added, "It puzzles me. Your timing. Just as we learn pregnancy might be in the offing."

"Think about it," Dan said. "It's the first time in months you're not in crisis—the first space when we don't have to gird ourselves for the next test, the next treatment. The first time we don't have some kind of obligation to stick . . ."

"To stick together?"

"Yes."

"Oh."

He looked at me. "Do you want to be married to me?"

"I do."

"Baby or no baby?"

"Either way."

"And you'll try your best? Give this marriage an eighth of what you've been giving to your treatment, and your search . . ."

"More."

He looked at me, his eyes filling. "I don't know if we can ever be happy. I knew that once. Whatever else I doubted, I didn't doubt that. I have a right to be happy, Jackie. Don't I? Even if it means ending our marriage. Don't I have a right to happiness?"

I could not refute this, only ratify it. We ate the popcorn. And then all three of us slept spoons that night in the king-sized bed, huddled as if we were in an air-raid shelter, or a lifeboat, and dreams capered around the room like imps.

Susan Reese, who has two adopted daughters—one who was a special-needs placement child because she is mixed race—ran the support group meeting on the subject of adoption. I went alone. We were all packed, ready to leave. There was nothing to do. So I went.

I liked Susan. She had a good throaty laugh and a fine sense of the cynical and the gift of putting us at ease with our foibles. She had been the distance on adoption, and could reconnoiter for us—she had tilted with the inescapable fact of her daughters' invisible parents and reported it was not insurmountable. She had warned me, one afternoon over coffee in her kitchen, to beware telephone company advertisements around Christmas. "I got a little misty last year, thinking that hey, all those people look like each other," she said. And then she snorted. "It took me a full minute to realize that those people were actors, they weren't related at all. Jesus, the games you can play on yourself."

I didn't mention it—I thought it would be presumptuous—but I had been noticing as Susan talked that her older daughter did, in fact, look like her. Same fair, freckled face, same strawberry hair. It was a weird quirk of adopted families I would come to notice often, later, and always with a start. Was it that the children moved in the same way as their parents, held themselves at like angles, used the same mirrored inflections, dressed like them? Or was it a function of everyone eating the same spices in the stew over time? They *looked* like their parents.

I had taken my last dose of Danazol on the night of the meeting; in a month, then, we could begin to try. But adoption had revealed itself to me, over the past few weeks, as something I wanted to do in any event, whether or not I could conceive.

Part of it, at the outset, was defiance. Selene, a woman friend of my father's whose teenager was adopted, had written me a long, heartfelt, and quite unsolicited letter.

"Your dad tells me that you're considering adoption," it began. "Please, honey, learn from my experience and *don't*. I don't know what it is—if it's taking on someone else's problems as your dad seems to think —or if it's just bad luck, but I know that if these two were my own they wouldn't be like this. They wouldn't be so bad. Adopted kids are only heartache."

There was an irony to this; it was only recently that I had learned that Selene's kid was adopted. Before that, I had marveled to my father, not entirely generously, how Selene's kid was a clone of her.

When her letter didn't seem to turn my head, Selene shared with me this homily on parental authority: "If you get one who acts up a lot, just do what I did with Timmy. Tell him, 'You stop that right now or I'll send you right back where I got you.' "

"Can you believe that?" I had asked my father. "Tim's no better than he should be."

While we were in Madison, I asked Mary if she could ever adopt a child. She hesitated. "I'm not sure. To be honest, Jackie, I don't know that I could, now that I've had two of my own."

Gail, when polled, told me firmly, "I couldn't. Some people can, and some people can't, and I'm lucky I had my two, because I *never* could."

"What if you were to adopt a baby and come to find out that there had been insanity in the family?" my grandmother asked me in her best poison-syrup voice.

"He'd fit right in," I told her.

"Don't look for trouble," she warned me. "Keep trying for your own."

I dithered; was I only naive? Blinded by the need to mother? My own, our own. Adoptive parents complained about the simple devastation of that two-word qualification; and I, already putting on their shoes, began to chafe under the irritation of it. In one of my books, I had read of a woman who told an acquaintance at a party that she and her husband soon expected another baby. She caught the man glancing at her flat stomach. "We're adopting a baby," she added hastily, and was horrified when a half-hour de-programming ensued in which the man tried to convince her that "it wasn't really the same" and it was much more special to have "your own."

Why did people regard adoption as so outré, yet still see couples who adopted as makers of sacrifice, as rescuers who "took in" what someone else did not want? I bridled when Mary, all well intentioned, told me how "lucky" a child would be that we adopted. It was we who would be the lucky ones.

But I could not argue with biology. There was an all but stupefying content—especially for people like me—inherent in the miracle of conceiving and bearing a child with my body. Of seeing the ancestral jaw and nose in cunning new configurations. The powerful assurance of

272

passing along the good genetics, the squeamishness about passing along the iffy. But were these not, as my aunt in New Orleans would say, lagniappes? Bonuses rather than essentials? Pregnancy lasted nine months in its bounty, breast-feeding perhaps another nine. Mothering lasted to the last breath.

Wasn't that so? I asked Susan at the meeting. Wasn't that the bottom line?

It had been for her, she said. Motherhood had been ninety percent of it for her. But there were plenty of people—smart, openhearted people—for whom the genetic continuity was essential. "I had to let go of pregnancy and birth," she said. "It was bittersweet. I had my family, but our family is not like others. And though I was a mother, I was still an infertile mother. I still had to endure the seasons when my friends were pregnant. Still had the urge to smack them when they came over to see my baby and chatted about LaLeche."

If the child is older, or racially mixed, that's another element that sets you apart from the bulk of families, she said.

"How do you make a ten-year-old part of the family? Can it ever be a real child-and-parent relationship? Or is it like a stepfamily—in which the love is there but it's impossible ever to feel the child really is yours? You're talking about a child with memories, even if the child is as small as four."Nancy smiled. "I think there's a decent likelihood that it can all be very positive, but we have to think about these things before we rush in."

I sat crenellating the corners of my legal pad with colored pen. The confidence that surged in me when I thought about adoption had kept me afloat; but was it a sham? I thought I could win any child, bind her to me, make her—except for looks, and who cares for looks?—mine, inextricably mine. Ours, I amended, with a small mental hand slap. It took an effort to give Dan a voice in these interior debates, he was by now so far on the perimeter of them.

But how would I handle it when my Korean or Pakistani or Micronesian child asked why she looked so different from us, wondered if Daddy loved Jocelyn more because she had his eyes, his smile. And would Daddy? And how about Mommy? Would I protect too fiercely because of that differentness, compensate too dotingly?

I told the group about my inquiries into finding a healthy white infant. Lester Cranshaw, the New York attorney, had sent an application. Processing the application, his secretary had written, would cost

$250. We should expect to spend about $15,000 on the total process, she wrote.

"The ironies kill me," I told the group. "We're talking about desperate people, people who only want what is after all a good thing—to have kids. And the situation is so tight that they're all but forced to go into outrageous debt or throw away their ethics because they know that if they don't, somebody else will be more than willing to."

"What about if you go the traditional route?" Ruth asked angrily. "Like the Children's Aid Society. You attend this meeting and that meeting and this meeting, and *then* you'll only be able to proceed if yours is one of the twenty or so names they draw from the hat every three years—out of thousands of names—and *then* there's no guarantee you'll ever get a baby, or that you'll still be young enough to qualify by the time you do."

And I, who had come over the course of these group meetings to dislike Ruth, to consider her a whiner, wanted to kiss her. I said, "It's as if we've already had it so hard, and the response is to say, 'You ain't seen nothing yet. Wait 'til you see how hard it can be.' "

"It *seems* that way." Susan made a time-out gesture with both hands. "It's damned easy to get pessimistic. To get defensive. Here you are, after all, good people—infertile people are, of course, superparents," she grinned. "We'll *never* yell at our kids. We'll *never* wish we had a moment to ourselves. Anyway, we're good people, and here we're forced to undergo all this scrutiny, reveal every detail of our lives to be judged by strangers, while Joe Schmo and his wife have fourteen kids and never have to answer to anyone. . . ."

She lowered her blond head. "And then you get a kid. And you know that someday that kid is going to want to know where he came from. . . ."

"I know of one group that finds babies," Ruth broke in, "but they require the adopting parents to accept a letter from the birth mother, to be given to the kid when he's old enough to understand it, and also require the parents to send the agency yearly photos and progress reports to be given to the birth mother. What the hell does that make me, then? A baby-sitter?"

"That's outrageous," Susan said flatly. "But if you adopt a kid, that kid is going to have questions. I still wrestle with it. And I'll tell you the truth, sometimes I think I'm going to tell my kids whatever I know, but if they want to go searching as adults, I'm not going to be all that comfortable with it. I don't intend to make any secret of the fact that I believe I'm their *mother* and their father's their *father."*

She made a slow circuit of the room with her eyes. "It ain't easy."

Back in Chicago, we were watching "60 Minutes" with Jocelyn. "I said I wanted to watch TV," she was griping. "You call this TV? This is just a guy talking." But Dan and I tuned her out. "The guy," Mike Wallace, was talking about another guy—an auto parts dealer by the name of Artie Elgart who lived in Pennsylvania and liked to call himself Mr. Stork.

It was not a misnomer, judging from the panning shot of the photos that lined the walls of his office. Elgart found babies for couples to adopt, and try as they might, Wallace admitted, the "60 Minutes" staff could not uncover any way he profited from it. Sure he profited, Elgart corrected, placing a hand on his chest. "Here."

Elgart's Golden Cradle put mothers who wished to offer their babies for adoption in touch with families for the babies—if the girls needed a place to stay, they often stayed with one of the adoptive families, though not the one who would receive that girl's baby.

The prospective parents paid for medical care, clothing, housing—they paid Elgart not a dime. The sequence was something of a minidocumentary on the difficulty of locating adoptable babies. A couple were interviewed who had advertised in papers all across the country, who had had a telephone installed in their home to serve strictly as an adoption "hotline."

But it came back to Elgart. To one of the birth mothers describing the sweet pain of giving up "the best part of me." To an auburn-haired adopting mother recreating the moment of the phone call—Elgart's "Congratulations! You're a mom." To Elgart's own wife and sons playing with him on their living room floor. They had adopted a baby, and six weeks later had learned they were pregnant.

"My husband had really wanted a son," said one of the adopting mothers. "And when the call came, and we knew we had a daughter, I was a little worried and I asked him, 'Are you disappointed? Even a little?' And he just looked at our little girl and said, 'She's . . . she's terrific!' "

Dan and I turned to each other, eyes streaming, as the sequence closed. "That'll never be us," I said. "Do you think that we . . . ?"

"Jackie, I hope so."
"You do? You honestly do? You're willing?"
"I'm willing." I threw my arms around his head.
"But why? Why now?"
"I don't know why. Don't ask."
"Geez," said Jocelyn. "You guys cry more than me."

Twenty-eight days after I stopped taking the Danazol, there was a spot of blood on my nightgown. "Good old body," I said. But that was it. There was no period. My basal temperature chart for the past month looked like the Grand Tetons. Clarke, when I called him in New Orleans, told me that it was not uncommon to skip an ovulation after completing the course of medication. I might have to be "started," he said. I would not do it, I told him. One of the qualifications for the VIP program for in-vitro fertilization was that the woman must never have undergone ovulatory stimulation. If it ever came to that, I would not be eliminated on a technicality.

Then wait, Clarke counseled. A few more weeks.

I waited. I used up bags of cotton balls, testing for blood. Took hot baths. I worked. I ate. I did not call Laura and made lame allusions to time-consuming projects when she called me. "I'm really getting involved with writing again," I lied to Laura. "It feels great." The fact of it was that I could never remember what any of the columns I sent weekly to Carol were about. And the book. The book was precisely seven pages long. I now had an agent, and I wanted to run every time she phoned.

It was a time for odd perceptions. Odd distances. I felt I had been cryogenized, an abstraction frozen in the shape of a woman, waiting to resume life. I watched the comings and goings of people with an alien consciousness, as if I were walking underwater, sealed off from their time, their oxygen, their reasonings and consequences.

There is one entry for April in my spiral notebook. My friend Hannah told me that she had not menstruated for two months when she stopped taking birth control pills—because she had become pregnant during the second month.

The rest of the pages are blank. I lay with the notebook on my stomach, looking at my bedroom ceiling, wondering how many overreactions added up to a psychosis.

Some redux.

My grandmother is going through my clothes closet on a Saturday morning as I lie on the bed, trying to sleep late.

"Why don't you sell this suit?" she asks me. My eyes are closed. Why doesn't she notice that? Would I ask someone questions whose eyes were closed? "Look at this pretty thing—the tags are still right on it. Why don't you just take a garment bag and bundle these things up and take them down to the encore store?"

"They're my clothes."

"But you don't wear them."

"They don't fit me at present."

"So, why don't you . . . ?"

"I intend for them to fit me in future."

"Ahhhhhh."

"What . . . ahhhhhh? What does that mean?"

"Just that, honey, you've had that extra weight for a while now. . . ."

"Nine months! Not long enough to start selling my clothes!"

"By the time you get back into them, they won't be in style."

"Tailored suits are always in style."

But the next week, I find myself taking out a few of the soft flannel slacks and blazers, folding the flowered lawn prairie skirt over a hanger (how long has it been since anyone wore a prairie skirt?). I am about to zip the garment bag when it strikes me that the last time I did such an inventory was in weeding my mother's clothes a month after her funeral. To hell with that! Back into the closet it goes—prairie skirt and all.

Gail's baby was christened on the first warm Sunday in April. Dan went to it alone.

31 WE HAD the sugar snow late one night, and woke up to its tracery on the windows of our room. They don't call it the sugar snow in Chicago. They call it a slow rush hour. This made Dan, who is weather-obsessed, feel fairly wistful as he set out on his long trek to work. He wondered aloud whether the bright green tongues of tulip shoots would be coming up in our driveway back in Madison. He said he would check.

"They'll survive long enough to be tulips for the first time," I said. "The dog isn't there to eat them. But we won't be there to see them, either."

After he left, I called Bellow for a summit conference. It had been seven and a half weeks since I had stopped taking the Danazol. I wanted answers. So what if he had never had a patient fail to resume ovulating after Danazol. Here was his first.

"Maybe you should ask Bellow to give you the fertility drugs, the way Clarke suggested," Dan had urged me. "What's the difference? Maybe it will improve our chances."

"But then what if my body came to require that stimulation?" I fretted. "That happens. Some women take it once, and then they can never ovulate again on their own. I'd never be able to have in vitro. The rules say it's only for people who never required ovulatory stimulation." Dan had clamped his lips. His position still was that unless I wrote a best-seller, or inherited wealth, in vitro was out of the question.

I had visited my dad's friend the gynecologist a couple of times. Once there had been a nagging knot of pain low in the left side of my abdomen. An instant's puzzlement had come over the fellow's face as he palpated my left side. Then he said, "Of course, the first thing I thought of was another ectopic. But there's no evidence of that, Jackie."

He'd suggested gas. Constipation. Maybe ovulation.

The second time I visited had been just a few days ago. My dad's friend couldn't say why I hadn't yet menstruated; he spread his hands wide in a gesture of helplessness. He wasn't an infertility specialist. But he had taken a long look at my temperature charts, which had been peculiar, unaccountably remaining high for the past ten days.

"When I see something like this, I normally think the woman is documenting a pregnancy," he'd told me. I had dropped by his lab for a blood test on the way out. The lab would call me in twenty-four hours with the results.

I mentioned it to Bellow now. "This guy seems to think I might be pregnant."

"Well, that's just wonderful!"

"Yeah."

"Yeah? You've been struggling to get pregnant for a year and thinking about hardly anything else and somebody tells you that you might be pregnant and you say, 'Yeah'?"

"I'm not pregnant."

"How can you tell?"

"No symptoms."

"It would be too early for symptoms."

I was not pregnant. I intuited that. But what the hell. Why not make the most of the feeling while it lasted? I had not told Dan about this before, but after I got off the phone with Bellow, I called him at his office. "Guess what? My dad's friend told me that my charts seem to indicate a pregnancy, and I just talked to Bellow and he thinks that might be true, too."

"Honey, that's marvelous. Wouldn't that just be the most miraculous thing? On our first try? That means the baby would be born around Christmas. Think what a Christmas present that would be. . . ." Poor love, I thought. I shouldn't have told him.

I had no important writing to do, so I decided to go to the exercise class I had signed up for when we moved. I had signed up, but I'd never as yet gone. "Are there fat folk in it?" I had asked one of my cousins, who lived down the street and had been in the class for several years.

The class met on the second floor of a reconverted school building. I put on my boots over leotards and headed over there. I wandered around the empty halls. Suddenly, I heard an approaching stampede. Around the corner came a gang of beautiful people in bright exercise togs, chatting and laughing as they huffed through the hall. "Okay!" cried the most beautiful of all, a sweet-faced blonde woman in peacock tights. "Let's get those heart rates up!"

In mid-leap, she caught a look at me, stopped, and studied my face. "Are you in the class?" she asked.

"Uhhhhh," I said.

"I know you," she said. "You're Bobby's sister."

"I am."

"I'm Katie Downey. Well, I was Katie Downey. Now I'm Katie Stankowski."

"Some change!" Some change, indeed, I thought. *This* was chubby little Katie Downey, who'd had a crush on my brother in the third grade? The last time I had seen Katie, she had been a round seventh grader in a cheerleader's uniform.

"I read your stories," she said. "About not having a baby."

"How did you . . . ?" In Chicago? Half the people in Madison didn't even read those stories, I thought.

"Bobby gave them to my husband. They play basketball together at the Y. Didn't you know?"

"I didn't. We just moved back here, and Dan still isn't in his new job yet, and I've been so busy. I haven't seen Bobby in a week. So, how are you? You're marvelous looking."

"Well, thanks," she said. But then, unaccountably, tears filled her eyes. "I'm actually not terrific. I just found out, about a month ago, that I'm not going to be able to have kids. My husband, Chuck, told your brother. That's why he gave us the stories. Endometriosis," she said.

The class gaped. "Go on, guys," she recovered, airily. "I'll be right with you." She turned back to me. "The thing is, I try not to think about it. I just put it out of my mind entirely when the doctor told me."

"Didn't you . . . didn't you know that there was something you could do about it?"

"Ecceek! That awful drug. Or surgery. No way. I couldn't do that stuff to my body." I could see why. It was sculpture. "I just kept thinking, what if the weight gain was permanent? God, I couldn't have stood that. Did you take it?"

"I did. I guess that's pretty apparent."

"Hey," she said kindly. "You're okay. It's easy to get skinny from where you are. I just . . . I admired you for the way you dealt with the emotions. I couldn't deal with them at all. So I just didn't. I just went on."

"For that, I admire you. That's what I'm trying to do."

"So you never did get pregnant?"

"Not yet."

"Well, good luck. Maybe someday, if it turns out to be that important to me, I'll investigate some treatment . . . I just don't know. My marriage seems fine the way it is."

"Mine was, too."

"What?"

"Nothing. Good luck to you, too." She bounded away, her ass the size of a baseball cap. Another, I marveled. The statistics must be wrong—one in six couples must be a conservative figure. The more people who knew I was infertile, the more infertile people I met. That was not so startling as the fact that they emerged from women I had already categorized as quintessentially normal—the stylish women in ads downstairs in my building, university professors, even my high school heroine.

I had met her at the cosmetics counter at Marshall Field's just after Christmas. Had it been seven years, or longer? Jennifer and I couldn't remember. The last time I had seen her, I had been substituting at a high school where she'd been assistant chair of the science department. We hadn't yet lost touch then, and she'd got me the three-week job. Now, except for Christmas cards, we scarcely communicated. Her cards were travelogues, résumés. They'd been to Japan, to Hong Kong, to Paris, more times than I could count. She taught physics at the university level now, was well, if discreetly, published, and was studying for her doctorate.

"It used to give me comfort that you were a year ahead of me," I told her, after we'd exchanged the obligatory have-you-seen, do-you-still-see news of old friends become acquaintances. "Now that standard has become sort of moot. Jennifer, I stand in awe."

She'd actually blushed, caught midway through a fantastic account of some seminar she'd attended in Nepal. "But you travel. . . ."

"Travel? My dear, the closest I've ever got to Paris is buying a steamship ticket with Laura a year after we graduated. We were going to rent a garret and hang around the Ritz bar, trying to absorb great-writer vibrations. But Laura fell in love a month before we sailed."

"What did you do?"

"Well, I fell in love, too."

"Mmmmm. Falling in love doesn't preclude doing something with your life."

"Now hold on a darn minute. . . ."

"I didn't mean that. Scratch that. I mean going places, doing things. Learning, when you're amazed to find you're not too old for wonder. . . ." I watched her, amused. She had been a titan in high school

—editor of this, queen of that, cheerleader, academic, athlete, National Merit scholar. Once, when she'd tried out for varsity cheerleading and taken a scholarship exam on the same morning, I'd asked her, "Don't you ever get nervous? With all of it?"

"No," she answered. "I always get what I want." It had offended me then. I'd heard in it an offhand slight. Now, hell, I couldn't argue. Perhaps attitude, as I read inside matchbook covers, was all.

"It's just a matter of priorities. You bought a house, I rent an apartment, the cheaper the better. When they co-op, we move. I was lucky enough to find a guy who shared my priorities. . . ."

"I guess our priorities, or mine, were having kids." I didn't have to explain. She'd run into my dad a few months earlier, and he'd given her the lowdown on me. "I thought you always wanted kids, Jen. Remember in high school, you said you'd want at least four, all boys . . . ?"

"That was a million years ago." She half-turned from me, fingering some wildly expensive jar of face cream on the counter. "I can't have kids," she said.

"How . . . how do you know?"

"Well, I've never used a thing, and I've never got pregnant. And . . . I . . . don't have many periods, maybe a few a year. I know something's peculiar."

"Have you ever seen a doctor?"

"Jack, I'm in science. And if that has taught me nothing else, it's that biology is damned hard to contradict. Whatever I have, it seems fairly profound, and starting some quest to treat it probably would only lead to frustration, not to mention a whole lot of expense. I just crossed it off." And then she smiled and said, as if she'd read my mind, "Half of always getting what you want is never wanting what you can't have."

I stood in the school hallway now, transfixed, watching the lovely exercise instructor. She and Jennifer are not all that different, I thought. It was a way. Not the way I had chosen, but it would take shutters over the eyes not to see the advantages of choosing to cope by avoiding. A person could live without children, a person could be damned happy.

There was an exhilaration in even thinking this—even in allowing myself to think of childlessness in terms of advantage.

I had been talking to some unmarried mothers recently for a possible story. We talked about the peer rejection they experienced, about the impossibility of a social life, about having the flu and a nine-month-old and wondering what to do with him while you threw up.

And, amazing to me, it had not been horrible. When one of the mothers complained that her family had called her selfish for willingly undertaking to raise a child who would never know his father, I found I could consider it. I could consider that there might be a circumstance in which having a baby could be selfish, that given the same opportunity, I might hesitate for the child's sake.

It was a kind of joy even to be able to give full face and value to these women's problems. A month earlier, I could not have done it. I'd have scorned them for carping about money and loneliness. Didn't they have *children*, after all? Didn't they have what I craved? Wasn't it craven to complain in the face of such richness?

But no. Of course it was not. As the oft-pregnant receptionist had schooled me, a season ago, parents have problems, too. Much as I still wanted their problems, I could look at them with some dispassion. I could pity Laura, whose beautiful Michael was now an awful baby, who screamed as routinely as he drew breath. When Richard traveled, which he had to, often, Laura literally could not put the baby down while he was awake. She could not shower. She could not talk on the phone. There was no one to spell her. I had tried, but Michael sobbed in any arms but his mother's. One look at his grandmother and he howled. "I love him so," she told me one day, "that sometimes I just cry for happiness at his being. But my God, Jack, it's not all roses. We're worn out. We take him for rides in the car at midnight, just to get him to fall asleep, and then as soon as we're back in the door, he wakes and cries. And we're off again, up those dark, quiet streets, exhausted. . . ." I offered to take Michael for a full evening. "Would you?" she breathed, and then, "No. It's no use. He'd just scream." But hadn't I thought of Laura's interrupted sleep with envy then? Put it down to hyperbole when she described waking in the dark, unaware that she'd slept, unsure whether she'd put the baby in his crib or fallen asleep while she held him and dropped him on the floor?

I told Dan about it that night. "I guess those are revelations to you," he said, smiling. "Don't get me wrong. I'm not knocking it. It's a healthy sign."

I awakened in the night, conscious of an odd, queasy heaviness, and went into the bathroom. When I came to bed, Dan was awake, sitting up. "I'm not pregnant," I told him. "But don't be sad." I took Bellow's tack. "If you can accept it, this is progress."

It did not feel like progress. As I lay in bed, I could feel the silence descending, the old separateness. Be gone, I told it. I'm through with you. Redux. Redux. But the next morning, I could feel it on me, a blight. Jennifer was Jennifer; I was I. It would take a hell of a peak in the Himalayas to erase this need from my spirit.

"Let's go away," I urged Dan. "Just a weekend. In a few weeks, when I'm fertile again. Make a baby in some nice old inn someplace." We hadn't been out of town, except to New Orleans, since July. Money had dictated a cancellation of our customary two weeks at my dad's place in Florida, slothful weeks of floating around on some seedy deep-sea fishing boat, of living in swimsuits. Susan, still feeling we'd put a whammy on her cabin in Door County, had offered us a free week up there in the still winter woods. But I still could not face that strip of carpet in the hall where I had lain my cheek, or that bed where I'd felt my life draining away.

Dan suggested we go back to Galena, a little town in Illinois where we'd spent our first anniversary. Galena is a river town, the hometown of Ulysses Grant, and has become over the years a sort of five-street antique shop. Dan could browse for Civil War regimentals in the bookstores; I could toast my toes in front of the fireplace in a room of the old reconverted mansion we'd stayed in before. It would be fun. Good memories. I booked a room.

Before we left, we had a visit with Dan's brother and his wife, who were up from Florida for two weeks. They'd hoped to take in a White Sox game, but it was cold and there were no good boxes available, so we made plans to meet at a Mexican restaurant on the north side. Dan phoned first to make sure hamburgers were on the menu; Rick's tastes did not run to the exotic. It was a family joke that he would eat no vegetables he could not certify were canned, and his wife considered it a major event in their marriage when he broke down and ate a stuffed mushroom on their anniversary.

We stopped on the way at Ann's house to pick up Gail and her husband; his mother was going to keep the kids overnight. Little Jason, now more than four months old, was lying kicking on a blanket in the living room. "He's changed so much," Dan said, scooping up his small nephew. "He's a real little kid now."

"What about you, Jackie?" Gail asked me pointedly. "Do you think he's changed?" I had not seen Jason for three months; I didn't know what was expected of me.

"He's certainly bigger," I offered weakly. Damn. What could I say?

Was his hair longer, his cheeks more plump? All I remembered of Jason was a fuzzy little head above a receiving blanket. I smiled, made small noises I hoped were appreciative. She did not offer me the baby to hold and I didn't ask. Ann grinned nervously and hustled Jason upstairs. Dan followed, and they talked a little business. Ann wanted to know if Dan was ready to go full-time. Dan still wasn't sure. I could feel Gail's eyes on my face, and wondered if I was forming frost. What was getting to her so badly? We had not been particularly communicative of late, and that was unusual since I had tried, since Dan and I married, to make Gail as much friend as relative—she had had her problems with Joan, small ones, granted, but I had not wanted to foster even a small breach. All this could not be the result of a few fewer telephone conversations, a few fewer visits.

I didn't ask. When Rick and Ginny met us, I let them do the talking. We admired drawings of the house they wanted to have built when they moved back to Chicago the following year. It would be great, Rick said, the brothers and sisters all in one place again.

We ate our tacos and drank our margaritas and Dan talked about his court case, coming up in just a few weeks. Joan had thrown a new wrench into the works. Jocelyn had just told us she was registered for Girl Scout camp, that week having been lopped off what was to have been Dan's time. "Mommy wanted to do it before you figured out when you wanted me in the summer," Jocelyn told Dan with childish candor.

Joan had been just as candid with Gail. "I don't know Jackie and I probably never will," she'd told her former sister-in-law. "But I just don't want Jocelyn brought up around her. If it was Dan on his own, I wouldn't mind how much time Jocelyn spent with him." Gail loyally reported the substance of the conversation to Dan, who took notes for his lawyer.

"It sounds like something any judge will have heard a time or two," Rick said now. "I think you'll have a pretty good shot."

We parted with kisses all around, and I was proud. I had not said a single word about babies or surgeries. I had smiled at all the right moments. I wanted Dan to pat me on the back. Instead, he said sourly, "You were magnificent. You didn't say a word all night."

"I wasn't unfriendly. Only quiet. Lots of people are quiet."

"But you're not. You used to act like a one-woman vaudeville team. Didn't you see how strangely they were looking at you?"

"Dan, I honestly didn't. Only Gail, I can't figure that out. . . ."

"Well, I can. She's told me. After the christening, we had this long talk. Lots of shouting . . ."

"Shouting?"

"Well, she's very angry, Jack. I had to try to calm her, and explain that you've been behaving strangely because of worry over the effects of the drug and all. . . ."

"Explain what? What have I done to Gail?"

"Honey, she's been pretty put off by your behavior around her baby. She has the idea that you tried to make her feel guilty about her pregnancy, and that you gave the baby dirty looks the single time you came to see him."

"Dirty looks? Oh, Dan, come on. I may be flaky, but I don't give four-month-olds dirty looks."

"I told her that I defended you. But she's just a very . . . she's a very emotional woman. You should understand that. And she feels you've been avoiding her and her baby as a personal slight."

"That's absurd."

"I think so, too. But hey, just fake it if you have to, hon. For the sake of family unity. Gail means well."

"When we get home, I'll call her, then. And I'll send a note to Rick and Gin. How's that?"

"Fine," he sighed. "Thank you."

We spent the evening stretched out on a huge cannonball four-poster at the inn, drinking champagne out of water tumblers and watching waves of flame leap in the fireplace. "This was a good idea," Dan said. "I wonder what the poor are doing tonight?"

"Probably freezing their toes, as I am." I got up from the bed to poke at the fire. "I can see why God made the space heater." He was silent. I turned to him. "What are you looking at?"

"You. Just wishing I could make love to you."

"You can make love to me."

"Okay. Now." He put out his arms.

"Not right now. Relax first."

Dan sulked. "You always put me off. You want a back rub. A hot bath. You're starting to remind me of Joan. One false move and a button goes off—'Not enough foreplay!' It used to be so . . . spontaneous with us."

"You mean you didn't have to put forth so much effort."

"You just used to be . . . you'd heat up faster. . . ."

"So now I'm slower. Big deal. I still get there. I've had a time of it,

Dan. I'm trying to reacquaint myself with sex, and I'm finding that the things that once turned me on have changed a bit. I'm thirty, Dan. Not seventeen. And where is it written that back rubs and necking on the sofa are the antidote to passion?"

"Okay. Relaxation you want, relaxation you'll get." He padded naked over to the chair where he'd thrown his coat and retrieved a joint from the pocket. "Present from Gail's husband," he grinned.

"Oh, Dan. I just said I wasn't seventeen anymore. Are we now going to be thirty-year-old druggies?"

"We're not druggies. But we used to be potties. Occasionally. Jack, it's not as if I pulled out a syringe and a spoon."

"It's not that. Pot affects the sperm count. You know that. And we're supposed to be trying . . ."

"Damn it. Woman, you've already got me wearing baggy underwear —I'm embarrassed to change my clothes at the racquetball club. I take lukewarm baths, when I prefer them scalding, I sleep naked, so as not to crowd the balls. Maybe if a man smoked dope every day, every week even, it would have an effect, but this is just a little toke. . . ."

I gave in. After a while, I asked, "Don't you wish you could sing?"

"I do," said Dan, staring at the ceiling. "I used to have dreams in which I was on stage with the Rolling Stones, and Mick Jagger was saying, 'Come on, man, we all know you've got a fantastic voice. . . .' "

"Imagine. Just opening your mouth and being able to sing. Or play a musical instrument."

"I'd like to play the banjo." We giggled.

"I'd like to pay the tonette. Anything. The spoons. But especially the piano. Couldn't you just see it, out at the end of the pier on a summer night . . ."

"Playing the piano?" He rolled me over at belly level, and I nuzzled his silky crotch. "Mmmmm, nice. Do that."

"Dan, we're supposed to be trying . . ."

"Just this once. Let's do it for us. Not pregnancy. Just us."

And so we did.

There was a note on the corkboard next to the phone. "Call Gail." I'd forgotten. Weeks had passed. Good weeks, though. It had been a glorious May, and it was a better June. Nights unbearable with clear moonlight, windy days of mile-tall clouds. I'd given Dan a used telescope for our anniversary—purchased at a steal from a gay dentist who was breaking up his entire household and moving to San Francisco in despair after splitting with his lover of nine years—and we'd spent midnights on my dad's roof. I had never seen the rings of Saturn, the amber bands on the surface of Jupiter. Dan delighted in making the introduction. "There's nothing wrong with us," Dan exulted, periodically. "Isn't it nice not to be miserable?"

Our first try at pregnancy had been of no avail. But there were plenty of rationalizations to be had—only one tube, remember; the Omega Institute estimated most pregnancies occurred between the ninth and eighteenth month after surgery. Physically, I had experienced what would be a familiar pattern. For the first ten days after I ovulated, I felt, or imagined, secret stirrings. Was it? Was it not? And then, three or four days before I was to have my period, I knew I had not conceived. There was no signal headache, no cramp, just a flaccid, giving-in feeling. A down afternoon, a needy night. Dan was good. The overall lightening of my mood gave him room for empathy. "Next month," he said. "Summer."

So, in an expansive mood one night after supper, I put aside my book work and called Gail.

"Hi," she said. And I noticed right away. She had not said, "What're you doing?" Gail always said, "What're you doing?" even if you jumped in and told her before she could say it, to head it off.

"Hi." Might as well get to it. "Honey, I called for a special reason. Dan says you've been upset with me. And I want to apologize. I haven't meant to put you off. . . ."

"That's fine."

"I mean, I never meant to hurt your feelings."

"It doesn't matter. It's pretty clear that you're ignoring me. You could not have been more obvious." So. This wasn't going to be easy. Well, I thought. Let her have her raps. For family unity. "The thing I didn't like is when you started taking it out on Jason. I know you have bad feelings, but I can't believe you could take those feelings out on an innocent child."

"Gail, I don't think Jason's old enough to realize whatever I felt. . . ."

"Oh, yes he is. You don't have kids, so you don't realize how sensitive they can be. When you didn't want to hold him, I was glad, Jackie. I didn't want him to feel all the negative things coming from you toward him."

"Negative things? I don't feel anything negative about the baby. If there was anything, it was only a sorrow. . . ."

"Ann wanted to take the baby upstairs last time you came over, out of your sight. But I told her, 'No way! I'm tired of kowtowing to her! I want to see how she reacts.' "

"And I reacted all right, I suppose. You know, Jason's adorable. . . ."

"All right? You wouldn't even look at him. Except to give him dirty looks." There they were. The "dirty looks." She was working herself into high passion. "That's why I kept asking you if he'd changed since the last time you saw him. I was asking you if he really was so ugly to you."

"I see."

"You don't know how many changes you've put me through. First, you entirely ruined my pregnancy. Here it was the most joyous part of my life, and you were ruining it. And you didn't even stop to think what you were doing."

But I'm stopping to think now, Gail, I thought, and I think you have a lot of nerve and precious little else. But I said, "That was never intended."

"Maybe not." She would give me that. Then, "But maybe so. I talked to Jeanine about this." Jeanine, a friend of Ann's, was a psychiatrist. "I had to, because every time you'd come over—or rather, Dan would come over, and make excuses for you. Nick and I would have horrible fights. Worse fights than we'd ever had before." Indeed, Gail, I thought nastily, recalling the several early bouts in their marriage in which the neighbors had called the cops to referee.

"Jeanine said I was dealing with some anxiety, but that I shouldn't take your reactions so personally."

"I think she's right."

"She *also* said you were in very bad need of professional help. Not that group, or whatever, that you went to in Madison. That is the worst thing you could do. Like a bunch of divorced people sitting around talking about how bad they feel, with other divorced people. You need someone to tell you to snap out of it."

"It seems you're doing just that."

"Okay, Jackie. It doesn't matter what you think of me. What I care about is my brother. And it's terrible for him, living with you."

"He doesn't seem to mind."

"What can he say? He tells me how it feels. It got to the point where

Nick told me that if I couldn't stop feeling this way, we just wouldn't see you anymore. And that if I wouldn't tell Danny, he would. Nick couldn't stand seeing me upset this way. If you had been a friend, reacting so negatively to my baby, you know, I would have said, 'Well, screw her.' But I couldn't, because you're family."

"Gail, don't you think you're reacting rather strongly? I've been terribly depressed, and I guess I've been fairly awful to be around, but look, I think you're making too much of it. . . ."

"Me making too much of it? Jackie, you're the one who's made too much of it. Rick and Gin couldn't have kids. But they didn't try to ruin other people's lives because of it. A couple of weeks ago, I tried to explain to them in the car what was going on with you—it was real plain something was going on—and they said they understood. That they went through some changes themselves for a while when they couldn't have kids. But they kept it to themselves. They didn't . . . spill it all over the place."

An embarrassment. An image of me spilling moans all over the place. "I didn't mean to do that."

"They *adjusted* to it. You haven't."

"Gail, I'm trying."

"Do you know what Danny said when I told him how I felt about all this? He tried to tell me that the way you felt about losing your baby was the way you would feel about losing a child! And that was the stupidest, stupidest thing I'd ever heard. As if you could care as much about losing a pregnancy as about losing a real, live baby. Something you've held and loved."

"Gail, believe me, it's hard to understand, but it's not so different."

"That's ridiculous."

"Gail, it's as if I were a . . . runner or something, and I'd injured my leg and couldn't run again. For a while, it just seemed as though I wanted to avoid those who could run. . . ."

"Well, that's all wrong. When Ann had her leg operation and couldn't ski, she still went to ski lodges." Don't be so fucking literal, I thought, angry now. Hear me. And then Gail said, "I don't think you really love babies. If you really loved babies, and you couldn't have any, you'd still want to be around babies. All the babies you could."

"Gail, if you were in that position, if you didn't have your own, I think you'd feel differently."

"No I wouldn't. At least I'd be coping with it."

Oh, yes, my dear. You are a champion coper. You and Nick, arguing in the gangway, kicking the doors of each other's cars. I won't hear this. I won't hear another word, I thought, but then I thought, Dan. Family. And I thought, you have done your share of raving, too.

And I said, "Gail, I love babies. I wouldn't have gone through all this mess if I didn't love babies."

"Are you sure it isn't just because for once in your life you couldn't have something that you wanted? Are you sure you aren't going to find out that it wasn't really children you wanted—only your own way?"

"That's unfair. I'm willing to listen, if you tell me rationally what's on your mind, but that's unfair."

"Unfair? You told your brother and Sandy not to have a baby before you did. That's unfair."

"I never told them that."

"If you truly loved your brother, you'd be glad he wasn't in your shoes. You'd want him to have what you couldn't have. How can you be so selfish? You made Bobby and Sandy feel really awkward about something that's none of your business."

"I agree it's none of my business. But I never said that to them." But had I? Between the lines if not in fact? In October, at the mailbox in Madison? Bobby's face, when he'd told me he and Sandy were ready to start a family. "At any rate, none of it was personal. None of it was intended to hurt." Or only a little of it. But Gail, you've got me cornered. I can't admit that now, I thought.

"Well, all right. I accept your apology."

By that point, I didn't want her to accept it. I wanted to bash the phone through the typewriter. Controlling the quaver in my voice, I told her good-bye, thanks for sharing her feelings, and put down the receiver. In an instant, I picked it up again. Called my brother.

He was entertaining a fraternity brother from out of town. They were just ready to leave for dinner. "Okay. But I have to ask you something. I just had a really remarkable conversation with Gail. She says . . . Bobby, she says I forced you and Sandy not to have a child. Did I do that?"

"I didn't tell her that."

"What did you tell her?"

"I told her we had decided not to try for a while."

"Why?"

"Oh, money. Wanting to change jobs. A lot of things."

"Mostly me?"

291

"Mostly you."

"But why? How could you have let me do such a thing to you? How could you have let me make you . . . ?"

"You didn't make us. We decided to."

"Why didn't you tell me?"

"Because, Sis, because I didn't want you to feel just the way you feel now."

I could not tell him how I loved him. How the inexpressible dearness of him filled my eyes. "You . . . just chose to make it easy on me, Sandy and you."

"Don't make a big deal out of it."

"It's a big deal. It's a very big deal."

"It's not so big. We just love you. You know?"

"Kiss Sandra for me."

"I will."

"Kiss yourself for me."

"That's harder."

"Tell Sandy to."

"Okay." He cupped the phone. "Wife, kiss me. There. Now, you take care."

"Bobby . . . I . . ."

"I know. Get pregnant. Is Dan home tonight? Go get pregnant."

"Okay."

I hung up the phone and put my head down on my typewriter and wept. Strange tears, thankfulness and resentment, and something else, old tears. As the poet Heine had written, tears left over from feelings felt long ago, belonging to another time. There had been a day last summer, when we were driving home from work and had come over the hill onto our street, and there, on the bank that sloped down to the lake, had been a group of toddlers in red and yellow slickers against the warm drizzle, tumbling chunky-legged down the lawn, chasing a group of ducks hightailing it for the lakeshore. Dan had braked, and we'd heard one little boy say, "And when we catch them, we will hug them, very hard."

And we had sat there, both of us not speaking, thinking, as surely as if we had spoken it, will ours be there? Next summer? In another summer to come? Will we come over the rise and see a brown-eyed one, with short legs like her father's and her mother's skinny spider fingers, dancing hatless in the rain?

And I had cried then, and cried now, for the knowledge that even if she never was there in fact, I would continue to look for her, in school yards, out of the corner of my eye—see her at three, at six, gradually dimming, but never gone. I could not outrun her.

But I could put her to one side! I could heal. These tears that pelted the dusty spaces between the keys were tears a life could be lived around. Not tears that burned, and threatened, that set me apart. I was ready to go back in, though the new world of my family would be full of new babies. I was ready for Jason. For Bobby's children when they came. There was relief in it. Let the world come.

"JUST lick them," I begged Dan. "I had them printed, I addressed them, and my licker is getting worn out." "Your licker is not being used to its best advantage," he told me mildly. But he acquiesced, and began sealing and fixing stamps to the pile of 150 legal-sized envelopes I had piled on the coffee table.

They each contained the same letter. I had composed it over weeks —in my notebook, typing it and retyping it, whittling it down to one tightly packed page, fussing over the language. It had to be supplicant, but not meeching—urgent, but not desperate. We had to sound like salt-of-the-earth but not sticks-in-the-mud. I had to be careful not even to seem to offer a money transaction. "Dear Doctor," it began. "This may be the first letter of this kind you've ever received, or you may have received a great many. In either case, please read it, please know that it is sincere, and consider whether you may be able to offer your help to two people in need of it."

I had photocopied addresses of obstetricians and gynecologists from the telephone books of towns all around the Midwest—Ohio, Illinois, Iowa—not Michigan, because as best as I could determine, Michigan did not have a law allowing private adoption. I avoided the listings for large cities; it seemed to me that urban doctors, with huge practices, would have ample connections and opportunities if presented with a child the birth mother wished to offer for independent adoption.

Not only that. The big public and private agencies held sway in the cities, and agencies cast a cold eye on private adoption. Not only were the occasions for abuse rife, it was the opinion of many agencies that private adoption drained away the precious few healthy infants they could offer to their duly certified and patient clients.

Yet an agency representative, from one of the Illinois diocesan organizations, admitted to me that couples who longed for a child virtually were being forced out of the mainstream into alternative tributaries by the waiting periods endemic to agency placements. Sometimes, by the time the paperwork was squared away, the infants they could place were up to four months old. "And that makes a great deal of difference to some people," he said.

And I said, "I couldn't see how it would." I was not a mother. Even six-month-old babies seemed impossibly little to me.

"You'd be surprised," he sighed.

I'd chosen small towns, towns that had perhaps a single gynecologist or family practitioner, a single clinic. My father's friend, the obstetrician, who had had no good news for us as yet, had suggested this. I pictured these independent doctors with their fingers firm on the pulses of their communities—aware, with laconic fatherliness, of who was expecting and in trouble. I pictured the towns peopled by hometown girls, not ignorant girls, but girls without the veneer of sophistication that would make a fast trip to the downtown abortion clinic the least troublesome alternative.

I pictured our baby growing inside one of them.

This struck Dan as among the more cockamamie of my schemes. "Do you think you're the first one to have ever hit on this idea?" he asked me. He got a kick out of our friend Michael, who was a printer, taking the letter to his plant under cover of darkness and printing out free copies for me on nice bond, and of me overworking the copying machine at my father's office nights, and rifling the yellow pages for towns with names like Bevier and Wauconda and New Scott.

Not the least of his concerns was that he considered my efforts wildly premature—we'd after all only begun to try on our own. "A year from now, I'd be willing to get behind this," he said. "Now, it just seems like a waste of postage."

"But say it doesn't work," I reasoned. "That a year from now, eighteen months from now, I'm still not pregnant. These things take time. I'm not expecting a doctor to get our letter and say to himself, 'Good gracious! Here is someone to give this baby I'm about to deliver.' I'm just hoping to plant a seed—no pun intended—in someone's mind. Maybe there'll be a doctor who'll keep our letter in his files. And maybe, a year down the road, if something should come up, he'll call us."

Dan and I did not travel in advantaged circles; we knew plenty of doctors and attorneys, but they were acquaintances, not intimates. We had no sister-in-law completing her residency; the closest to that was Joan's husband, Jerry, and though he was a kindly man, it seemed far-fetched to think he would canvas his colleagues to help find his wife's ex a baby. Yet I had taken Peter Briggs' advice about trying to establish a network. My brother had alerted his huge office full of engineers. My cousins in Minnesota and Florida had shown my letter to their doctors and their friends. My father had told all the physicians at his club. Even my housekeeper, Joanna, back in Madison, was keeping her ear to the ground at college.

None of these avenues, however, seemed to augur well for getting a baby, and that made for frustration. I was not convinced that I would never eventually become pregnant, yet some indefinable sense kept telling me that eventually, if it came, was many more months and complications distant. I wanted to begin our family, as Shapiro had put it, yesterday.

How to convey that in a letter, without seeming to indicate that Dan and I were drowning in our marriage and viewed a baby as some sort of living life preserver? That was not true, or at any rate, true no longer. The first frantic need had subsided. It had been as much a need to reestablish myself as normal, to convince me that what had happened constituted only a detour, that my dreams would wind out uninterrupted, as it had been a desire to have a child. Now infertility was a fact of our lives. But the wish to love our own child shone through, clear and unshaken. I thought we would be wasted on childlessness.

The letter was of the essence. It would have to set us apart, and on paper we sounded like Mr. and Mrs. Middle Class Average. Nothing stood out. I had taken care to place myself on the national computer registry intended to find American Indian homes for Indian children, but I lived no more as an Indian than I lived as a Hindu. We had two little cars, a little boat and a big dog, and a paucity of prospective grandparents. It was a nice enough setup, but how could I draw, with a few words, the nurturing that would be attendant on the raising of a child—how we would try to instill, but not force, on him our love of reading and seeing and discovering?

I decided to emphasize that which I liked best about Dan and me. We liked a laugh. Our family loyalty was paramount. We were openminded people. We were generous. We were healthy.

It would have to do. We sealed up the last of the envelopes, and Dan told me he would like to have a cardiac surgeon standing by when he presented them for stamping at the post office. I expected to get perhaps ten responses. I would receive four, myself, and another unknown physician would send a copy of the letter to authorities of the state, asking if what we were doing was illegal. It was not, of course.

About the same time, my cousin Sally, one of my Aunt Pat's daughters in Louisiana, wrote to my grandmother with an offer. She wanted to suggest to Dan and me that she was so moved by our plight that she was willing to act as a surrogate mother for us. She would allow herself to be inseminated with Dan's sperm, and bear the child for me. She would ask nothing for it, except some help in buying clothes for the pregnancy. She simply, she wrote, wanted to make us a gift of her love and health. And to experience birth without the attendant responsibilities which Sally, having just divorced her childhood sweetheart, was not ready to take on. She had not written Dan and me directly, she said, because she could not gauge our reaction. She feared we would think her presumptuous at best, loony at worst. But it was a genuine offer, she insisted, and she asked my grandmother to broach it with me.

My grandmother, whose view of the adoption process was strained through the point of view of earlier generations and a Georgia girlhood, and who was in a sweat over the possibility that I would blithely adopt a whole houseful of babies in varying skin tones, thought it was the perfect solution. Dan and I were less sure, not because it wasn't an exciting thought—it was, particularly because Sally and I, as second cousins, were sufficiently closely related that the baby could not help but inherit a few eccentric Dvorak genes along with the Allegretti ones— but because we thought it was a terrifically large decision for a twenty-two-year-old to make. It would certainly affect her social life, and possibly imperil her health, and we would bear responsibility for that. And Sally would be forced to know the baby she had borne with her body as a little niece or nephew. Was she prepared for that ineffable conflict of emotion? I wrote to her, "You have made me aware once again how blessed I am with such family as you and your mother, and the largeness of spirit and depth of love in your offer leaves Dan and me speechless. . . . We want you to take time, think it over, allow us to think it over —pray about it if you pray—and make sure that this is a firm and considered decision. Call me anytime, collect, and we'll hash it out together, as well."

I put my letter to Sally in with the bundle headed for the doctors. We would experience a bittersweet relief months later that we had not taken her up on her gesture abruptly, because in September Sally and her estranged husband reconciled, and remarried, and planned children of their own.

There was a welling of peace after sending the letters. The end of the preliminaries had been achieved; I had done all I could do, and the rest would be for the future to unveil. The agency home studies would wait until after I could see what the letters would bring.

But the habit of industry was impossible to break. I turned it on work. The National Conference of the Women's Political Caucus was meeting in early July in San Antonio. My friend Hannah, who then was an aide to Congressman Robert Kastenmeier, was lobbying me to persuade the paper to fund my attendance, as a special project.

"Not only will you get the jump on substantive issues for '84," she said, "but think of the Mexican food, the plazas, the nights along the Riverwalk, sipping margaritas . . ."

"I don't think Carol and Dave are going to be entranced by the vision of me sipping margaritas on the expense account, Hannah."

But Hannah would not give up. She had come a few credits shy of becoming an ordained rabbi, and the woman could sermonize. Who would write about gender-gap issues for the election, if not an informed woman reporter? Who would cover the struggle for pay equity? Reaffirm the stance on abortion?

What finally sold me was my ignorance; I had no idea what the hell she was talking about. A reporter would have to have lived on Mars for the past nine months to have missed the phenomenon of women, even formerly apolitical women, falling away from Ronald Reagan's policies like dominoes; but that was a fair description of my condition. I could virtually quote paragraph summaries of stories about Dr. John Buster's work in embryo transfer at UCLA, but I had not the vaguest idea how John Glenn differed from Walter Mondale and Mondale from Cranston. Hannah was appalled. "And you are a women's issues columnist," she intoned.

"I'm a *human* issues columnist," I protested feebly.

But finally, in the middle of June, when I was sure it would be too late to budget a trip, when I was convinced that the convention would no longer accept press registration, I mailed a memo to Carol.

"Whereas," it began, "I have toiled for this paper for lo, these six years, and whereas in service of this paper, I have never traveled more than 180 miles round-trip for a story (except for once interviewing a fellow in Chicago over a weekend, and I was here half the time anyway), and whereas others, notably but not exclusively my fair-haired spouse, have crisscrossed the nation on assignments, and whereas at least one reporter—again, my spouse—is rumored to be planning a winter foray to Honduras and Nicaragua, and whereas my font of columnar wisdom has grown dry . . ."

"Whereas," Carol memoed back, "I think you have a point, I will budget the trip. Have a good time and file many stories. Repeat, file many stories."

I was flabbergasted. Hannah was elated. "But it's my fertile time!" I told her over the phone. "I can't miss a time."

"Have Dan send it UPS. I was going to be able to do bris, maybe I can do artificial insemination."

I decided to skip a month. It was a fairly agonizing decision; but I figured a baby deserved a mother unchained from an obsession. There would be next month, on our camping trip—ah, with Jocelyn, I remembered in consternation, but Jocelyn could be dispatched on a long berrying expedition with the dog.

Dan's court date was coming up the following Thursday; I had planned to go with him, at least to offer support, but now preparations for the trip meant backlogging columns and doing legwork for a medical ethics series Dan and I were planning together. I was to do work in Milwaukee, talking to experts there.

We were excited about it. Technology had given rise to a slew of troubling questions, and none beyond euthanasia had been treated in depth by our paper. There were ethical quandaries surrounding what the press called "genetic engineering," fetal research, late-term abortion following amniocentesis—several fetuses had been live-born at a Madison hospital, causing a terrific uproar—and my own favorite, in-vitro fertilization.

We would attend a conference together the following Friday and Saturday, and there were several university specialists we wanted to touch base with first. It was a rare and welcomed occasion to work together. Dan and I had made it a point to keep our personal relationship, once the early, bloody months of whispered conferences in downstairs halls were past, well to the background in our professional setting. There were reporters at the paper who didn't even know that we were married, since we had different last names, and Dan's contacts in the community were continually being surprised, when they asked if he knew me, to hear him say, "Really rather well. She's my wife."

Dan took off for court on Thursday, and I took off for a Wisconsin convention to pick up an award the infertility series had garnered. It was a tedious day, notable for frothy speeches and rubbery quiche, and I couldn't wait to get home.

When I walked into the house just after dark, I was frightened by the silence. Not a single light burned, and the dog was lying, curled tight in a corner under the table. My father and grandmother were conspicuously absent. Mournful messages. I knew Dan had to be home.

I found him in bed, literally with the covers over his head. "Go away, now," he told me, his voice not only muffled but slurred. "I don't want to talk."

"But how did it go?"

"I said I don't want to talk."

I sat in the living room, turning a book over in my hands, too wired to read, until, at nine o'clock, he came out into the kitchen, passed me without even a glance, and began clattering about with the coffee maker. "What's the matter?" I asked the dark, softly.

"I'm drunk, for one," he replied. "And I'm disgusted, for another."

Joan and Dan had met in mediation with a court representative. Joan had presented an elaborate list of summer activities planned for Jocelyn —a dance recital, special tumbling lessons, vacation at Grandma and Grandpa's farm, a week at Jerry's plush cabin in the northern woods, Girl Scout camp. Dan had been armed only with a father's desire. He wanted to do small things with his little girl—take her on walks with the dog, teach her to swim underwater, make ice cream, pitch a pup tent for her on my dad's terrace. Take her to Madison.

"They put me in the position of seeming to refuse what would be best for Jocelyn," he told me, his voice cracking. "As if by wanting her to be with me, I would deprive her of all these good things." Finally the counselor hinted that it seemed that for this summer, at least, plans had been set, and that to disrupt a child's expectations was never the optimum route. And Dan had given—as it seemed to me he always gave, the poor, dear sonofabitch, to the point of hurting. Joan had got everything she asked. Magnanimously, she had found an extra three days among the summer's festivals, and granted it to Dan as her one concession. Dan left Daley Plaza in Chicago feeling as if he'd lost his shirt and his dignity. He'd picked up Gail and headed for some corner tavern in the town where they'd grown up. Poured out to his sister, as one can only do, perhaps, to the person who has seen you coming up in life, a terrible sorrow.

We sat in the dimness of the kitchen and made plans for our four weeks. We'd intended to go to Canada, to expose Jocelyn to my dotty Montreal relatives and then head for Quebec City, possibly by rail. But now we decided that the time was too short; it would be wrong to take Jocelyn from the kids on the block who anticipated all her visits with such honest eagerness. We would vacation in Madison. Make a camping weekend, instead of a week. Contrive to crowd all the emotions and experiences that should unfold with natural timing into the allotted space.

A second court date had been set by the attorneys for the following February. "Honey, I'm not trying to butt in," I advised Dan, clearly trying to butt in. "But this time, plan. Muster our plans."

He gave me a weary look. "How can I muster our plans? If nothing else, Jack, it's clear that we're in a period of . . . flux."

On the day following the hearing, Dan and I drove to Marquette University in Milwaukee for the medical ethics seminar. The conference, we already were aware, was being sponsored by the right-to-life forces, but judging by some of the names on the program, we foresaw a lively exchange of viewpoints.

I had waited for a speech by Dr. Donald DeMarco, a Toronto psychologist and moral philosopher and a doctor of theology, who would speak on in vitro among other topics. He intended, he said in his opening remarks, to help philosophy serve as a "moral compass" in the minefield of biotechnology, "to help us determine what human life is, and how to further humanize it."

He commenced his discussion of in vitro with a question that clued me immediately. "Does a human being have a right to another human being?" The question of whether parents have a right to children, he said, was only a subset of this larger question. He said that there *was* a way for parents to have children without violating the "canons of justice" and that was by intercourse. "It represents, at its climactic moment . . . an abandonment of ego, an unconcern for control, and an attitude of submission to something beyond the individual."

Now, he went on, with in vitro, we have "serious problems." Not the loving abandon that allows life to enter the picture as per biological order, but this pesky question of parents acting on the belief that they have the right to another person. People fall into the trap of considering that not having another person—that is, infertility—is a disease. It's not, Dr. DeMarco pointed out, it's a desire. Do we not make a mistake in asking the medical profession to "prostitute" itself by treating a desire rather than a disease?

He did not mean to imply that he considered all efforts to reverse conditions that prohibited conception immoral; in fact, he mentioned laser microsurgery, and the high rates of success publicized by Dr. Heiss in New Orleans.

But in vitro was another matter. It meant assuming the moral burden of bringing a child into the world to make oneself happy. The point was to have children to make *them* happy. "You cannot expect another person to make you happy," Dr. DeMarco explained blithely. "You alone can make yourself happy. You should expect only to make others happy." Making others happy had a name—love. Expecting a child to make you happy also had a name—greed.

I was furious. This philosophical tap dance had me scribbling in my notebook: "He is saying that you alone can make yourself happy, and you alone can make others happy. So how can anybody, by that logic, make anybody else happy? Isn't the logical extension of this that infertility specialists, particularly those involved in in vitro because it's the court of last resort, are the most loving fellows on the ark, because it is their aim to make others happy?"

"It seems," DeMarco concluded, "that the great moral problem associated with in-vitro fertilization and implantation—apart from all the embryo wastage and apart from the degradation of parenthood and the violation of the two-in-one-flesh intimacy of the parents, and all the possible harm that attends the child to be, and the frustration and the economic cost and the exploitation of women's feelings and so forth—is this idea that we're taking a path of exploiting rather than following out a commitment of love."

A psychiatrist in the audience rose to pose a question: Did not in vitro serve a medical function, was it not in fact treating a disease, if it eased the psychological distress of infertility by a successful outcome?

"I'm in no way demeaning the seriousness of the desire to have children," DeMarco replied mildly. "Morality deals with means. We want to have children so how do we get them? Sexual intercourse? Or the black market, or in-vitro fertilization, or steal them or kidnap them?"

Ah. Little Elizabeth Carr's face swam before my closed eyes, a picture of her as she had played happily with the papers on a desk during an airing of the "Today" show last October. The faces of her parents, overwhelmed by love—these parents who with great pain and sacrifice had "kidnapped" Elizabeth's life out of their great greed and self-interest. The grandparently faces of the Joneses, who had opted to "prostitute" themselves as physicians.

I kept popping up; Dan kept pulling me down by the elbow. I had no idea what I wanted to say, wanted to ask, only that I wanted to rail at that smug face spouting such perfunctory moralities. DeMarco went on to suggest adoption as the most hopeful and healthy solution for the childless. Abortion rates were spiraling, he told us. Would it not be better to put our efforts toward keeping those children from perishing by adopting them, rather than encouraging a financially wasteful enterprise such as in vitro?

"I guess putting a halt to in vitro would convince more women to opt for adoption rather than abortion," Dan scribbled on my notes.

When I finally got the opportunity to ask a question of DeMarco, I asked him if he would further expand on his assessment of the medical and psychological needs of infertile couples. How they could be addressed. "I think rather strongly that if a couple who doesn't happen to have children is experiencing stress or distress, it's . . . not because they don't have children, but because of some other problem. I imagine a very immature couple, who feel that if they don't have children, they have not been able to validate their sexuality as man and woman—and out of their immaturity and selfishness they want to have a child simply so that they can be reassured that they are a potent husband and wife. Stress in this case is connected with selfishness."

"I see," I said. "And so you object to any artificial means of enhancing the likelihood of pregnancy. Some couples are instructed by their doctors to time their intercourse, for example, for the best chance at fertility. . . ."

And Dr. DeMarco said, to the restrained titters of the audience, all but a few of whom seemed to be smack in his camp, "Perhaps they might wish to time it for after dinner rather than before. As to other timing, no."

I stalked out of the meeting. I had wanted to screech at the man, "Do you have five or six kids at home? And did you get them the old, deity-approved two-in-one way? And did the ease of that so blind you to the pain of others that you were able to explain away their suffering as greed, their longing as the urge to degrade parenthood?"

Dan and I went to a German restuarant for a break. He ordered drinks. I told Dan I was thinking maybe I really should finish my book.

July 5 was a Tuesday. Dan had the day off and was at home, sleeping in. I was out with my grandmother. The telephone rang.

Dan is not a great riser. He stumbled to the phone, nearly dropped it, and mumbled, "Hello?"

"This is Dr. Joe DiMaggio's office," said a female voice. Dan groaned silently. Our outrageous friend Michael, the printer, who often announced himself as a representative of Richard Nixon's Thought Police, obviously had inveigled some female cohort into this early-morning mission.

"Michael," he said, and almost added, "this is Eleanor Roosevelt."

"Michael?" The voice was puzzled. "This is Dr. Joe DiMaggio's office. Is this Dan Allegretti?"

"It is."

"Are you and your wife still interested in adopting a baby? I don't know how you heard about us, but we've been updating our files, and we may have a baby . . ." Dan was awake, wide-eyed, instantly.

". . . a baby?"

The voice identified itself as Mrs. DiMaggio. She explained in a rush that Dan, struggling to find a pen and make notes while cradling the phone, was hard put to keep up with. Mrs. DiMaggio was a nurse, she pointed out, and she and her husband, who practiced in a small rural county north of Chicago, had for some years placed babies for adoption. Perhaps a dozen of them over fifteen years. Dr. DiMaggio's efforts in placing babies privately were fairly well known in the area, which is how she assumed we'd got their name, and very recently she and her husband had been given temporary guardianship of a baby that they now were attempting to place. "My kids all want us to keep the baby ourselves," she chatted on, "but we have six, and the youngest is twelve, and it would just be too selfish, we couldn't do that, but the kids are just in love with the baby." The baby was two weeks old, healthy, white. She would not specify whether it was a boy or girl. "We sometimes hear from a couple who is very precise about wanting a boy—or a girl—and we just think that's awful, I mean, when you have one, you don't know what you're going to get, right? So at any rate, I was going over your letter . . ."

"Why did you choose us?"

She hesitated. "I don't know. It certainly wasn't the most detailed one we've ever got. Most people send long letters, and references and pictures, and medical notes. It was just something about the letter. I don't know, something subjective." She laughed. "Maybe that your name ended in a vowel."

Dan closed his eyes and sent up a prayer of thanks for an Italian surname. Mrs. DiMaggio went on to say her husband would be screening the names on file over the weekend—could we send something more? Some letters of reference perhaps? And a more detailed description of ourselves, our hobbies, our plans for the future? And a photo. They would like a photo of the two of us.

"Of course, " he said. "We'll do that right away. And, uh, thank you. Very, very much. I apologize for my stumbling about at first. I'd just got out of bed."

Mrs. DiMaggio laughed again. "That's nothing. You're interested, then?"

"Oh, so interested," Dan told her, and didn't stop to reflect until he'd put down the phone that he didn't know if that was fact, but that the thought of a healthy baby, so close, had filled him with eagerness, with hope. That he wanted the baby—it was ridiculous, it was too soon—but he wanted the baby. It seemed right, meant, like one of my omens.

When I came home, he met me at the door. "The strangest thing just happened," he said. "A doctor's wife just called me, and she thinks they might have a baby for us."

I screamed. I half lifted my grandmother, who gave me a sour look and headed for her room. I ran into the study and began to write down Mrs. DiMaggio's information requests. Tapping my teeth, I tried to figure how I could fulfill all of them by sundown.

I called Carol for a letter of reference. I got my boss Elliott up out of a sickbed to write one. I made a rush call to Hannah and she promised to send one on paper with the congressional frank. I gave them all the DiMaggios' address. "It has to be today," I pleaded. "While it's on their minds."

Hannah called me later to read me what she had written. "Dan and Jackie will make proud and devoted parents," she read. "They will raise a child with grace and joy."

Tearful, I told her, "May we be half so good as you make us sound."

"You are," she assured me. "Doubly. The thing I want to know is, are we still going to San Antonio? Or is it off for you now?" I had forgotten about it entirely.

"Well, of course, I can't . . ." I began, but then reconsidered. "Dan or my grandmother would be here if the phone rings, and there isn't going to be any decision before Monday at the earliest. And we'll be back Monday night. Sure. Let's do it. See you at the airport tomorrow."

The biography I assembled was a marvel of detail. I included my vegetarianism—that was healthy—and Dan's outdoorsiness. Then I wrote it all over again. We sounded too wholesome. I found a friend with an instant camera, and we posed for a smiling picture. And then I called the courier.

"Don't lose it," I fussed to the uniformed man who picked up the folder.

"Lady, if we lost them, we'd be out of business," he told me gruffly.

There was nothing left to do. My clothes for the trip all were ironed. My column was done, and mailed. But what would I do to occupy my mind until tomorrow afternoon when we left for Texas? I was bursting the walls. I was babbling.

So, though I had promised myself to tell few people, so as to cut down on the disappointment all around if nothing came of it, I called Mary.

"Oh Jackie, you don't know. I prayed and prayed. I kept asking God to give you a baby, or a pregnancy, before my baby was born." Mary was in her ninth month; the last time I had seen her, she had been huge. "And there wasn't much time. But it looks as if He's going to come through."

"I'd like to talk to Him about it."

"We can do that."

"Oh, Mary. Come on."

"Well, we can." Mary's faith was as breezy and matter-of-fact as anything else about her; she had no qualms about praying with a friend or a relative in need, even while her kids and her husband tromped through the living room and the television blared away. And so we prayed, the two of us, 150 miles apart, as if she were holding my hand. "I hate always to go to God like I'm passing the hat," I told her afterward.

"Silly. You pray all the time. You're just not aware of it."

I felt myself folding up under Mary's serenity. I would accept the grace, but did not deserve it. I was no atheist—had neither the stomach nor the moral fortitude for it—but I knew that my relationship with God was heavily laced with mythology. I was willing for God to possess my heart, but mystified to divine how I would know when it had happened. It was more like a child's concept of Santa Claus; I invested God with miracles—I figured He knew when I was sleeping and knew when I was awake, and whether I'd been bad or good. Goodness, however, did not come to me as second nature, the way it did—all their protestations to the contrary—to Mary, to Laura. I had to wrestle with a sharp tongue and a short fuse. But I tried to be good. That was why, for so long, I had rooted about in my past, in my psyche, for the one inevitable inky spot of evildoing that had won me all this travail.

Perhaps the account had been settled. I hoped.

That night, Dan insisted we call Todd and Leah and tell them the news. "I don't know, Dan," I said. "We told everyone before, and look what happened." He dismissed it.

"We won't tell the rest of the family. We won't tell Jocelyn. But come on. You already told Mary. I need to tell someone."

They were buoyant. Leah got on the extension and the four of us had a nearly incomprehensible round table. In the middle of it, Leah said, "Andy's here. He wants to talk to you."

"Tell them about the Emancipation Proclamation, Andy," Todd urged the little boy, and whispered, "Wait until you hear this."

Andy got on the phone. "Well," he said. "Dan and Jackie, Lincoln was a very great man. He freed the dwarves and made them eagles."

And soon this would be mine, I thought. A kid who, even when all else failed, made life a weekend. "You know what?" I told him. "If I have a little baby, I hope he's just exactly like you."

Andy fell silent. And then, somberly, he said, "You know, I really hope you have a very beautiful baby soon, Jackie. And you know something? I think that even when he is a grown-up man, he will still need you."

"Where does he get stuff like that?" I asked Todd in awe, after Andy had trundled away to brush his teeth for bedtime. "He's five years old."

"Search me. I think he'll be a priest," his father sighed.

We sat at the airport, waiting for Hannah to arrive, fiddling with club sandwiches neither of us had the appetite for, and talking baby names. Laura had offered tiny clothes, a portable cradle, lamps and mobiles and assorted other pastel paraphernalia, but we had decided to accept not a single thing until we were sure. "I could see us with a newly painted room with a border of yellow duckies and then come to find out someone else had been chosen," I'd told Dan. "It would be the stuff of a Gothic horror novel."

"Not to mention that your father would have to explain the duckies to all his friends."

But a casual airport discussion of names did not seem too much a temptation of the potbellied gods. "If it's a boy, how about my name?"

"Jacquelyn?"

"No. Mitchard. We would call him Mitch. That's a nice name, Mitch Allegretti. Good byline."

"I'd consider that. What about if it's a girl?" There is a scarcity of girl's names that sing with Allegretti, and one of the best ones was already occupied. "How about Claudia?"

"*Claudia?* Ye gods, why not Gloria? I can't stand Claudia. It reminds me of a girl with dyed-red beehive and pink pedal-pushers."

"Don't take on. I'm not going to dig in on it."

"How about Anna?"

"Anna Allegretti sounds like the needle got stuck on the record."

I pulled my hole card. "How about Francesca?" I watched for the slow smile that would spread over his face, and was elated when it came. "We could call her Frankie, and my favorite little girl name in the whole world is Frankie, like *The Member of the Wedding.*"

"I never read that."

"You never read *The Member of the Wedding?*"

"I confess. I'm culturally impaired. I like Francesca, though. But we never decided. What about a boy?"

"What would you like?"

"How about Joey?"

"I love Joey, but my family would flip. We talked about that last time." Joey was the name of my older brother, who had died in a riding accident as a child, and I knew my family well enough to know they would consider that name freighted with all manner of ill luck.

"Well, I'll tell you what I really want. If it's a boy, if you wouldn't mind too much, I'd like to name him Daniel."

The cherishing washed over me. "I'd love that. Daniel it is. Dan, think of it. There's a baby sleeping in a cradle somewhere this afternoon that doesn't even know we are its mama and daddy."

"Go slowly, honey."

"I can't. I'm high."

"Go slowly. I don't want you to hurt. I'm excited, too, but let's try to contain it. Later on, if we're lucky, we can celebrate for the next ten years if you want. But Mrs. DiMaggio did say that there were a lot of other couples. . . ."

"But not us."

"Not us. But good people. And anyway, what the hell are we?"

"The best prospective parents . . . in this airport."

Hannah and I fell in love with San Antonio. It's a bewitching city, and the conference was jammed with substance—reporters had the opportunity for leisurely conversations, not press conferences, with Gloria Steinem, Bella Abzug. All seven of the Democratic hopefuls appeared to court the NWPC, and Walter Mondale covered himself with grace while Gary Hart's imperiousness made for decent color copy to send home. I filed by phone every morning by eight, writing pieces on the language of the nuclear age, on the caucus president's denunciation of Ronald Reagan and the Reagan representative's lame defense, surprising myself with my avidness for politics—something I had placed always outside my ken.

At night I would phone Dan. Any word yet? No word. My grandmother had fallen in the Quick-Stop grocery and cut her eye. I was not to worry, she told me, but have a nice time. Still, it was clear that I had committed the unpardonable sin of going out of town when I was needed. "Are you sure your family isn't Jewish?" Hannah asked me, when I quoted my grandmother to her.

She and I did not have much private time, but we made the best of what we had. We went alone to the Alamo late one evening—it was closed, but a young Texas Ranger on guard in the park unlocked the gates and gave us a quiet tour of the exterior of that famous silent white facade. At Dan's request, Hannah used her Kodak to photograph the brass inscription reading, "Thermopylae had its messenger of defeat. The Alamo had none."

As we walked across the plaza to the hotel, she asked me, "Are you thinking about it?"

"Not as constantly as I thought I would. But, yes."

"I used to have some pretty good connections up there," Hannah told me, taking my arm. "It's been a long time since I was a rabbinical student, but I'm doing my best for you."

"Keep doing."

We had begun the trip as coffee-acquaintances; we came home feeling like sisters, energized by the conference and by our newfound closeness. Dan picked us up at the airport on Monday night. Hannah took a bus home. "I called Mrs. DiMaggio today, and she was in a great rush and couldn't talk," he told me first thing. "But she said to call tomorrow, that she hoped the decision would be made by then."

I got through the next day, toiling over a wrap up of the conference. Phoning it in. There were good reasons not to fasten onto the Di-Maggios' deliberations a few minutes' drive away—Jocelyn was coming, and Dan and I were taking a week off. We would all be together for the first time in months, and that togetherness would stabilize Dan and me. But there was no bologna in the house, no macaroni and cheese, no cherry Kool-Aid; the kid would starve. I finished the wrap up and headed for the supermarket.

In the late afternoon, I made the call. "Mrs. DiMaggio? This is Jackie, Dan Allegretti's wife. And I'm calling about the baby, the baby that you . . .".

"I know," she said. And stopped. I could all but feel her discomfort. "Jackie, that baby has been adopted."

I will not cry, I thought. This was only the first try. We have so many other options. It was only luck, after all. We'd been picked out of a hat, more or less. I will not cry, I thought, but my voice broke when I asked her, "Was it us? Was it something about my husband and me?"

"Oh, honey, no. It was a most difficult decision. I shouldn't tell you this, but it basically came down to yourselves and one other couple, out of a great many names we had in our files. The other couple were a bit older, and they were never, ever going to be able to have a baby by any other means. They'd been waiting five years. . . ."

"I'm glad, then."

"I know it must hurt . . . but listen. I want you to stay in touch with us. There's a possibility—I shouldn't be telling you this, either, my husband would brain me—but we may have another baby for placement the middle of August. It's not firmed up yet, but there's every indication. And if we do, you two would be very strong candidates."

"That's fine. That's great."

"Call me August first."

"Oh I will. You can bet I will."

Dan came home late that afternoon. He didn't have to ask. He saw my face. "B., oh, B. I'm sorry. For you and for myself. I . . . had got used to the idea. I had let myself want that baby. Did you find out anything about him or her?"

"That it was a girl. A little dark-haired girl."

"A Frankie."

"Yep. But not our Frankie."

Laura and I took a walk at dusk. "Have you told everybody?"

"Yes. All the people who wrote the letters for us. They hated it."

"I hate it, too."

"It's funny, Laura, but I don't. I keep having this image of what Mrs. DiMaggio told me, about the mother setting eyes on the baby for the first time—she almost fell down, her knees gave way. I can feel that woman's joy . . . and I know that somewhere tonight there's this couple just mad with joy, just spending the night on their knees thanking . . ."

"And you aren't good." She hugged me. "You're *so* good, because if it was me . . ."

"You'd feel just the same."

"I don't think I could."

But we are veterans at being disappointed, Laura, I wanted to say, realizing before I did how unintentionally smug it would sound. Dan and I, if nothing else, do disappointment very well. Because if there is any good thing about all this, it is that surviving the worst early on cushions what comes later.

We thought that. We honestly did.

If a genie had formed that moment out of the plume of my cigarette smoke, he could not have convinced me there would be a time when we would take the lowest moment of the past year back willingly, and call it a good trade.

33 JOCELYN was having a very grown-up summer. She still needed her Chou-Chou, the polar bear puppet, and her Furry (which was, as best we could determine, a scrap of someone's aged rabbit-fur collar) to sleep with at night, but early on in her visit, one night while doing the dishes, she announced that she was in love.

"How can you tell?"

"He lets me use his calculator. We gave each other four cookies at the cookie exchange. We write love notes."

"Love notes? What do they say?"

"*You* know. 'I love you.' "

"You're too little to be in love. You're eight."

"No, I'm not." She sloshed the sudsy water about in the sink, ruminating for a few moments, and then said, "I know I'm in love in another way."

"Don't tell me."

"I kiss."

"You *kiss?*"

"On the head."

"Oh."

"And the lips."

"*Dan!* Don't you think eight is too young to be in love? How old do you think is old enough to be in love?"

"Thirty," he said. Like Ward. Coming up out of the mists and smiling at June and adding something really substantial to the discussion.

"Well, tell your daughter, then, unless you want to sign consent forms for her to finish middle school after the wedding."

"What's this?"

"Jocelyn's in love. She kisses."

"Jocelyn, you can't be in love and there's an end to it."

"Too late, Dad. I already did it."

"Did *what?*" Newspaper reporters are prey to terrible visions—preteen sex rings, pubescent porn in the kickball court.

"Being in love. Kissing."

"Now, Jocelyn, I want all this kissing talk to come to an abrupt halt. Eight is old enough to have boys for friends . . ."

"Three is old enough to have boys for friends."

"Right. But kissing at your age is silly. . . ."

"If it's silly, how come three—no, five—other girls in my class have kissed, too?"

"None of them should have. Kissing is for older people, not eight-year-old people. . . ."

"How about eleven-year-old people?"

"*Eleven?*"

"When I'm eleven, I can date."

"Who says?"

"I just figured. Just to McDonald's."

"Jocelyn, you cannot go to McDonald's with a boy when you are eleven. You can go to McDonald's with a boy when you are . . . fourteen. If we drive you. You can go to a school dance when you're . . . fifteen. And you can't go out, on a real date, until you're sixteen and a sophomore." I was making this up as I went along. I hoped she didn't spot it.

"*Sixteen!*" Suds flew all over the drain board. "He'll never wait for me."

"He who?"

"Fred."

"Fred?"

"My boyfriend. That I kiss."

"Kissing," I sighed, "is for older people. I mean, boyfriend-girlfriend kissing. Married people kissing."

"Yeeeech," cried Jocelyn, blowing soapsuds from her hands, in huge pink Playtex rubber gloves. "That's sickening."

"What is?"

"Married people kissing. Jerry and Mom do it all the time. They're always lying around on the couch kissing. I have to push them apart to even talk to them."

"I'll bet they love it when you push them apart," said my dad, passing through on his way to his study.

"They tell me to go play."

"Mmmmm."

"I would never kiss like that."

"Well, that's part of what being in love is. You'll like it when you're big. You're not *supposed* to like it now."

"But I love Fred. First my friend Glenna started loving him, then I started loving him, then Bridget started loving him, but he can't stand Bridget, and you know, she shouldn't have just budged herself in our being in love like that. Now Jill wants to love him, too. But, you know, Jill doesn't have boyfriends. I mean, she knows how to get boys, but she doesn't know how to keep them."

"Jocelyn, what do you mean?"

"Oh, not write on them. Share your Rollos."

"Oh." But then without missing a beat, she smiled and said, "I know what real sex is."

". . . indeed."

"I do. Bridget does, too. Men want it. Women don't, though."

"Who told you that?"

"Mommy." Dan and I traded looks. "Yes," Jocelyn went on. "Real sex is not like *Snow White.*" I had taken her and Bridget to see the movie just a few days before.

"No, not much."

"Men do want it, don't they?"

"I guess."

"Except Daddy."

"Oh, of course."

"Bridget's dad does. So does Jerry. But not Daddy. Bridget doesn't think so, either."

"Why not?"

"Because he's so funny. He plays with us and stuff." She dipped a plate experimentally into the rinse water. "Jackie, you didn't have to do sex to get Daddy, did you?"

"Do the dishes, Jocelyn."

"Is real sex in love?"

"Real sex is in love, but love is not always in real sex."

"Huh?"

"Jocelyn, we are ending this discussion now. You are too young to be in love, which is what started all this, because you only stopped believing in Santa Claus one month ago. In fact, I think you still do."

"No, I don't. But, anyway, those are two different things, Jackie. Being in love doesn't have a single, solitary thing to do with believing in Santa Claus."

"Oh, yes it does, Jocelyn. Believe me."

Later that night, as we lay in bed, Jocelyn-in-love long asleep with her stuffed animals and her Jesse by her side on the floor, I told Dan, "Forbear with that stuff. Remember, you are an idol."

"I'm a weary idol," he said. And then he raised himself up on one elbow. "Jackie, we have to talk about something. The public relations thing isn't going to work out. Ann knows it. I know it. I've agreed to stick around until she finds someone she really wants, but I'm never going to want to leave newspapers for good."

My stomach turned over. "So you want move back. Right away."

"I'd love it. You don't know how much I'd like to normalize my life. I hate this back and forth stuff. I hate living with the whole army. Though I have to give your dad credit. He's been really good about this."

"And what about my grandmother?"

He smiled. "Your grandmother has been your grandmother. Your grandmother is you in thirty years."

"What does that mean?"

"It means I've learned to live with it. But honey, the thing is, we need our own space again. There's a word I never thought I'd hear come out of my mouth. But we do. We need to live alone in our own house. Wherever that is."

"I know that. I know that. But the thought of moving—all my files and my junk, and changing all the mailing addresses and papers all over again . . ."

"That's not what really bothers you, is it?"

"No."

"It's that you don't want to move away so long as there's even a possibility of the DiMaggios having a baby for us in August." He let out a long whistle of breath. "Well, I'm not going to insist on it. I know how much it means to you. You'd never forgive me. But I hope you can appreciate what I'm doing to make it so we can stay. You know, I never would have given Ann's proposal more than a passing thought if it wasn't for the look on your face when you brought up what that friend of your dad's had said about adopting."

"But I thought you were at least attracted to the job. I thought . . . you never told me. You should have told me."

"Should I have?"

"No."

"I'm trying, B. I'm really trying. I want you to have what you want."

"What I want?"

"What we want." He paused. "Yes. What we want. You know, it wasn't until we lost the chance to adopt that baby that I realized how much I really wanted it. I was really excited about the possibility of being a father again. And I didn't only feel sorry for you when it happened. I felt sorry for me."

"I didn't know."

"The one thing I've never been able to make you understand is that I do want a baby, too. A baby with you." He rolled over onto me. "It's just that I could have lived without one."

"And now?"

"And now that the chance seems so close, well, we have to take it."

"But what if we did get a chance to adopt? We'd still have to stay here, live here."

Dan sighed. It was late summer in Wisconsin. He longed for it, his beloved adopted home. He was homesick and heartsick. "I'll tell you what. If this thing turns out, I'll find some kind of permanent job here. I'll commute until I do. And we'll get a house. And we'll live in the city and I'll be miserable all the time, thinking about how we could walk across the street to Lake Monona."

"But we would have a child."

"Right," he said. "And someday, we could get another place by a lake. A place out in the country. Maybe a cottage up north."

"And our kids could run around."

"That would be a good thing."

We went to Wisconsin and camped with Bobby and Sandy at Tomahawk Lake a few weeks later, having finally found, after years of successive tries, a campground that satisfied all of us, where Sandy could take hot showers and plug in her blow-dryer and Bobby could use the toilet without terror. Roughing it, to my brother and his wife, meant three consecutive days without cream rinse. Here Jocelyn could play on a swing set, and yet Dan could have access to a champion fishing lake.

We set up the campers and waited for the monsoon. It didn't come. We were astonished. Our camping trip was an annual ritual. Once, there had been flash floods. Another time, a bona fide tornado had whirled up out of nowhere and sent half our gear, nearly including the late Jeb, then a pup, into the trees. And last year, we had counted ourselves lucky that we got nothing more than three solid days of rain; we'd sat in Sandy's

316

father's camper, playing UNO and eating taco chips for seventy-two hours.

"It's because we were going to go July fourth and had to put it off," Bobby said, cracking open a beer and surveying the cloudless starscape above our campsite. "There's no other explanation. We have defied natural law, and beat nature at its own game."

It was a good respite. Being with the two of them always made a picnic.

Still, the weekend had a sad-colored border. Jocelyn would be going back to her mother at the end of it. Jerry and Joan would be meeting us in Madison and taking her north to their vacation home. The time had swept past us. It was always the same when Jocelyn was with us; for a few days, we were tentative—we felt the pull of conflicting schedules and values. Then, abruptly, she'd always been there. Her sign would go up on the door of her room, newly crayoned: "Jocelyn's Room—Love It or Leave It—Knock Before Enter." The house would bulge with kids; under Jocelyn's leading, we lived healthier. When we were in Madison, we went to the beach every day there was sun, and when there wasn't sun, we sometimes even ran about outside in the warm rain. We threw ourselves into the world of Flintstone vitamins and bedtime stories and tummy aches. And then, just as abruptly, wrenchingly, she would be gone. And the house filled with silence, overlarge. The dog would whimper at night at the door for his playmate.

We used to leave her sign up, glancing at it whenever we passed, until the edges began to curl and the tape lost its adhesive, and then we would take it down and one or the other of us would fold it away, next to the ones she'd drawn at Christmas—of three hens with T-shirts reading "I'm French"—in Dan's miscellaneous dresser drawer.

We decided to make the last day of the camping trip a blast. We let her plan it.

All morning, we paddled up and down in the shallow water, throwing Frisbees. We found an isolated corner of the shore and took Jesse swimming. In the afternoon, we piled into the boat, determined to catch ourselves a fish dinner to share before leaving. We fished. And fished. And at length, after better than three hours, Dan began to haul in nice-sized crappies—three, then five, then what was approaching a meal, when Bobby said, "There are a great many very large thunderclouds right over there."

We glanced at the western sky. So there were. Huge ones, fifty-thousand-footers piled up like doom and looming. "Well, that's only because of the heat," I explained. "By the time those get here, we'll be on the road for home."

"Those are very big clouds, Stepme," Jocelyn whispered worriedly. "And I see lightning in them."

"Ah! Don't worry. It's from the heat."

It was on us in moments. We putt-putted frantically along at a stately two knots, all the boat would do with its unaccustomed load, the wind tearing at the slickers we held vainly over our heads, the sky splitting and rolling green above us, with Sandy yelling over the howl of the wind, "We have defied the natural order, right, Bob? We have beat nature at its own game!"

We made the shore, thunder bombing all around us. "Run for the car!" I told Jocelyn, who snapped the dog on his lead and began to make tracks. The four of us tried to anchor the boat. It kept twisting away in the wind, lurching, and every time we would get it near land, lightning would crack and one of us would let go of the aluminum side, and the boat would snap back to the end of the rope.

Jocelyn came running back, drenched. "It's locked!" she hollered. "The car's locked!"

"Give me the keys!" I shouted to Dan, who was standing, feet braced, tugging on the boat rope. He motioned for his pocket. I searched. No keys. Bobby raced up to the parking lot.

"I can see the keys!" He shouted back. "They're right in the ignition!"

We crowded under a tree, windbreakers stretched in a continuous tent from arm to arm. "I don't think you're supposed to sit under a tree," Sandy cried nervously.

"Right you are!" my brother answered, and he threw off his windbreaker and waded through a foot of water to the boat and retrieved a six-pack. He popped beers all around. "Let's drink to the majesty of nature. . . ."

"Shut up," said Sandy. "This reminds me of last year, when we went camping with my cousins. It was a beautiful day, just like this one—it was this same weekend, I think—and all of a sudden there was hail the size of birds' eggs, all over the picnic table—do you remember that storm? It was right near here. You must have had hail in Madison."

I wiped the rain out of my eyes, straining to remember. "I think we were still in Door County, then, so . . ."

"We were still in Door County," Dan said, his voice flat.

I looked at him. It was July 31. One year to the day. "This was the night that . . . " I began then.

"We remember," said Bobby, with a sharp look at his wife. "I'm sorry we brought it up. I remember, we didn't find out until Monday, no one could reach us."

"It's okay," I told them. "It doesn't matter now." The rain had slowed to a sprinkle. "You can't avoid anniversaries."

Bobby looked at the storm clouds mustering for a new assault on the horizon. He lifted his beer. "Fitting," he said. And then, "We'd better try to break into the car before the next deluge."

The holiday was effectively over.

The next afternoon, back in Madison, a gloomy trio of little girls sat around the dinner table, supposed to be enjoying a treat of cantaloupe while waiting for Jocelyn's mother to come, but actually only pushing the melon about on the plates.

"I'm so saaaaad," Christin moaned, with seven-year-old angst. "We hardly got to see you at all this year."

"You guys are mopes," Dan said brightly, his own eyes ringed with small, suddenly apparent lines. "Jocelyn had a nice visit. Not like last year, but very nice. Now she's going up north to Jerry's cottage with her mom and is going to have lots of fun!"

Jocelyn stared at him. "It isn't that much fun, Daddy."

"Oh, I'll bet it is," I put in hastily. "You forget, Jocie, that you're sad to be leaving your mother when you come to Dad and then you're sad to be leaving your dad when you go back to Mom."

"That isn't the way it is. I'm there *all* the time." Oh shut up, Jackie, I thought. Haven't you learned anything about demeaning someone else's pain?

"Look, Joc," Dan said. "Mommy's here."

"Terrific," Carrie, Jocelyn's other playmate, said sourly.

Joan and Jerry were fairly ill at ease in our kitchen, so we contrived to get the suitcases on the landing and all the good-byes said in short order. But the three girls wanted to finish their melon, so the four of us adults stood around, making awkward small talk, Joan in pink linen slacks and a brief white T-shirt and me in one of my summer-weight bags. I must never eat again, I thought idly. I went into the washroom to brush my hair.

At length Jerry asked, "About ready, Jocelyn?"

"We're dawdling," Christin explained, "because we don't want Jocelyn to leave. We wish Jocelyn could stay with us all summer."

"Well," Jerry replied, with the hint of a frown, "we would rather have her with us the whole summer, too."

In an instant, Jocelyn was at my side in the washroom, her eyes wide with panic, her lip quivering. "Christin ruined everything! Now my mommy is going to be so sad that she won't let me be with you for even four weeks next summer! Maybe she won't let me come at all. Oh, Jackie, why did Chris have to say that? It's going to make my mom so mad!"

She clung to me, her closeness and her fear squeezing my heart. What a fool I had been. Joan and Dan should never have parted. It was none of it worth the price Jocelyn was paying—forced, at eight, to second-guess adult motives, assuage adult passions. Dan and I could have fooled around if we had to, and then the ones who would have been hurt would have been ones old enough to bear responsibility.

"Listen," I told her. "First, wash your face." She did. "Now, I'm going to tell you something and I want you to listen, and then I'm going to give you a very special thing to seal the promise—like a token in fairy tales. Okay?"

"Okay."

"Did I ever, ever tell a lie to you?" Jocelyn's face sank into a study; she would not let this pass without scrutiny.

Finally she said, "No."

"Well, I'm telling you something now that I want you to believe. And that is, I promise you will be able to come next summer for just as long as you like. And that no one will make you feel sad for it, and you won't have to tell Daddy or Mommy because I will tell them for you."

"Really?"

"It's a promise. So, you must promise me not to worry anymore." She promised, and then I ran into my room and fetched a nice rope of fake pearls I had got on sale at some State Street boutique and put it around Jocelyn's neck. She was entranced.

"Oh, Jackie . . ."

More often than not, when we would pick her up for overnights thereafter, she would have the pearls looped around her neck, and would touch them and nod at me with a closed, conspiratorial smile. She did not understand, she told me in September, why her mother objected to her wearing them to school.

Dan was inconsolable after Jocelyn left. I was all sympathy, but then a greedy emotion snaked its way to the surface. "Your love for her is so overpowering," I told him. "Do you think you could ever love another child as well?"

"Of course, Jackie," he snapped. "But if we had a dozen kids, I would still grieve when Jocelyn left." I retreated to the bedroom, and packed up a few trifles feeling quite the chump. He followed in a few moments. He put two cigarettes in his mouth, lit them, and handed me one. We had not smoked all the weeks Jocelyn was with us. "Paul Muni," he said.

"Was that Paul Muni?"

"I think so."

"Why ask for the moon, we already have the stars?"

"Yes, that was it."

"Except mine isn't lit. I think you're more like Paul Winchell."

"Ass."

"Well, do you want to do something? Take a boat ride? We still have time."

"No."

We sat on the couch together, reading, listening. I threw down my book after a while. "Why aren't we doing all those carefree things childless couples are supposed to be able to do?"

"Because we're parents, Jack. We're parents even when we don't have a child," he said. "Might as well leave." So we did.

I called Mrs. DiMaggio August 1. She was too busy to talk, apologetically curt, but she said nothing had happened regarding the possible other baby, and that she was taking two weeks off to ready her college kids for school so she would not be in the office until the sixteenth. I should call her then if I hadn't heard from her. She gave me her home number.

I called her again on the morning of the sixteenth. Nothing had happened; she wasn't even sure of the birth mother's present status. Yet we chatted for a long while. She said she had got a call from a woman nearby who'd adopted a baby the previous year through a physician and attorney in Chicago. Now she wanted a second baby. That struck me as selfish.

"Me, too," cried Mrs. DiMaggio. "But you should see the people we hear from. People who have three children but are in their late thirties and don't want to go through another pregnancy who say they'd really just like one more son. The nerve! And I try to tell them about all the childless couples we try to help, and it just doesn't seem to make any impression. Sure, maybe they've got more money, and could give a kid more advantages, but the love parents give the only child they may ever have is so much more than any *money.*"

I told her I was glad she thought so, since we had plenty of the former but not much of the latter. "Well, it won't cost you much," she said. "You'd be expected to pay the doctor's bill, and whatever your lawyer costs. There's no fee from Joe."

"Why did he start doing this?"

"I'm not sure. It was years ago. He had seen a fair number of patients in his work who couldn't have kids for one reason or another, and it always haunted us, because we loved having kids—I guess that's obvious, since we had six. Patients would tell him about how long the agencies made them wait, how the babies that did get placed were sometimes in foster care for months. Joe doesn't think that's right. He thinks a baby should leave the hospital in his mother's arms."

"Think of it. Leaving the hospital with a baby in my arms."

She was silent for a moment. Then she said, "Sometimes, Joe likes to talk personally with a couple. . . ."

"We could drive there today."

"No, that isn't necessary. But could he call you? Maybe in a few days."

I waited a few days—a few days, I judge, is three. Then I called back. Jane DiMaggio was pleased to hear from me—"You're eager," she said—but the doctor had been so busy he hadn't had a chance to review our letters and documents once again. "He'll call in a few days," she promised.

Fifteen minutes later, the phone rang. A voice that sounded so much like my father's I thought it must be him said, "So you want to be a mother, huh?"

"Who is this?"

"This is Dr. DiMaggio."

"Dr. DiMaggio! Hello! I didn't expect . . ."

"Okay. So you'll get the next baby."

I judged the distance between myself and the sink, sure I was going to throw up. "We? Will?"

"Otherwise my wife will never leave me alone."

"God bless her."

"The mother is due in a week to ten days. She's still a little small, and that concerns me—I haven't been in on the case the whole way—but she's healthy otherwise and she already has one kid. Altogether, the expenses should come to about four thousand, maybe a little more. If the mother has to have a cesarean, of course, that's the adopting parents' responsibility."

"We can handle that." How can we handle that, I thought.

"And there's one other thing. If the child has any abnormality, cleft palate, anything, I won't place that child. That child will have to be placed through an agency by the birth parents. That is just the way I've done it. Okay?"

"Okay."

We hung up. I put my face down on the kitchen table and cried. Then I stood up and jumped for about two minutes. I called Dan at the office. He'd already left. He wouldn't be here for two hours. I called Mary, just three days home from the hospital. Peter Carl had been born July 14. Then I called Laura. Then I called Gail. I was still talking with her when the back door opened. I threw down the telephone and jumped on Dan.

I was working at the newspaper office in Madison early on a Saturday morning, August 27, when the desk rang me and said there was a call for me on the main line. "Where have you been?" a faraway voice cried. "You're in so many places you're impossible to track down. I've been trying to call you since two o'clock in the morning!"

". . . what?"

"This is Dr. DiMaggio. You're a mother!"

"Oh my God."

"Congratulations."

It was real. It was happening to me. It was happening to Dan, working unawares across the room, getting up to run downstairs for coffee. We were parents. There was no description for it, no joy, no liquor, no promotion, no honor, that equaled this transport.

But I didn't know whose mother I was.

"Is it . . . ?"

"It's a little boy." I had a son. A Danny boy. "It's a very little boy," Dr. DiMaggio went on. "Only four eleven. But he's doing very well."

"What were his scores?"

"Oh, you know the lingo, huh? They were nine and nine." That was fine. Leah had told me there were no tens, so far as she could determine.

All her babies had been nine-and-nines.

DiMaggio talked on, while I struggled to pin myself to the seat, to hear him, not to fly off. The baby would need to be in the hospital for three days, the birth mother had seventy-two hours to change her mind, but he was certain she would not, I should contact our attorney today, I should get a cradle—he laughed, here—and the chromosome analysis and other tests would be back from the lab in a couple of weeks.

I sobered. "Chromosome tests?"

"They are routine," he explained. "I always do them. Not on every baby that I deliver, but on every baby that is to be placed."

"Do you suspect there's anything wrong with him?" I had been reading Luella Williams' *A Haven for Carolyn* fairly obsessively over the past weeks. I had, for some reason unknown to me, read it twice, dumbfounded with pity and admiration for the mother of the little girl all the physicians had called normal at birth, but who had, in fact, sustained mid-brain damage.

Strauss syndrome, I thought. Anoxia. Birth injury. No.

"Of course not," said DiMaggio. "He's just fine. I've delivered a baby or two before, you know."

I relaxed. "What does he look like?"

"He looks little and red. What you do think he looks like? He has lots of very dark brown hair . . . you'll see him soon enough."

Of course, it could not be soon enough. "Doctor, I can't thank you. Because I don't know how to begin to thank you. This is . . . our life is . . ."

"Don't bother. Just love him."

"You don't know."

I ran downstairs. Dan was sipping coffee at a cafeteria table. Early sun from the plate-glass window striped his beard, grown bushy since winter, the beard he would not shave, his talisman. He lifted his shoulders, raked his hair in the tic that was essentially Dan, and I thought, savoring the moment, drawing it out and memorizing it, we are for life now, you and me. Yesterday you had one child. Now you have two. I wanted to enfold him, bundle him with my joy.

"Sit down," I instructed Dan, coming up behind him. He grinned. He already was sitting. "You have a healthy baby son."

"No," he cried. "You're kidding me. Don't kid me. . . ."

"I'm not kidding. DiMaggio just called."

"But the baby wasn't expected . . ."

"Babies come when they feel like it."

"Is he . . . ?"

"He's fine. He's ours."

We held each other, crushing, as if to exchange skins. It was no different from the blast he had felt, Dan told me later, when Jocelyn was born before his eyes—if anything, it was stronger, more hard won than when he was young and parenthood was a thing that seemed to him to happen more or less uneventfully to everyone.

"This is tender. And in the cafeteria." It was Todd, passing by with briefcase and car keys on the way out. We opened a corner of our circle.

"Shower me with congratulations," I said. "I just had a baby."

Todd's eyes popped. "But that's marvelous! You sonofabitches!" We hugged, the three of us. "I have to call Leah. . . ."

"Let me call her. No, you call her. I have fifteen or sixteen thousand phone calls to make. We have to get a cradle. We have to get back home."

"You've got a cradle. I'll bring it over today."

"But that's a handmade, family . . ."

"I'll bring it over today."

"I have to call my dad, and tell him to make room."

"He'll love it," Dan said, rolling his eyes.

"Maybe we should rent a place then. And the book! I have chapters due on the book. . . ."

"Slow down. We'll handle it."

"And money. It's Saturday! How are we going to dissolve our certificates on a Saturday?"

"Your dad could float us a loan."

"Oh, sure." My father, informed we'd soon go ahead with an adoption, had been predictably dour. An awful chance, he had said. Who knew who the parents were? Someone else's problems, he said, otherwise, why would anyone give up a child? His sole experience with adoption had been through his friend Selene, whose dire predictions held his ear, in spite of my airy assurances about nurture over nature.

"We'll have to ask him. And he'd have the money in a day or two."

"He'll say we didn't prepare."

"How could we prepare? We thought we had all next week at least."

"Maybe the baby wasn't quite full term."

"DiMaggio would have said so."

"He said a funny thing, Dan. That he was going to do a chromosome scan. It made me think that, maybe because of the baby's small size, he thinks there might be some damage. . . ."

"I'm sure he doesn't. Did he say he thought that?"

"No. He said it was routine. But . . ."

"Do you want me to call him?"

"I'd feel better. I'm a fretter, I'm half nuts. . . ."

"You're a new mother is all." Dan called. DiMaggio, more amused than irritated, reassured him.

Meanwhile, I was on the phone to Hannah, to Mary, to my brother and Laura, to my boss, my grandmother, my aunt in New Orleans, my other editors and their wives.

Hannah's mazel tov reached our house in Madison before we did. We found it on the porch in a brown paper bag—an offering of heart and cedar chest. Her five-year-old Shira had drawn a "Welcome, Daniel Robert" poster—the baby was to be named for Dan, and for my brother and Dan's late brother, as well as my father, if he would have it. Hannah's other daughter, Francie, three years old, had put in her treasured Superwoman ring, a gift to Jocelyn in honor of big-sisterdom. There were blankets and sleepers in impossibly small sizes, a book on the first twelve months of life, a pair of Jordache rompers, brand new, and cradle sheets.

Mary showed up, with a Huggies box full of little clothes her huge seven-week-old had already outgrown; and by the time we had loaded the car and driven home to my dad's, my sister-in-law Sandy was there, with a case of formula, a box of diapers in the smallest size she could find, a bunting, undershirts, and a box of plastic covers to put over the floor outlets. "I don't know why I bought that," she explained, bewildered. "That was from the first run through the store. I was buying choo-choo trains and jogging suits . . . when we got to the counter, we had about a hundred and eight dollars worth of stuff. So we had to take some back. I just lost my mind."

And then my brother came in, walked across the kitchen in a single huge stride, and lifted me off my feet and asked, "Are you going to be happy now?"

I said, "Yes."

We had interviewed. We had signed papers. We had visited the courthouse, shepherded by our attorney. We had visited the DiMaggios, with kisses and handshakes. We had wedged the cradle next to a double bed in the house, and laid out the tiny clothes on the coverlet. We had packed a bag with a diaper, the magnificent Italian knitted baby gown Ann had given Gail for Jason's coming home, and Gail had given us, and soft mohair booties. Dan had run out the previous night just before the stores closed to buy a rattle that had "My Boy" painted on it.

We sat in the hospital administrator's office while she squared matters with our attorney. Then the administrator, Sister Frances Quillan, a small, twinkly, white-haired nun in a modified habit, said, "Come along. This is the part I like."

We were left, gripping hands in a waiting room, while she bustled down to the nursery to inform the nurses we were ready. "How do you feel?" I asked Dan.

"Scared."

Sister Frances motioned to us from the doorway. "We're ready." We walked around a corner in the corridor. A large, red-haired nurse was holding a tightly wrapped bundle in her arms. She lay the bundle on a white table and motioned for me to put my hands through an opening like a bank teller's slot in the Plexiglas viewing window. "This is your baby," she said.

"So tiny." It would echo for days on everyone's lips. Danny's head was the size of a tangerine, feathered with thick brown hair the nurses had washed and brushed into a curlicue. He yawned and opened a petal hand in a dream. I thought, he is too little to have been full term. There is something wrong. . . . But then my eyes blurred, and I stretched my hands out to our first touch, my son's and mine, and I thought, there is nothing wrong with him my love cannot heal. I will make him strong and well and hardy. There is nothing I cannot do for him.

I had forgotten my husband, and now moved to make a place for him, while the nurse dressed Danny in his gown and bonnet, and while the other nurses crowded round and cooed, "Doesn't he look lovely in that?"

The red-haired nurse waltzed with practiced ease around the barrier and told me, "Put out your arms."

"I can't bear it," I told her. And looked up, and saw her eyes were wet, as well.

We held him between us, Dan and me, awkwardly, then with assurance. Dan brought out his camera and took a picture of me, smiling as if my face would split, and though I have never seen the photo, I remember the ache of my jaws, the unaccustomed strain of grinning and then wanting to grin again. We handed the lawyer the camera and he took a picture of all of us, and then the nurse walked with us out to the elevator, and we waved and smiled at the administrator, who was brushing at her eyes and calling, "Happy two o'clock feeding!"

The nurse helped us strap the baby, whom no amount of bobbing awakened, into his federally approved baby car seat between us in the car my father had lent us for the air conditioning—the day was in the nineties—and gave us instructions.

He would probably need the preemie nipples the hospital had provided us for some time. He should eat every three hours, because he was so tiny; when he was hungry, he would let us know. Danny like to sleep swaddled, for the security of it, she said, and showed me how to wrap the blanket with secure strokes. He took his bottles at room temperature. He'd still a trace of jaundice, so I should place his basket in a sunny window until a press of his nose—she pressed the tiny button it was clear would be a major nose someday years hence—showed no yellow tone. A few days, she supposed.

Then she hugged me. "Congratulations, and all the luck."

"We have had the luck."

"It's wonderful," she agreed.

We drove out of the covered parking lot into a sopping rainstorm that thickened the air and made it hard to breathe. We got lost, because the area was unfamiliar to us, and because we had to marvel whenever the baby flickered an eye or sighed. We turned on the car radio, and in a few minutes, Kenny Loggins' "Danny's Song" began to play. Such omens.

We drove to Joan and Jerry's house so that Jocelyn would, before anyone else in the family, be the first to set eyes on her brother.

As we pulled up to the curb, the clouds cleared for a brief space and Jocelyn came running. "Oh," she whispered. "Oh, Daddy. Oh, Jackie. Is he ours for good?"

"For good and all," Dan told her. "When he is six months old, we will go back to court with him and make it final, but that doesn't matter. He's ours."

My father and his friend Alice were on the terrace of the house when we arrived—hours late because of the weather—standing in the rain. Alice shouted, "They're here!" and all of our family rushed out, save my grandmother, who was in Michigan visiting her brother, and began to wave. Gail and Sandy hugged each other.

Dan turned off the car. "It is so amazing. He's mine. He's already my son. Who'd have ever believed it could strike you this way? Instantly?"

"Is it the same? For me, it's beyond everything. But then, I've never been before."

"It's exactly the same. Exactly." He kissed me. "Mama."

"Dada."

And then the relatives were on us.

"Miracle" became a commonplace. I undressed Danny and memorized his ribs and tummy—the whole ridge the size of a man's palm—with my fingers. I stroked the new silk of his cheeks, his winged black eyelashes. I fed him as he slept. Laura drove over the first night alone, while Richard stayed with their baby. As the two of us hung over the basket, Danny opened his eyes, fluttered them, hiccoughed, and began pumping his arms and legs furiously.

"That's his early-warning system," said my brother, the biologist. "See? He's quieting now. All systems are go, this is only a test."

But I had seen Danny's slanted, milky-blue eyes open for an instant, and had fallen into them.

"He's marvelous," Laura breathed. "Isn't it all here now? For us? Just as we dreamed?" We went misty together, over the baby book she had brought us—made for an adopted child by Hallmark—over the bit of sentimental verse by Michael Anderson on the flyleaf, "Welcome home, child; at long last, welcome home."

It had been at long last. Upscale, well-modulated emotions would not do—we needed the syrupy old ones, greeting card emotions, great gobs of them. There was much talk of answered prayers. "Isn't it wonderful?" asked Gail. "I never imagined I could feel this way . . . I thought it would somehow have to be different with an adopted child. But it's just as if he'd come from you two. I know that sounds stupid; but I had always assumed that if I couldn't have my own, I wouldn't want any. I was so *wrong.*"

My father astonished us. The one time the baby cried, startled by a slamming door, it was my father who got to him first. Cradling the baby on his own huge stomach, my father walked through the halls and around all the rooms, crooning inaudibly about horsies and doggies. "Maybe you were right," Dan told me. "Maybe he did want a grandchild."

The nurses had told us to take advantage of the first nights—when Danny would sleep almost round the clock—because those nights would cease soon enough. But Dan and I hovered over the basket, inserting our fingers into the clutch of the baby's fists, crying out low to each other whenever he moved, tasting his cheeks, absorbing him. It was midnight in a moment, and then it was dawn.

"Who needs sleep," Dan asked, "when you have Danny?"

There was an abundance of nights and days to be spent; and in time, we told each other, we would learn to spend them carelessly, as did other parents. He would put his face in the oatmeal, and bring me smeary valentines, and drum his heels on the floor in a tantrum, and regard our faces, puzzled, when we explained to him that another woman had borne him for us, but that we were his mommy and daddy sure as stars are sure.

But now, we had to lie awake to be sure we did not dream, to be sure that Danny was here, that the bad year had ended—nearly to the day —that we were in harbor, safe, a family for good and all.

34 IN THE MIDDLE of the second afternoon we had him, Danny began to have trouble sucking. That did not concern me very much; he was so small-sized the nipple overwhelmed him. But I could not rouse him. Through the night, he had not waked for feedings; I had awakened him, and got only a couple of ounces down.

I undressed him, I tickled his feet, I stroked his cheek. Nothing. He didn't stir.

"He's cooked," Dan told me heartily. "He's sleepy from lying in the sunlight, just as you would be sleepy if you lay in the sun all day."

But I was not convinced; Dr. DiMaggio had told me Danny was active in the nursery. This stillness . . . I called Laura. She was puzzled. Michael had always been eager for his bottle. At four o'clock I called the hospital.

"I just brought my baby home yesterday, and it seems that I can't rouse him to feed," I told the nurse who answered.

"What's the baby's name?"

"His name is Daniel Allegretti, but I don't know what his birth name was—we've adopted him. . . ."

"Oh. I know which baby you mean. Well, have you tried rubbing his back, or tickling his feet? Some newborns will just sleep and sleep if you let them."

"Yes. And it doesn't do any good."

"Well, he has to eat. He can't go for very long at his size. Keep trying, but if it lasts until tomorrow, get in touch with your pediatrician."

Ann was coming in with Gail and her husband to see the baby, and they were going to drive with my father to Chicago to see a White Sox game. I'd convinced Dan to go as well, since there was an extra ticket. Now I wasn't sure I wanted him to leave me.

I called my dad. "It's probably nothing," he said, "but let me give Sam Skolnik a call." Sam Skolnik was an old friend of my father's, a pediatrician who worked in the area, and he had agreed to do Danny's early care. But it was Wednesday night; Dr. Skolnik would not be in his office. I didn't know how my father could find him.

My father called back fifteen minutes later. "He'll meet you at his office in an hour. I found him at his golf club."

"Dad, do you think he minds?"

"I didn't ask him to do it for nothing. I'll pay him."

"Still, it's an inconvenience. . . ."

"Look, honey. Sam's been a doc for forty years. If you're scared, you should have him take a look at Danny."

My father arrived at the house not long after, at the same time as Ann and Dan's sister and her husband, who had brought Jocelyn over for the evening, and Ann painstakingly coaxed the baby to take an ounce of formula, while I sat across the room smoking and weeping.

"I'm so afraid, Dan. There's something wrong with him."

"Jackie, this is your pattern. The first little thing . . ."

"Dan, I can't help it."

We discussed the ball game. I told Dan he should go; he would not hear of it. Déjà vu. "The last time you convinced me to go to a ball game against my better judgment, I had cause to regret it," he said.

"Jackie," Jocelyn whispered, tugging at my arm. "There isn't really anything wrong with Danny, is there?"

"I don't think so really, sweetie."

Ann and my father and Nick and Gail set off for the game. They would call us during the seventh inning, they said.

We found Skolnik's office, in a little suburban office center, without much trouble. We were early, and the heat, as we sat in the parking lot, was terrific. "It's so hot, that's why the baby's asleep," Dan kept repeating, wiping his face nervously. "That's why."

Dr. Skolnik arrived, a tiny, natty old man in bright golf clothes, driving a huge, powder-blue Lincoln Continental. He shook our hands, and asked after my dad, and unlocked the office door. We told Jocelyn it would be best if she waited in the waiting room—she could read the kids' books—but she would not. It reminded her too much of when we were in Door County, she said.

"Now Mother, undress the boy," Sam Skolnik instructed, and as I did, I saw the doctor's face change from its studied benignity to something sharp, alert; and I wanted to run, to take Danny and run to Madison, to Canada, and beyond, as if I could run far enough and fast enough. . . ."

"This is not a full-term baby," said Skolnik. "This baby is very premature, perhaps two months. I thought your father said he was full term?"

"That is what Dr. DiMaggio told us, the doctor who placed him with us," Dan said. "And we didn't know . . . he did seem so small. . . ."

Skolnik bent over the table. He straightened Danny's arms from his sides and let them flop back, and turned over the baby's hands to examine his palms. "Look at the shape of his head," he murmured. "No, this baby is quite premature." He sat Danny up. Danny did not wake. "A baby should wake up when you rouse him. . . ."

"Should he be in the hospital?"

"No, there doesn't seem to be any need for a respirator or . . . but there is something else here, possibly, some indications of a genetic abnormality, perhaps. . . ."

Dan says that I staggered, that I reached behind me for the chair and it was not there. He caught me by the elbows, and I heard Dan ask, "What? Doctor, what?"

"He means the baby has Down's syndrome, Dan." My voice was clear, far-off, as if it came from a tape in another room.

Skolnik looked up abruptly. "That's right," he said to me. "But I'm not sure. I can't be . . . there are some indications." He bustled off to the back of the office for a medical book.

"He's wrong," Dan whispered hoarsely. "Look at Danny. He's not mongoloid. Look at him." Dan looked at me. "Jackie, sit down. Are you all right?"

I said I was fine. And then Skolnik was back and showing us pictures in books, terrible pictures of blank, tiny faces with protruding tongues —oh, but Doctor, this is not a case in a book, this is our son, whom we have waited for so desperately, please tell us you were wrong after all, or if you cannot, give us some pills, a great many, enough for all of us, because it's true. I know it's true.

"Do you see the line on his palm?" Dr. Skolnik showed us Danny's tiny hand, his petal hand, with a straight crease across it. "This is called a simian line. And he puts out his tongue—not too much—and the shape of his eyes . . ."

"But many newborns have slanted eyes, Doc." Dan is strangling; he seems to choke over his voice.

"That's absolutely true. I just can't be sure. The fold on the back of his neck—there are some characteristics, but not all of them. They aren't pronounced." He smiled kindly at us. "If I had to stake all my money on it right now, I would say that this is *not* a Down's syndrome baby. That's what I would say." He paused. "What about the doctor you say placed the baby with you? Didn't he mention this?"

"He said the baby was normal," Dan said.

"But the chromosome tests, Dan . . ."

Skolnik's eyes snapped. "He did a chromosome test?"

"He said it was routine."

"Well, it is not routine."

"Do you think he knew? That he suspected and he represented this baby as a normal baby to us anyway?"

"I'm not saying that. No, of course not," Skolnik said soothingly. "Was the birth mother an older woman? Do you know that?"

"She was eighteen."

"Ahhhh. Well, then, perhaps we have nothing to be concerned about. Long ago, maybe twenty-five years ago, I told a father I suspected Down's—I would not tell the mother, because I knew it would devastate her—and I was utterly wrong. That family still sends me pictures of this lovely, bright girl . . . doctors can be wrong. We will hope in this case that it's just a coincidence. . . . But let me have this Dr. DiMaggio's number. I'll call him as soon as I get home, and ask him about this test and when the results are due."

"Weeks," I told him.

"Well, if you don't want to wait, I know a man you can see." He rummaged in his desk file. "Here. Dr. Chang. He is a top-notch genetics specialist. And I'm sure he could tell you just by examining the baby. If you want me to call him and set up an appointment for you . . ."

"We'll call. It's no trouble," Dan told him. "Just let us have his number."

Dr. Skolnik wrote the number on a bit of paper. "I'll call you tonight after I talk with Dr. DiMaggio. For the time being, you go home, and treat the baby just as if he were your own, thin the formula with a bit of water if he has trouble keeping it down." He patted my hair as I dressed Danny, who still lay dreaming. "Try not to worry."

He turned to Dan. "But don't finalize the adoption yet. Please. Because if it's true as Jackie's father said, that the two of you may not be able to have more children . . . I don't know what you know about Down's, but this can be a very difficult, heartbreaking situation for parents."

"I know what it means," Dan said flatly.

We drove, not speaking. Dan says that after a few minutes, I lifted

Danny from his car seat and began to rock him, and sing to him, "I knew this would happen. I knew this would happen," as if it were a lullaby; but I don't remember that. Nor the drive. I remember only vaguely Jocelyn's leaving, faint smudges of blue under her bright eyes, someone offering to drive her home. I remember the phone ringing, and Dan telling Gail, "The doctor thinks Danny has Down's syndrome." And then repeating, "Down's syndrome."

Gail would tell me later that she made her way through the crowds at Comiskey Park back to the boxes and told the rest of them. "It was so loud out there I couldn't hear. I thought that Dan said the baby might have Down's syndrome. But he couldn't have said that." It was the seventh inning—the score was seven to six, the Sox trailing, with three men on base and two outs. It was a crucial pennant contest. They got up and left. They were in the door a half hour later. I don't know how they made it; they must have driven ninety miles an hour without stopping. Gail told us, "Oh, the game was boring."

I had been afraid of what my father would say. I could already hear him. Someone else's problems. You didn't know this DiMaggio character; you wouldn't listen to me. But he came into the room, and I ran to him and put my head against his chest, and he said nothing like what I had expected. He only stroked my hair and said over and over, "Little girl. Little girl."

I slept for an hour, my hand on Danny's cradle. When I awakened, the house was full. My brother was there. And Sandy. Dan was on the phone, trying to reach Dr. DiMaggio. He had called four times. The first time, one of DiMaggio's teenage sons answered. "We have a terrible problem here," Dan told the boy. "The baby your father placed with us may have Down's syndrome. I have to reach your father right away." The boy was vague. He thought his father might still be at the hospital. Dan called the hospital. It was ten o'clock. Dr. DiMaggio had not been seen. He spoke with a nurse in the nursery. The baby had been lethargic, difficult to feed. The nurses had suspected, but then, Dan must understand, it was not their place . . . he said he understood. Dan asked about Dr. DiMaggio's reputation. The nurse was noncommittal. "Oh, God," she said. "We feel for you. You are lovely people."

Dan called DiMaggio's home a second time. The phone rang and rang. "He's not at the hospital now, the sonofabitch," Dan muttered. "He's sitting right there, letting the phone ring, talking to his lawyer."

Dr. Skolnik phoned us. DiMaggio had returned the call Skolnik had left on his service. DiMaggio told the pediatrician he had suspected Down's syndrome from the first. He had done the chromosome tests. But the mother had been so young, and had had a normal child two years before, and the pediatrician who had checked the baby, he said, had not seemed concerned. DiMaggio had decided to go ahead.

"But if he had even the smallest suspicion, he should have told us," Dan pleaded. "Isn't that true? He told us that if there was anything wrong with the baby when it was born, he would not place it. How could he do this to us?"

How could he do this to us? Dan asked me. "He couldn't have known," I insisted. I was not ready to see monsters.

"Maybe he knew," Gail put in. "Maybe that's why the mother gave the baby up in the first place. Maybe they all knew."

"He knew you guys wanted a baby so badly," Nick said. "Maybe he figured you wouldn't find out until it was too late. . . ."

"It's too late now. He's our baby," I said. And everybody stared at me.

"Jacquelyn," my father said, warningly, "you can't . . ."

"I don't know yet what we can or can't do. Maybe we won't have to decide. But so far as DiMaggio's duping us is concerned, where would be the profit? We didn't pay him a dime. Why would he risk his reputation . . . ?"

"You could sue him," Nick suggested.

"Sue him? I'll break his goddamned neck," Dan said darkly, and I thought, unkindly, how easy it is for him to overreact when it is his problem as well as mine.

"Dan . . ." I said.

"But Jackie, I can't. This is my worst fear. This is my nightmare, happening. . . ." He walked, ran, from the room. I found him in the baby's room. He had lifted Danny gently from the cradle and knelt beside the bed, his arms encircling the baby. "Please, little baby. Please be well. This is Daddy, Danny. Please be okay."

He would tell me later, "I prayed. I hadn't prayed in twenty years. I offered God years of my life, my health, anything He would demand, if only He would give Danny a normal chance. . . ."

We reached Mrs. DiMaggio at eleven o'clock the next morning. Dan said she feigned surprise at the news; I can't be sure whether she did. "I'm sure the doctor will say it's fine for you to keep the baby," she told

Dan. "I know if my little Tony got Down's syndrome, I'd love him just as much as I do now. . . ."

Dan cupped the phone. "Bitch," he said. "She's talking like she doesn't even know what it is. This woman is a *nurse?*" And he said to Mrs. DiMaggio, "You don't seem to understand. Danny was presented to us as a healthy infant. This is the most terrible thing that has ever happened to us. We don't know what to do."

She promised to have her husband call us right away. DiMaggio phoned an hour later. He'd been on the line to the lab in California, he said, and there was some goddamned problem with the sample sent for the tests. He wanted to take another test; would we bring the baby to the hospital? "It would be better for us to keep him until we know for sure," he told Dan. "My wife will care for him, and as soon as we're sure, we'll call you and you can have him back. I checked with my lawyer, and it'll be okay. I don't want you two to continue the bonding process with him. . . ."

But Dan had checked with a lawyer as well, a woman who worked with my sister-in-law Sandy. And she had advised us, before we'd even asked, not to give the baby back to the DiMaggios in any case; we'd been given legal custody, and if a lawsuit should develop, we did not want to stand in any shady areas. "We'll just keep Danny, thanks," Dan said sharply. "Unless you want to admit him to the hospital, we can't legally place him in your hands. We will bring him to the hospital, and you can take the test, and then we'll bring him home."

DiMaggio was silent. Then he said. "Fine. Whatever you want. Jesus, Dan, I'm so sorry this happened."

"You should have told us."

"I never thought . . . it was a judgment call."

"It was a judgment call that's destroying me and my wife." We made plans to meet him at the hospital later that day. But when Dan put down the phone, he abruptly picked it up again and called Dr. Chang's number. "I'm not going to rely on his fucking test. He may say he can rush it through the lab and have results by Monday, but it could take weeks, and then I'm not sure I trust the guy enough to believe the test results whatever they are. I want a specialist to look at Danny. I don't give a shit what it costs."

"I'd like to speak with Dr. Chang," he told the medical center operator who answered.

"Dr. Chang is in a consultation. But I can let you speak with Dr. Wang," she said.

337

"Fine."

Dr. Wang said Down's syndrome was not his area; we wanted Dr. Wong. Dan rolled his eyes at me. "It sounds like a comedy team," he said. Dr. Wong came on the line, a crisp, heavily accented young voice.

"But this is terrible," he said when Dan explained our situation. "I can't be sure what I can tell you by seeing the baby, but you can bring him in tomorrow. I'll make time for it."

We thanked him.

We set out for the hospital with Danny. Jane DiMaggio met us in the lobby, along with Sister Frances, who looked drawn. Mrs. DiMaggio put out her arms to me, and I walked into them, letting her motherliness enfold me, forgiving her. Dan watched in distaste.

We waited, listening anxiously to Danny's sharp cry as the technicians took blood from his tiny arm. "We're in love with him back there," a young nurse told me, as she placed the baby back in my arms.

"So are we," I told her.

We talked with the DiMaggios in the lobby. Dr. DiMaggio had brought a personal check, made out to the amount of all our expenses for the adoption, which he insisted we take. "This is my responsibility," he told us. "And if it turns out that Danny has Down's, you'll want to rescind the adoption."

"We're not sure of that," Dan told him.

"Dan, I know you love him, you and your wife, but you're talking about a kid here who may not thrive, who might develop problems that would shorten his life, not to mention the retardation. . . ."

"I know that."

"Let's just wait on the tests." We had not told him about Dr. Wong. "If it's bad, then you'll have the next baby that becomes available."

"That's kind of you," I said. Dan shot me a baleful look.

"It was kind of him," I said in the car.

"It was the only goddamned thing he could do," Dan shouted. "Jackie, do you know what he's done here? I don't know if it's malpractice, but he's admitted he knowingly committed a fraud. He told Skolnik he suspected the baby had genetic damage, and he went ahead anyway. He smells a lawsuit, that's all."

"But Dan," I asked again, "if he does, why would he have taken such a risk?"

"Maybe he thought we were stupider," he paused, "than we are."

Dan was on the telephone the rest of the day—with the lawyer at Sandy's company and with the lawyer who had processed the adoption.

The phone was his comrade, his reporter's sword that cut down the wrongdoers. He used it to keep the terrors at bay.

I did not put Danny down—when he slept, he slept curled on my stomach. He had perked up over the past day, and regarded me gravely with his bright, hazel eyes. I bathed him on his bath sponge, dabbed his circumcision with Vaseline. Brushed his long, fine hair into a topknot. "Come and have something to eat," Dan told me. He had rushed through a delicatessen on the way back to the house, picking up packages of this and bags of that, unsure whether any of it went together. He'd laid it out on the kitchen table, stuck spoons in the mustard pots, tried to make a nice picnic. I stared at him. "I can't eat."

"You have to eat."

"I want to be with Danny."

"Darling, he's asleep now."

"But I have to watch him sleep. I have to watch him," Dan told me later that I said, "because I may not have very long."

Gail found a baby-sitter the next day. She wanted to drive to Dr. Wong's office with us. "You needn't," I told her, wanting her to, wanting someone, anyone with Dan and me if we had to face the worst. I worried for Dan.

He had held the baby, wide-awake and utterly fetching, up to me the night before. "Look at this boy. This boy is just a regular boy. Nothing is wrong with this child. So his eyes are funny. They are just like Daddy's." Dan's eyes and Jocelyn's had a definite tilt to the lid, more pronounced when they were tired. He would not admit there was a strong possibility that Skolnik's suspicions were accurate. "You know how you have feelings? Well, I have a feeling. I have a feeling that Danny is fine."

The geneticist's lab was in a huge complex; the hospital was one of the largest pediatric facilities in the Midwest. It took us an hour to get there, and the baby fretted in the heat.

Gail waited in the hall while Dr. Wong examined the baby. "Strange," he said, turning Danny on his side, on his tummy, "I . . . I can't be sure."

He walked out into the hall and summoned a tiny brown woman in a long white lab coat. "This is Dr. Sommers," he said, and the woman smiled at us. "I would like her to take a look at him."

Dr. Sommers examined the baby. "Not traditional," she told Wong, tracing the line in Danny's palm.

339

"This is not what we'd call a typical simian crease," he explained. "This is a kind of line that some quite normal people have. I think you could go downstairs and into a roomful of medical students and find one or two that have this very same configuration."

"But the eyes," said Dr. Sommers. "Does the baby poke his tongue out often?"

I was at a loss. "Fairly often."

She shrugged at Dr. Wong. He went back out into the hall, and came back with a graying Oriental man, a man he held, by his gestures, in high regard. "This is Dr. Chang. Doctor, this couple have begun adoption proceedings on this baby; he was presented to them as a healthy infant, but there is some question . . ." Dr. Chang leaned over the baby. He reached for his stethoscope.

"Do the baby's lips turn blue when he cries?"

"No."

Chang listened for a moment. "His ticker seems fine." He picked up one of Danny's feet. Shook his head. "Don't finalize the adoption," he said. I reached for Dan's hand; he snatched it away, raked his hair with his fingers.

"Do you think that he has Down's?"

Chang nodded, briefly. And left.

Dr. Wong faced us across his desk. "Now, you know that Down's syndrome is not one condition, there are many different degrees and variations. It may be that all of the genes have the abnormal chromosome configuration, it may be that only some of them do. Some children who have only, let us say, fifty percent abnormal, do . . . rather well."

"But there is always retardation."

"Yes. Almost always."

"Is there no test you can do? The doctor who placed Danny with us did a blood test, and he said it would take three weeks to get the results, and then he did another one and said it would be back to us by next Tuesday."

"That's impossible."

"The test always takes so long?"

"Well first of all, it's Labor Day weekend. And secondly, such a test means hours of counting chromosomes . . . it's just impossible."

"Doctor, we are . . ." How could I explain it? "We are in a great deal of pain. We have waited for a baby for what seems to us a terribly long time, and this was our greatest joy. . . ."

"Let me excuse myself for a moment." He walked back out into the hall and summoned Dr. Sommers. They held a whispered conversation. Wong came back in, smiling. He glanced at Danny, nestled in my arms, and said, "We will do a test. We will stop everything here for it. It will be ready by, perhaps by late Wednesday afternoon. If the blood cultures properly." Dr. Sommers swabbed Danny's foot with alcohol, and a lab technician took his blood.

"So tiny," said the lab technician, stroking the baby's fist.

"I want to be optimistic," said Dr. Wong. "That is how I am. Dr. Chang . . . he's more cautious. But let me ask you this, you are young —why do you adopt? You could have your own children."

"We have had . . . an ectopic pregnancy, and other troubles," Dan explained.

"But maybe these can be fixed. There are many new techniques."

Dan gave Dr. Wong a weary smile. "Believe me. We're trying all of them."

"Then maybe you will have your own children if you do not adopt this baby." His smile evaporated. "It is my business to counsel parents on raising a Down's child. It is my business to help them. But it is also my business to see that these kinds of children are not born, do you see? If the baby has Down's, I am going to have to get in touch with the birth parents, so that they can be warned about future births. If they are young people, this probably is a congenital matter. I am trying to say to you, you have a choice. Don't choose this. It is a more difficult thing than you can imagine."

He folded his long fingers on his desk blotter. "There. We will have a test for you soon. Not long to wait. Are you happy now? It will turn our lab upside down to do it."

"We're not . . . happy," I told him. "But we are grateful to you."

The test cost $275. Dan presented his MasterCard at the desk. We wondered how we would pay for it. Gail, who'd waited in the hall for the whole ninety-minute consultation, finally asked, "For God's sake, do they think he has it?"

I did not want to answer in front of Dan. But he said, "Gail, I think it's going to be bad news." She put her face in her hands and cried.

We had a doctor's appointment that afternoon. Physicals for the adoption. We did not know if we should bother. As Gail held the baby in our living room, Dan and I huddled on the bed. "What should we do?" I asked him. "What if the worst is true? Can we raise Danny?"

"It would mean a change in every area of our lives. One of us would have to give up working, I think, because a retarded child has a great many more needs. . . ."

"And we have to think about special schooling. We'd want him to be able to achieve as much as he could."

"But Jack, what if he could achieve nothing? Some Down's kids learn to read and write. But there are some who can never even feed themselves."

"Dan, I don't know if I can go the distance."

"I don't either."

"I hate myself for admitting this, but I wanted to teach my child, to read to him and help him make up stories. I wanted to take pride in his schoolwork. . . ."

"That's no crime. But it isn't that part of it that bothers me. It's . . . what if he should develop some other physical complication? What if he should die at the age of ten? I could perhaps, if I had to, give him up now. It would kill me, but if I had to, I would do it. But I could never give him up then, not after years. If it feels like this after three days . . . oh, God."

"Honey, honey. You can cry."

"I can't. I'd never stop."

We sat in the parking lot of the doctor's office after our physicals—wanting to drive home, dreading it. We'd gone ahead with the appointment on the chance the tests would be negative—and on the off chance that in the future, we might want to adopt another baby DiMaggio found. "I don't know why I agreed to this appointment," Dan said bitterly, "because if it turns out Danny has Down's, I'm never going to want to see DiMaggio's face again. I won't adopt another baby through him. I couldn't ever trust the man."

"Dan, Dan, he's only trying to help us. I know that the impulse is to blame . . ."

"Blame? Jack, I could do murder."

We drove back to the house. The tree-lined blocks teemed with children—children running through sprinklers, hopping curbs on their bikes, sweet brown bodies in bright shorts and sunsuits. "This is the last week of vacation," I remembered suddenly. "Jocelyn will be back in school next week, a third grader. Dan, does it seem possible . . ."

"Oh, Jesus. This is going to destroy her!" he burst out. "Every time

I call her, she asks, 'Is the baby all right yet, Daddy?' She thinks we can give him some medicine and he'll get well."

"It's as if we'd been teaching her that nothing is permanent, not pregnancies, or marriage, or baby brothers."

"Her face, when she saw the baby. She kept telling me, 'I'll never be an only child again. . . .' It's not just the thing itself happening, it's the choice. . . ."

"I know, as if the pain weren't bad enough, it's as if we're being told, 'It's not enough that you suffer, you have to choose your mode of pain.' " Like Sophie. The gods, when they wanted to punish, gave a choice. A choice was the cruelest, I thought. It made you bear not only grief, but the responsibility for the grief.

"But we're grown. What about him? What kind of life will he have?"

"With or without us, he'll probably be a happy child, Dan. Everything I've ever read about Down's children indicates they are happy children. He'll probably have a childhood that lasts . . . years."

"You say that to soothe yourself."

"How can I do anything else? How can I think of having him hurt? Or needing? Needing me, who could give him up. . . ."

"Oh, darling, don't beat yourself. I'm sorry. I'm just on edge. I can't think."

Gail said, as we walked into the house, "Call Dr. DiMaggio right away. He called half an hour ago!"

I took the baby from her. Dan went to the phone. It can't be the results. Too soon. But I held Danny tighter, so tight he began to struggle faintly.

I heard Dan's end of the conversation. "Well, that is . . . good of you. Thank you for letting us know. But as you can imagine, we're not interested in hearing about that right now." He paused. Lit a cigarette. "Well, we will think about it. And we'll be in touch with you right after we hear from Dr. Wong. Yes, we did have another test done. We couldn't wait. Yes, one will serve to confirm the other."

He put down the phone and turned on the television.

"Well, what did he say?"

"He said, and I quote, 'Well, Dan, somebody up there must like you.' "

"Huh?"

"He said that at two o'clock in the morning, one of the nuns called him from the hospital and asked him if he wanted to place another baby for adoption. There was a girl there in labor, telling them she wanted to place the baby."

"And he said . . . ?"

"He said he did. He went over there, and he delivered the baby. And it was a little boy. A perfectly healthy little boy." Dan's eyes burned from blue hollows; his whole face looked bruised. "He said that if we decided to rescind the adoption, we could adopt this baby. 'I'm sure this time,' he said. He already called the lawyer, and the lawyer told him it was a peculiar circumstance, but that it could be arranged, that we wouldn't have to go through any other interviews. . . ."

"And you said?"

"I said we couldn't think about that just now." My heart knocked.

"Are you sure?"

"I'm sure."

"You could *never* do that," Gail piped up. "That would be the most horrible thing. When you first told me another baby might be available in a matter of months, even then I was horrified. You can't just . . . trade babies."

"Of course not," I said.

"You would never consider that, would you, Dan?" she asked. "After all you've been through . . ."

"No," Dan answered. "And furthermore, I don't believe a word the guy says. Doesn't it sound awfully damned peculiar to you that this guy makes a terrible, unconscionable mistake and then suddenly—out of the blue—there's this other, perfect, healthy little baby boy to make it all right? Convenient."

"Maybe he just went out and bought a baby," Gail suggested. "That's what I thought this was when I first heard about the whole thing. A baby-selling racket. People don't just . . . give up babies. This doctor's got to be crooked."

I wanted to smack her. Let us all leap then, hand in hand, off paranoia peak. "If it's a racket, it's a hell of a poor money-maker. Think, Gail. Why would someone buy babies and then basically give them away? We didn't pay Dr. DiMaggio anything."

"Maybe just to get his fees paid."

"But they would be paid. Even if the birth mother was on welfare, *somebody* would pay him. His fee for delivering Danny was five hundred and fifty bucks, Gail. Do you think anyone would be so stupid as to risk his license, his practice, everything, to get five hundred and fifty bucks?"

"Well, I don't know. But I think the whole thing stinks."

"Maybe it does. But you'd have to show me a better motive . . ."

"Well, now, the motive would be avoiding a lawsuit," Dan said. The investigative reporter. "I'm going to make a few calls."

But nothing turned up. Dan and Merill McCann, the attorney who worked with Sandy, made phone calls all evening and part of the following day. Those they talked with who knew anything about Dr. DiMaggio said he seemed to be a decent guy. That he simply had good rapport with the nuns at several large Catholic hospitals, and that they turned to him when they counseled single mothers. His work was well known. Our attorney for the adoption, whose own suspicions were raised by the appearance of the second baby, did some checking on his own. The circumstances were as DiMaggio had described them: an eighteen-year-old college girl already in labor came into the hospital with her mother. The physician who had done her prenatal care was unavailable, so DiMaggio, who was on call, did the delivery. After a long conference with her parents, and then with her parents and a nun, the girl had decided to offer the baby for adoption. It was an uneventful birth. The baby weighed six pounds and one ounce. The DiMaggios had petitioned the county court for temporary custody of the baby boy, and received permission to take custody pending his adoption. DiMaggio told Dan that he had screened a couple who were eager to adopt the baby. But he would wait on our word.

"What would you do in the event that Danny has Down's, and that we decided we could not keep him?" Dan asked me. We were sitting on the couch, staring out at the quiet street late on Friday night. Danny lay in his basket, wearing the yellow cap the nuns at the hospital knitted for preemie babies, who are prone to heat loss. I had held him on my knee, a half hour before, while Dan took pictures. He'd been wiggling and grimacing—and then suddenly, with newborn ease, he'd gone limp. Asleep.

"I didn't know that we'd decided."

"I talked to Todd today. You know he has two retarded kids in his family. He told me what his parents went through raising Mary and Patrick. How difficult it was. The guilt. And the worry, now that they're growing up, and Todd's parents are in their sixties." He turned his cigarette in his fingers. "You know, Jack, we didn't get started all that early on parenthood. What if we keep Danny, and then when he's thirty, if he lives that long, I die? We'd have to make plans for his care for the rest of his life. . . ."

"We would have had to do that if we'd given birth to him."

"But we didn't. However we feel, we didn't give birth to him. We don't have the obligation . . ."

"Stop that."

"We don't."

"It's too cruel."

"All of it's too cruel. At any rate—I was telling Todd about DiMaggio offering us another baby, thinking out loud, I guess, about adopting both of them. And Todd said, don't. Better to take neither. Because, he said, we would do as his parents had done. We'd favor Danny. We'd say, in effect, the normal ones will do all right on their own. And Todd said for two little boys the same age, both adopted, that would be devastating. To the one who was not retarded. He'd feel like . . ."

"Like dessert. Not the meal."

"In a way."

"It was good of you, though, to consider it."

"I know you want a normal baby. I can't blame you for that. And I've asked myself over and over, should we consider this other option? Will we ever have another chance? Will we kick ourselves someday for turning it down?"

I also asked myself, Dan, I thought. I know that we will. But . . .

"But I could never forget Danny, honey," Dan said. "I would see his bright, slanted little eyes in my mind for the rest of my life. If we took this other baby, I couldn't be his father. It would be your baby alone. And that would be wrong. There is just . . ." His eyes spilled, and he looked into mine, unmindful of the tears. "There is just no more room in my heart. . . ."

"You once thought that about Jocelyn. That you could never love another child."

"I thought it. I thought it up until the moment you placed Danny in my arms. He was so helpless, so tiny, more tiny than any baby I'd ever seen. And that might have been part of why . . . I gave all I had to him in that moment, Jackie. There's no more left to give."

"Then tell DiMaggio." I would not cajole him, not beg him to think it over yet again, though I thought, with fearful intensity, of putting the tiny clothes back into their bags, stripping the sheets from the cradle and putting it back into the truck, taking the cradle to Leah and Todd, wondering how such things could be done.

"I will," said Dan. "I'll tell him. But not yet. If it were up to you, you'd take the other child, wouldn't you?"

"And give Danny up, too?"

"I guess that's what I was asking."

"I don't know, Dan. It seems more callous than a person could be. Perhaps if we could raise both of them . . ." I shook my head. "But we couldn't do that. I don't know what to do. The chance to have a healthy infant doesn't come along every day, not even every year. It might never come again. This . . . it seems two of them born in such a short space is impossible. But, Dan, I might take the other baby. Even if we had to give Danny up. I won't stop wanting a child."

"I want this child," said Dan. "He's my *son*, Jackie, he has my *name*." He groped for my shoulders and held them, as if I could keep both of us afloat.

35 MAY WE never again have such a weekend. May whatever disasters poised over the arch of the years we have to pass through fall swiftly, decisively, and let us scramble out from under if we're able.

It was a weekend of stopped clocks—clocks glanced at on the striking of the hour that an hour later by the body had moved ahead only five minutes. We did not sleep. An hour here or there, lying close together, and then waking—seeing the shape of the cradle in darkness, or hearing the dear urgency of the baby's hungry cry—and then dusting off the sleep, and finding under it the reality. After a while, we did not bother. I didn't eat, and when I next stepped on a scale, five days later, I had lost twelve pounds. Dan ate doggedly, joylessly cleaning out the refrigerator, running out for milkshakes and pinwheel cookies. We both smoked—the drapes and pillows stank of it—packs of the cigarettes we had sworn we'd give up forever, once we had a child.

Our friends called. Sharon, a woman I had known from work, called Saturday morning. "I hear there's a new man in your life," she began, teasing, jubilant.

"Yes, yes Sharon, but wait . . ."

They could not believe it, our friends. What could they do? What could they bring? They would come . . . no, we told them. We were managing. We would let them know. We thanked them.

Todd called daily. On Saturday afternoon, Dan was asleep. "I hate to wake him," I apologized.

"Don't. Dan's not doing very well, Jack. He fancies himself a stoic but this is tearing him up. Jesus, what did you guys do to deserve this? It's as if every time you turn around, some fate or the other has to take a turn pissing on you."

"Karma. In another life, I must have been Vlad the Impaler."

"Did you hear any more about the other baby?"

"No. Just that we can have him if we . . . if . . ."

"Have you decided?"

"We can't decide. We can barely talk."

Laura called two, three times a day. I called her as often. "Have you thought about DiMaggio's offer anymore?"

"Laura, Dan won't consider it. And I half agree with him. It would make me a monster."

"Jackie, no! You have rearranged your lives around having a baby. What are you going to do with these months?"

"What I would've done if no other child had ever been offered. Write the book. If we don't get to keep Danny, I'll just . . . bide."

"But babe, you want to have a baby. Is that some sin, now? You've known now, what it can mean to you to have a baby. If you come out of this with nothing but empty arms and an empty cradle, I fear for your sanity. Not to mention your marriage . . ."

Bobby and Sandy came over every night. On Sunday afternoon, Dan said wearily, "I just want to be alone. I can't bear to talk about it anymore. When Bobby calls, tell him that, honey. He'll understand."

Bobby called. "Dan's at rock bottom," I said. "He just doesn't want any company tonight. He just doesn't want to see anybody else."

And my brother, my dearest, said, "Fine. Then we won't bring anybody else. We'll just come." And as he had been so often in the past year—so often in our adulthood, if I was honest—he was the elder, the soother to me that weekend. This was what I had wanted for Jocelyn, the utter, ineluctable support of a brother, who when you are alone, when your hair is dank and stringy and smoke-smelling, when there are hives on your hands, and you have worn the same dress for two days without taking it off, touches your cheek and says, "You look better. You're doing just fine."

He remembers Sunday night, when he stayed with me, when my dad insisted on taking Dan to his club picnic—"This man needs a beer," he said—and Sandy had to go someplace with her mother. He fell asleep in front of a baseball game on television, and when he woke, it was dark, and I was not in the room.

He found me on the side of the bed, rocking Danny in his cradle, and he told me later that he could not see me in the darkness, but he could hear me, and I was saying, "No more. No more. No more."

"Why does this have to happen to you?" he cried. "You're a good person. You don't deserve it. Oh, Sis, if I only could take it away."

"Poor Dan."

"Poor all of us."

"Dan doesn't want the other baby, Bobby."

"I know. I've wanted to talk to him. But it isn't my place. The poor bastard. Oh, but Jack, you need to be parents. You'd forget . . ."

"We'd never forget."

"But in time, you could live with yourselves again. And then you'd have a child. You're going to think that I'm a coldhearted shit, but try to look down the road. Three months. A year. This will fade from your mind. Okay, you'll never forget. But what else could help you heal more than a healthy baby? Honey, that was the point of all this. The point of all this worry, and work, and this . . . your campaign over the last year was to have a healthy child. You want that. Dad wants it. Even I want it."

"If only it can be Danny."

"I pray for that. But Jack," he took my hand, "if you search yourself, you know that no matter what Dan says, the tests are just a formality. Once you know that there is something wrong with Danny, and you look at him, you can see the signs. They're there."

"I love him. I love him no matter what fucking thing is wrong with him."

"I know you do. I love him, too. But we are talking about what amounts to a life sentence here, Jack. You want to write. You've told me that you'd work at a newspaper until you dropped down dead one day after deadline, that you'd never retire. That would be over, Jack. You're not talking about one life here. You're talking about three lives. Four, if you count Jocelyn's. About changing all those lives for something that, please forgive me for this, that wasn't your doing, and that you never asked for."

"Plenty of people adopt handicapped kids."

"People who know what they're going into with their eyes open. People who are prepared for it. Not people who have just struggled through the lousiest year of their lives, and nearly lost their marriage. Raising a handicapped kid puts an unreal burden on a marriage, Jack. You can't destroy yourself and Dan for this child."

"DiMaggio called today. He said he has a couple who wants Danny. Who've already adopted two other handicapped kids. I believe the father, or the mother, I can't recall, teaches retarded children. . . ."

"There you are."

"It's not so simple." I am his mommy, Bobby. I can't say that, because I don't want to wound you; you are doing your best. But it would mean giving up my own child.

"Just promise me you'll think about it. Do you want me to talk to Dan?"

"No," I told him. But he did. And later in the weekend, Dan said, "I've been thinking it over. I don't want to make any decision yet about another baby. I want to keep that option open."

"I'll go with what you decide," I said.

"That would be a first."

On Monday afternoon, Dan wanted to bring Jocelyn to the house. "Dan, no," I protested. She'd only be able to be here for a short time, and she has school tomorrow . . ."

"She wants to see the baby."

I exploded. "What? Play with the puppy that might have to go back to the pet store? He's not a thing, to be shown off while he's around. He's a little boy, a not very well little boy. . . ."

"He's fine. Even if he has Down's, he is just fine, Jackie. And I don't believe he does. I just can't believe he does."

But he called Jocelyn. And said she would have to wait for another time.

We slogged through Monday. On Tuesday Dan called the newspaper and arranged for a few weeks of open-ended leave. His editors were glad to give it. "Whatever happens, we're here," Elliott told him. "Take the time. No matter how it goes, you're going to need it."

On Wednesday morning, I had warmed a bottle and given it to Dan to feed to the baby in the bedroom, and was washing my hair in the sink when the telephone rang.

"Mrs. Allegretti?"

"Yes?"

"This is Dr. Wong." I sat down, hard, in a hard chair. "Are you alone?"

"I'm . . . my husband is here. In another room."

"Mrs. Allegretti, I have the test results. And I cannot tell you how sorry I am to have to say that it is as we had feared. . . ." I could not hear him. The pounding of the blood in my ears, like canals bursting their walls. "Mrs. Allegretti?"

"I'm here."

"Have you decided to terminate the adoption?"

"I believe . . . that we have, yes."

"I think that is best for you."

"We have no way of knowing."

"But I want you to know this. I intend to follow this case. The kind of Down's syndrome the baby has is a relatively rare phenomenon, a translocation . . ." He named it. "And this has been a special area of study for me. We want you to know that we will do all we can to help him thrive. . . ."

"Thank you for that. Thank you for all your help."

"It was nothing. I hoped the news would be good." He coughed. "I have contacted Dr. DiMaggio."

"He knows, then?"

"Yes, and Dr. Skolnik as well."

"Thank you."

"Dr. DiMaggio has said that he will speak with attorneys so that you may surrender custody of the baby to them while the order to . . ."

"Yes, yes, of course. He has told us that another baby is available."

"A healthy baby? But that's wonderful. You need to be happy, then."

Happy.

"We'll try. Good-bye now."

I sat holding the telephone until the warning whine began to sound. You must put one foot in front of the other, I told myself. You must take perhaps ten steps down the hall. You must tell Dan, and then be ready for whatever he hands you, because he will be wild with grief. You must put aside anything you feel. Later, you may have your turn.

But it was not necessary. I felt nothing. As if the nerves had been nipped at the source of the pain, in the way some physicians favored doing with terminal cancer patients, there was only numbness. I walked into the hall. I could hear Dan singing, off-key, "Danny Boy."

It turned out I did not have to say the words. "Who was that?"

"Dr. Wong."

He looked up. He held the baby against his chest. I shook my head. He keened. There is no other good word for it. He keened and rocked himself back and forth. I took Danny gently from him, fed him the remainder of his bottle, changed his diaper and wrapped him in his pink cotton blanket, and put him down to nap.

And then I called my brother at work. "I'll be there right away," he said.

But it would not be right away. He had a half-hour drive ahead of him.

Dan and I were alone, as we had not been all weekend. He did not talk. I made calls. I told Gail that we were planning on bringing the baby back this afternoon. She asked to talk to her brother. Dan shook his head at the phone. Gail said she would be at the house by noon; Lord, I thought idly, what we are costing our family in gas mileage.

I called Laura. "Can you do it?" she asked. "Tell me for real if you can do it."

"It wouldn't be right to let anyone else do it. Mrs. DiMaggio just called and offered to pick Danny up. She has papers for us, from the attorney . . . but I told her no."

"I think you're right, but only if you can do it. How is Dan?"

"He is . . . just . . ."

"Do you want me to come? Richard is here."

"No. Thank you. Laura, there's just this . . ." My brain seemed to be dividing in lobes—the part that has mothered Danny, the part that must let him go. It is a bizarre ache, the brain dividing, I thought.

"What is it? The movie? I'm trying to think of this bit of dialogue . . . his mommy of the heart, that's it. I was thinking last night, that you would always, no matter what, be Danny's mommy of the heart."

The tears came then. All the old cliché-loads of tears. Buckets. Showers. Dan came into the kitchen as I put down the phone and stood above me. "Cry," he said. "Cry hard." I looked up at him. His eyes were overbright, dry, an illness in them, a cachectic shine. "Cry, because this is all your fault."

"Dan, no."

"You and your fucking rotten luck. You, who had to rush to adopt a baby. Couldn't stop to consider what might happen. You pushed me, you pushed me, and now you have pushed me to this." I put out my hand. "Get away from me! I want to move. Now. Do you hear me? No more babies, adopted or otherwise. I want done with you. You're a . . . goddamned albatross. No one should have to live around you. I can't wait to get away from you, and live my life as a normal man. You're a . . . pariah . . ."

"I'm your wife. And I know that this is the worst thing that has ever happened to you. But nothing should make you say such things to your wife."

"They're true."

"They're not true. And you mustn't try to make me believe them."

I ran into the washroom and closed the door. Sluiced my face with cold water. Not a minute had passed before he was knocking. "Honey, forgive me, forgive me."

Bobby arrived, his shirt sticking, tie askew; he'd driven hard. Gail arrived, eyes red-rimmed, and went immediately to the cradle, to sit beside her brother. "Will you come with us?" I asked Bobby.

"That's why I came."

It was not so far in miles. Not even a proper outing for parents taking their little son for a ride on a sunny summer day. It was far in other measuring. Far to hear Gail's moaning in the back seat, where she sat next to her brother, "I should adopt him. I don't see how you guys can do this to him. I mean, so he's retarded? It's not as if he were mongoloid, like my girlfriend's baby. . . ."

"That's exactly what it is, Gail," I said, biting the words.

"Oh no. Down's syndrome and mongolism are two entirely different things."

"That's exactly what it is, Gail."

"Dan . . . ?"

"It is, Gail," he said. What she must think of me. This interloper. Who has dragged her brother over sharp rocks, willy-nilly, and seems not to care. It was all I could do to stare ahead. I counted buildings. I counted license plates with letter As in them. Dry-eyed, I stroked Danny's face as he lay, fed and fast asleep, in his car seat between Bobby and me. I rolled down the window and breathed in great swallows of overheated air. Gail wept quietly.

We pulled up at the curb in front of Dr. DiMaggio's small clinic. You will unfasten the straps—no, my baby, I will not, my son, this is not possible—and then, one foot in front of the other, you will walk in the door.

I walked past the desk, where an inquiring young woman in white asked me who it was I wanted to see, past the examining rooms to where I knew, without ever having been back there, Dr. DiMaggio's private offices were.

Jane DiMaggio and her sister, whom we had met the day we adopted Danny, were standing between a pair of huge polished wood desks. At the back of the room, I could see a bassinet had been set up. "Is that for Danny?" I asked.

Jane DiMaggio said it was. "But I will take him."

"Wait," I told her, literally holding up a hand. "Dan? Gail?" They came forward, bent. It is a funeral, I thought, here—pay your respects.

. . . Dan kissed the baby, crying hard. Gail cradled him for a moment against her cheek. I looked up at my brother, whose face was inert but for his eyes, and he shook his head.

"In this bag," I told Mrs. DiMaggio, "are two of his bottles. And his teddy bear. And his music box. These are his, and I want him to have them. . . ."

"Oh, honey," she said, her eyes moist, "please, stop . . ."

"He takes three ounces if you are very patient. He may spit some up. He takes his bottle at room temperature. . . ." Jane DiMaggio grabbed me. She caught Danny between us, and motioned the others away. Alone in the room with her, I kissed the baby's two cheeks. I told him that I loved him, and that I knew he would have luck in the world. And then I told my son good-bye, and placed him in Mrs. DiMaggio's arms.

And then walked out of a steel side door that seemed to be made for an emergency purpose, and to my brother, who was waiting outside in the alley for me.

They left us alone. I don't know how long the time was. Through two interfacing windows in the building, I could see Dan and Dr. DiMaggio talking in the courtyard. Dan was leaning on a trash dumpster, DiMaggio on the fender of his Cadillac, and both of them were smoking and looking at the ground.

"He kept trying to cheer me up, and I resented the hell out of it," Dan would tell me, long after. "I kept asking him, 'Don't you see how I feel? Don't you understand what is happening to me?' It was as if he could not bring himself to admit it, because if he did, he would have to bear the guilt. . . ."

Jane DiMaggio came to the fire door after a time. Her sister had taken Danny home to the DiMaggios' house, she said. She would contact the prospective parents, who would not be able to take him for several weeks, since the mother was in the hospital with an injured back. "We will take the best care of him in the world," she said. "He'll be with a physician's family, after all. . . ."

Bobby and I looked at her, and her voice faded. She asked me if I wanted to see the other baby. "No," I said. We would pick up the second baby, if we picked him up at all, tomorrow before court. Dan had arranged, just before we left the house, for Dr. Skolnik to meet us at Skolnik's hospital on the way to the courthouse, so that he could do his own examination of the baby before we proceeded.

"Please," Jane DiMaggio pleaded. "He is so beautiful. People will stop you on the street with this beautiful son. . . . Don't punish yourself. Just look at him. You can look at a baby. It won't hurt you."

My brother took my elbow. "Go ahead," he urged me. "I'll take responsibility for you if you flip."

Jane DiMaggio led us into one of the examining rooms. There was a baby scale—one of the huge, old white sort—pushed against one of the walls, and a large cardboard box sitting on the scale filled with blankets, and boxes of neat blue files stacked on tables, and a glass-fronted cabinet lined with medical samples. If there was a baby here, I couldn't see him.

I heard him. He gave out a cat's cry. In the box, surrounded by blankets, he was lying, flailing, kicking his feet, wearing an oversized striped sleeper with a patch on the pocket that read "Little Slugger." I heard my brother, standing behind me, draw in a breath. He was an astonishingly beautiful baby, with a round, broad brow that made me think of Swedes, and oval eyes that already were a clear blue. Everything about him was blond—the down that covered his cheeks, his fuzzy hair, with a hint of red, his infinitesimal lashes. "He may have red hair," Jane DiMaggio said, as if that worried her. "He is Irish on both sides."

I remember thinking, what a lovely, lovely boy. And making not one move to touch him. Jane DiMaggio began busily to remove his sleeper, and I saw his fat small legs churning, and then she turned to me and put her hands on her hips and said, "Here. You do it."

My hands moved as if they were marionettes attached by sticks to the ends of my arms. I reached out, and the baby twitched and wet all over the front of my dress. Bobby gave his silly, high-pitched hoot of a laugh. "He's yours now for sure," he said, his voice all hope.

I changed the baby. Poked his big feet back into the sleeper socks, feeling, guiltily, the health and soundness radiate from him. Though he was a very small infant, he seemed to me huge after Danny, who had been miniature, and madly active after Danny's limpness. But this, Jane DiMaggio was telling me, was how babies acted. Most babies.

Dr. DiMaggio had brought Dan in. Dan glanced at the baby, his mouth working. "He's . . . lovely," he said helplessly. He would later tell me, "*That* is what I still want to sue somebody for. For robbing me of the elation of that first look. That I had had with Danny. And with Jocelyn." But he could not touch him. And Gail was already waiting in the back seat of the car, her head forward on the backrest.

We began to drive home; it was rush hour in this small border town, and the hot streets were clogged. Bobby threaded his way slowly toward the expressway, cursing softly. At one point, he pulled over, yanked the baby seat out of the straps, and locked it in the trunk. "Sorry," he told me as he slammed the door on his side. "I'm not a stone."

And as if she had been cued, Gail said then, "You should put all of that stuff away. Bobby, will you help them? Just put it out of your minds. . . ."

"What, until tomorrow?"

"Tomorrow?"

And Dan, who was sitting shrunken against one side of the car in the back seat, his hands hanging between his knees like a small old man, said, "We've decided to adopt the other baby."

Her gasp was a whistle. "No! But you said . . ."

"I know what I said. But Jackie knows more about these things than I do, and she thinks that we have to take this chance, because we may not get another. . . ." Thank you, darling, I thought, tasting ash, for that nice vote of confidence. Burden neatly shifted. Proceed.

"You can't do this! What do you mean, you decided? You didn't decide! Jackie decided, like she decides every other thing."

We lingered on the roadside. "I figured the way it was going," Bobby told me the following week, "that I might as well not move, in case anyone wanted to get out and box."

"Gail," Dan remonstrated, weakly. But he could not help but feel championed. He could not help but hear echoes of himself in her defense of him.

"When I heard that DiMaggio might have another baby for you in a few months, I was astounded that you could even consider such a thing after so short a time. But I thought, 'Maybe it will work out. I couldn't do it, but maybe they have to.' I never dreamed you would consider this other baby. Danny, speak up for yourself. . . ."

"Gail, I wouldn't have done a thing without your brother's consent."

"Consent! Of course, he has to consent. He loves you. He wants to save his marriage. No matter what it costs him. You know, I've had about enough of this. The poor guy puts up with your bullshit for a year, and then you fix up this adoption, which was probably crooked to begin with . . ."

"Gail, it wasn't crooked. The papers are in the glove box if you would like to peruse them."

"It was fishy as hell! And now you want to drag him into this thing, one day after he loses his son. . . ."

"Dan? Are you being dragged?"

"What do you expect him to say? If he says no to the adoption, you'll never forgive him. You'll bitch at him for the rest of your life. I know what you said, Jackie, I know you said about the first adoption that if he didn't agree to it, you'd leave him."

"I said that? Dan, did I say that?"

"You said that."

And then I remembered. The cold feet night. When Dan had said the timing was all wrong, our finances were impossibly snarled, couldn't we just wait . . . and I had. I had laid it down. I had told him that he would be proving to me, by giving me a child, his stake in the marriage.

"You don't love him!" Gail was in high gear. "You just want a baby. You want a baby no matter if it's against nature, or if you have to break my brother's heart. . . . I told Ricky the other night, she'll leave him. I told him, 'She'll leave him as soon as she has what she wants.' "

My brother reached over and turned off the radio. "I don't believe," he said, deceptively mild, "that I am going to let you say that to her. Jackie has gone through hell today. And if you had the slightest bit of consideration for that fact, you would hear yourself, and realize how you're making her feel."

"Well, so have I gone through hell. And more to the point, so has my brother." She glowered at Bobby in the rearview mirror. "Well, I wash my hands of it. I could never look that kid in the face. Never."

"Gail," Dan began again, his voice impossibly small and weary. "Cool off."

"Well, Dan, someone has to say it. I've held it in long enough, when she abused you, and threatened to leave you . . ."

"Do you know what your brother told me this morning?" I purred. "In the very kitchen, do you know what he said? He said he wanted to get as far away as he could from my rotten luck, that I was an albatross, and a pariah. . . ."

"He didn't mean that. He was half crazy. You should have understood that."

"Oh. So, he can be upset and spout off, but I cannot be upset and

spout off. When I spout off, I mean it, and am later quoted. Set down
the rules, Gail, before we play."
"It's you who play. With lives."
"I see."
"With little Danny's life."
I said to her, "Fuck you, little girl. I don't have to take this from you.
And I have decided that I won't. So be still with your silly mouth."
"I know that you can't stand me, Jackie."
"You are trying me, Gail."
"I know . . ."
"It's apparently you who can't stand me. All this is quite a revelation.
Though I should not be surprised. Let's make it easy. Since I allegedly
give your baby dirty looks, don't present him to me for my dirty looks.
If you, or any other Allegretti present or not present, do not feel you
will be able to look at me and my kid, when I have him, don't look. Let
me make you a present of it."
"You'll be a wonderful mother, Jackie," she hissed. "You treat babies
as if they were baseball cards. You got a Willy Mays, and you wanted
a Mickey Mantle, so you just took it back. . . ."
"That is it," said my brother, throwing the car into gear. "We're
leaving now. We're driving back. Anyone who wants to ride, shut up."

Dan and I went to bed. Bobby spent the night on the couch. At
eleven o'clock, drugged and groggy, I heard Dan get up, and I made my
way out to the kitchen and clattered around on the unfamiliar shelves,
looking for coffee.
Dan went out to sit in the living room. I could see the red end of his
cigarette in the dark, hear the sofa creak as Bobby swung his long legs
up off its short length.
"How are you?" Bobby asked.
And Dan said, "Living."
"Gail was quite incredible today."
"It was an incredible day," I put in hurriedly. But I could not resist
it. "So far as the art of kicking one when one is down goes, however . . ."
"Jack," Dan said. "She was irrational. She was as upset as any of us
by this. She . . . takes things very personally."
"She's not the only one."

"So," said Bobby into the breach. "I'd like to sleep at least until Christmas. I never had a day like this day. Sleep that knits up the ravel'd sleave of care . . ."

"Shakespeare! Out of your mouth?"

"Not all engineers are dolts," he told me.

"Only most." A joke. Lame and wee. But a joke. Redux. Or is this double redux?

"What are you going to name the baby?"

"Oh, I don't know. We already named our baby what we wanted to name a baby. Dan, what do you think?"

"You liked Cody for a boy," Dan said, looking out of the window.

"That's a good name," Bobby said. "Uncle Forrest's horse was named that."

"Is *that* where you got it?" Dan shook his head.

"Thanks, Bob," I said. "Well, we talked about giving him my last name as a first name, if we had a son."

"Mitchard?" cried my brother. "Jack, that's appropriately bizarre, but come off it. . . ."

"Well, what then? Joshua? So he can be the fourteenth Joshua in the first grade?"

"We could name him Robert Daniel," Dan said softly.

"I like that a great deal," my brother said.

"Figured you would."

"Not because it's my name. Well, partly because it's my name. But it's a great sporting name. That kid has catcher's hands. I can hear the chanting now as he steps up to the plate. 'Bobby! Bobby!' "

"Robert. Now there's a really unusual name," I said. "I had in mind something more bookish. . . ."

"Bookish," Dan snorted.

"It's a name," my brother said then, "that nothing horrible is attached to. It's a name the gods won't notice."   ·

"So he can just grow up," Dan mused. "Like all the other little boys. . . ."

"Right."

"Robert Daniel it is," Dan said, in a voice that brooked no disagreement.

"You don't have to say it's after me," Bobby began, in his mock-wounded voice.

"But it is. The second baby Bobby," I said. "It will be after you. And we want you to be his godfather, don't we, Dan? And Sandy his godmother?"

"If we must have him baptized."

"We must."

"Then, of course. You will, won't you Bob?"

"Proud to," he answered.

	WE MET Dr. Skolnik at the hospital at eight. We stood
36	around fretting in the lobby, Dan compulsively creasing the leg of his slacks, until the DiMaggios arrived with the baby. Jane DiMaggio was right. The lobby full of nurses and technicians fluttered about him like so many doves.

"He's so beautiful!" "You surely can tell that one's a boy!"

Dr. Skolnik motioned us into the examining cubicle. He did not have much time; it was Rosh Hashanah and he was expected at temple. This exam was a gift from Sam to my father—the omens surrounding this adoption were very clearly circumscribed, and we could trust no other doctor's word.

I undressed the baby. "Ah," Skolnik began right away, "this is not a full-term baby either. . . ." He turned to me. I had not breathed. "Don't worry, Mother. That doesn't mean a thing. I would say he arrived sometime during the first week of the ninth month. This is called 'immature' rather than strictly premature." He continued, making small tuneful murmurs as he thumped the baby's chest, peered into his shells of ears over the pin light of his instrument, listened to his heart, and fingered his tiny, rosy genitals. "Mmmmmmmm." He spread his hands at us, and lifted the baby off the table. "This is a beautiful boy. This is a perfect baby. A gift. Now, Jackie, don't cry. . . ." He put his arms around me, this little birdlike man—I towered over him, and I am of no particular height—and kissed my hair, and took Dan's hand in both of his. "Congratulations."

I wanted to give him roses. A plaque. A shiny silver Lincoln to complement his blue one. He had said my soon-to-be-son was—nothing so spectacular, nothing that was not being said at this minute in delivery rooms the length of the country, in pediatricians' offices, to parents who expected as much and were not surprised—normal.

"Now take good care of him," he grinned at us, as we left with the baby. He struck his forehead. "As if you would not."

"Good holiday, Doctor."

I prattled in the car, "Hannah said on the phone last night that Rosh

Hashanah is not only the new year, but a turning away from the past toward the future, and how fine a gift that it was the day of the adoption, and how she would mention Bobby in her women's service today . . ."

"I love Hannah," Dan said. "But religious babble is religious babble."

He looked like death. His hair stuck up in spikes, and his clean clothes seemed to have rumpled as he put them on. The Mitchard way was to plummet and peak; the Allegrettis plateaued and built slowly. My family was ready to embrace a fresh emotion. Dan and Gail—who I was certain would never speak to me again—would live the past weekend for months.

I was weighted by the obligation to do the same. To hold the grief and shape it, regard it from all sides. But I had not the will for it. I wanted to put it away from me—whatever manner of human that would make me. The rupture that had taken place over Danny had begun to close; I could see no good in stopping it. Here was a child I could love without reservation or fear. Yet I hurt for Dan. For him, the insults of the past year had been once removed—only in Danny had the grotesquerie of ill luck targeted him personally. It had been for me the most stunning blow in a series of blows. For Dan, it had been the knockout punch.

"But it's so unfair," Laura had wept on the phone last night. "This little boy deserves for this day to be the happiest day of his parents' life. He didn't cause this. It's so damned unfair. . . ."

Me, Dan could forgive. But not DiMaggio. He had handed him back his check—DiMaggio had paid all the costs of the second adoption for us, over our obligatory protests—and shaken his hand wordlessly. And not God. The pray-TV folks earnestly told the viewing audience that Jesus was their personal friend; they took Jesus everywhere with them —even to the supermarket. Dan had not bothered God with helping him find a good bargain on pork roast; he had called on Him once, and God had not heard him. He said that he had felt yesterday as he had felt one other time in his life—when an aunt had called him, four years before, and told him that his younger brother had been killed the previous night in an auto wreck.

For me, the spiritual was inescapable. That baby Bobby should have been born when he was, unexpected, in the midst of a calamity that seemed unassailable, filled me with hush—it smacked of high wonder.

"I suppose no one can ordain how your prayers will be answered,"

Laura had said. "But of course, they were answered. Nothing could change Danny's chromosomes, but wasn't it as if you were being told, 'Here is what you prayed for, if you can bear it . . .'?"

I repeated this to Dan, feeling the ninny. "What was it," he replied, "that St. Theresa said about answered prayers?" I shut up; he was happy we had got the baby. It would have to be enough. He was not ready for more.

We drove to the courthouse.

Our attorney met us on the steps. "My assistant filled in the papers," he said, handing them to us. "Are you two holding up? This is a helluva thing . . . can I see the baby?" I presented Bobby. "Isn't he wonderful." The attorney told us he had been an infertile father for many years. After dozens of treatments, they'd had a son. Now his wife, who was a judge, was bugging him to call DiMaggio and get on the list.

I glanced over the papers, and suddenly saw the birth mother's name had not been inked out. I opted not to mention it; Bobby might need that name one day—not for love; I hoped not for love, but perhaps for blood, or marrow or history.

"The child's name is wrong," I told him. "This baby is Robert Daniel."

"But I thought . . ."

"That was another person. That was Danny's name."

The lawyer trekked back across the street to his office, and his assistant typed in the change. We initialed it.

At the sheriff's department in the courthouse, I held Bobby while a deputy tapped his head with the adoption papers. "You are served," she smiled, "with this order of adoption."

It was over in fifteen minutes.

We drove back to the house. "I'm going to go to Madison for a while," Dan said. "I need to unwind. Maybe get in touch with Dick and do some fishing. Get back to work. There's no reason to take any more leave. . . ."

"But we just got him."

"He'll be around for a long time." Dan made as if to reach for his cigarettes, but we'd agreed to quit, and he could only pat the empty pocket. "I'm not ready for him, Jack."

"But . . ."

"Let me do this in my own way."

"When do you want to leave?"

"Later today. As soon as you're all settled. Your grandma will be here to stay with you. And your dad."

"*Today!*" I pitched a fit. "Everyone is coming to see the baby. It will look just terrible if you run off . . ."

"I don't care how it looks. I need some time alone. I'm sure I'll . . . love him. In time. It's just too soon." Icicle in the throat. He is to be my child alone after all. Dan, don't go, I begged him silently. Because you are not the only one. When I close my eyes, I see Danny's face, as if his face had been superimposed on my own—when I yawn, I see his mouth open. I feel him. Don't leave me. Because I can't love this baby as much as he needs yet. He deserves it, this innocent . . .

"He certainly is beautiful," Dan said, as if he were admiring a rosebush or a brand-new car. "He's so *strong*. Danny was so small and needy. . . ."

It made me angry. This small boy can't help it that he is sturdy. He should not have to pay for it.

"Couldn't you just stay the night, Dan? We're both so tired. I'll let you sleep. . . ."

"No reason to."

"For me."

He sighed. I knew he would stay.

My father was wild about the baby. Relief, regret, helplessness—here was an outlet for all of them, all inexpressibles for my father, and better still, it bore his name. I marveled. He carried the baby through the halls of the house, fed him his bottle, rocked him to sleep, and when I tried to take him and put him down, my father growled, "Just leave him. He's fine right where he is."

Tears formed in his eyes when I told him that I had dreamed, the previous weekend, that my mother had come into the room where I lay beside Danny's cradle, not shorn and gaunt as she had been when last I saw her, but healthy and full, the light from the street shining through her brown hair, wearing a long white nightgown—my subconscious, on short notice, had put together an angel as best it could—and that she had lain down beside me, smelling of Jungle Gardenia, and held me. When I had tried to explain all of it to her, she had put up a warning finger. "I can either talk with you, or hold you," she had said. "I decided to hold you. So be still."

"Your mother would love him," my father said. "She wouldn't let you within ten feet of him."

"Dad," I asked then, ever the hunger for approval, unshakable. "Do you think we did right?"

"You did just right." For the first time in better than thirty years. No qualifier.

We drank my father's champagne that night. Fourteen people came —among them Laura and Richard and Michael and Richard's other son, my brother and Sandy, Sandy's parents. We toasted and toasted, to Bobby, to the end of pain, to Dan—who smiled wanly, and clinked his glass on mine. I drank a great deal. Felt high.

And then unexpectedly, Gail and Nick showed up. "I don't know if we're welcome," she began.

Dan kissed her. "Of course you're welcome."

And then she asked, "Jackie . . . ?"

"Gail." She would have to do this herself.

"I said a great many things I didn't mean. . . ."

"And some you did."

"And some I did. At the time. But I should not have, and I'm sorry. I feel like a fool."

"People are foolish. I'm sorry, too. It was awful for all of us."

"May I see my nephew?" she asked. "I promise not to give him dirty looks."

When all of the guests left, so did Dan. He said that the dark drive north would soothe him. He kissed me good-bye; he would return on the weekend, picking Jocelyn up on the way. "Won't you kiss the baby, too?" He brushed Bobby's small head with his lips.

"Take good care of him."

"I will."

I sat in the darkness, holding him after he finished his bottle. He curled one small hand around the strap of my nightgown and sighed. I thought he slept. But when I looked down, he was staring up at me gravely with his great gray-blue eyes, as if he could see me through and through. "Let's do our best to love each other," I told him. "It's just you and me."

Finally, it was not Jocelyn that accomplished it for me, though Jocelyn was heartrending.

She came tearing up the stairs, ripping off her raincoat. "Where is he?" She leaned over the basket, her hands clasped in eight-year-old melodrama. "He's so cute. Can I hold him?"

We installed her, bolstered by pillows, on the couch. "Is he really ours? This time for sure?"

"For sure."

She stroked his hair with a finger. "Oh—my brother, my brother. Jackie?" she said. "Do you know what? I don't want anyone to ever tell him about Danny."

"Why not?"

"Because he would think that he was second choice. He would not understand, because he's only little."

"Maybe when he's big."

"Why?"

I could not think of a good reason to rake up that pain, years hence. "Perhaps you're right, Jocelyn."

"And no one must ever tell him that he's not my *real* brother, because he's adopted."

"Who ever would?"

"Mommy said that he's my stepbrother." Ah. Joan-ever-vigilant.

"Well, he's not your stepbrother. Jerry's kids are your stepbrothers. Some people would say that he is your half-brother, because he is only the child of your father, and not your mother. . . ."

"Do I have to say that? Can't I just have him as my real brother?"

"Of course. That's the way Daddy and I would like it to be. Someday, he'll be a pesky little boy, following you around the way Uncle Bobby followed me, and you'll be telling him to get lost. . . ."

"Oh, Jackie." She was aghast. "I would never tell him to get lost." I never did, either, Jocelyn. Perhaps we will both of us be doting, much older sisters.

"Most sisters do," I told her.

"Well, I won't." She bent her neck to rub her soft cheek against Bobby's softer one. "I will protect him all my life." And then she said, "Jackie? Do you remember what I used to say about the dog?"

She liked to remember it. She was old enough now that her malapropisms of three years before no longer embarrassed her; she thought the little girl she once had been was cute. When Jocelyn was five, and just starting school, she had got into a period of pining vocally for a baby brother. Dan and I were not yet even married; babies had seemed a long way in the future. "But look, Jocelyn," I had told her then, to divert her, "you have your good Jeb."

"Great," she had said glumly. "I'm the only kid in kindergarten whose baby brother is a dog."

She rocked the baby, and said now, "I used to say that because I hated being an only child. Everyone used to say that: 'She's an only child.' But now, I'll never be an only child again. For sure." She kissed her brother.

I had to turn away then.

But it was not even that moment that sealed it. It was the next morning, a Saturday, when my brother and I took the baby for his belated circumcision. Dan was working for Ann and unable to break away, so Bobby tolerantly got up at six, so we could be at the hospital by eight. I had dithered over it. Every tenet of enlightened medicine now held that circumcision was not necessary, a little extra hygiene would do the trick. But did I want to nag a six-year-old to remember not only to wash behind his ears, but beneath his foreskin? Did I want his to be the only hooded weenie in the seventh-grade shower? I decided to go ahead, in spite of the fact that it would now have to be done in a minor-surgical unit, since Bobby was more than a week old and fast coming out of the newborn vapors. I was to bring a couple of bottles and a pacifier, which mystified me, until a nurse told me the baby would need them to comfort him after the pain, and then it terrified me.

My brother signed us in. And a pregnant young nurse came to take the baby, who was fast asleep. We guzzled coffee in the waiting room, talked idly about my brother's master's courses, and stared at the white door behind which we were certain we could hear thin wails.

"It's taking a hell of a long time," Bobby whispered.

I flipped through my mental file of horror clips. One slip, and it will be Roberta. I got up and began to pace. In a few moments, my brother joined me, and up and down the room we went, from the coffee machine to the magazine rack and back, eight steps, then a turn . . .

A nurse appeared in the door. "Who's the baby's mother?" she asked the room, which was lined with patients of various description.

I hesitated for a blink. And then it blossomed. "I am his mother," I said.

She brought Bobby to me. His hands, his outsized baby catcher's mitts, were twined prayerfully under his chin. His pacifier was bobbing furiously in his mouth, and two perfect tears trembled on each lash.

I held him to my chest, a rush so powerful I felt it must knock me flat. I could tear down buildings with my fingers, climb rocks barefoot, walk through rapids without a guideline, for this boy. My son. Not of me, by a technicality, but in me now, as certainly as if he had been.

I held him, rocked him, joined the mother-motion that waved slowly over the world, over time, back and forth.

Rapture.

I went with my brother to pick my grandmother up at the bus terminal later that day. She had not come home sooner—I had asked her not to—in the midst of the furor over Danny. "I don't want to see him, anyway, and then have to say good-bye to him," she had told me. "It's better this way. You don't know what this is doing to me, Jackie. It's a curse. That's all it is."

My brother had told her, over the phone, about the second baby. I could not. It sounded too bizarre. If she had been overjoyed to hear about Danny, she was something less about Bobby, my brother had reported. "I have a very bad feeling about this," she had told him.

"Gram," he had said, "you have a very bad feeling about everything. You remind me of R2D2."

So I did not know how she was going to react. I had asked for a great deal of tolerance from her in these months, and she was not given to excesses of tolerance. She had never known an adopted child.

We took the baby with us, though he was feeling punk. Perhaps she would be disarmed by him—snuggled in his federally approved car seat in his blue-dotted sunsuit; perhaps she would not. She might be determinedly cool; the frosty family glance that could speak volumes. But I would not care, I told myself. I would not let it rile me. Wouldn't it be just like her, to take a measuring look at Bobby, and then look away? Let her do it, I thought. This baby has love enough.

My grandmother came out of the terminal, tottering under the weight of her case—irritated, I could see already, that my brother was not there to take it from her—and I was struck by how frail she looked, my old adversary, my old champion, in her gray silk dress and her very correct gloves. She got into the car and kissed my brother in the front seat, and she did not look into the back. So. There it was.

But I had to make a try, and so I said, "Grandma. There is someone here to see you." And the baby opened his eyes.

She swiveled in the front seat. "But, Jackie!" she cried. "I didn't even know he was here!" She clasped her hands, then she tore off the gloves. "Why, he's the most gorgeous thing I've ever laid eyes on. So tiny! The darling. Come here, you little chunk. Come here to your Nana. Oh, how could you have found such a beautiful baby?" She lifted Bobby out of the car seat and cradled him, while lines of cars honked for us to move aside. The baby began his hiccuping newborn sobs.

"I'll take him," I said quickly.

"Oh, no, you won't," my grandmother cried. "I'll just give him his bottle, there, sweetheart. You don't know a darn thing about taking care of a baby, Jacquelyn, and you're going to have to learn to . . ,"

I leaned back against the seat. She would give Bobby a kind of caring even I could not—utterly without reservation, without criticism. She would save the criticism for me. That was all right. He would give her years.

The following weekend, I was in the kitchen making bottles. It had taken me an hour the first outing. High science. Separating confounded sterile plastic sleeves without ever touching the insides, fouling up two for every one successful; laving the formula can with soapy boiling water, reboiling each nipple that slipped for an instant from the tongs.

But over the days I had grown able to put down my Dr. Spock for full hours at a time. The baby did not get sick if I brushed the nipple with my fingertip before it went into his mouth. I relaxed. I could sing "Rockabye Baby" without emotion closing my throat. I could diaper one-handed with a bottle propped under my chin.

I was in a rush today only because Bobby was fussy—fussy is too petite a word for it; he was in a full-blown fit. He sat wailing in his swing, curdled milk flecking his lips, his little face a beet.

Dan was out there with him, but no amount of Dan's bouncing and holding had quieted Bobby. "He wants his mother," Dan called out. "Let me do that."

I didn't want it to be that way. I wanted Bobby to hush at Dan's touch as he had just lately begun to hush at mine. Be nice, son, I instructed him silently. Make your father your father as you have made me your mother. Turn on the charm.

He turned on the charm. There was a horrible gurgling eruption, a wild bubbling, and then a fierce, sharp cry. Dr. Spock, consulted later, called it projectile vomiting, but it was horror-movie fare for me, and it scared the baby, who promptly opened his mouth in a soundless, breath-holding cry.

I dropped utensils. Grabbed a towel. Headed for the door, arms reaching, already forming soothing sounds. . . .

But Dan was there. Scooping the baby out of the swing, wiping the slurry on Bobby's face away with his hand, cradling him against his chest. "Don't cry, small boy, don't cry. No need to cry. Everything is all right," he said. "Dada is here. Your dada is here."

I let the door close softly on them, so as not to disturb the future.

Afterword

 I FEEL a motion. Not Dan's broad turnings in bed. Something little, barely filtered through sleep. A mouse. I open my eyes, wade up through heavy water. Dark. A small mound between the pillows. "You put him in our bed again."

"Shhhhhh."

"He's almost four months old. He shouldn't even be in the room. . . ."

"Little kids like to sleep with their parents. See? How he snuggles up?"

He snuggles remarkably, cunningly, his tiny butt mounding the comforter, my human kitten, who can banish snarling broken sleep with his smile.

But I should not be up. This is Daddy's night for bottling. I had finally succumbed; I, who vowed that complaints about the demands of a baby would never sully these lips, had begun to moan of late. I needed a break —a dream or two—mental health demanded it. And Dan had grudgingly given up his weekend sleep marathons for the present, and now he mentions that there can be . . . something in these private spaces of stillness between him and the baby in the nights.

There cannot be too many complaints. He is a marvelously good-natured person, Bobby—a jumper, a grinner—who offers his fruity-voiced, Germanic coos and squeaks to each of us equally. I regret not having been able to nurse him, until I see how he melds to his father at feeding. There are compensations for losses.

We have almost recovered from the first jolt of him, dropped into our lives as if by the mythical stork—unprepared for, though we'd believed ourselves prepared. Undreamed of, in his constant casual revealing of wonders. Parenthood isn't what it was cracked up to be. It's more.

We managed one night out. After the movie, we drove around. Wouldn't it be nice to stop for a drink in some quiet piano bar, observe the dress, gossip about work, plan the larger house we must buy someday soon if we move back to Wisconsin, and probably we will . . . but the

car made its way home of its own accord. Bobby is the hottest ticket
in town. Three hours away from him was about our limit.

It is not only his constant needs, I tell Laura, that exhaust me. Not
only that sleep has become more a philosophical concept than a daily
event. It has been falling in love, around the clock, day after day, for
months. This is demanding, this new love. Man-woman passions temper
after the first headiness of discovery; lovers can tear their eyes from each
other and fall back into everyday step. But a baby is a black hole; he
absorbs tenderness with a voracious capability—and then, when the
limit has been reached, he changes, he pats my cheek on purpose for
the first time, and there is a new enchantment.

With Dan as well. With seeing Dan firsthand in the complexities of
fathering a child. I can see new planes and possibilities.

I came upon them one day, in the bedroom. Dan did not know I was
there. "Lemur-eyes," he was crooning to Bobby, who was gazing gravely
at his father. "Little lemur-eyes." I made a move to leave, and he heard
me and looked up. "Go away now," said Dan, "we're bonding."

Later he told me, "You know, I really do feel differently about having
Bobby from the way I felt about having Jocelyn." I tensed. "I know this
is going to make you mad, but I have to say it." A sinking in the middle
of my stomach. But Dan said, "He's a little boy. And Jackie, little boys
really are different from little girls. . . ."

It is part of the process of acquaintanceship—both of us with Bobby,
and Dan and I with each other. It is as if, as Dan has said, we had been
on long, independent journeys and have only just returned home. We
expect euphoria, and are tense when it lapses. I overcompensate, flustered, when we have any small disagreement. "Don't worry," Dan
temporizes. "Seventy percent good is good for now. We can try for
eighty-five percent. Give it time. We're fine, considering." Considering
that once the tension between us rang in the air of the house as if it were
a third voice speaking—like a television left to run for so long no one
heard what it said any longer. It's silent now.

Yet we don't have the hot, sweet connection we had before my
ill-fated pregnancy. We thought it might return, with happiness, and it
did not. There is no sexual desert; but the loving has to be spaced
between laundry loads and other urgencies. What we have now is a
marriage, for good or ill. It seems to me now that what we had before,
under the name of a marriage, was a romance that lasted longer than

we had a right to expect it to last—and by lasting so long, it seemed that it would last forever. If we had had the child we first conceived, the cooling down might have happened anyway. Perhaps we could have drawn the romance out longer; we can't know. I miss it. But I do not think that—however much we talk about second honeymoons in hot, white-sand paradises—we will have it, exactly like that, ever again. Still, we had it. There are compensations.

There have been times, even since the baby, that we believed we might not have a marriage at all. There was no express lane that we could find from the wounding of the past year to happily-ever-after. We had inflicted terrible wounds on each other, and they did not miraculously heal. Some outside help, some well-armed psychological intervenor might have blunted some of them. I think now that at the worst of it, when I seemed to be able to do little except slash at Dan, and he seemed to be able to do little except retreat, leaving defenses against me piled up behind him, we should have taken ourselves to help, shouted for it.

But if we were too proud, we also probably were too afraid that we would emerge from counseling with two healed selves ready to go in separate directions. Infertility had spaded up issues that had nothing to do with my inability to have a child—such as my obsessions with Joan, and the tensions attendant on our marriage. If our marriage had proceeded as planned, these were issues that might have worn themselves out over time. But they rebounded with new, blistering significance when our plans were turned on end.

Our plans continue to be turned on end. There was a space when we thought we had it all whipped—we had Bobby, the surgery had been a success, and we could hope, in time, to conceive another child.

Then, on the day before Christmas Eve 1983, I went to Madison and Dr. Bellow for a "second look" laparoscopy. There was no particular urgency about it, but since I was between projects for my various employers, and the book was coming along, I decided it would be as good a time as any for the procedure that is not an uncommon step when a woman has had tubal reconstruction and then not conceived after a year.

I went back to the same-day surgery unit, gave my spiel about bad veins, and received the unpleasant blessing of gas, and when I came fully around after the surgery, Bellow was already in the room, talking with women in beds on either side of me who had had the same procedure. His steps had a sad redundancy—they were a dance I could have choreographed from memory. He spoke to each of them, reassuring them in turn that "everything had looked normal in there," and then he turned to me.

We walked up the hall to the conference room. "I wanted to be able to talk with you in some privacy," he began, "because . . .

I said the words with him, "The results were not normal."

"I figured," I told him.

He hadn't figured. He was puzzled. The X ray, months before, had looked splendid. So it was not a case of the laser surgery not having worked, precisely, and there was no evidence of endometriosis having returned, nor of any other "process" that was new. . . .

Yet the dye did not go through. The tube was closed.

Was that it, then? Bellow wasn't ready to say so. "I would try to dissuade a patient from a second try at surgery in most circumstances," he said. "The reason for that is that it's usually evident that if the tube closes, something else is going on, or there's other damage that would make a second surgery impractical." But he held out some hope that a second microsurgical attempt might reopen it; everything else seemed sound enough that the odds probably would be no worse than they had been the year before.

I know what I would have done at that moment, if that moment had fallen just three months earlier. I'd have crumpled. I'd have scurried, like a frightened lab rat run up against yet another door in what looked like the way out of the maze, to make another surgical appointment. I'd have plunged backward into the frantic helplessness I had learned so well.

But now I was a mother. An infertile mother, but a mother nonetheless. The sorrow of realizing that I might never, in fact, bear a child with my body was anesthetized; I could feel the pressure but not the pain. As Susan Reese had told me, adoption was not the cure for infertility. But it was the anodyne. I had a child who depended on me, so the risks of another surgery could not be undertaken lightly. I could sorrow over the loss of my reproductive ability, but they would be tears of simple regret—tears, I had learned, a life could be lived around.

More than that, I was complacent, unready to gear up for another assault. Unaccustomed as the feeling was for a compulsive striver, I liked my life as it was. I was labile, unstoic, about the thought of more physical pain. I had thought that part was done.

Yet a sibling is a fine thing; I've had good experience of it. I do not want Bobby to be raised as an only child, with periodic visits from his big sister—one of them having to suffer that parting is bad enough, though there is nothing I can do about that—and with all the well-intentioned smothering a woman of my makeup would visit on an only son.

Jocelyn is a good girl, a grand girl, but she struggles with a fair case of ringmaster's disease. She has not been able, at least not yet, to learn the lessons of openness and compassion for others that a full time sibling makes easier. She warms to people slowly. I believe a kid needs an in-house ally.

And conceiving a child still is the surest way to increasing a family. We had an incredible bolt of luck, with all the costs, in finding Danny, and then Bobby, so quickly, and in a manner that we could afford. And I am selfish. Having once traveled the inexpressibly starry road of seeing an infant grow from a tiny, floppy doll into a laughing chunk of individual, I want it again. I don't believe I have a right to it, but I want it.

And so we discussed a second surgery, Bellow and I, while I huddled with a hospital blanket around my waist, and my teeth knocked from chill and the after-effects of anesthesia. Discussed it rather dispassionately.

He was surprised when I told him that I would like for him to do the surgery, if I should have it again. He had assumed that I would want to go back to New Orleans or have it done in Chicago. He was not in favor of New Orleans—at every visit, for months, Bellow had made it a point to bring up laser microsurgery and his doubts about it. Not that he believed it was more risky, or even less efficacious than traditional methods. He simply thought it was being glamorized, overemphasized. The rush for hospitals to equip themselves with terribly costly miracle machines, to compete fiercely for patients through technology, was in itself dangerous, he said.

He could foresee a day when a sought-after surgeon might offer to do all his surgeries in one hospital in exchange for that hospital's purchasing a laser for microsurgery—and having a much better chance of having that request granted than if he requested, say, three extra nurses on a floor. Bellow left no doubt about which request would better serve patients.

It was the skill of the surgeon, he told me over and over, in reconnecting the tubes that was the critical factor—not the tool used to remove an obstruction. He shuddered to think of would-be microsurgeons flocking to the laser and expecting it to replace painstaking skill.

But it was not only Bellow's doubts, nor his presentation of figures from around the country that seemed to indicate that success rates using the laser were about the same as those without it, that influenced me. I had been in contact periodically with Orin Clarke, the New Orleans surgeon who'd done my first operation. He'd left the Omega Institute.

"I still think the laser is the best method by far," he told me. The shorter time spent in surgery and the quicker recovery were benefits to the patient that could not be discounted. But the laser was not the technological end-all it seemed to be, he admitted.

But in spite of the outcome, and all the strain of it, choosing to go to New Orleans for the surgery is not a thing I regret. Events might have unfolded more or less as they did if I had chosen to have the surgery in Madison or Chicago, or someplace else. But the way we felt about the odds given us allowed us to approach a fairly rough go with confidence, and we needed the confidence only slightly less than we needed choice.

Choice. It's the loss of it that staggers so many infertile couples. The lifting away from them, bit by bit, of control over the most intimate arena in their lives. My obsessive comparison shopping for options wore Dan down, but it afforded me a measure of control.

The choices we made, the control we exercised, may have affected outcomes only tangentially, or not at all. But even symbolic gestures of control over one's own life are salutary.

The course we had been plopped down into led toward attrition—toward the progressive removal of possibilities. We snatched hope by refusing to surrender to the facts.

It was not always the wise course. By far not the smooth one. I liked to believe the people who told me I was brave—all those operations, all that pain—but I was not brave at all. The courage to close the book, as Susan had, as others had, with some dignity and peace, to press away childbearing between old pages, with other dreams I had that did not pan out, eluded me. It still does.

I still must run after options—another surgery, embryo implant, which has a hopeful ring to it, perhaps even in vitro. I must talk about in vitro again with Dan, who has not changed his mind about it.

The difference from the first panic is only ephemeral, but it is crucial. We have time. We had it before, but I could not see it. And so I crashed blindly ahead, in a desperate beating of the medical bushes for the missing member of the family. Bobby has given us the time to talk.

There are many things we need to talk about still. Tears in our fabric that are sturdily patched, but need to be made seamless. Infertility did not better our marriage. We are not better people for having rubbed elbows with our personal monsters. Perhaps we are more capable of empathy, of trying to see under the surfaces of others; Yoko Ono was a woman Dan thought he would never forgive—she had displaced his musical hero—but now his heart is turned when he reads about the Lennons' struggle to have a child. He can put his hand out and touch that pain.

Pain. Why so much, and so corrosive? Much worse things had happened to people. I had health, I had brains, I had not been disfigured or physically limited. Yet even all of the psychological elements that add up to the life crisis that is infertility, taken singly, do not seem to add up to the violence and relentlessness of my reaction. There is something I cannot yet put a name to in learning that you will not have children, if you want them—in learning that that center of your life has been cut out—that has made people through history prone to all manner of desperate folly.

The biblical Rachel cried, "Give me children, or I die!" And her husband, Jacob—like every other husband of an infertile woman— yelled back angrily, in effect, "Hey! Don't blame me!"

Blame and rage and the torpor of depression—neurotic is a word that I've always understood rather well, but my reaction, I learned, differed only in the details from the reactions of the many other women and men I met. And part of the reason I decided to write this book was that each of them believed at first his or her reaction had been the most over-blown, the most shameful.

It is modern to gain through pain, but we did not. Pain remains to us something to look back upon, having survived it—best avoided if at all possible. A great deal of the pain we visited on ourselves and each other was the worst kind of pain, the least healthful, the most pernicious, because it bred nothing but more of itself, and the knowledge of ourselves it gave us was knowledge we could have done without.

Yet a great deal of it was unavoidable. A great deal of it, for ourselves and our families, was simply being caught in the fallout from an explosion of dreams.

A rabbi I met in one of my hospital forays told me, "Suffering is good for the soul. But only if you do it *right.*" We did not always do it right. But when we did, when we let our families and our friends support us, they gave in measures they would not have believed they had in reserve. They circled the wagons. They would not let us isolate ourselves. They say they learned from it.

There was learning for us, as well. Not only in the pronunciation of Latin pathologies. It continues. The child we gave up, we have been told, has a home with fine parents. He thrived, Mrs. DiMaggio told us, during his weeks with them, and it was the consensus of DiMaggio's colleagues who saw him that his handicap would not be profound. The couple who adopted him were in their twenties; they had an older adopted daughter who was blind. They had had a Down's daughter; she died at the age of two. They were overjoyed at their first sight of Danny; he still bears that name. The mother spoke with Mrs. DiMaggio about us: "It seems that they have the baby they lost, and we have the baby we lost."

The guilt that I could not be such a woman is inescapable, but there is a comfort in the knowledge that my baby of the heart has parents who were wise and tough enough to want him just as he is. There are people stronger than we are, but we are stronger than we thought.

Dan and Jackie have one thing we did not have in the summer of 1982. And that is perhaps the realization, awfully arrived at, that our marriage was not the convenient bit of sociology we may have believed it to be when we made it—a tidy legal picture frame that would surround the house and the car and the children when they came. It is a richer covenant than that, something we have learned that we both want terribly, worth a good fight to keep. Many people do not need tragedy to teach them that; perhaps we did.

And something else.

He lies here, between us.

My grandmother likes to ask me if he was worth all the search and suffering, the expensive outlay of energy and resource. But of course, there is no reckoning of worth. The very word falls bizarrely out of context in the face of a child. But price—price might be a word. If I had known there was to be a price exacted—from the first blast of the ectopic through all the stitches and tears to be paid out over the months —or else no Bobby, I would have paid it. It would have been a very small price, seen from this vantage. He beggars it. I would pay it again and again, as long as flesh was able. I think what my grandmother means when she asks is whether he would have meant so much to me without the price, if I had come by him easily. I don't know, I think he would have; perhaps the little jealous gods know better. But I am a lion of a mother.

He lies here, and I reach out over my pillow to cradle his head—not to touch him, for he is a light sleeper, and a touch might startle him —but to circle his small head and feel its heat. And I find another hand there, limp in sleep, his father's. And so we can make a bridge over him with our two hands, we can shield him.

I can sleep. Our son is here. He is in the world with me. He is here as I drift off, and he will be here in the morning when I wake up.

January 1984